MY ROAD TO ITHACA

A TWENTIETH CENTURY SMALL HISTORY

MICHAEL PANAYOTOPOULOS
AS TOLD TO BEVERLY BUNN

This book purposely retains the speech patterns, idioms, and expressions of the author, to be read and heard as the words were spoken.

My Road to Ithaca
A Twentieth Century Small History
All Rights Reserved.
Copyright © 2023 Michael Panayotopoulos as told to Beverly Bunn
v3.0

The opinions expressed in this manuscript are solely the opinions of the author and do not represent the opinions or thoughts of the publisher. The author has represented and warranted full ownership and/or legal right to publish all the materials in this book.

This book may not be reproduced, transmitted, or stored in whole or in part by any means, including graphic, electronic, or mechanical without the express written consent of the publisher except in the case of brief quotations embodied in critical articles and reviews.

True Adventure Publishing LLC

ISBN: 979-8-9868182-0-7

Library of Congress Control Number: 2022915677

Cover image: Shutterstock. © 2023 All rights reserved - used with permission.
Cover design: My Vision Press © 2023 All rights reserved - used with permission.

PRINTED IN THE UNITED STATES OF AMERICA

Photo credits

1) Greek Machine Gun Team During the Greco-Turkish War: Creative Commons CC0 License, Milliyet {{PD-US}}   https://commons.wikimedia.org/wiki/Category:Hellenic
Proussa1921: Agiasofia.com; http://greekmilitary.net/konstantinoupoli/thisdayofyear/general_papoulas_proussa.jpg

2) Map of Greece: nationsonline.org
Turkish Flagship: PUBLIC DOMAIN CC0 Wikipedia.org {{PD-Art}}

3) Greeks Escorting Bulgarian Prisoners in Trenches WWI 1918: Alamy.com
https://www.alamy.com/stock-photo-greek-soldiers-escorting-bulgarian-prisoners-in-1918-during-ww1-greece-170543259.html
Venizelos Reviewing Troops at Serres 1918: PUBLIC DOMAIN via Wikimedia Commons
Greece, Red Cross Nurses 1921: Library of Congress, No Known Restrictions. Greece, June 1918
https://www.loc.gov/item/2017674647/

4) Takis Panayotopoulos with Adolf Hitler: Private Photo Author Owned
Berghof: creativecommons.org/via Wikimedia Commons, Bundesarchiv, Bild 183-1999-0412-502 / CC-BY-SA 3.0
Goering Hunt: PUBLIC DOMAIN via Alamy.com
Hermann Goering: Franz Langhammer, PUBLIC DOMAIN via Wikimedia Commons
https://commons.wikimedia.org/wiki/File:Hermann_G%C3%B6ring_by_Langhammer.jpg

5) Gordonstoun: LarchOak, PUBLIC DOMAIN CC BY-SA 4.0, via Wikimedia Commons
https://commons.wikimedia.org/wiki/File:Round_Square_and_Gordonstoun_House.jpg
Urquhart Castle: PUBLIC DOMAIN CC0, George Hodan via PublicDomainPictures.net,
https://www.publicdomainpictures.net/en/view-image.php?image=187721&picture=urquhart-castle

I

Melina Mercouri: PUBLIC DOMAIN https://picryl.com/media/griekse-actrice-melina-mercouri-arriveert-op-schiphol-80b645

6) Paris Match N° 959 DU 26/08/1967 - La Terre a Tremble

7) Venizelos: PUBLIC DOMAIN CC0 via Wikimedia Commons https://commons.wikimedia.org/wiki/File:Venizelos_in_1919.jpg
Metaxas: PUBLIC DOMAIN via Alamy
Papadopoulos: CC BY-SA 4.0, via Wikimedia Commons https://commons.wikimedia.org/wiki/File:Georgios_Papadopoulos.jpg
King Constantine I: Megos Andreas, CC BY-SA 4.0, via Wikimedia Commons https://commons.wikimedia.org/wiki/File:H.M._King_Constantine_I_of_Greece.jpg
The Colonels: Alamy.com https://www.alamy.com/stock-photo-1962-the-3-strong-man-of-the-republic-of-greece

8) Greek Newspaper: No Known Restrictions
Phryne before the Areopagus. (1861) By Jean-Léon Gérôme. PUBLIC DOMAIN via Wikimedia Commons
Gloria Root: Playboy Magazine December 1969: Not available for third party licensing.
Helmut Schmidt: Photograph Hans Schafgans, 1977, CC BY-SA 2.0, via Wikimedia Commons
Medal: Order of Merit: Oğuz Gemalmaz PUBLIC DOMAIN, via Wikimedia Commons
Certificate: Order of Merit: Private Photo Author Owned

9) Penney—Panayotopoulos Marriage Publicity: New York Times February 21, 1971; April 25, 1971, used under license Portraits by Bachrach Photography

10) Vouzas Hotel: https://vintage-files.blogspot.com (photos file - Billy Files)
Castalian Fountain: PUBLIC DOMAIN Louis Dupré via Wikimedia Commons
Archbishop Iakovos: PUBLIC DOMAIN White House Photo, via Wikimedia Commons
Queen Frederica, Jackie Kennedy: Helmer Reenberg YouTube https://www.youtube.com/helmerreenberg

Table of Contents

1. Proussa, Asia Minor 1
2. Statesman vs. Monarch 11
3. The Greek Swimmer Founds a Fortune 14
4. The Split, a Disunited Greece 24
5. Serres: Ninety Men Equal One Division 35
6. Thessalonica Hospital 44
7. Reporting for Duty and a Duel 53
8. A Dozen White Sheets 61
9. End and Aftermath 68
10. Greece's Due, Lost 76
11. The Greek and Goering 88
12. Family and Business 96
13. Rescue from Exile 103
14. Prelude to War 108
15. Wartime Athens 116
16. Escape to Scotland 126
17. The Keep at Urquhart Castle, and Gordonstoun 134
18. Return to Athens 146
19. With the Argyll and Sutherland Highlanders 156
20. Becoming a Mining Engineer 166
21. Greek Army Boots and the CIA 179
22. The Family Enterprises 187
23. A Congo Mercenary 196

24. The Colonels 207
25. Moscow: Blue Jeans in the Diplomatic Bag............................. 219
26. Bonn, *un post du combat* *227*
27. Six Months Ago, She Was a Man 234
28. Phryne and the Playmate of the Month 240
29. Emery, Whips and Education 245
30. Commercial Women.. 253
31. The Spy 258
32. Living the Good Life 264
33. The Highest Decoration 282
34. Archbishop of the Americas 290
35. Apollo, the Jewish Baby 295
36. The Cultured and the Culture Minister 301
37. The Sabra, and Sophocles 306
38. Kissinger's Doctrine: Greece is Dispensable........................ 314
39. Meeting Miss Kim 321
40. Job Insecurity... 327
41. Becoming a Fugitive 335

ITHACA HAS GIVEN YOU THE BEAUTIFUL VOYAGE.
WITHOUT HER YOU WOULD NEVER HAVE SET OUT ON THE ROAD.
SHE HAS NOTHING MORE TO GIVE YOU.

KONSTANTINE KAVAFY 1911

Preface

I am Greek, after all.

The Fates keep me from making plans and the Muses affect my life.

There are only three things in my life I have never tried, I have never injected myself with heroin nor taken crack or the like, and three, I have never been the passive part of a homosexual pairing. I have also never committed treason, although some Greeks might give you an argument on that.

Like my uncle Socrates, I know one thing: I know nothing. I cannot prove he was my uncle, but nobody can disprove it either.

I haven't come up with an original idea. I haven't written anything that hasn't been thought of before. I am like a parrot, I can repeat what I have read or observed.

Through the eyes and the ears of my father I have experienced years more than my own life, and I know every detail. Through my father, who served as Military Attaché in the Greek Embassy in Berlin from 1936 through 1940, I have another viewpoint of history. My father was a personal friend of Hermann Goering since 1921 and had first met Adolf Hitler when he was a nobody at the Bierhalle in Munich.

While I am a great-great grandson of the Duke of Argyll, and descended from the Earl of Inverness, and my mother is a Dame of the British Empire, I am not a gentleman.

Though I am rude, I have not said anything that I know to be untrue.

I have related events as my memory serves me.

This is my journey on the road to Ithaca.

Michael Panayotopoulos
2022

ITHACA

When you set out on your journey to Ithaca,
pray that the road is long,
full of adventure, full of knowledge.
The Lestrygonians and the Cyclops,
the angry Poseidon— do not fear them:
You will never find such as these on your path,
if your thoughts remain lofty, if a fine
emotion touches your spirit and your body.
The Lestrygonians and the Cyclops,
the fierce Poseidon you will never encounter,
if you do not carry them within your soul,
if your soul does not set them up before you.

Pray that the road is long.
That the summer mornings are many, when,
with such pleasure, with such joy
you will enter ports seen for the first time;
stop at Phoenician markets,
and purchase fine merchandise,
mother-of-pearl and coral, amber and ebony,
and sensual perfumes of all kinds,
as many sensual perfumes as you can;
visit many Egyptian cities,
to learn and learn from scholars.

Always keep Ithaca in your mind.
To arrive there is your ultimate goal.
But do not hurry the voyage at all.
It is better to let it last for many years;
and to anchor at the island when you are old,
rich with all you have gained on the way,
not expecting that Ithaca will offer you riches.

Ithaca has given you the beautiful voyage.
Without her you would have never set out on the road.
She has nothing more to give you.

And if you find her poor, Ithaca has not deceived you.
Wise as you have become, with so much experience,
you must already have understood what Ithaca means.

Konstantine P. Kavafy (1911)

CHAPTER 1

Proussa, Asia Minor

THE SHELLS WHINE and burst furiously around and amid the eleven remaining men under the command of Lieutenant Takis Panayotopoulos, most of them wounded. Still, they grimly determine to fight till the last drop of their blood, till the last breath escapes their shattered lungs hurting awfully from the blasts of the infernal explosions caused by the incessant Turkish artillery barrage. Panayotopoulos' machine guns, legendary French St. Etienne's, grow red hot from continuous firing and the men urinate upon them in an effort to cool them somehow and prevent them from malfunctioning. The Tenth Greek Infantry Division is decimated by the waves of Turkish attacks. But the Duz-dag Hills have to be defended or else Proussa, only twelve miles to the west, will fall.

A terrible deafening explosion hurls Panayotopoulos yards away from his smashed machine gun, his right index finger still pressed on the trigger.... his right arm separated into a mess of torn flesh, bones, and blood. The eleven men who only hours ago were 130 are now three, and no machine gun fires anymore.

Has it been minutes, hours, days, or an eternity since that hell of an inferno when Takis Panayotopoulos feels strong enough to open his burning eyes? He can hear no sound, but no wonder to that, the blast next to his ears has probably deafened him. It can't be...he is hallucinating, or he is dead and landed in Paradise...there are no angels with beautifully deep violet blue eyes in the mountains of the Turkish hinterland. He tries to focus, his eyes and everything else hurt so much.... he is in a room with whitewashed walls, and he is lying in a blood-stained bed, but yes, next to him stands a cherub, or rather a girl, the most divinely gorgeous girl he has ever seen in his life, dressed in the uniform of a Greek Red Cross nurse. She pauses, looks at him with angelic blue eyes, large and intelligent blue eyes, and it seems to him that they are filled with sorrow, the tears ready to descend the alabaster face.

"Are you real, or am I in Paradise?"

She starts at the sound of his voice, and hastens out of the room, a ward of the field hospital set only three miles from the front. In a few minutes she is back with Surgeon-Captain Nicolas Prossas.

"I have both good and bad news for you, Lieutenant, or rather *Captain* Panayotopoulos," says the smiling doctor. "Your stubborn resistance on top of the hill saved the day for us. The Turkish offensive has been broken, Proussa is safe. The Turkish dead at the foot of the hill you defended count in the hundreds. You have been promoted for outstanding bravery and so have your surviving men. As soon as you recover enough to withstand travel, we are to ship you to Athens where the King is to decorate you with the Order of Valiance. The gold medal. His Majesty himself!"

The smile faded, "Now for the bad news. When your three boys dragged you here, they also brought along what was left of your right arm. But I am a simple surgeon, not a magician, and I don't know how to stick it back together."

"It's alright, doctor, don't blame yourself. After all, I was a lousy draftsman. I may take up conducting or dancing where one hand is plenty enough." Moving his head, his eyes follow the girl. "But I have something to ask you. Since when do you have angels in your hospital? From what part of heaven did *she* come?"

But suddenly an appalling piercing ache overtakes him and also the realization that he is missing his right arm, pain and nausea, and the world turns black. He is unconscious.

The time is March 11, 1921. The place is that part of Turkey known as Asia Minor and the town is Proussa, called Bursa by the Turks, inhabited at the time by twenty thousand Greeks, seventy thousand Turks and another five thousand Jews, Armenians, and other nationalities. The battles tearing that country apart are an extension of the First World War.

The fact was that an inspired, rugged, and tenacious Turkish general, Mustafa Kemal Pasha, was not about to admit his country's defeat or to accept the treaty signed by a decadent and corrupt government in Constantinople, the Sevres Treaty, which ceded vast areas of the once glorious and serene Ottoman Empire to Greece, France, and Italy. The presence of the Greek troops, on the other hand, was the proof of the determination of Greece to enforce the treaty, safeguard her newly acquired land in Asia Minor and protect the large ethnic Greek populations which had inhabited the area since the beginnings of history. The Greeks were furthermore determined to realize the centuries-long dream of reinstating the long-gone Byzantine Empire, a dream which, thanks to the victory in the First World War, seemed very much attainable and almost fulfilled. The only remaining obstacle was Kemal Pasha—Pasha is a Turkish honorific title—and 150,000 of his loyal soldiers.

Had that been accurate, then in all probability there would be no country known as Turkey today, and Greece would be a vast, powerful empire exercising tremendous influence in world politics. If Kemal were really the only obstacle, he most certainly would have been defeated and forgotten. But because of support from other powers, he is instead praised in Turkish as well as in world history as the Father of Modern Turkey—Mustafa Kemal Ataturk—a great warrior and leader and reformer of international repute. He took the title Ataturk in 1934.

So, what other obstacles prevented the Greeks from fulfilling their centuries-old dream? Politics, both domestic and foreign and the theory behind diplomacy of the times: the balance of power. If Greece were to crush Kemal, efface Turkey from the map and conquer all this land, she would certainly become both economically as well as politically a world power.

Great Britain appeared as a placid observer for the most part of the struggle. Greece was well anchored as a British satellite; the King of Greece, Constantine I, was the first cousin of the King of Great Britain. The mainstay of Greek economy was her merchant fleet and most of this business was conducted in and from London. Greece owed both political as well as financial favors to Britain. And Greece, even a very powerful Greece, constituted no danger to the venerated, and to the British soul, sacrosanct, free routes to India. On the contrary, a strong Greece would be a safeguard against any future expansion of Russia towards the warm seas, another pillar of British policy, and it would certainly curb any dreams of Italian or French expansion to the Middle East. Britain secretly encouraged the Greeks in their effort to force Kemal to his knees and did not acknowledge Kemal as the true leader of Turkey.

The destruction and partition of the Ottoman Empire in the First World War was almost exclusively an accomplishment to the British, Indian, and colonial armies, and after the annihilation of the Turkish Army in the Battle of Halep—or Aleppo, the British were not particularly concerned with the demoralized and shattered remnants of that army. The lion's share of the bisection of the Ottoman Empire went to Britain anyway; Mesopotamia, today known as Iraq, Palestine, and Trans Jordan, were either British protectorates or colonies and the remnants of the defeated Turkish Army constituted no challenge and no threat to British imperialism. This is probably the reason why the British neglected to enforce total disarmament and demobilization to the remaining armed forces of Turkey, which under the Kemal Pasha— the hero of Gallipolis—found both inspiration and leadership.

France and Italy, on the other hand, saw things from an entirely different perspective and subjected their policies *vis à vis* Kemal on their own aspirations and plans which had no resemblance at all to the policies of Great Britain.

France had formed with Great Britain the '*entente cordiale*' the cordial alliance because she felt threatened by the rapid growth, industrialization, and efficiency of Germany, but she was also a vast colonial power. In many respects and areas of Africa, French and British policies were on a head-on collision course. France also had aspirations in the Middle East, proof of which was her acquisition of those parts of the Ottoman Empire known today as Syria and Lebanon. Even though France and Greece were good friends and allies, it did not fit in the French empirical plans to have a powerful Greece standing fast in the eastern Mediterranean as the guardian of British interests.

Italy's policies bore a striking resemblance to the ones of France. Italy was the youngest member of the club of superpowers. In spite of her most humiliating and devastating defeat suffered in Caporetto at the hands of the German army, she emerged as a victor at the end of the war, and her greed was unsurpassed ever or since till the possible exception of Stalin's Soviet Union. She collected a disproportionate amount of reparations from Germany and Austria plus the German-speaking territory known as South Tyrol, and a province in Asia Minor, south of Smyrna. Incidentally, the French helped themselves also to a neighboring province.

The Italians also had a dream: they wanted to resurrect the Roman Empire at the expense of parts of Africa and Greece. They laid claim to the Greek Islands of the Ionian Sea; they had already taken the island of Rhodes and the twelve adjoining Greek Islands known as the Dodecanese, and most certainly a strong, great Greece was definitely not to their liking. Albania was also a part of Europe where Greek and Italian interests and aspirations conflicted. Italy had turned Albania into her protectorate and advance base. Greece, on the other hand, claimed the southern part of that most primitive and backward Moslem country because it was inhabited mostly by Greek-speaking Christians who acknowledged Greece as their mother country.

The obstacles to the realization of the Greek dream were not only the ones which were of purely international political nature. Greece had also at the time a domestic problem which was dividing the nation. Half the Greeks, mostly the ones from the south, were Royalist, backward conservatives loyal to then King Constantine I—a Dane; and the other half were Progressive, liberal republicans devoted to a genial politician from Crete—Eleftherios Venizelos. Both the King and Venizelos were men of strong character and stubborn conviction, and there is no doubt that they both had the interest of Greece deep at heart but their methods and polices were contrasting.

In 1912 Greece joined the Balkan Alliance in a war against the decaying Ottoman Empire. The Alliance comprised Serbia, Bulgaria and Montenegro, a country later devoured by Yugoslavia. The purpose of the Alliance was to fight the Turks and force them out of their remaining European provinces: Bosnia and Herzegovina, the Banat, Epirus, Macedonia, and Thrace. Many islands in the Aegean like Lesbos, Samos, Chios, and Crete were still under Turkish rule. In all these provinces and islands, the inhabitants were mostly Christian Slavs and Greeks, with slight Turkish minorities. The true purpose of the Alliance was to liberate fellow Christians from the Turkish yoke and increase the national territories.

Since, with the exception of the islands which were purely Greek, many of the provinces were claimed by more than one member of the Alliance, Macedonia being the most notable example, the agreement was 'takers keep.' Thessalonica, the largest city in Macedonia, was coveted by Serbia, Bulgaria, and Greece. Constantinople was the immediate target of Bulgaria, but Greece felt that old Byzantium should rightly be hers since it had been for over a thousand years the capital of the Greek Empire, prior to the Turkish conquest. The Balkan Alliance was rather loose, with many conflicting interests, but with one communal characteristic: the mutual hatred of the Turkish oppressor and the strong wish to increase one's territory at Turkey's expense.

When the Balkan War started in 1912, Constantine was the Crown Prince of Greece and the Commander in Chief of the Greek armed forces. Venizelos was the Prime Minister, head of government, and Minister of Defense. In the Balkan Alliance, Bulgaria seemed to be the senior partner since her army was the largest, 200,000 strong, and supposedly the best equipped and trained. In fact, the Bulgarians were called at the time the 'little Prussians of the East.' Serbia's army ranked second with 150,000 men armed and trained by the Austrians. The Montenegrin Army numbered only 25,000 but was formed of brave, rugged mountain men who were superior in their terrain to anyone. The Greek army comprised 80,000 men with inferior equipment and armament compared to the Bulgarians, but Greece was the only member of the Alliance which had a navy, and this navy was the ace of trumps of the Alliance because it was supposed to block the Turkish fleet out of the Aegean and Mediterranean seas and prevent the Turks from reinforcing their European garrisons with troops shipped from Asia. The Greek Navy was very much up to this task because, even though smaller in numbers of men-of-war to the Ottoman Navy, it had some modern units, and the training and ability of the Greek sailors was superior, possessing a millennia-old seafaring tradition that the Turks lacked. The Ottoman Army was 800,000 strong but mostly poorly trained and ill-equipped with antiquated methods of warfare. Most significantly, the bulk of this army was deployed along the Russian border, and it would take it at least two months to reach the Balkans.

The initial victories of the Balkan allies were beyond even their wildest dreams. It took the Bulgarians less than a month to reach Tsaltaza, a small town only ten miles away from Constantinople. At the same time, the Serbs and Montenegrins had smashed all Turkish resistance in Sarajevo, the Dalmatian Coast and Albania. The Greeks had liberated most of Epirus and were a few miles away from Thessalonica. The Greek Navy had proven her worth by defeating the Turkish fleet in two engagements and forcing them to retreat in flames behind the sanctuary of the Dardanelles. The Aegean was now a Greek lake, and all the islands were liberated one after the other.

Constantinople seemed doomed to fall to the Bulgarians but a cholera epidemic in Tsaltaza stopped their advance and gave the Turks some very valuable time and respite. By December 1912, they had managed to reinforce their line in Thrace so the danger of Constantinople falling to the Bulgarians was averted. Meanwhile, the Turks had gathered some 300,000 troops in Smyrna ready to be shipped to Macedonia. The Turkish fleet attempted another sortie on December 3, 1912. On that day the Greek Navy, with the ultra-modern 15,000-ton battle cruiser, *H.M.S. Averoff*, destroyed two Turkish battleships, the *Mesudi* and the *Hamidi* and severely injured the best unit of the Turkish Navy, the battleship *Hayderedin Barbarossa* which, burning, fled the encounter. That battle sealed the fortunes of the Turks in this war; the troops they had amassed in Smyrna could not be transported anywhere where they could be of any use, and as far as the Turks were concerned the war was over, with all the remaining European provinces of the empire having fallen to the hands of their ex-Balkan slaves. One after the other, the Turkish units still fighting surrendered to their victors, except for the defenders of Constantinople who held their front against the Bulgarians and were constantly reinforced.

It took the Balkan nations only four months to fulfill the dreams of generations and boot the hated Turkish tyrant out of Europe. The Turkish garrison surrendered Thessalonica to the advancing Greeks. Ahead of his army, the Crown-Prince Constantine entered and occupied the city to the frenzied delight of the 90,000 Greek inhabitants. The glory, prestige, and adulation of the crown-prince had reached superlative dimensions. Since the glorious days of Byzantium, no Greek war leader was so hailed by his adoring people. Constantine was now the incorporation of the fulfillment of the hopes and aspirations that the Greek nation held sacred for all the centuries of enslavement to the Turks. The Phasma of Phoenix, the mythological Greek bird that revives out of its ashes, seemed reality.

The prestige of Venizelos also had reached its apogee because it was he who had insisted and accomplished the modernization of the Greek Navy and it was he, in his capacity of Minister of Defense, who had conducted the behind-the-scenes strategy. In those four months there had been many a time that Crown-Prince and Prime Minister had clashed in total disagreement concerning the conduct of the war and what should be the top priorities, but the unexpected collapse of the Turkish resistance, the continuous advance, and the enthusiasm of the people obscured the fact that these two men were diametrically opposed, and their characters could not mingle. Victory was so swift and total that the people thought that the two were a winning team set by Providence to glorify Greece.

Serbia, Greece, and Montenegro doubled their territory as a result of this war and Greece came out with the top prize: Thessalonica. The Bulgarians, on the other hand, who had fought the best units of the Turkish Army and had sustained the most casualties scored only modest gain in real estate and were stinging. They signed a separate cease-fire with the Turks and decided to turn against their allies in order to also double their own territory, at the expense of their allies.

In February 1913 Bulgaria issued Greece an ultimatum ordering the evacuation of Thessalonica. Greece stood fast, so the Bulgarians attacked. Now was the time to settle very old scores with the most evil and devious enemy of the past, and the enthusiasm, the will to fight of the Greeks was insurmountable. It is true that on paper the Bulgarians looked like a most formidable opponent. Their army was bigger, better armed and better equipped that the Greek Army. Furthermore, they were trained by Prussian professionals, and they had already defeated every one of their neighbors in recent wars, be they the Serbs, the Romanians, or the Turks. Bulgaria, being mostly a fertile plain, was also richer than rocky, arid Greece. So, in all probability, Greece did not appear to have any chance in this encounter and consequently the Serbs decided to be peaceful observers and not provoke the Bulgarians.

The initial battles between the Greeks and the Bulgarians were terribly bloody, brutal, and ferocious. The centuries-old hatred rekindled by recent Bulgarian atrocities and massacres in Greek-populated villages in Macedonia brought forth the worst in the combatants. The fighting reached savage proportion and no quarter was offered by either side. Luck was on the Greek side; the Bulgarians committed the cardinal sin of underestimating their opponent. They frontally attacked the Greeks on all fronts, expecting the Greeks to crumble and retreat. Instead, the Greeks counterattacked, and in less than a month the backbone of the Bulgarian Army was broken. The surprise and disappointment of the Bulgarians for their failure was followed by panic and a disorganized retreat. Even their commanding chief, General Hesapsief, was captured prisoner. The élan of the Greek Army was suburb. The Greek attacks and in-depth penetrations were so swift that in another month, the Greeks had crossed the old Bulgarian border, liberating Greek populations in Macedonia that had lived through a nightmare under Bulgarian rule. The Bulgarians were incapable to organize even a token resistance to the advancing Greeks.

Bulgaria's neighbors, Serbia in the west, and Romania in the north, upon observing the unexpected routing of the Bulgarian army by the Greeks, decided to act and settle their scores with their old adversary. They both invaded Bulgaria and marched into the territories that Bulgaria had conquered in the past from them. Bulgaria's position was desperate. The Greek Army had reached the outskirts of Sofia, the capital, and was preparing for a triumphant parade into the city. King Boris of Bulgaria begged for the intervention of his uncles, Kaiser Wilhelm of Germany, and Tsar Nicolas of Russia. Both monarchs readily responded to their nephew's appeals and a cease-fire immediately ordered.

It was time for peace in the Balkans and a treaty with Turkey, because at least in theory, the war with Turkey was not yet over. The Greek Army was deprived of its triumphant entry into Sofia but the jubilation and euphoria of the Greek people at having so decisively defeated and humiliated in so short a time, two of the most hated enemies reached no end. Athens was the site of continuous celebration, merriment, and excitement. Day and night people were dancing in the streets and praising their leaders to the sky.

Meanwhile, the old king, George, had been assassinated under the most mysterious of circumstances and to everybody's puzzlement, because he was a popular and loved king. Constantine had ascended the Greek throne while leading his army in the heart of Bulgaria. No man has ever become king under more opportune conditions. Constantine's popularity was unsurpassed. His people admired and adored him. He stood next to God in their adulation, and he would lead them back into Constantinople.

The legend was now quite clear: Under a Constantine Emperor we lost her, and a Constantine would take her back. People were already fantasizing the Patriarch crowning Constantine Emperor of Byzantium within the walls of the greatest church in the sacred city: the Hagia Sophia. He was the personification of every Greek dream held dear during the more than four hundred years of Turkish rule.

Greek soldiers with French St. Etienne Mle 1907 machine gun, used by my father at Proussa.

THE GRECO-TURK WAR 1919-1922 – GREEKS FOUGHT TO ENFORCE THE TREATY OF SEVRES THAT RETURNED TERRITORY TO GREECE AT THE END OF WWI, BUT WHICH THE TURKS REFUSED TO RECOGNIZE.

At Proussa (Bursa), Asia Minor, in spring 1921, General Papoulas, Commander in Chief of the Greek Army, overlooks the city my father helped liberate.

CHAPTER 2

Statesman vs. Monarch

THERE WAS ONLY one man in Greece whose popularity ran in a parallel course to the one of Constantine: Eleftherios Venizelos. He was, to many, the architect of the victory, Constantine the tool. Had it not been for Venizelos, Greece would not have so powerful a navy and then the outcome of the war might have been different. The more sophisticated liberals in Greece did not share the people's love for Constantine. They saw him as an undesirable foreigner: his father was a Danish prince, the brother of Queen Alexandra of Great Britain, and his mother was a Romanoff princess. They were secretly accusing him of having orchestrated the assignation of his father.

The negotiations that ensued the cease-fire in the Balkan wars did not turn to Greece's benefit. Upon the insistence of the Kaiser, who was Constantine's brother-in-law, most of the territory taken away from Bulgaria was reinstated to her and then some. Bulgaria, at the insistence of the Tsar, was even given an outlet into the Aegean Seas in spite of the fact that that particular area was inhabited by almost exclusively Greek populations. Further, Greece had to withdraw from north Epirus because that province became part of the newly created country of Albania, engineered, incidentally, by Italy. In spite of adverse developments in the negotiations, Greece came out with having more than doubled her territory and added half a million Greeks to her population.

In the beginning of 1914, elections were held throughout Greece; the liberal party of Venizelos was returned to power by an overwhelming majority, especially in the newly acquired areas. His political opponents rallied to the King for solace and support, and so the beginning of a split of the nation was in the offing at the dawn of World War I.

In the interim period between the end of the Balkan War and the Great War, Greece signed a friendship treaty and military assistance alliance with Serbia, which meant that in case either country was attacked the other should rush to its assistance.

In 1914, hopelessly entangled in alliances, the fate of Europe was sealed with the fatal shots fired in Sarajevo at the Austro-Hungarian Crown Prince, engaging another bloody and devastating conflict for four horrible years. As the murder occurred by a Serb in a Bosnian town, Austria demanded exaggerated, humiliating compensations from Serbia that no country with honor could possibly meet. Serbia threw herself to the mercy of Russia for protection. Russia warned Austria that if she invaded Serbia, Russia would take it as a declaration of war against her. Russia, as part of her pan-Slavistic policy, was the self-appointed champion of all Slavs. Germany warned Russia that of she initiated hostilities against Austria, then a state of war would exist between them. France informed Germany that she was bound by the *Entente Cordiale* to fight at the side of Russia should she be attacked. Great Britain was also bound by this alliance. Italy, who had signed a treaty with the Central Powers, Austria and Germany, did not make a move, waiting for further developments, wishing to throw her weight to the winning side.

The bleeding and decimate Ottoman Empire was at a dilemma. Traditionally her best protector had been Great Britain with which she shared common interest in Egypt and the Sudan, but Britain's protection was offered whenever Turkey was threatened by Russia. Britain's foremost policy was to never allow the Russians into the so-called 'warm seas,' and the Straits of Hellespont securely in Turkish hands was a safeguard of this policy. But now Russia and England were allies against Germany who was admired by the Young Turks, a military-political coalition of young officers who were determined to reform Turkey and bring her into the 20th Century.

Since the Young Turks had, by means of a military coup, taken over the government of Turkey, the ties between the two countries had been strengthened and Germany considered Turkey as being within her sphere of influence. The Turkish Army and Navy were now trained by German officers and Germany was financing and building a railroad connecting Berlin to Baghdad all across the Ottoman Empire. The British did not like the idea of a railroad which would bring the Germans so much closer to India. Turkey decided to bide her time and wait but was hoping in case of war that Germany would be the victor. Bulgaria felt in equal terms. Russia had always been her protector and she owed her very existence to Russia, but in recent time, Germany had come to her assistance. German officers were training her army and Germany was admired much more than decadent and old-fashioned Russia.

Greece was faced with a dilemma because of King Constantine's delicate position. Greece's traditional allies and friends were France, Great Britain and Russia. She shared financial interest with Britain, cultural and trade interests with France, and a common religion with Russia. Her traditional enemies were leaning to the side of Germany. She had recently signed a treaty with Serbia that made it unavoidable to take Serbia's side in case Serbia was invaded by the Austrian Army, so where was the dilemma? It seems that the future Greek policy and the path she would have to walk in case war broke out was clear: at the side of her friends and allies. But this was not so, as far as the king was concerned.

King Constantine I was married to the Kaiser's sister, Sophie Hohenzollern and was devoted to his brother-in-law. He personally believed in the invincibility of the Prussian Army. He felt contempt toward the French and had promised his brother-in-law that, in case of war, he would keep Greece neutral. The people who adored him did not share his admiration for Germany but were willing to rest on the recently acquired laurels, savor the great victory and have faith in their king's political criteria. After all, the man who had led them to victory knew best what was in the interest of his country. Venizelos, on the other hand, was determined that, should war break, Greece would come to Serbia's assistance, and he was enraged by the Kaiser's partiality in favor of Bulgaria during the Balkan negotiations. He felt that Greece had nothing to expect from the Germans and much to lose.

The war came in August of 1914 engulfing almost the whole of Europe. Serbia was overwhelmed by the Austrians and was desperately appealing for assistance to her Greek ally. Venizelos demanded of the King to allow the Greek army to march to Serbia's rescue, but the king dismissed him. There was only one alternative for Venizelos. He resigned and charged the king with violation of both the Constitution and the honor of Greece. The king proclaimed elections, but Venizelos and his party refused to participate on the grounds that no elections were needed since the Liberal Party enjoyed an overwhelming majority in parliament. The king went ahead with the election without the participation of the largest party and the resulting government was a minority government comprised of court lackeys. The fuse of political passion and dissent was now lit in Greece. The split of the people was total. Father against son and brother against brother.

CHAPTER 3

The Greek Swimmer Founds a Fortune

THE PANAYOTOPOULOS FAMILY in Piraeus was a strong supporter of the Liberal party and its leader Eleftherios Venizelos. The family engaged in shipping, banking, trading and the manufacture of abrasives. Most of their trading partners were in England, the British Empire, or France. Their ships were sailing to the British, French, and Dutch colonies and bringing home to Greece tea, coffee, cocoa, spices and all such products known as 'colonial ware.' They were storing the imports in large warehouses in Piraeus and distributing them to their dealers all over Greece and the Balkans. The children of the Panayotopoulos family were educated by private tutors and were all fluent in French.

This branch of the Panayotopoulos family had been established in Piraeus since 1842 by Captain Michael Panayotopoulos, my great-great grandfather, who was born Michael Rapitis. He had participated in the Greek war of independence against the Turks of the Ottoman Empire in 1821. The war had lasted eight years and ended, through the intervention of Britain, France, and Russia, with the granting of independence to only the southern part of Greece, a miniscule proportion of the area within the Ottoman Empire that was inhabited by Greeks.

Captain Michael had excelled during the war and had acquired the fame of a hero because, being a native of the island of Chios, he could swim, surprisingly, a rarity. He was an illiterate young fellow and may have been born in the year 1800. It was he who would be chosen by his superiors to navigate the Greek fireships and attach them to the sides of the Turkish ships of line and set them afire. Being a swimmer, he could then swim back to safety.

In 1821 some Greeks organized and rebelled against Ottoman rule, and the island of Chios also joined the rebellion against the Turkish Sultan. This rebellion came as a surprise to the Turkish establishment because the Greeks had a certain degree of autonomy at the time. They prospered, pursuing their traditional business of shipping. Chios had a privileged position as a royal gift to the harem, because Chios is an island that produces gum out of mastic trees, and the women in the harem loved chewing gum. Chios was very important to them. The Sultan was incensed that Chios rebelled against his rule, so he ordered the inhabitants of Chios to be massacred. In the Louvre, there is a big painting by De la Croix which shows the *Massacre of Chios*. Most of the men of Chios were on board their ships so they were not there when the killing occurred, but about 15,000 old men and women and children were massacred and the few survivors were sold to slavery.

Greece, rebellious Greece, decided to take revenge on that. They waited until the Ramadan, the Islamic holiday when for forty days the Moslems fast, and then they feast. Even though alcoholic beverages are not allowed in Islam, on the day of Ramadan, most Turks are drunk. On that particular day the Greeks sent a fireship to go and blow up the largest unit of the Turkish Navy, which was a three-line battleship. Michael Rapitis was chosen to pilot the fireship because he would be able to escape by swimming. It happened there were two ships, anchored side by side. He anchored his fireship between the two Turkish ships of the line and the explosion of the one broadcast the fire to the other, so the two top units of the Turkish Navy were blown up. The burning debris flying from those two exploding ships transmitted the fire to other Turkish ships. The entire Turkish fleet was maimed, if not totally destroyed, on that day in Chios. So, Chios was avenged, and Michael Rapitis became a national hero.

He did not have any further success even though he attempted to blow up Turkish ships in Rhodes, and even in Alexandria in Egypt. But his first and only success in the island of Chios made him immortal in the annals of Greek history. When Greece, a very small proportion of what used to be the Hellenic world, became independent in 1829, in recognition of his service, he was given ownership of a brigantine, which during the war he had taken as a prize. He became the owner-skipper of the 40-ton merchant ship.

Rapitis, with a crew of ten, would sail his ship to Odessa in Russia, load it with wheat and sell the cargo in Marseille or Livorno in Italy or Trieste, an Austro-Hungarian port in the Adriatic. He was making a fair living in the wheat business and had reached the age of forty-two still a bachelor. It seemed that he was immune to female charm, and no woman had managed to attract him, until the inevitable happened.

After an unusually successful sale, he and his crew went to celebrate in a Trieste *café chantant*, as saloons were known in Europe at the time. A very young and very pretty blue-eyed blond Hungarian girl called Julitska was dancing and singing at the establishment and, for a certain fee, was also willing to entertain the patrons in private. Michael Panayotopoulos was mesmerized by her youth and beauty, and he invited her to sit with him at his table. He ordered his men to go aboard ship and prepare for sailing in the middle of the night, though this was unusual and not in accordance with port procedure. Offering the girl twice her usual fee, he asked her in very bad Italian if she would consider coming with him to his ship because he felt uncomfortable going to a room in the saloon. The girls were not supposed to leave the premises with their customers, but Captain Michael was so handsome, so robust, and strong, and his pouch was so filled with gold coins that Julitska felt she could allow an exception.

When she awoke next morning, happy, content and richer, thanks to Michael Panayotopoulos' generosity, she felt a peculiar movement. The ship was under sail, and she was in the open sea in the middle of the Adriatic. Her protests were to no avail. Captain Michael has set course to Piraeus and that was where she would spend the rest of her life.

In Greece, he married Julitska and that changed his life. Julitska turned out to be a magnificent wife and mother and brought Michael good fortune. She was literate and she could speak both Hungarian and a little bit of German and she became the beacon of the rest of his life. She managed to make him a major ship owner with four-masted schooners that would go from Greece to the Dutch East Indies and to China, and bring back to Greece spices, tea and other so-called colonial wares. Julitska convinced him that he should also create a fleet in the Danube, so many of his wares that were imported from the colonial ports would find their way to Bratislava, to Budapest and to Vienna. She gave birth to many healthy children.

There was only one shadow in his married life. The origins of his Hungarian wife and her profession were the subject of considerable gossip in the small and restricted Athenian society. No matter how rich and successful a businessman he turned out to be, he was never accepted and never invited to the Royal Palace, and his heroics in the war were watered down to appear almost insignificant. He was no longer considered a hero of the revolution and a factor for the independence of Greece. For that, he developed a profound hatred toward the ruling dynasty and the people of the court.

In defiance, he even determined to change his name. Since his godfather's name was Panayotis, which in English would translate into 'James,' he changed his name to Panayotopoulos, which means 'the son of James.' He died in 1862, a wealthy and happy man in his eighties, with a large family, a bank, a warehouse, barges that traversed the Danube, and a fleet of six oceangoing merchantmen, all bigger and faster than the modest brigantine with which he had started his career. When Michael Rapitis died, he didn't die as Michael Rapitis, he died as Michael Panayotopoulos.

From then, it was decided that if the Athenian society was to ignore the Panayotopoulos clan, they would ignore the society and marry foreign women. That deprived them of the very convenient Greek custom of receiving from the bride's father a substantial dowry, a custom obsolete and forgotten in the rest of Europe, but the Panayotopoulos family maintained that they were rich enough and did not need their wives' money to make it in life. Their form of inverted snobbism kept them active and agile in their endeavor to excel in business and acquire more wealth and the power that comes with it. Their daughters were given in marriage to their foreign business associates, and the men married whomever they pleased.

One exception to that practice was Captain Michael's grandson, also Michael 'Mickey' Panayotopoulos, a very promising young man extremely interested in the business and politics of the time. He fell in love with a Greek girl from the island of Aegina, Helen Peppa. Born in 1872, she was quite an exceptional girl for her time. She was, for a Greek woman, unusually tall, almost six feet, a rarity, and she was also an intellectual.

Girls were then considered mostly a burden, and their function was to bear children. A woman was supposed to live in the shadow of her husband, to be seen but very little heard, and they had practically no rights or privileges. Very rarely would a Greek family spend the money to educate their daughters beyond the absolutely essential knowledge of how to read and write, and some superficial learning of a foreign language, and a little piano. It was considered at the time, a disgrace for a family if any of its girls worked, and only the very poor and destitute had their girls working as maids or seamstresses—women did not buy their clothes readymade, they had them made at home, and those who could afford a seamstress hired one—or in menial and domestic jobs.

Not so the Peppa family. They were not rich, but most were highly placed civil servants, judges, and government functionaries. One of Helen Peppa's uncles was a Supreme Court Justice of Athens, the *Areios Pagos*. Another was the abbot of the largest monastery in the holy mountain, Athos, which is a Monk community. On the island of Aegina, about thirty-six miles south of Athens, Helen Peppa's father had a ten-acre pistachio grove. That was all he had. But he also had three daughters. Daughters, at that time, needed dowries to get married, and ten acres of pistachios could not produce enough dowries for three. The two who were pretty, their father thought, would manage on half the grove to get them husbands. The third, who was too tall for a Greek woman, and not as pretty, he would educate, so that, as a spinster, she could make her own living.

The family exerted influence and enabled Helen to be admitted to the Athens University, where she became the first woman to be graduated from the University and obtained degrees in Philosophy and Literature in 1892. Helen thus enjoyed the best education possible in the primitive Greek public educational system, but she couldn't get a job. She was staying then in Piraeus at the house of a relative. She decided to write Primaries, textbooks for elementary schools, as she couldn't become hired as a teacher, in order to make a living. The Primaries she wrote were accepted by the Ministry of Education of Greece for use in the public schools run by the state, possibly through the influence of her relatives, but the royalties out of Primaries were not a large revenue. She thought, since she couldn't get work as a teacher, she would have to open a school of her own. But for this, she needed money.

The biggest and best bank in Piraeus at the time was the Bank of Piraeus of which my grandfather, Michael 'Mickey' Panayotopoulos, was owner and Chief Executive Officer. As Helen entered the door of the bank, a guard moved to bar her way. Unescorted women were not welcome. But Mickey had seen her enter and was intrigued.

He approached her and said, "What do you do, what do you want, Madame?"

Helen spoke unhesitatingly, "Well, what do people do in banks? I came to ask for a loan."

"Come to my office," he invited. "but you can't apply for a loan without your husband."

Settling herself, she admitted, "I am not married."

"Well," he offered, "your brother or your father, then".

She responded calmly, "I don't have a brother, and my father is in Aegina."

Incredulous, Mickey's voice rose, "This is uncalled for, for a woman to walk in public and enter bank establishments!"

Quietly, she answered, "Be it as it may, I came here because I was told your bank is the best bank in Piraeus."

"Yes, my bank is definitely the best bank in Piraeus. But it is unheard of to give loans to unescorted women. What do you need the money for?"

She declared, "I want to open my own school."

"On what grounds do you think you are eligible to open your own school?" he demanded.

"I have a degree from the University of Athens."

Mickey had never heard of a woman obtaining a degree from the University of Athens, but he believed her. "Alright," he proceeded, "In order to obtain a loan it is necessary to have collateral. What do you have?"

"I have royalties of the books I am going to write."

Helen's confidence was startling to Mickey, and he continued patiently, "Banks don't give loans on future or imaginary income. What do you have now?"

"I don't have anything."

Almost with exasperation, Micky asked, "What does your father have?"

Nonplussed, Helen replied, "He has an orchard of ten acres of pistachio groves."

"Do you think your father will co-sign a loan on the basis of his pistachio groves?" Mickey frowned.

"I doubt it," was her response.

Confounded, Mickey, the banker, concluded gently, "There's no way you can obtain a loan."

Then, drawing a breath, he said, "Please, stand up." She gracefully rose from her chair. He said, "Please, turn around." She turned around. Skirts back then were down to the ground. Mickey wanted to ascertain whether she was wearing high heels because she was at least three inches taller than he. Finally, he asked outright, "Are you wearing heels?"

She balked at that. "I came to your bank to ask for a loan, not to discuss my footwear."

"I have an idea," he began, "Instead of having a school to teach other people's children, why don't you teach your own?"

"I told you I'm not married, how can I have children?" It was her turn to be exasperated.

"Well, you get married and have children and teach them." His voice, his look, created an intimacy between them.

Catching her breath, but without coyness, she said, "Is that a proposal?"

He nodded, "Yes. My mother is Italian, my grandmother was Hungarian, and I think it's time we put some Greek blood in the family, and you being tall as you are, we shall have tall children."

At the age of twenty-five, a very late age then, Helen Peppa married Mickey Panayotopoulos, and she not only towered over him in height, she was, compared to him, an intellectual giant. She wrote poetry, short stories, contributed to the literary pages of the Athenian newspapers and magazines and authored many textbooks for elementary schools. But Mickey was a business genius. The bank was only one branch of the business. Mickey had an ocean going fleet. He had a very large fleet of barges in the Danube, and he had already started the emery—the abrasives—factory in Piraeus. And he was also a junior partner in a munitions factory, so he was quite well to do. The business and the money came to him from his father, but he augmented the fortune. Mickey was the one who started the emery quarries in Naxos by using convict labor, meaning labor didn't cost him much because he was hiring convicts from the state.

Their marriage produced four sons and a daughter born in exact intervals of two years apart. It was their second born son, Takis, who was the handsomest, liveliest, most mischievous, and rebellious of the lot. Their third son, Alexander, was shy and timid, but he had a tempestuous temperament and was highly intelligent and very inquisitive. At the age of seven he showed a great interest in the business of the Panayotopoulos clan and instead of playing with children of his age, he was spending his time in the warehouses taking inventory, or in the bank counting money, or if a ship of the family was in harbor, he would board it and have the Master explain to him the handling of a ship. It was obvious to everyone that he would be the most suitable heir to take over the business and expand it even further. Alexander inherited his father's business genius, and was an exceptionally astute businessman, intelligent enough to always be on the fence of legality but not on the other side. In fact, he obtained a law degree at Athens University, then the only university in Greece, and he used it to keep himself out of trouble.

Alexander and Takis did not get along well together and were of entirely different character. Alex was very tight with his allowance, saving most of it, while Takis never had enough to spend. One was very much the introvert while the other was extremely extrovert. They were both tall and handsome and displayed equal ability in absorbing their lessons, but in different fields. Takis displayed an aptitude toward French, history, literature, and geography, while Alexander was better in mathematics and science. When, at the age of twelve, Takis was caught having sex with one of the young maids, he was flogged by his austere father, who could not tolerate any misbehavior in his household, and getting a maid pregnant was no small matter. His mother, on the other hand, always forgave him no matter what he did; he was her favorite son and she loved him dearly.

By the time Takis was fifteen years old, it was 1914, the year the Great War started, he was six feet, three inches tall, very handsome with brown curly hair, and looked much older. His was a debonair and carefree life, and he enjoyed it to the hilt as long as it could be concealed from his father. He had inherited his mother's literary talent and under a pseudonym, was writing plays and limericks for burlesque shows. His lustful targets were the female members of the cast who at that time ranked not much higher than ordinary prostitutes. His affairs and adventures with that type of girl had reached scandalous proportions for a teenager. He was spending way more than he was allowed to, but his mother was covering for him. Eventually his reputation reached his father who was infuriated and disgusted.

Mickey Panayotopoulos was now Mayor of Piraeus and could not afford any scandals concerning his son. Certainly, the stories of a teenager spending all his time in the burlesque surrounded by chorus girls and can-can dancers would make excellent copy in the Royalist press that always accused the Liberals of decadence, low morals and unprincipled behavior. Mickey Panayotopoulos saw that the only solution for his son's unruly style of life was the Military Academy. Unfortunately, they were admitting only young men who had already finished high school, and Takis was a long way from that. But money could buy everything including a high school equivalency diploma, and so Takis was propelled into the *Scholi Eyelpidon*, the prestigious Athens Military Academy. It was destined for him that the army would be his future.

It was the time that the Greeks were bursting with national pride and enthusiasm. They believed that sooner or later their country would join the Allies in the war and were looking forward to fight it out to the end with the Bulgarians and the Turks and teach them a new lesson. Even though Takis and his father did not see eye to eye in most things, their politics were identical. Takis was an enthusiastic follower of Venizelos and was eager for the day Greece would enter the conflict.

He was a brave lad and anticipated the day he would be called to arms. Unlike his brother Alexander who thought the war was bad for business and a waste of time. So, even though the Military Academy with its harsh discipline and restricted liberties was a burden heavy to bear, Takis took it in a sporting manner. The flashy blue and yellow uniform of the cadets was very appealing to girls and the army would be a convenient home to a rich officer.

He was soon to realize that he was in the wrong place. He was punished and disciplined every day, sometimes twice a day. The more he rebelled and resisted the worse it was for him. All his liberties, little as they were, had been suspended and he never had a day off. As is the custom of practically every military academy in the world, the boys of the senior class treat the novices like dirt and subject them to the most humiliating tasks. Takis got more than his share in hazing. His reputation as a playboy had preceded him, and most of his seniors who had not even kissed a girl were red with envy. There was also the fact that most of the boys in the Academy belonged to Royalist families, and Takis was the son of one of the most ardent supporters of Venizelos.

Life had changed to hell for Takis. He tried to escape a few times, but his father would not offer him any help and his mother, for once, told him that he should prove his manhood by enduring the torture and becoming the best cadet. He was also warned that if he ran away again, he would be expelled by the academy after court martial and sentencing. He was so desperate that he was considering suicide.

It was during this time that events were taking place in the theatre of the war that would change the fate of the world and of Takis Panayotopoulos.

Source www.nationsonline.org

GREECE

Piraeus was the hub of the family trade and shipping fortunes, and islands held our mines and minerals.

My father played medal-winning roles in a WWI battle at Serres, and at Bursa (Proussa) in 1921 in the Greco-Turk War.

A burning Turkish flagship in the 1821-1829 Greek War of Independence against the Ottoman Empire, such as one my great-grandfather Michael fired after covertly swimming to it, making him a hero.

A ship he captured as the spoils of war, he later used for trade, thus founding the family fortunes.

CHAPTER 4

The Split, a Disunited Greece

GREECE HAD REMAINED, by Royal Decree, neutral during the initial years of the war and it appeared that she would remain so for the duration.

After the initial successes of the German Armies both in France as well as the eastern front, both Turkey—the Ottoman Empire—and Bulgaria had joined the Central Powers and were engaged in the fighting: the Turks in the Middle East against the British, and the Bulgarians against the Serbs and the Romanians. Italy waited a little longer and once the war in France reached a stalemate after the German defeat in the Battle of the Marne, joined the *entente* after negotiating in advance with the hard-pressed Allies what she would get if she joined. Now the peaceful Alps were the scenes of battles between the Italian and Austrian armies.

Germany held the upper hand, and it was fair to believe that she had a good chance of winning. Hers were the best soldiers, the best generals, the best weapons, the more advanced technology—mustard gas—and the most disciplined and cooperating civilian population. Even at sea she was challenging the British supremacy with her Grand Fleet and her submarines. German Zeppelins were even bombing British cities.

Of all the Allies, the most vulnerable was Russia. Not only had her Army been dealt a severe blow in 1914 by General Hindenburg in Tannenberg and the Masurian swamps, but they were also losing against the Austrians, and now with Turkey in the war she had opened a new front in Armenia defending against the Turks. In fact, her combined fronts were over a thousand miles extending from the Baltic Sea to the Carpathian Mountains and all along her border with the Ottoman Empire. The Russian Army was the worst equipped; most of its soldiers reached the front without a rifle and no training whatsoever. Russia was almost beaten to her knees. There was a British military mission in St. Petersburg that was offering the Tsar twenty-five *kopeks* for each new recruit he was sending to the front, which probably explains why most Russian soldiers had no rifles and had never been trained. They were rounded up like cattle in the villages and railed directly to the firing line.

Russia had to be assisted at all costs or else it was a matter of little time before her fronts would collapse, and that meant more German troops in France and an assured German victory. But helping Russia was not an easy task. It was impossible to send her the needed munitions and other assistance across the Baltic Sea because it was dominated by the German fleet. The north ocean was frozen most of the time, and the Russians had only the most primitive and inadequate port facilities there. A possibility existed in shipping assistance to her through her Pacific port of Vladivostok, but that involved extremely lengthy sea and land lanes and it would take an inordinate amount of time. Some help was reaching her from India through Iran, but there were practically no roads there and that route proved inadequate.

It was in February 1915 that Winston Churchill, then First Lord of the Admiralty, proffered the idea of forcing the way through the Dardanelle's into the Black Sea by using the tremendous power of naval fire. His plan was to pulverize the two forts that guarded the entrance of the Straits and proceed upward towards Constantinople blasting everything that offered resistance on the way. The plan might cost a few obsolete battleships, but once it succeeded Russia could then be regularly supplied from her best port, Odessa on the Black Sea. The supplies would arrive at a spot close to all the Russian fronts, and with satisfactory means of transportation and fast dispatch. The second advantage of the plan was that Constantinople, the capital city of the Ottoman Empire, would be under the mercy of the formidable guns of the British Navy and in all probability the Sultan would sue for peace. In order to implement the plan Britain and her allies needed a port facility in the area that could accommodate such a large concentration of naval ships.

The Bay of Moudros at the Greek Island of Lemnos, only sixty nautical miles away from the entrance of the straits, was the ideal location. Great Britain, France and Russia made overtures to the King of Greece to grant port facilities at Moudros and join the Allies in this venture. Britain even offered the island of Cyprus, then under her control, to Greece in order to entice her to enter the Alliance. King Constantine obviously knew that the request for port facilities was purely symbolic, and the British would occupy Lemnos no matter what he did if their mind was set to force an entry through the straits. So even if he granted the British request, he was safe with his brother-in-law who would not take it as a breach of his promise of strict neutrality.

Venizelos on the other hand, was thrilled by the unique opportunity offered to Greece to join the Alliance, with Cyprus given freely as enticement. He had a strong feeling that he had the Allies over a barrel and that he could negotiate much more than just Cyprus. He felt that Constantinople was the most he could ask for and given the circumstances he would probably get her. The Greek participation was needed for Churchill's plan to have a 100 percent chance of success because there were no land forces available to the Allies. Even though the plan was based on an exclusively naval operation, still some land troops would be needed to guard the coasts and capture whatever the navy had pounded. Furthermore, unknown to either Churchill or King Constantine, there was a Greek plan at the Greek general staff conceived by Colonel Metaxas during the Balkan War, which provided for a swift amphibian action with Constantinople the target. The combination of the humble Greek plan with the might of the British Navy spelled for sure success.

It was during Venizelos' tenure of the office of Defense Minister that he had authorized Metaxas to draw a plan for the conquest of Constantinople via the straits and forestall the eventuality of the Bulgarians getting there first. Metaxas, who later became Dictator of Greece, was considered a genius tactician. He had finished first in his class at the *Berliner Kriegsakademie,* the 'West Point' of Prussia, which was acknowledged as the foremost military school in the world. In fact, the Kaiser himself had been in the same class with Metaxas, and he and other classmates and fellow cadets used to call Metaxas 'small Moltke' after the greatest general in the annals of Prussian history. 'Small' because Metaxas was a short fellow, but amply compensated by brains what he lacked in height.

After the formal request by the Allies, Venizelos rushed to the palace and met with the king. He tried to persuade him and presented the Metaxas plan to him. He cajoled him, besieged him, begged him and threatened him, to no avail. The king was determined to remain neutral. Venizelos even had Metaxas attend the meeting, who stated that his plan with the added might of the British and French fleets had no chance of failing. Metaxas supported the king because he, too, loved the Kaiser, and thought that even if Turkey were out of the fight and Russia reinforced, still the Germans would win the war and Greece would be on the losing side. It was after this meeting that Venizelos resigned and temporarily withdrew from Greek politics, accusing the king as a traitor and violator of the constitution.

Events followed as expected. The king granted the Allies port facilities at Moudros, on the island of Lemnos but declined the offer of Cyprus and declared that Greece was to remain neutral. Events proved that the

German general staff had anticipated Churchill's plan. They very inconspicuously had mined the straits and installed 40 cm. caliber mortars in the valleys and ridges on both sides of the Dardanelles in such positions that it was practically impossible for the naval guns to hit because of the steepness of the angle. The mortars were deployed in such a manner that it was very unlikely for a ship to clear the minefields and not get hit by a mortar, considering the narrowness of the straits, an average width of 1,200 yards. Some of the best Turkish troops under the command of Kemal Pasha were also stationed in the area to guard the mortars from amphibian assault. The Germans were determined to prevent the British from forcing their way and they succeeded. After the British and French Navies sustained very heavy losses, either because of the mines or direct mortar hits, they concluded that the only way to force their way to the Black Sea was by landing an army and capturing the mortars.

That also turned into a fiasco because the Australian and New Zealand troops that landed were small in number, and the Turks were prepared for them. In less than a month of fighting, over 15,000 brave Australian and New Zealand Army Corps, the ANZACs, had strewn with their bodies the outskirts of the Turkish town of Gallipolis. The Turks counterattacked and the British were forced to evacuate the insignificant gains in occupied land that they had secured. When it was too late, new troops arrived, but they were no more needed. The plan to force a way across the straits was abandoned. Churchill had to resign his office and join the fighting in France as a colonel of the British Army.

At the same time that the Allies were suffering this devastating defeat in Gallipolis, another calamity befell them. The Serbian Army was totally defeated and overwhelmed by the Austro-Germans, and the Serbian remnants were now retreating in panic toward the Greek border. The King of Serbia asked the King of Greece to offer sanctuary to his retreating troops, but Constantine declined stating that such a sanctuary could be interpreted by the Germans as an act of war. Greece was not in a mood to fight Austria for the sake of a few thousand Serbian soldiers. The Allies decided to take action on that issue, Greek neutrality be damned. Since they had some 40,000 idle troops at hand in Moudros, they used them for a landing in Thessalonica and deployed them along the Greek-Serbian border at the same time they occupied the Greek island of Kerkyra (Corfu) and used it as a sanctuary for the Serbian army and a place where the Serbs could lick their wounds and reorganize.

The flagrant violation of Greek sovereignty and neutrality appalled the Royalists in Greece. Not so, the Venizelists. The king protested but declared his determination that Greece was to remain neutral. The people were split, and civil war seemed very possible. Meanwhile a Balkan Front was established with the Allies fighting the Germans and the Austrians on Greek soil. Along the Greek-Bulgarian border, the best two Greek Army divisions were deployed and in the initial phases of the Balkan Front, the fighting was confined on the Greek-Serbian border only, but it was a matter of time when the Bulgarians would join the fighting. Indeed, the Kaiser, through his ambassador in Athens, informed his brother-in-law, King Constantine, that in view of the fact that the Allies had occupied Thessalonica, and were constantly reinforcing their positions, it became imperative for the Central Powers to also violate Greek neutrality and attack the Allies through the Greek-Bulgarian border.

King Constantine was advised to order the two Greek divisions guarding that border to surrender and was given the Kaiser's word that the men of those divisions would be taken to Germany and treated as guests of the German state for the duration of the war. The king complied with his brother-in-law's demand and the two Greek crack divisions surrendered. No shot was fired. And the century old, most hated enemy, the Bulgarians, were roaming unresisted in Greek Macedonia terrorizing and massacring Greek populations. Most Greeks, even some Royalists, couldn't tolerate that. They were disgusted and furious at the king's action. Two Greek divisions were surrendered without a fight when the very lives of hundreds of thousands of newly liberated Greeks were at stake. Shame, disillusionment, humiliation and anger filled the heart of almost every Greek. This was the drop that filled the cup as far as Venizelos was concerned. He left Athens for Thessalonica proclaiming a new provisional government, declaring war on the Central Powers, and inviting every Greek to join him in fighting the hated enemies that had oppressed Greece for centuries. Venizelos' call to arms was accepted with unprecedented enthusiasm. Thousands of young men were rushing to any and every means of transportation to join the ranks of the army of 'New Greece.' One after the other all the units of the Greek Army were joining Venizelos, and some of the Navy. And that was the opportunity that Takis Panayotopoulos was hoping for.

The day of Venizelos' proclamation in August 1916, Takis Panayotopoulos jumped over the fence of the Military Academy as a second-year cadet, to return after three years as the most decorated and youngest Lieutenant in the Greek Army.

The moment he cleared the grounds of the Academy, Takis stole a bicycle and rushed to Piraeus, seven miles away, hoping to get passage to Thessalonica. He was in luck. The whole First Attican Regiment had appropriated the passenger steamship *Angelica* and was embarking. He was wearing the fatigues of the Academy when he presented himself to the first commissioned officer he saw and requested permission to board. The officer took him to the commanding officer, Colonel Papamandelos, and introduced him. The colonel was an avowed Venizelist and knew of Takis' father. He said, "You came at a most opportune moment, Cadet, because I need a sergeant in the Third Company of the First Battalion. Go find your men and your superior officers, Sergeant Panayotopoulos, and assume your duty." Takis was thrilled. Not only was he on his way to the fighting, he was in the army, and even a non-commissioned officer.

The passage from Piraeus to Thessalonica took usually two days and nights but, in this case, it took a little longer. In the first night of sailing *Angelica* was torpedoed by a German submarine off the coast of the island of Euboea. Takis was a good swimmer and had no difficulty reaching the shore, but quite a few of his comrades drowned or were lost in the blast. In his first day in the army, he already had received his baptismal in enemy fire, albeit of a different nature than what he had anticipated. The war had reached Greece for real. The first casualties had colored the water of the Aegean with their blood. Two British destroyers arrived the next day and picked up the survivors of the Attica First Regiment, delivering them the morrow in Thessalonica with no incident.

The harbor in Thessalonica was a tower of Babel. British, French, Italian, Moroccan, Indian, Australian, New Zealand, Rhodesian and South African troops were either disembarking or mingling with the ones already on the quays. All the allied troops were under the command of French General Francois d'Espret. Takis' regiment was immediately ordered to march and bivouac at a village twelve miles north of Thessalonica. His hopes to spend the night in the arms of a girl, after so many months, were shattered, but in a war, everyone has to suffer. All the men in Takis' platoon were veterans and at least five years older than he. He was the youngest in the regiment, but also the tallest and that was some compensation. The training and harshness of the Military Academy stood him in good stead, and it did not take him long to earn the respect of his men. He was an excellent shot and a good all-around athlete. Hunting and fencing had been his hobbies apart from his insatiable desire for women. The regiment remained in the village of Asprovalta only six days, enough to count its casualties from the torpedoing, reequip and get ready for the front. The Bulgarians were advancing; they had already occupied Serres and only shadow resistance was offered to them by the very thin French lines.

In the very first encounter Takis was up to the expectations of his men and proved to be a fearless warrior and clever leader. His men were unhappy with the fact that they had already fought three years ago in the same region and had to spill new blood for the same real estate, but their casualties were slight while the Bulgarians they had ambushed fled, leaving ten dead and twenty-six wounded. His men were about to cut the throats of the wounded prisoners, but Takis ordered them to put the bayonets back into the scabbards. "We are Hellenes, the children of Leonidas and Pericles, not barbarians who murder their prisoners," he told them.

His men said that it was common practice during the Balkan war to kill all Bulgarians. "They were doing the same to us."

Takis was adamant; his would be a clean, chivalrous war. Some of the Bulgarian wounded understood Greek and crawled to his feet, kissing his boots. This episode impressed his men very much and they realized that young sergeant was something special, a gentleman. Most of them were simple half illiterate peasants from the vineyards around Athens and the war had made them even rougher, but they were moved by Takis' humane attitude toward the helpless wounded enemy. They carried the wounded prisoners back to the regimental headquarters and the staff officers were very glad that they had prisoners to interrogate. They were even more surprised at the willingness of those prisoners to cooperate and respond truthfully to their questioning. They knew it had to be the expression of their gratitude to the young sergeant who had spared their lives.

The action at the Balkan Front was swift and in a very fast pace. The battles followed one another rapidly, and as the Greek troops poured in with increasing rate day by day, the Allied positions were secured and capable of counterattacking. Takis was engulfed in battle and the continuous fighting and toll had no ill effect upon him. It was not quite a month since he had joined the fighting that he received a field promotion to first lieutenant for outstanding gallantry over and beyond the call of duty. He was also awarded the Greek Military Cross. To obtain his commission and medal, he traveled to Thessalonica where Premier Eleftherious Venizelos himself handed him his officer's stars and shook his hand in congratulation. As if that were not enough, the French Commanding General gave him the Order of Knight of the French Honor Legion and kissed him on both cheeks.

Takis was elated, but also a little taken aback. He did not think that he had performed anything unusual or outstanding. It was the thirty men of his platoon whose reliability and bravery should be rewarded. It was thanks to them that he had been able to attack a whole Bulgarian company, push them off the hill they were defending, and capture the heavy artillery battery that was stationed behind the hill. It is true that he had no idea how to fire a heavy 105 mm. caliber gun but one of his men had served briefly in the artillery and knew how, so, thrilled with their new toys, they turned them around and fired them at the Bulgarians. It was a lucky shot that landed four miles away in the old school where the Bulgarian Chief of Staff and his headquarters were stationed and killed them all. This one lucky shot created such panic among the Bulgarian ranks that they abandoned their positions and ran away, but he did not feel that he deserved all the credit for that.

He was much more delighted with Venizelos' handshake and took the opportunity to chat with the great man. He told him about the soldier who had been in the artillery and without whom they would have never been able to shoot at the Bulgarians with their own cannons. Venizelos assured him that the man would be rewarded with the Bronze Medal of Distinguished Service and promoted to sergeant.

Venizelos insisted to have the full account of Takis' action and Takis was more than eager to tell him the whole story with every detail just so that he could prolong his stay with the admired man.

"Well, Your Excellency, our Second Battalion had attacked the hill the previous day and took a licking, so my captain said that it would be our turn to make a frontal assault first thing in the morning. He ordered me to take my platoon by sundown and reconnaissance the foot of the hill, which I did. Then I had the idea to take advantage of the obscurity and climb the hill a little higher. We then saw the Bulgarian sentries before they saw us, so we sneaked as close as we could and stuck them with our bayonets. I had some of my men dress in their uniforms and pretend they were the Bulgarian sentries and the rest of us hid in the surrounding bushes. When, after a few hours the replacement sentries arrived, we very swiftly ambushed them and slit their throats.

"It was past midnight when we crept up to the top to the hill where the Bulgarian machine guns were posted. We waited until dawn and attacked them with our bayonets. They were so surprised that they hardly fired at us. In less than five minutes we had taken all their machine guns and we were firing them at the rest of the Bulgarian company. They obviously thought they were outnumbered and fled. Then we used the machine guns to kill the men of the artillery battery on the other side of hill. The whole thing was over in less than an hour. It was no big thing, Your Excellency, just a piece of cake. I really don't deserve all this praise and medals, but I'll take them."

Venizelos was smiling under his moustache, and he was really beaming inside himself. He was very pleased with this young officer who was the son of one of his closest political friends.

"Do you know, young man, that your parents are very anxious about you? Your father thought that you might have joined me, and he wrote a letter asking me to make inquiries and let your mother know, who has gone out of her mind. Why haven't you written to her? For that, I penalize you to take no leave, return to the front immediately and keep the good work going. But before you go, I order you to sit there at my desk and use my stationary and write your mother a letter. When you are finished, don't seal the envelope. I want to add a few lines to her myself."

Takis was overwhelmed. He was treated as friend by the foremost man in Greece.

As the Greek ranks continued to increase, the Austro-Germans and the Bulgarians started losing the initiative, and by the winter of 1917, the Balkan Front bogged down to the trench warfare that prevailed in all the other fronts.

Meanwhile that ridiculous condition whereby half of Greece, the southern part from Mount Olympus down to the Peloponnese, was neutral, ruled by the king and his appointees, while the north part, mostly the areas liberated during the Balkan War and all the islands, under Venizelos and his friends, was at war, could not continue. Unfortunately, the Allies did not leave it up to the Greek people to find a solution. They forced one themselves that created much bitterness among the Royalists. Once Venizelos established his government in Thessalonica and the Greek troops joined the Allies in the fighting, the French acted to expel King Constantine I from Greece. It was in their interest to turn Greece into a republic after the French model, and so turn her into a French satellite, rather than have her remain a kingdom with a ruling dynasty related by blood to the British crown.

Without provocation the French fleet blockaded the port of Piraeus and isolated the southern part of the country. Trade was now down to nothing, and all businesses suffered. That had an adverse effect to what the French expected. The Royalists hated this foreign intervention and rallied around the king. That disappointed the French who hoped that after a few weeks of blockade, the Greeks would rebel against the king, so they decided to invade. They landed their marines at Phaleron, a bay and sea resort only four miles south of Athens and began to march toward Athens. To their surprise and dismay, the French marines were attacked by the Royal Guards at the shores of Phaleron and a blood bath ensued. Over 500 French marines were killed and the remaining captured.

The French admiral in charge of the ships enforcing the blockade was enraged. He never suspected that the few troops still loyal to the king would have the effrontery to oppose France. He presented the king with an ultimatum: either he order the Royal Guards to surrender, or the admiral would open fire with his naval guns and pulverize Athens. The king by now, knew that his days as monarch were counted, and in order to avert any further needless and futile bloodshed, asked for British intervention in the form of free and secure passage for himself and his family and close friends to Switzerland. His cousin, the King of England, obliged and a week after the Phaleron massacre, a British cruiser took him to Venice, and from there he went to Zurich. Most Greeks were relieved, but the whole thing had left a bitter aftertaste. The Greeks felt hurt and humiliated that foreign powers were treating them like their underlings in African colonies.

In a pandemonium of celebrations and parades, Venizelos moved his government from Thessalonica back to Athens. Greece was reunited, content, and optimistic of the future, but was presented with an unprecedented constitutional problem. She was a kingdom without a king. The French suggested to Venizelos to proclaim Greece a republic and name himself as the president. Venizelos politely declined. He was a political leader, not an opportunist, and he in no way intended to violate the constitution. Obviously, Venizelos could see the French motives and was not about to alienate Greece from her best friend, Great Britain. He had an idea how to solve the constitutional problem of the vacant throne, even though his idea would certainly create another but much lesser constitutional discrepancy.

The second-born son of King Constantine, Prince Alexander, was married to a Greek woman, Aspasia Manou. Hers was a prominent and respected Athenian family, but according to the Greek Constitution, no Greek national was allowed to bear any title with the exception of the members of the royal family. If Prince Alexander were to become king of Greece, then his wife as queen would personify a breach of the Constitution because only a princess of royal blood could be queen. When Prince Alexander married Aspasia he surrendered all his rights to the Greek throne and consequently had no place in the list of succession. On the other hand, he was very popular in Greece because he had married a local girl rather than some princess from abroad. So that was Venizelos' idea: to invite Prince Alexander to ascend the Greek throne by national acclaim. He felt sure that such a development would bridge the chasm that divided the Greek nation in two feuding camps, the Royalists, and the Liberals.

When the invitation reached him in Switzerland where he was living with the rest of the royal family, the prince was inclined to decline. After all, he was the second born, and he had surrendered his right to the throne in order to marry the girl he loved. His father, though, encouraged him to accept. The wrong king was better than no king at all in his opinion, and some day in the future, especially if the Germans were victorious, his son could abdicate on his behalf without hassle and problems of succession or constitutionality. Constantine was also afraid that if his son rejected the offer, then either Greece might turn into a republic, or a British or another prince might be offered the throne of Greece. That would spell the end to his dynasty. So, with his father's blessing and to the delirious happiness of the reunited Greek people, Prince Alexander returned to Greece. He was crowned 'King of the Hellenes,' and his wife was to be addressed as 'Royal Spouse,' not Majesty or Highness, so the constitutional problem could be somehow patched up.

Of course, to the common folk that made no difference, they were happy with their Greek pretty queen. In all Greek or Byzantine history, there seldom has been a king crowned under happier circumstances. The people were united and jubilant; Venizelos had redeemed himself in the eyes of the Royalists by proving beyond dispute that he was not against the monarchy or the throne, but only against the person of the former king, and that his motives were dictated exclusively by the national interest; the Balkan Front was stabilized, and the Allies were on the offensive. King Alexander and Venizelos were destined to lead Greece to the fulfillment of all her dreams. Or so the people hoped.

CHAPTER 5

Serres: Ninety Men Equal One Division

THIS WAS THE summer of 1917, and the war did not seem to end. True, the Allies had scored some significant victories: the French in Verdun and the British in Jutland, but the Western Front was still touch and go, the Italian front was a stalemate, and Russia was about to collapse. Only in the Balkan Front and in the Middle East were the Allies the undisputed victors, but that was more of a side show and would not decide the fortunes of war. Or so the strategists of the day thought.

The first of the Central Powers whose fronts showed signs of collapse was the Ottoman Empire. In spite of their initial successes in Gallipolis and in Kut, a small town in Mesopotamia, where in a licorice factory, they annihilated the whole Black Watch Highland Regiment, they were now retreating. Jerusalem had fallen to Lord Allenby's Australian and New Zealand Army Corps, ANZACs, and even the Russians had scored a victory against them in Armenia and the Cossacks were advancing toward Sampsun, a Black Sea town.

Trench warfare was not Takis' preference in waging a war. He now commanded ninety men of the First Company, First Battalion, First Athens Regiment attached to the 56th French Infantry Division, to which also a British brigade was assigned. His restlessness and adventurous disposition were not meant for the static, patient, miserable, and so lacking of heroics, type of warfare to which he was now subjected. His nerves were tried time and time again when he had to crawl in the dirt like a rat while the position of his regiment was pounded by enemy artillery fire. Even the defense or attack stages of trench fighting disappointed him because he felt that mowing down so many young lives, so many tons of blood spilled in each and every major attack, for the dubious gain of a few hundred yards of terrain, was really not worth it. Now that he was in charge of ninety men with three light machine guns at his disposal and hundreds of *troblons*—a French invention, the forerunner of a portable mortar—he believed that, given a free hand, he could conquer half the world.

There were a few compensations. There was frequently presented the opportunity of patrol skirmishes, which by now was his specialty, and he enjoyed visiting his neighboring units and trying his French words with the real Frenchmen. He preferred the company of the British who were the cleanest of all, their food was the best of all, and their cigarettes smelled best of all. But unfortunately, he could not speak a word of English, and that restricted his attempts to make friends among his British comrades at arms. He was, in fact, intrigued by the peculiarities and idiosyncrasies of the English language throughout his life, and mildly resented the fact that the English do not bother to learn any foreign language.

His first unpleasant encounter with English was when after a few months of trench fare, he got down with a very nasty case of dysentery. The British had, in that part of the front, the best hospital facility and they were permitting Allied officers to come there for treatment. Takis was taken there and the first thing he had to undergo was an enema. The British orderly proceeded with the initial stages of this delicate undertaking and let a trickle of hot water through the pipe, looking quizzically at Takis for his reaction. The water was burning hot and Takis shouted in pain, in Greek, "*Och! Kotei!*" which translates, "Ouch! It burns!" The British orderly heard "Okay," because that is how the Greek words sound. So, he said, "Is it okay, luv? Now, that's a good lad," and opened the water valve all the way, resulting in Takis fleeing out of the room with his pants down, and the pipe trailing behind him stuck securely in his backside. This was his first victimization by the English language, but through the course of his adventurous and eventful life many were to follow to his everlasting astonishment and dismay, because he felt a genuine love and admiration for the British.

By the end of summer, 1917, Takis had collected, apart from the Military Cross, the Silver Medal for Distinguished Service, the Silver Medal for Gallantry, the Medal of Honor, and Bars to his Military Cross. He had already a French distinction, and now the British also honored him with their Military Cross. He had more medals than any other officer in his regiment with the exception of the colonel. Most of the captains and the major in the First Regiment were green with envy and called him Don Quixote behind his back. They hated him for always volunteering for any and every dangerous mission, and for the loyalty and willingness of his men to follow him no matter where.

It was then that he conceived a plan that ordinarily would take a whole division to accomplish, but he thought ninety brave and dedicated men was all that was needed. He decided to take the Greek town of Serres, which was only five miles behind the German-Bulgarian trenches, all by himself. He did not discuss his plan with any of his superior officers because he knew it would be turned down. He only discussed it with his men, and they were very skeptical, but they agreed that they would cooperate. The plan was very simple and very daring. In their patrols they had discovered a weak position along the German trenches where the barbed wire was not securely anchored to the dirt. They thought that on a moonless, dark night they could sneak under the wire, crawl into the German trench, avoid any contact with the enemy, if possible, and then keep on crawling to the second line of trenches. There was the danger that they might be crawling through a minefield, and they had no idea what this second line looked like. However, once the night was calm and no shooting was heard from the front line, the second line would have no reason to be alerted, and playing it by ear, they might clear the second line with no incident. If that were accomplished then they could reach Serres and ambush whoever was there, capture the town, and hope that the Allies might take advantage of the certain disorder than such an action would create among the enemy ranks, and attack all along the front.

It was very bold on Takis' part to choose a German sector of the front for his enterprise, because the German machine guns and the men who operated them were definitely the best, and so far, no one had managed to break a German line in the Balkan Front. Fortunately, there were very few German units available in the Balkan Front. Most of the fighting here was being done by Bulgarians and Austrians. Even though Takis' plan seemed extremely simplistic and frivolously superficial, it worked. It was both a model of insubordination because nobody had any idea what was going on, and of daring, since no commander worth his salt would expect three platoons to take and hold a major town.

When Takis and his men reached the outskirts of Serres, it was still dark. Most of his men had been, and fought, in Serres and the surrounding area during the Balkan War only five years earlier, so they were familiar with both terrain and town. They suggested that in all probability the largest building in town, the Municipal Building in the main square, would be the headquarters. Opposite the Municipal Building was the Greek Orthodox Cathedral and they thought that they could hide there until daytime. Luck always favors the bold, and indeed they made it into the cathedral without being detected. There were sentries standing guard outside the Municipal Building and patrols marching in its vicinity, so obviously some higher ranks of the Bulgarian military leadership must be there.

A deacon and the sexton of the church saw them coming and they were about to start cheering, because they thought they were being liberated. Takis and his soldiers had to restrain them and ask for their silence and cooperation. They placed their machine guns—portable French Hotchkiss—at the belfries, and the men who more proficient in the use of *troblons* were deployed along the roof of the cathedral. Now they had a commanding view of the whole town, and once light broke, they could see every move and enemy approach. The rest of the men and Takis would assault the Municipal Building and kill as many as they could. The deacon told him that the Bulgarian commanding general, and his chiefs of staff, and headquarters were all in that building, as well as many of the German and Austrian liaison officers and their staffs.

At dawn, the deacon and Takis climbed to the belfry, and the deacon pointed out to him the various houses and buildings where enemy soldiers were stationed. Groups of men were detailed to attack every one of them. Once the sun started rising, the main square of Serres became the hub of military activity: riders, cyclists, carriages and even motorcars started coming and going in all directions. It was then, at six o'clock on the morning of September 14, 1917, that Takis gave the order, "Fire!"

The machine gun bursts from the belfries had everyone on the square dead in no time. The men who fired the *troblons* aimed them on the windows of the Municipal Building and in less than a minute that part of the building facing the square was afire. Whoever ran to investigate what was going on was mowed down by the machine guns. Takis and twenty of his men dashed across the square and entered the building. In less than ten minutes they were out, their bayonets dripping with blood. The Municipal Building was a conflagration, and some Bulgarians were jumping out windows and off balconies to land on the cobblestones of the square. All the while the men on the roof of the church and the machine gunners in the belfries, from their commanding position, were shooting at everything moving or attempting to approach the square.

The sexton had a hidden Greek flag, and it was now proudly flying from the cathedral's flagpole. The sight of the flag produced dozens of white flags all over town, and hundreds of Greek flags, since there were at least 15,000 Greek inhabitants in Serres, and they all thought that the day they had hoped and prayed for had arrived. They were once more free.

As Takis and his men emerged from the flaming building into the square, groups of Bulgarian soldiers were approaching holding white flags and their hands over their heads in surrender. This was one time that Takis would regret his lecture to his men about murdering defenseless prisoners.

It had been common practice during the First World War for snipers to shoot the enemy officers, and one of the Bulgarians who was approaching, with his hands up, was holding a grenade—the best he could do at sniping at that moment—and was determined to throw it at an officer. The moment he spotted Takis, he let go. The grenade exploded a few feet away from Takis, killing instantly one of his men and wounding two more.

Takis did not feel any pain, but in a reflex action he hurled his bayoneted rifle at the Bulgarian who had thrown the grenade, as if it were a javelin. The blade went right through the man's heart and emerged from his back nailing him down to the surface of the square. At the same time, all Takis' men on the roof of the church opened fire at the surrendering Bulgarians cutting them down like wheat ready for harvest.

Once the firing became more sporadic, the thousands of the Greek population, singing and dancing and praising the Lord for their deliverance from the hated oppression, congested the square and embraced and kissed the Greek soldiers, their liberators. It was then that the flowing blood covered Takis' eyes and he also felt a stinging pain to his left leg. The grenade had caused some severe scratches on his face, and a splinter was embedded deep into the bone of his leg, having gone through the hide of his boot. His helmet had a few holes, but otherwise he was intact.

It was now eight o'clock in the morning. The shooting had stopped altogether; the people were celebrating their liberation, turning the square into a scene of celebration and festivity. But from the front, no sound at all. Takis had been taken to the house of the best Greek doctor in town who was ministering to his face and leg, while dozens of other jubilant people were competing who would spoil him most. Similar was the treatment of the other Greek soldiers who had joined in the merriment of the celebration and were too aloof to their dangerous situation.

Takis was very concerned, because if a Bulgarian company were to attack them now, they would all perish, and nothing would have been accomplished. Well, almost nothing. Fate had it that for a second time in a year, Takis had exterminated the whole forward general staff of the Bulgarian army, had killed over two hundred Bulgarians and Germans, mostly officers, and the Greek flag that was flying from the cathedral's pole had been spotted by the enemy lines and had caused panic. The Bulgarians thought they were surrounded and fled, forcing the Germans and Austrians to follow them in retreat rather than having their flanks exposed. The couriers who were sent to town never came back, and the few who reached the front lines from the town reported that the whole town was under attack by superior forces and that the headquarters were burning. No wonder that they decided to flee, assuming that they had been outflanked from a distant sector of the front, by an operation whose secret had not been intercepted by their intelligence.

It was late in the evening that patrols reported to the Allies that the enemy had abandoned their positions and that the trenches were empty. Certainly, they also had heard the shooting coming from the direction of Serres, but it had lasted for less than an hour. There had been no artillery fire which, according to this war's dogma, always preceded any kind of attack, so they concluded that some uncoordinated reconnaissance action in force had occurred to test the enemy farther north. They had nothing to do with it, so they didn't care. Now that the patrols reported the enemy trench empty of occupants, things looked different. It might be a German ruse to lure them forward, and from pre-arranged positions surround them and destroy them. The Germans had done that so often in the Western Front that it had lost its originality. Still, they sent a few platoons to occupy the vacant trenches and see what happened. Of course, nothing happened. Except that from their new positions these platoons could hear the sound of distant music and celebration coming from the way of Serres. It is fortuitous that the Greeks are among the loudest of people when it comes to dancing and singing. That was reported to divisional headquarters, so still very cautiously, some platoons were sent further east.

The first to enter the town was a French patrol of ten men and they thought they were hallucinating. The whole town was celebrating; the main square looked like an enormous festival with thousands of people dancing and singing. Once they were seen, they were engulfed by the joyous crowds and became part of the celebration. Their leader, a corporal, was taken to Takis, who to his great dismay was ordered in bed by the doctor. He told the Frenchman that he, Lieutenant Panayotopoulos, *Chevalier de la Legion d'Honeure* (Knight of the French Legion) had taken the town and was inviting the French general to join him. There is no way to describe the corporal's amazement. He would rather stay there and enjoy himself, but he felt it was his duty to report back and see the expression on the faces of his superiors. After gulping half a bottle of *ouzo* that was offered to him, he took some of his men—others were too drunk to walk—and made for the Allied lines.

It was almost midnight when the French general, the British brigadier and Colonel Papamandelos arrived in Serres. The *panygiris*, the Greek celebration, was still going on as strong as ever, by now having been joined by hundreds of allied soldiers. The commanders repaired to the doctor's house to see for themselves who had the audacity to counter all the principles and accepted practices of modern warfare, and dared surprise them like that in the middle of the night.

Only Colonel Papamandelos was not surprised. Since it had been reported to him that Panayotopoulos' group was missing, he instinctively knew that something unusual, or funny, or tragic might happen. But even he could not imagine that ninety men could possibly sneak undetected for five miles of solid, well-guarded, enemy ground and, to boot, get into so important a town where the top Bulgarian general was quartered. He was also very happy, because he knew that his regiment would accept all the credit for the taking of Serres and the breach of the whole enemy line. Panayotopoulos' antics, in all probability, had gotten him his long-coveted general's stars. He intended to level with Panayotopoulos and make him agree that he was acting under his orders. One could always excuse the lack of coordination among the Allies to language problems.

Takis, upon seeing the French general, felt if wings were about to sprout from his shoulders. He was elated beyond belief. He addressed the general in French, begging to be forgiven for not being able to stand in attention and properly salute him. The Frenchman flushed in irritation, and he was so confused that he could hardly utter a word. The British brigadier, sporting a beaming smile, said, "Well done, m'boy," but that was lost to Takis. Colonel Papamandelos winked his eye, and smiling, said to him, *"Mou tin eskases pali bayassa,"* which roughly translates to, "You did it to me again, you rascal."

By now the Frenchman had found his composure and the same thoughts which were in Papamandelos' mind surfaced in his own. All the credit for so incredible and successful an action would go to his division. Since this Greek brat had already been decorated by the French commander in chief, and obviously spoke fluent French, he could claim that he had acted under his direct orders on a topmost secret mission for which he had volunteered. The French general's features turned into the personification of benevolence. There, on this bed, lay his promotion and his ticket to Paris.

"My most heartfelt congratulations, my brave and fearless lieutenant," he said. "I somehow knew you would accomplish the mission I entrusted you with, and I must admit you did not disappoint me. You performed magnificently and I thank you. As a token of my appreciation, please accept this." And removing from around his tunic's collar the medal he was wearing, he placed the *Medaille Militaire* around Takis' neck. This was one of France's topmost decorations: the Military Medal was given in very rare and outstanding occasions of exceptional gallantry in the field and was the supreme award for leadership, being awarded to generals and admirals who had been commanders-in-chief. The medal was considered superior even to the grand cross of the *Legion d'honneur,* and, in contrast to such medals as the *Croix de guerre*, was one of the rarest French decorations to be bestowed upon foreigners. The French general had earned it in Marne. Takis' eyes were moist with emotions of amazement, gratitude, and pleasure.

"*Mon General*, I do not deserve to be with the French immortals. I'm just a lad from Piraeus doing his duty. Had it not been for you who encouraged me to take the risk, we would still be sitting in the old trenches." Having said that to the French general, he looked at Papamandelos and winked back. The French general missed the wink and was very impressed by the young Greek's intelligence and presence of mind. He felt he could like this impertinent colt and decided to take him under his wing.

"I shall have the ambulance take you first thing in the morning to the French Military Hospital in Thessalonica and once you recover, I shall have you transferred to Saint Syr for advanced training in the new weapons and tactics." That was the French Military Academy from which such greats as Lafayette and Napoleon had graduated. Takis had no objection to be treated in the French hospital, where he had heard were some very pretty French nurses, but the idea of going to France while there was so much fighting right here, did not appeal to him. He thanked the French general for his consideration and said he would be grateful to be treated in the French hospital. After some more pats on the shoulder and handshakes, the high-ranking officers left, and Takis slumbered in a blissful sleep wearing the *Medaille Militaire*.

My father, Takis fought in the trenches against the Bulgarians at Serres in Greek Macedonia in 1917-1918, and in an insubordinate act used the trenches in a surprise attack that took the city. Greek soldiers escort Bulgarian prisoners through a trench.

Prime Minister Eleftherios Venizelos, shown with the troops at the front, visited the wounded Takis and the king bestowed the medals.

Volunteers served in Greek Red Cross field hospitals. Takis' great love Jeannine was one who died in a shelling at Serres. My mother was one, and first saw my father as she assisted in the amputation of his right arm after the battle of Proussa.

CHAPTER 6

Thessalonica Hospital

BY THE TIME he arrived in Thessalonica early in the evening he was weary and sick. His leg was hurting intensely, and the wound was bleeding. There were no paved roads in northern Greece in 1917 and the motorcars, even the ambulances, had compact rubber tires, not inflated. The road was bumpy and the ride terribly uncomfortable. But the French general had made all the arrangements, and when the ambulance eventually arrived at the hospital, there was a detachment of French soldiers in two tiers along the entrance presenting arms to the *Medaille Militaire*. That compensated for the discomforts of the ride, that, plus the sight of the first French nurse he saw, who was exactly as he expected her to be, pretty and buxom.

It was anticipated that many dignitaries would be visiting him, Takis was taken to a small ward all by himself. Only very high-ranking officers were treated with such honor, but it seemed that the *Medaille Militaire* knew no limits in French preferential treatment. Takis was glad to be by himself. That, he hoped, would enable him to explore in depth the lode of French nurses. He had been for over a year without a break, continuously in the first line of the front, and he looked forward to some, almost forgotten, decent female companionship. His very few and sporadic brief visits to the villages in the immediate vicinity of the front had been uneventful and boring. A village widow now and then, but he longed for better fare.

The very first visitor was no other than Eleftherios Venizelos. He stayed with him for over an hour and wanted to know every aspect of the daring operation. He also wanted the truth because both the French General and Colonel Papamandelos claimed credit for the capturing of Serres and the breach of the enemy line. Takis told the Greek leader the truth: neither of them had had any idea, for the simple reason that had he entrusted them with his plan, they would both most certainly reject it as impossible and order him to stay put and let the commanders do the planning and the conducting of the war.

Venizelos said that he had sensed what the true story was, but that the situation was quite delicate and the feelings of the French General and Colonel Papamandelos should not be hurt by calling them liar. Venizelos advised Takis to write in his report that he had acted under the secret orders of the French General Guillemot, but that he had also informed his Greek superior officer, Colonel Papamandelos and had obtained his permission and blessing.

Venizelos mockingly scolded Takis and pulled his ear like they do in Greece to punish naughty children, but he could not conceal his gratification and pride for so fine and brave a young officer, who was entirely dedicated to him and his cause. Venizelos told him that when the news of the fall of Serres reached Athens, he ordered a special train to take him in all dispatch to Thessalonica, and that the train had brought someone else who had come specially to see him. His mother. After all the official talk was over and Takis was given his instructions concerning his report, Venizelos opened the door and invited Helen Panayotopoulos in.

Mother and favorite son had not met for over a year and their reunion was moving and full of tears of happiness. She told him all the news of the family; how his elder brother, Dimitri, was doing in Paris where he was attending the law school at the Sorbonne; about his only sister, Sophia, having almost married a French naval officer; and the progress of his younger brother, Alexander, in having almost completely taken over the business from their father. Takis had had very little contact with his elder brother, their only common characteristic being that they both liked girls. He somehow resented the fact that while a war was going on, his brother was a student, rather than a volunteer in the Greek Army. He loved his younger brother, Alexander, even though they were so very different in character, and he adored his youngest brother, Paul, a lad of nine years of age. The French nurses had to interrupt the visit because it was late at night, and this was Takis' second day in the hospital, and they had to prepare him for his surgery next morning. They almost had to forcibly send Helen out, but she promised she would stay in Thessalonica for at least as long as he would be in the hospital. Takis was pleased to see his mother, but his hopes for the advantages of his privacy seemed to be dwindling with his mother ever present.

The grenade splinter was imbedded deep into the bone of Takis' leg and the French surgeons thought that if they removed it, it might cause complications that could force them to amputate the leg, so they decided to leave it there and let the wound heal with the piece of metal in it. It worked, and Takis lived the rest of his life carrying that splinter in his leg as a reminder of Serres.

His handsome forty-five-year-old mother was his constant companion for the remainder of his stay in the French hospital, to both his joy at having her there with him, and his disappointment for not having a chance to acquaint the French nurses. They were flirting with him and teasing him, and that made him lusty. He wanted to grasp hold of them, but out of respect to his mother he restrained himself. Little did he know that the nurses shared his eagerness, and their desires were very mutual. He was the only topic of discussion at the nurses' quarters. Especially after two French generals arrived to visit him.

The Commander in Chief François d'Esprait, and General Guillemot, came to congratulate him and present him with the parchment of his promotion to Commander of the Order of the French Legion. Now, whenever he would be in formal dress, he would also have a wide blue, white and red ribbon to put across his chest. The French generals told him that the arrangements had been finalized, and as soon as he was released from the hospital, he could be on his way to France to attend Saint Syr. Takis thanked them from deep in his heart but had to summon all his tact to avoid offending them with his rejection. He told them that he felt his duty was to rejoin his fighting men, and he wanted to reserve the right to go to France after the war had come to a victorious conclusion.

The two Frenchmen were impressed. They suggested that, instead, he could remain for four months as a convalescent in Thessalonica and attend a French military school there, where the new weapons and tactics were taught for the allied officers in the Balkan front. They advised him to grasp the opportunity because every career officer needs all the schooling he can get if he wants to advance. "Don't worry," they told him, "the war is not going to run away from you in four months." Takis thanked them for their advice and promised to attend the school, but in his impish, mischievous manner, he also said that he was not so overly concerned about promotions, and that if the war were to last a couple of years, he would accumulate enough field promotions to make it to general. "After all, *mon Generaux*," he said, "I am only eighteen, and look at me, already with Commander of the French Legion and *Medaille Militaire* to boot." The generals were speechless but pleased that so daring an officer was fighting on their side.

Everybody in the French hospital, from the most menial orderly to the chief surgeon, was impressed by the visit of the two top French Generals. It had never happened before that two generals at the same time would come to the hospital and pay a visit, an extended visit, at that, to one low ranking foreign officer. It had not happened even when they had colonels in treatment. And how very extraordinary that so young a man, actually a boy, would be the recipient of so high a French decoration. Who was this Takis Panayotopoulos? There were thousands of brave young men risking their lives every minute in the various fronts. What was so special about him? The French doctors were puzzled and amazed. It had never happened to a Frenchman as far as they could remember. Why should it happen to a Greek? Of course, they had heard various accounts of the capture of Serres, and how the Greeks had been lucky and destroyed the Bulgarian headquarters, but after, all, it was the French division that had broken the enemy line. So why all this commotion about a simple Greek lieutenant?

The discussions in the nurses' quarters were also along those lines but there, instead of envy and amazement, there was primarily curiosity and attraction.

"Well, obviously he is a good soldier, but how is he in bed?" "Most of those super-brave ones have no idea how to treat a girl and behave like school children."

"This one, though, he seems to be interested. His eyes sparkle when he sees me."

"He is so handsome and tall."

"If only his mother would go home earlier."

It was obvious that Takis had stirred tremendous interest among the nurses because all of them would invent reasons and excuses to go to his room and attend to him. His mother was quick to realize that her son was much more than the object of the professional attention and care that exists between patient and nurse. That pretty blonde, Jeannine, was particularly attentive to her, and always eager to please. Perhaps she had set her eyes on her son. That evening, Helen decided to leave earlier than usual. She was a very understanding mother and knew her son's weakness. She was not particularly concerned or anxious. With the exception of a few medical professionals, all those French girls were Red Cross volunteers and belonged to good bourgeois or even to aristocratic families. It was commonplace during the First World War for girls of good homes to volunteer to the Red Cross of their country. This way they felt that they performed a duty to the country just as much as their brothers who had volunteered to the ranks. Besides, all the boys were at the front.

Helen Panayotopoulos early departure was like an inaudible alarm throughout the hospital, and especially in the nurses' quarters. Jeannine de Beaufort was 'passing by' Takis' ward when his mother made her departure and she escorted her to the main door, making small talk and assuring her that she would take extra care of her son, and not to worry.

Helen smiled beneath her serious expression and knew that her son was about to spend a good night. She thanked Jeannine for her courtesy and good intentions, and before leaving her, she said, "Sister, please bear in mind that he is wounded and make sure he does not put any stress on his leg."

Jeannine blushed. "The old hag has read my mind," she thought, "but then, who cares?"

She turned around and rushed to Takis' room, where, to her disappointment, Yvette Duclos and Brigitte Routier had preceded her, and were tending to all Takis' needs, actual and imaginary, mostly imaginary. There was one need that she was determined to attend to herself. She approached the bed and started arranging his pillows, the same pillows that had already been arranged twice in the past few minutes, while making sure her breast touched, but very slightly, his face. She approached his ear and whispered, "In two hours, I am off duty and then I shall come and keep you company, *Cherie*. Just wait," and bit him softly on its lobe.

Takis was overjoyed. He could hardly believe what was happening. That was exactly what the other two nurses had also told him, except that Yvette would be off duty in one hour. He liked Jeannine best, who was taller and had long honey-blond hair, and blue eyes, and whose nipples were almost piercing through her uniform, but Yvette was alright. So was Brigitte, for that matter. And so was Monique. So was Suzanne. And so were the others.

In his anticipation, it seemed a long time before he saw Yvette opening, very quietly, the door, and looking right and left before entering. The confounded door did not have a lock, but Yvette deftly placed an armchair under the handle and secured the door. She then approached the bed, sat, and buried her hand in his curly hair in a tender caress. Takis was too excited to respond in kind. It had been years since so pretty a girl had been so close to him. He clasped her neck and pulled her face to his, while his other hand was running up and between her thighs. They embraced with a passionate kiss, tongues touching, exploring each other's mouth as his fingers reached their moist target. Yvette was a red-hot blooded girl from the Mediterranean, born and raised on the Cote d'Azur. She instantly responded to Takis' touch, and shedding her uniform, joined him under the sheets. All her middle-class inhibitions dissolved, and at once they were engaged in a fierce, explosive, yet tender, lovemaking.

Immersed in their passion, they did not hear the door being pushed back. Brigitte and Jeannine had arrived almost simultaneously and had heard the moaning, love cries and Takis' heavy breathing. They knew what was going on behind the door. They were both resentful of Yvette for having beaten them to Takis' bed, something they had been dreaming of and longing for in the past six days. They both pushed on the door, and it was the sound of the armchair turning over and falling on the ceramic tile floor that brought Takis and Yvette back to reality. They were embarrassed with the presence of the other two nurses in the room. Yvette's blush of shame was lost in the darkness of the room, and she hated being found by her colleagues in so compromising a situation. Takis' embarrassment lasted only briefly. *More is better*, he thought, and finding his composure, he invited the newcomers to join him on the bed.

Jeannine asserted her powerful personality and ordered the girls out, threatening them with expulsion from the Red Cross if they revealed what had happened. At twenty-one, she was the oldest of the three, and outranked the other two both in seniority in the Red Cross and in social standing. Her father was an Ambassador of France and an aristocrat. Takis was puzzled, but when the two murmuring, protesting nurses reluctantly left the room, and Jeannine stayed, he beamed happily.

Jeannine replaced the armchair under the door handle and did it more effectively than Yvette. Turning to Takis, she said in a severe tone of voice, "I told you I would come as soon as my shift was over. Couldn't you have waited a little? Shame on you. I thought you cared for me!"

"Of course, I care for you. I have been crazy for you ever since I set my eyes on you when I first came here. I have been dreaming of you every single night. It is you I like best, but since Yvette was kind enough to join me in bed, I could not be so impolite and ask her to leave. Besides, thinking always of you made me very lusty. I hope you forgive me."

Takis' words, with their peculiar foreign accent, fell sweetly on Jeannine's ears. She determined to tame and possess this unusual and unique fellow. She was a very headstrong girl, in spite of her otherwise innocent though seductive appearance, and in all her life she got what she wanted. Now, more than anything else, she wanted Takis. She was sexually proficient, and very demanding, and their lovemaking lasted until the sun was about to rise. They were so immersed into each other that hours passed like minutes, and they were both exhausted. They found themselves head over heels in love. Takis had loved many girls before, but never with such a passion and abandon. This was genuine. He was captivated. But that was exactly how Jeannine felt. *"Le coup de foudre."* She had never given herself so utterly and completely to any man before, and there had been quite a few. She was already making imaginary plans of marriage. It was daylight and neither of them had slept at all. She dressed as quickly as she could, and kissing Takis with unsated passion, left to begin her day's duties. Not until she was gone did Takis realize how tired he was, and how much his leg hurt.

A trickle of blood was oozing from his wound. That did not bother him at all. If he could prolong his stay at the hospital and be treated every night so magnificently by Jeannine, he thought he wouldn't mind staying there forever. The first nurse to come to his room this morning was Yvette. She saw the blood on his leg and ran for the doctors. By now there was enough gossip about the orgy of the previous night, throughout the hospital, that everyone knew some kind of exaggerated story. The doctors ordered a plaster bandage to be wrapped from the waist down, covering both legs and leaving only the wound free. This way his movement would be restricted, and the wound would heal faster with no sexual interference. By the time his mother came to visit, Takis was buried in plaster bandage and looked very pale and unhappy.

When Jeannine came with the dinner tray, Helen Panayotopoulos told her, "Mademoiselle de Beaufort, I am very disappointed with you. Obviously, you ignored my advice of last night."

Jeannine blushed furiously, and said nothing, but the adoring way she stared at Takis spoke volumes. His mother teased him about his adventurous and clearly amorous yesternight and advised him to be careful. In her typical way of taking opportunities to display her profound knowledge of ancient Greek, she told him, *"Meden agan, speude vratheos,"* meaning, "Don't rush into anything."

She told him that she had anticipated that he and Jeannine would sooner or later become involved, and she had already made inquiries about the girl. She was three years his senior and was almost engaged to a French officer who had been wounded and treated at the hospital six months ago. It seemed that her family was one of the richest in France with many land holdings and political influence and was favoring her affair with Marcel de Montcalm.

"So, my dear son, Takis, be wary and don't let yourself be hurt, because it seems to me that you have bitten the metal plate," using a Greek expression for being desperately infatuated.

Takis said it was much more than that, he was in love and would like to marry the girl and go live with her in France. His mother was disturbed hearing this, but thought it was the typical reaction of a hungry teenager after so many months being deprived. Takis' immobilization with the plaster bandage did not deter Jeannine. Now their pleasure was confined to oral sex instead, which Jeannine preferred anyway. After all, she was a true blossom grown in the heart of France.

In a few weeks Takis was on his feet and discharged. He had confronted Jeannine with his knowledge of her affair with Captain de Montcalm, but she assured him that it was nothing serious, and besides, it had been long over. They were very much in love and determined to live the rest of their lives together. Jeannine had insisted that he should accept the suggestion of the general and go to Saint Syr. Her family owned an estate close to the school and she could arrange for them to be together in France.

Takis' mother, on the other hand, had—with the assistance of Venizelos, who paid him another visit at the hospital—persuaded him to stay in Thessalonica, and while convalescing, attend the French Military School there. "Men like you are rare, Takis, and I need you here," Venizelos said, and that was more than a command for Takis. He felt like he had grown into a giant when the greatest man of Greece complimented him in such a manner. Besides, if he stayed in Thessalonica, he would be with Jeannine whenever she was off duty.

He first went to the paymaster's office and collected a year's pay that had accumulated there all the time he was at the front and had no use of money. It was a small fortune, over one thousand *drachmae* in gold. He had never had so much in his life. He had heard that the French Consul in Thessalonica was being transferred and was selling many of his items. The French Consulate was his next stop. The French guards at the door were reluctant to let him through because he was still wearing his soiled and blood-stained battle uniform, and they thought upon seeing him, and seeing the *Medaille Militaire* he was wearing around his neck, that he was a deranged person who had stolen the medal.

The consul had met Takis at the hospital and scolded the guards and invited him in. He advised Takis to go and buy a proper uniform. But first, Takis wanted to buy the consul's car, even though he had not learned how to drive. The car, a Pik-Pik, was a huge two-seater with compact tires, and to start it, one had to crank it from the front with a rod. It was an awkward car to handle, especially for someone who had never driven before. He also bought a 12-gauge double barrel hammerless shotgun. The consul kindly took him for a drive to show him the handling of the car. After they motored back, the consul had many doubts as to how long the car and Takis would survive together. Takis thought that if his eldest brother, whom he considered inadequate, could drive, so could he. With some difficulty and to the pedestrians' horror, he found his way to the best tailor in town and had half a dozen uniforms ordered, one for each occasion, and dozens of shirts, underwear, and everything else a dandy needs to be presentable at all times.

He then drove to the hospital and insisted that Jeannine accompany him for dinner. By that time, the French doctors considered him a kind of menace and in order to see the least of him, allowed Jeannine to leave before her duty was over. Fortunately, Jeannine knew how to drive since both her father and brothers had Pic-Pics, thus they arrived a seaside restaurant with no major incident. They drove back to Thessalonica and repaired at the best hotel in town, the Mediterranean, and were engaged once again in their marathon lovemaking. Neither could have enough of each other's amorous overtures and their pairing was so passionate and intense as if that were their last night. Their bliss was total and delightful.

The invitations started pouring in and soon they were the talk of the town. The young hero and his French princess. He received a most unusual invitation from the British consul that intrigued him, like almost anything British. Unlike the accepted norm of the time, it was printed in English rather than French and he could not read it. The invitation was for ten o'clock in the morning, so he could not take Jeannine along, who loved every opportunity to display her charms and her escort. Takis was now seen by Greek standards as a topmost catch.

Takis drove to the British consulate. The guards there stood at attention and saluted him, and he was greeted at the door by the consul himself. The consul spoke very accented French, but some communication could be established. He took him to his office and gave him a piece of paper printed elaborately in English. Then he opened a safe and gave him one hundred forty-four pounds sterling, twenty-four in gold, and the remainder in paper notes. The consul smiled and poured Takis a cup of tea and offered him a cigarette. Takis was the image of bafflement. He had not the slightest idea what was going on. He drank the tea, which he didn't like, smoked the cigarette, which he liked, and after a period of long silence, he stood up, trousered the money, said *"Merci beaucoup,"* and left.

Late that evening, he picked up Jeannine at the hospital, and she read the English letter. It was a commendation of His Royal Britannic Majesty's government congratulating him for his deed and in appreciation of the lives his heroic action saved, he was begged to accept this mild token: one hundred forty-four pounds. His love and bewilderment for the British was further augmented after that. Why one hundred forty-four, and not one hundred, or even one hundred fifty pounds? What an amazing race of people. How they could manage to rule half the world was a mystery to him. Next day, he made the rounds of jewelers in town. Thessalonica was, at the time, the largest Jewish town in the Balkans, with over 90,000 Israelites, so he hoped he might get a good bargain in a diamond ring for Jeannine. For merely twenty-five pounds, he purchased the best brilliant cut diamond available in Thessalonica and had it inscribed especially for her.

CHAPTER 7

Reporting for Duty and a Duel

BY NOW HE had spent ten days in total extravagance enjoying every minute, and he hadn't even bothered to officially ask for leave. He had always been a spoiled brat and although he did not want to take advantage of his fame or his friendship with Venizelos, he knew he could get away with ignoring bureaucratic authority. In a war, it is the fighting man's turn to bend the rules, and the pen pusher has to acquiesce. In peacetime it is the other way around.

It was the time of Jeannine's menses, and she had a fetish about making love during that time, so Takis thought it an opportune occasion to report at the French Military School. It was located six miles north of town and it took Takis almost an hour to drive there. He had still not quite mastered the intricacies of his automobile. He was told by the school's quartermaster that he had been expected ten days ago, right after his discharge from the hospital, and they had already reported him to the headquarters of the Greek Tenth Infantry Division as a deserter.

He was to be placed under arrest pending the investigation of his whereabouts. Takis had never heard of a Tenth Division. All Greece had were nine divisions and most of them undersize. He told the quartermaster that he had not deserted, that he was in Thessalonica all the time and very much visible, and besides he had nothing to do with a Tenth Division. His was the First Athens Regiment and it was attached to the 56th French Division.

The Quartermaster looked at him in loathing. "Don't you even know that your regiment has been promoted into a division? If you are so senseless, how can we possibly teach you anything here?"

Takis was offended. "I can be a good officer and lead my men to victories without your teachings as my record, and this, proves," he told the Frenchman, pointing to his *Medaille Militaire* and the rosette of the

French Legion. "I can prove to you I did not desert. All you need to do is call on the telephone General François d'Esprait. I had dinner with him last night."

The Quartermaster, Major Duval, who had never fired a shot at an enemy, and had never been close to the fighting through the twenty-five years of his career in the French army, was so angry that he turned scarlet, and his frontal vein alarmingly enlarged. He hated this impertinent foreign brat and envied him for his French decorations while he, a French high-ranking officer, stood no chance of ever coming near them. He wanted to leap from his desk and strangle this insolent Greek, but his potbelly and his fear of being at the receiving end, plus the fact that it was not becoming for a major to disgrace himself by quarreling with a junior officer, and a dirty foreigner at that, deterred him.

"Lieutenant Panayotopoulos, you shall confine yourself to your designated quarters and stay there until otherwise ordered," he said, and instructed a French orderly to take him to the room that was the worst in the dormitory.

The news Takis had missed, being devoted body and soul to Jeannine de Beaufort, was that his colonel had been promoted to major general (there was no rank of brigadier in the Greek army prior to 1943) and his regiment had been enhanced into a division, the Tenth Infantry Division. It was also designated the 'Serres Division' to commemorate in years to come the feat of the men comprising the division who had captured Serres single handedly.

The regiment, now division, was temporarily stationed in Serres and withdrawn from the fighting to give its men a long-needed rest, and a month furlough. Most of the honors and decorations went to the regimental flag and the commanding officer, now General Papamandelos. A special medal commemorating the heroic capture of the town was minted and awarded to all allied ranks involved in that sector of the front. Only a few officers and some non-commissioned officers stayed at Serres, training the new recruits and volunteers, and doing the necessary paperwork and logistics of expanding the ex-regiment to divisional strength. All other ranks had gone to their hometowns and villages in Attica, the province where Athens is located.

General Papamandelos, on his way to Athens, stopped for a visit at the French hospital, but it was the day Takis was being treated and plaster bandaged so he missed him because, had he waited to see Takis, he would be too late for his train.

Takis was glad to know that he was now serving with the Serres Division and that thanks to him, his commanding officer was a general.

The only thing he didn't like was that, whereas the Allies had bestowed him with an avalanche of honors and decorations, his own country, and more specifically his friend Venizelos, had given him nothing in comparison. Yes, he did get the Serres medal like everybody else, and more bars to his Military Cross, and laurels to his Medal of Honor, but no promotion, or a Greek gold medal. His only compensation was that some of his men were promoted to non-commissioned officers and that most of them had been decorated.

He did not stay long in house arrest in his new school because the French General Guillemot came the day after he arrived to visit him. General Guillemot wanted to bid him goodbye since he was leaving for Paris and, having been promoted to lieutenant general—equivalent to a three-star general in the U.S. army—he was given the command of an army corps in the Western Front. The French general himself introduced him to his tutors and superior officers in the school and ordered then to take good care of his young Greek protégé. Major Duval, who was the only one Takis had already met, was fuming in anger and envy, but in front of the general, he was all kindness and reassurances that he would personally make it his primary concern to make Takis' stay a comfortable one.

The school was supposed to teach captains and lower ranking officers the use and applications of heavy, water cooled machine guns, 61 and 81 mm. mortars, the 20 mm anti-aircraft fast firing cannons, the 1.37 cm. anti-tank rifles, flame throwers, new technology about nerve and other poisonous gases, the new anti-personnel and anti-vehicle land mines, co-ordination tactics between tanks and infantry, new systems of telecommunications, and whatever else man had invented to destroy man faster and more efficiently. Most of the pupils were low ranking officers who had been wounded in battle and were in the stage of convalescence before reassignment to the front.

The majority of the students, naturally, were French, but there were two more Greeks, a few Serbians, some Italians and one Australian. His name was David Townsend, and mysteriously, he could speak French. Takis made a point to meet him and at last penetrate the British mentality. He was a veteran of Gallipolis and Jerusalem, where he was wounded, and now his unit had been transferred to a Balkan Front, and that was how he got himself to the school. They felt a mutual affinity and become close friends for the rest of their lives. Attending the school was also Captain Marcel de Montcalm, Jeannine's former paramour, and as far as he was concerned, he did not like being in the 'former' status. He hated Takis. He also had no difficulty to commute the hatred to his fellow French classmates who envied Takis for his fame, success, and the French decorations.

Marcel would miss no opportunity to demean or insult Takis and make his life at school very hard. The tutors and trainers were all French, veterans of the Western Front, ranking from colonels to non-commissioned officers. They all knew of his affair with Jeannine and resented it that the prettiest French girl in Greece, and possible one of the prettiest in the whole of France, was involved with that Greek upstart. Takis avoided the company of the French and was spending most of his free time with Townsend, or the other Greeks, and the Serbians. Fortunately for him, he had good aptitude for learning, and, although he was youngest among the trainees, he had more combat experience than most, which changed the attitude of some of the non-commissioned officer trainers. All that Takis was learning was meant for the static trench warfare, while he was the born commando raider—but that was a war too early. He put forth all his effort to do well and soon he proved his worth by out shooting everyone, including the trainers, with the machine gun. In a written test about ballistics of mortars, to his own surprise, he ranked fourth, mathematics never having been one of his favorite subjects.

The nights were very boring, and he was missing Jeannine, who in over two weeks, had written to him only four letters. He wrote to her a letter every day, and sometimes two. Was it just a fling, and now that he was gone, she was offering her attention to some other patient? His only consolation to this thought was that Marcel's hatred had not the least abated and, he being a captain, had more free time to go to Thessalonica and spend the night there, so would gleefully know if Takis were spurned. Takis would get his first free day after a month provided he passed the appropriate tests. It was the happiest of days, when the third Sunday since he had been attending the school, Jeannine, riding a horse, appeared at the gate of the school, and asked for him.

According to regulations, he was not supposed to leave, even for a few minutes, and women were not allowed into the compound. Takis was both very happy and very irate. He went to the commandant of the school, an ancient colonel and begged him to let him go for at least an hour. He was so desperate that tears erupted, but the Frenchman was adamant; he could make no exceptions.

Takis had to talk with Jeannine across the gate, while all the time he yearned to embrace her and ached to kiss her. Eventually the commandant sent an orderly to ask Jeannine to leave because, with her presence, she was causing a disturbance. Most of the young trainees had gathered at the gate and were staring at her, and some were making vulgar remarks. Jeannine was incensed, but before riding away she promised to come and see him next Sunday. Takis went to his dormitory cell, bit his pillow, and cried. He was so enraged he wanted to kill half the French army. At mess that evening he was discussing with Townsend Jeannine's visit, saying how concerned he was that Jeannine had ridden unescorted, and that so beautiful a girl could be raped in the fields between Thessalonica and the school, with so many drunken soldiers in the area.

"I wouldn't be at all concerned," interrupted Marcel. "That slut would enjoy to be raped by all the soldiers of the world."

Takis had endured enough abuse by Marcel so far, but that was the limit. He hit him straight in the jaw and when he fell, he kicked him in the head. Townsend and a few others grappled with Takis and restrained him, otherwise he would have killed the French Captain there and then. Takis had committed a court martial offense by striking a superior officer, although Marcel's conduct was definitely unbecoming a gentleman, especially referring to a young woman he had intended to marry. He was unconscious in the moments after the beating he had received and his French comrades were attending to him, trying to stop the bleeding from his nose and broken teeth. They were saying among themselves that it should be a matter to be dealt with between the two offended parties and not to allow the matter to reach the court martial, where they knew their friend's comment would get him into trouble and would stigmatize his otherwise immaculate career.

When Marcel recovered consciousness, they suggested to him that his was a matter of honor and should be dealt with as such. Dueling had been at that time prohibited by law in almost every civilized country but on rare occasions, and only between gentlemen, it occurred, especially in France. Marcel was angry and felt humiliated for having taken such a beating by an inferior and a foreigner in front of the whole mess. He told his friends that he would never consider dueling with someone who was not a gentleman. He would take the Greek bastard to court martial and see him stripped and dishonorably discharged. He would not soil his hands with the blood of an inferior Greek half ape.

Takis had by now recovered his composure and very calmly, holding the rage inside him, he addressed Marcel, "As to who is a gentleman, and who isn't, the whole mess can determine that, because they all heard how you described your former fiancé. But if we were to judge realistically who between the two of us stands higher in the eyes of your own country, it is I who am the bearer of two of France's highest distinctions, whereas you have none. So, it would rather be me who should have to demean myself and descend to your level. The real reason, however, why you want to avoid facing me on the field of honor is very simply that you are a coward."

At this, the French officers now insisted that Marcel duel with Takis. They threatened that after this challenge, should he decline, they could not support him, would withdraw friendship. In matters such as this where the honor of a wellborn lady is involved, the French officers' corps was very strict. Marcel realized that his friends would spit on him if he declined, so grudgingly he consented to duel with Takis.

It was unanimously agreed among the officers present in the mess, that the most offended party was Marcel, so his seconds, or witnesses, would have the choice of weapon. His two best friends chose pistols because they thought Marcel to be a better shot and it was agreed that the duel would take place at six o'clock in the morning at a yard behind the main building. That was half an hour before reveille.

Takis had never dueled, and he was not aware of the various customs and practices connected to dueling. He did not know that the whole purpose was to draw blood, not to kill. Killing was considered ungentlemanly. The better the shot, the more superficial should he try to make his opponent's wound. After blood was drawn, the victor should feel satisfied and shake hands with his adversary and the matter was closed. Only in very rare occasions the drawing of blood would not satisfy an opponent. This was the unwritten gentleman's code in the first quarter of the twentieth century.

Since nobody had brought dueling pistols at school, it was agreed that the adversaries would use their service pistols. This was a severe breach of the dueling code, but in times of war, one has to compromise. Takis had discarded his Greek military issue pistol for a German 08/15 9 mm. Luger he had taken from the dead body of a German officer in Serres, and he had not as yet familiarized himself with it. Marcel was using a Belgian 7.75 mm. Browning automatic that he had since the beginning of the war.

It was still dark in the early morning of November 26, 1917, when Takis and Marcel, their backs touching, cocked their pistols and waited for the signal to start walking in opposing directions. It was agreed by the witnesses—Townsend was Takis' second—that the duelers would take ten steps, turn around and fire once. The chief witness gave the signal and started counting. At the final word, Takis turned like a flash, aimed straight at Marcel's heart, and fired.

Marcel collapsed to the ground in the same instant. It was over before anyone had a chance to even consciously think that a duel was in process. The witnesses rushed to Marcel. A small hole on the left breast side of his shirt was turning wet and red with his young blood. The ground where his body lay was pooling with red even faster. Takis' bullet had gone through his heart and exited from his back. Marcel was dead. The two French officers, Marcel's witnesses, looked at Takis in dismay and utter disgust.

"No wonder he did not want to duel with a plebian," one of them said.

Townsend looked at Takis, astonished, and a little hurt. "Now *that* was not necessary," he said.

Takis felt a little sorry, but he was primarily perplexed. In all the cinema films and the romantic books with which he was acquainted, a duel was supposed to end with one's life. Starting with Hamlet all the way to the three musketeers, duels ended usually with loss of life. Why all this resentment?

The two Frenchmen carried the body of their dead friend into the building. Even Townsend left, leaving Takis there all alone holding the pistol whose muzzle was still smoking. The whole thing had lasted less than a minute. Takis went back to his room and sat on his bed wondering what he had done wrong. Was he supposed to let Marcel fire first? What if Marcel killed him? It didn't make sense. In a while Townsend came to his room.

"The frogs are going to arrange everything," he said. "They will report it as an accident, but they shall insist that you leave immediately. By tomorrow the whole Balkan Front will know. You are now a marked man and if I were you, I would avoid French officers like the pest. Someone is about to get you."

Then, "Really, Takis, why did you do it? Surely the beating you gave him last night in front of his friends should have been adequate satisfaction. Killing like you did puts you in the same ilk with pimps and assassins. I am disappointed in you."

Takis voiced his astonishment, and eventually it dawned upon Townsend that Takis did not know the dueling code.

"Well, old boy, in that case, I can't blame you. It was they who suggested the duel in the first place. When they asked me, I said I favored fisticuffs according to the Marquis of Queensbury rules. They rejected my choice of weapons as not becoming gentlemanly. Now they've got a dead gentleman instead of a badly bruised one." He added in Aussie English, "Nice shooting, mate."

By the time reveille sounded the whole school knew. It was officially reported that Captain Marcel de Montcalm's death was caused by an accidental discharge of his pistol, because duels were prohibited even among officers and gentlemen according to the French Army code. A French non-commissioned officer and a soldier came to Takis' room and told him to stay there because later the colonel would want to speak to him. About an hour later he was escorted to the commandant's office. The commandant told him that he was expelled from the school for behavior unbecoming an officer and a gentleman, unworthy of the company and comradeship of such, and that a car leaving now for the front would take him under escort and deliver him to his unit in Serres. He had ten minutes to pack his things and go. He was dismissed.

Takis was disheartened, but on the other hand, he was relieved. He had never enjoyed his stay at the French school. His only concern was how to communicate with Jeannine to let her know. He rushed to find Townsend and asked him to deliver his car to Jeannine and tell her what had happened. Townsend promised to do so, and Takis, reassured, embarked on his journey, and looked forward to his reunion with his men.

CHAPTER 8

A Dozen White Sheets

AS THE WINTER of 1917 approached, the situation on the Balkan Front showed signs of deterioration. The Russian revolution had created chaotic conditions in that country, and the Eastern Front was crumbling now that the Russian Army was under the leadership of soldier committees known as soviets. Once the peace Treaty of Brest-Litovsk was signed between the German and Austrian Empires and Lenin, things turned very bleak. There were now three German and three Hungarian Armies available to reinforce the other fronts. The German Army group under General August von Mackensen attacked with all its might the weak troops of Romania defending their northwestern border, while the bulk of the Romanian Army was engaged in a fight in the south with the Bulgarians. In a few days they destroyed and eliminated all the Romanian Army, forcing the country to surrender. Now all the Bulgarian units fighting the Romanians were thrown to the Balkan Front.

Von Mackensen's next move was Italy. For almost two years the Alpine front was something of a joke. Neither the Austrians nor the Italians had undertaken any major offensive. They claimed that the mountainous terrain was not suitable for trench warfare and that there was no place where one could deploy considerable formations of troops needed for so gigantic an undertaking as breaking through the Italian defensive line securely anchored on the peaks of the Alps. It took Von Mackensen and his Germans, who, incidentally, were not Alpine troops and had no knowledge of mountaineering, like the Austrians or the Italians, a week to break the Italian defensive line all across the front and engage the fleeing Italians in a horrific battle in Caporetto where most of the Italian Army was destroyed. Two and a half million men were dead, wounded, missing, or taken prisoner, and the few remnants dispersed, disorganized, and panicked. Now the Allies had to divert troops so desperately needed in the Balkan and Western

Fronts in order to avert the total collapse and occupation of Italy.

Those were the circumstances prevailing when Takis rejoined his division in Serres. He was given a hero's welcome by the population of the town, but this time there was no time for festivities. The casualties were mounting; the Bulgarians and their German and Austrian allies were on the offensive and the Allies were losing ground. The Serres Division was by now 7,000 men, still very much under the normal strength of a typical Greek division of 12,000 troops. It was assigned the sector of the front that was previously held by the British brigade and an Italian regiment, who together had been 10,000 strong. Those two units were rushed to Italy to help stop the German avalanche.

Takis was given a command of a machine gun company, under strength, comprising 130 men, mostly volunteers from the area, inadequately trained, and with only about fifteen of the men of his original platoon, who were by now nearly all non-commissioned officers. The only advantage was that his new men were from Serres and the adjacent villages and worshiped him as a legendary hero. They called him 'the liberator' and were ready to follow him to hell and back.

The Allied casualties were mounting at an alarming rate and the front showed signs of collapse. The only respite came from the Serbian Army which by now had recuperated from its terrible defeat and reorganized in the sanctuary of the island of Corfu. They were only 45,000 men, but in so desperate a situation every bit counts. The Serres Division, even overextended in its given sector of the front, and with no reserves, gave a good account of itself and did not lose any significant ground.

Takis' role as a machine gun company commander was even more static than when he was ordinary infantry. His men were assigned no patrol duty and did not participate in attacks. Their duty was to repel attacks and keep the machine guns firing. There was no opportunity for heroics, and patience, of which Takis possessed precious little, was the best virtue. Patience and endurance. Before any attack it was the machine gun positions that received the lion's share of artillery barrage. Takis saw his men dying much faster than they could be replaced and hated the passivity and inertia of the situation. He yearned for real action and mowing down the disciplined and dedicated formations of enemy infantry while they were trying to cover the distance of no man's land and engage the defenders in hand-to-hand combat was not his penchant. He repeatedly asked to be transferred to light infantry, but his superiors told him he was doing, under the circumstances, fine, and declined his requests.

New Year's Eve of 1918 was cold and the whole area was under a thick carpet of snow. There was a pause in the otherwise continuous fighting, the men on either side of the front had temporarily laid their weapons at their sides and were celebrating the coming year with hopes of victory and homecoming.

Meanwhile, a French field hospital had been stationed only six miles west of the front, and Jeannine de Beaufort had volunteered for duty in the advanced line and was serving there. She could just as well have stayed in Thessalonica because she had been so close to Takis for over two weeks, and they had seen each other only once for a few minutes. Takis planned to take advantage of the temporary lull at the front and go see her. He also had another plan and he hoped she would be able to help him. When he reached the hospital after one hour of walking, it was getting dark, and she was not very busy. In fact, she was anticipating his visit and had made some plans of her own.

It was past midnight when Takis made his way back to the front, but he was happy and satisfied that he had at last been able to hold his beloved in his arms and elated because she had been able to provide him with a dozen fresh white sheets from the hospital's inventory. His plan was to choose ten of his veterans who had joined him in the capturing of Serres and have them cover their uniforms with the sheets so they could advance across the no man's land—which in that part of the front was less than a mile wide—undetected, reach the Bulgarian trench which would be less carefully guarded after the drinking and rejoicing that had preceded, ambush them and capture their trench. The objective was not as grandiose as Takis' previous undertakings, but it would save hundreds if not thousands of lives.

By three o'clock in the morning they were ready and started crawling along the open expanse. Takis had instructed his remaining men that if they were successful, he would fire a green light signal and they were to rush ahead with all their equipment and properly occupy the captured trench. Upon seeing the signal, they were to inform the neighboring units that a breach had been forced in the enemy line, and they also should attack. Luck was again on Takis' side and his plan succeeded, one hundred percent. He and his men totally surprised the slumbering Bulgarians and took 161 prisoners including one major and two captains. They killed and wounded at least another thirty and many ran away, spreading panic. After his signal was received, and once the whole division attacked, over six miles of enemy trenches and ten artillery batteries were captured. The Bulgarians lost some 600 men in casualties and 2,000 were taken prisoner. Takis had done it again, thanks to a dozen sheets and a small group of loyal, determined, and brave men.

General Papamandelos jokingly called him 'Alexander the Great,' and that nickname stuck. The significance of the operation was of way more consequence than Takis anticipated. The enemy had planned a major offensive for the third of January, and the breach of their line, plus the capture of so many field pieces, destroyed their plan. Now they would have to work until April to put another such plan together. For his deed, Takis received the Order of Phoenix and the Cross of the Redeemer, plus a compliment of bars and crossed swords to his existing medals. To his great satisfaction all his men were decorated and the ones who had joined him in the 'ghost march' were all promoted.

Papamandelos felt that Takis also deserved a field promotion, but he was afraid that entrusting him with the command of more men might make him even more daring and that he might attempt to win the war by himself. Instead, he arranged with the French Chief Surgeon for Jeannine to get a week's leave of absence and granted Takis the same. That indeed pleased him more than a promotion.

The two lovers drove in the Pic-Pic to Thessalonica. Jeannine was at the steering wheel because she said she wanted to arrive safely and make the most of her unexpected vacation. They again repaired to the Mediterranean Hotel in the same suite they had occupied on previous occasions, and they were only seen again when it was time for them to motor back to the front line. The more they were together the more, if such were possible, their mutual love increased. They believed they were predestined to become one of the famous pairs in history. They had now time, in the short intervals between their lovemaking, to discuss at length Marcel's death and the bad impact that the duel had caused among the French community.

Jeannine was treated like a leper and her compatriots reviled her and blamed her for the tragic incident. Takis explained to her that he had never before been involved in a duel and had no idea that he was not supposed to kill his opponent. Duels were very rare in Greece because, although the people are hot tempered, their anger does not last long, and they are by nature forgiving.

"Anyway," he told her, "if your countrymen hate you, mine adore you and since you will be my wife, Greece will be your country, and you shall shine there like a luminary of beauty and grace.

"Besides," he added, "Marcel asked for it by calling you a slut." "But I am a slut. At least in the opinion of most Frenchmen, for going so openly with a foreigner who is not a noble. Besides they say that your great-grandmother was a prostitute and that is why you like me."

Takis was not surprised that such malevolent talk had reached Thessalonica. "Gossip," he remarked, "is a common characteristic among people all over the world. Especially if you are famous, people always try to disparage you behind your back. Usually, the same people who prize you so high in your presence."

They agreed to ignore the gossip and enjoy each other and look forward to the end of the war and the beginning of their own family. Here they had their first disagreement. Takis wanted many children, but Jeannine was more concerned with preserving the exquisite lines of her figure.

"What do you care?" Takis said, "After all, I'm the only one who is supposed to see you naked, and I like you no matter what."

Poor Takis, he so very much wanted to have many children and even though he married five times in all, he sired only two.

Their one week of total bliss was over much faster than they cared for, and on the fifteenth of January 1918, they were back to their respective duties. Takis was told upon arriving, that big caliber, heavy artillery, long-range guns had made their appearance on the Balkan Front. The enemy was also using poisonous gas at every opportunity the wind was blowing west, probably in order to compensate for the loss of their trenches. That meant that on top of all the other miseries of life in the trenches, the men now had to wear the gas masks for hours on end and increase their suffering. The news was bad from the Western Front. The Germans, after knocking Italy out, were now attacking all along the line in France and Belgium and were advancing. They had reached so close to Paris that they were bombarding the capital city with their very heavy long-range cannons. Now the only hope to stop them was fresh and abundant cannon fodder from the United States, who at last had joined in the fighting.

Things were critical but not desperate on the Balkan Front. The line was mostly stabilized, but in some sectors very thinly occupied and there were no reserves. In case of a major offensive, it would probably break with no available troops for a counterattack. The collapse of Italy had increased the pressure on the front north of Thessalonica where large formations of Austrians had been transferred. The front-line trenches were under constant artillery fire, but also locations as far as twelve miles away from the front were being hit.

It was on such an occasion that a few heavy shells exploded in the French field hospital, and among the dead was a pretty, blond nurse, Jeannine de Beaufort.

Takis was at the front when he learned. He felt the world collapse around him. His life was not worth living without her. Until this moment his bravery and daring exploits were the results of his vanity and vainglory in conjunction with his strong sense of patriotism and his desire to please. War for him, was a deadly sport whereby if you win, you get medals, and if you lose, you die. His attitude and conduct were not contaminated with hatred. Jeannine's premature death filled him with hatred. In this instance he turned into a non-compassionate and maniac killer. He was also instilled with a horrifying death wish. He did not intend to commit suicide, but he was taking from now on uncalled for risks in hope that an enemy bullet would put him out of his misery. He would fire his machine gun standing erect, or he would jump out of the trench and engage in close combat with numerous enemy soldiers any time the opportunity was presented. His men knew that he wanted to die, and risking their own lives time and time again, they were doing their best to protect him from himself.

Fortunately for Takis, in a counterattack that the machine gun company had no business being part of, he got a flesh wound in his right arm caused by an enemy bayonet. His men were relieved. The wound was deep enough to keep him in the hospital long enough for him to at least partially recover from his more severe wound, the one caused by Jeannine's death. This time he was also very severely reprimanded by divisional headquarters for insubordination and threatened with discharge should a breach of discipline occur.

He was taken to a Greek military hospital in Serres where the local population went out of their way in an effort to sooth and please him and make his stay there as comfortable as their means allowed. Takis appreciated the friendship and concern of these simple people who worshiped him but was inconsolable. He spent most of the time thinking of Jeannine and weeping. His wound was infected and presented complications and he had to be transferred to a bigger hospital in Thessalonica.

His mother came again from Athens, where the family had recently moved from Piraeus, and her company and wisdom did alleviate somehow his suffering. It took him three months to recover from his wound, and even then, he felt very weak, but his real pain had not eased. Even though some of the Greek Red Cross nurses tried their best to cheer him up and entertain him, he was totally aloof to their charms and ignored their presence. His mother was concerned because that was not like the son she knew.

He never forgot Jeannine throughout the rest of his life, but his passionate nature and his vigorous youth eventually overcame. After his release from the hospital, he was given a week's leave that he decided to spend in Thessalonica with Yvette. She, as well as the other French nurses, came frequently to visit him as soon as they found out that he was wounded and lying in the Greek military hospital in Thessalonica. Yvette was a very poor substitute for Jeannine, but she showed great compassion, and her Mediterranean blood and spirit proved to be the best cure for Takis' broken heart. She insisted they go to a different hotel because she knew about the suite in the Mediterranean and did not want Jeannine's interference with her pleasure of Takis for a second time.

CHAPTER 9

End and Aftermath

BY NOW THE Central Powers had unleashed their major offensive and in spite of Takis' absence, they had been beaten back with appalling casualties. They had lost so many men they were unable to replace, that after their offensive lost its momentum, they began retreating even before a counterattack was mounted. The dawn of a final victory was almost there.

Things didn't show any promise for the Germans on the Western Front either. After their spectacular successes in the initial phase of their winter offensive, the front had been again stabilized and the ever- increasing presence of the American doughboys in the trenches spelled ominous doom to come for Germany and her allies.

The Germans were not losing the war at the front. Although they had lost over 7,000,000 men in those three and a half years, they had inflicted three times as many casualties on their adversaries. France had also lost 7,000,000 men. Great Britain had lost 2,500,000 home troops and almost 1,000,000 Colonials. Italy had lost 4,000,000 and Russia—it was hard to tell, but it was claimed that their casualties reached 15,000,000. The United States had just joined the fighting, so their casualties so far were negligible in comparison. Germany, though, did not have another 8,000,000 men to sacrifice. She was bled white, but the United States had a tremendous reservoir in men, and if they were determined to take the war seriously and fight it out to the end, Germany knew she could not last much longer.

On the other hand, if the American casualties were to reach the dreadful numbers that the other Allies had already suffered there was hope in Germany that such terrible carnage would cause an uproar in Congress and that President Wilson might be forced to withdraw from a war that some thought the United Sates had no business fighting in the first place, and except for financial advantage to their industry and agriculture, they had nothing of everlasting value to gain. Wilson had claimed that pure idealism has prompted the American people to fight in this war and that they were determined to win and put an end to all wars. The Germans thought that if a couple of million American boys were to die in the first six or seven months, then 'idealism' which was making the rich even richer, might give way to more realistic considerations like the oceans of tears of the mothers and sweethearts who were losing their loved ones.

Where Germany was losing the war was in Germany itself. After their defeat in the sea battle of Jutland, where in spite of the fact that the German fleet sank three times as my ships as it lost, they had to flee from the battle else they stood a chance of losing all their ships. The mastery of the seas was indisputably in British hands. The British effected a very successful blockade of all the Central Powers and not a single freighter could reach their ports anymore.

That created shortages in everything, essential or not. The civil populations in Germany and Austro-Hungary were suffering of all kinds of deprivations. Their economies were in shambles and their industries were reaching a standstill, not only because they were deprived of the needed raw material, but primarily the lack of working hands who were all now fighting at the front. Unlike World War Two, it was thought in the beginning of the twentieth century that women were incapable of doings 'a man's job' so instead of being invited or recruited to staff the factories and industrial plants, they sat at home helpless, dismal and reflecting how tragic this war was, how much misery and suffering it had inflicted upon them and shedding everlasting tears for the loved ones they had lost.

By the middle of 1918, the Allies were out-producing Germany in everything. For each shell the Germans could fire, the Allies could shoot twenty back. The Allied tanks were reaching the front in ever increasing numbers, changing constantly the balance to their advantage, whereas the Germans could only produce a trickle in comparison and their tanks were much inferior. The same was also true with airplanes and all kinds of motorized vehicles. Nerve and poison gas was a two-way maneuver and now they were taking as much as they delivered, and more. Their only advantage in this respect was that the wind blows more frequently westward than eastward in France, but now gas was delivered in shells, so the wind was not a decisive factor.

But it was in Berlin and Vienna that Germany was losing the war, not in the fields of Champagne or Picardy or Flanders where the valiant soldiers stood fast and made a fine show of themselves in spite of their worn-out weapons and scarcity of munitions. They were less than sixty miles away from Paris and no force on earth could break their lines and make them flee. It was true, a well-coordinated tank attack could create a temporary breach in some sector of their line, but tanks then were clumsy, and their range was very restricted, and a direct hit was putting them instantly out of action. So, they concentrated in shooting their light guns more accurately and devised some very effective and efficient anti-tank cannons.

When Takis rejoined his unit, the whole Balkan Front was on the offensive. In the north sector the French, British and Serbs were chasing the Austrians back to Belgrade. In the Eastern sector, the Bulgarians were forced to surrender the Greek towns of Drama and Kavala and were now retreating to their old border. Victory was very much visible now. The Greek Army had reached its peak by the middle of 1918 in organizational efficiency, manpower and equipment. It was 200,000 strong at the front and had 120,000 in reserves. In July 1918 the Greek Army mounted its own major offensive against the front held primarily by Bulgarian troops and pushed them out of the coasts of the Aegean and way behind their old border.

Takis, upon meeting some Bulgarian peasant girls, determined that they were the shapeliest and healthiest of all the females in the Balkans. He had not met any Romanians as yet, so his opinion was restricted to present experiences, but he was impressed. It is a pity they were our enemies because they could make good friends, he thought. He was put in charge of the occupational forces in a small rural Bulgarian town deprived, because of the war, almost entirely of its male inhabitants, and soon he had own little harem of eager and playful Bulgarian girls. It was this kind of spoils of war that he enjoyed.

The first to sue for peace were the Austrians because their multinational and loose Empire was about to crumble, and the Allies were preparing plans for an offensive with Vienna as the target. The Germans felt betrayed. It was like a dagger striking them in the back. A day later the Bulgarians sued for peace, followed by the Turks. Germany stood alone. On the basis of the famous 'Fourteen Points' of President Wilson's declaration, Germany agreed to the signing of the Armistice on November 11, 1918. The German lines were still only sixty miles from Paris and their troops were still fighting as bravely as ever. But now there were over 1,500,000 million American troops engaged in the fighting on the Western Front and more coming every day. Germany had nothing to lose by accepting the Fourteen Points of Wilson. Such items as self-determination by the people of disputed territories, was in fact to Germany's advantage in almost all the areas that Germany claimed. Holstein, Elsas and Lotrigen—Loraine in French—, Memel, and East Silesia were provinces with solid German populations and undisputable Germanic traditions.

Unfortunately, Wilson's Fourteen Points remained on paper. The Allies were not willing to forgo the opportunity for obtaining as much land and money as avariciousness could get them. Gradually Germany was betrayed and eventually disarmed and forced into the fiasco and charade of the Treaty of Versailles. President Wilson was personally conducting the peace negotiations in Paris, but he was both extremely naïve and ill advised by his equally naïve, uninformed, and inept aides. The theology professor and former Dean of Princeton University did not possess the experience, stamina, or the fortitude for interminable discussions with such cunning and able political giants like French Prime Minister Georges Clemenceau, Britain's Lloyd George, or Italy's formidable Orland. He was unskilled in the company of the professionals, and although he could see that idealism and the noble thought of laying the foundations for an everlasting, equitable and just peace were discarded by the Allied leaders in favor of extracting all they could from the defeated Central Powers, he was incapable of averting the severe and reprehensible injustices committed during the peace negotiations in Paris.

The German, Austrian and Ottoman Empires lay prostrate on the table of the peace negotiations and the victors, like vultures, were devouring them. Wilson hated what was done before him and in spite of him but did not have the personality or the mettle to avert it. The French have an axiom, *'en mangeant viens l'apetit'* which means 'the more you eat, the more your appetite increases,' which appeared to be the political creed prevailing in the peace negotiations. It is true that there were ethnic groups and whole provinces within the territory of their Empires who were foreign to the nationalities of the German or Austrian or Turkish people, areas that had been conquered sometime in the past and had never been restored to their appropriate national niche. But the Allies became frenetic.

Italy enigmatically claimed and obtained south Tyrol, a characteristically Germanic province of Austria. Poland, which until the war ended did not even exist as a sovereign country, was created out of the carving of Austria and Germany and some vast areas wrested out of the Soviet Union, who, preoccupied with her civil war, had not the adequate power or means to defend that territory. Out of the demolition and dismemberment of the Austrian Empire sprouted new countries like Hungary; Czechoslovakia, which was given a mass of Germanic territory called the Sudetenland; and Yugoslavia, which emerged from tiny Serbia by annexing the vast areas of Croatia, Slovenia, and Dalmatia, was made overnight into a giant. Italy got back all of the parts that once belonged to Venice, like the province of Istria, but seized also areas that had nothing to do with Italian nationalism.

The Ottoman Empire was probably the biggest victim of all in loss of territory. Syria and Lebanon and a province in Asia Minor were taken by France. Mesopotamia—now Iraq, Trans-Jordan, Palestine and all the Emirates in the Persian Gulf—were turned into British protectorates or mandated territories. Italy acquired a province in Asia Minor opposite the island of Rhodes, an island inhabited exclusively by Greeks, which Italy also had already annexed. Venizelos, who also attended the peace conferences, was given the provinces surrounding Smyrna, but that was of little consequence since these provinces were inhabited mostly by Greeks. He was also given the province of Thrace, but Constantinople was excluded. That was to remain the capital of the Sultan and the puppet government that the Allies had imposed in Turkey.

Constantinople, though, was to acquire an international status, which meant that the 200,000 Greeks living in the city would now be free and unoppressed. Venizelos made sure of that by obtaining the authority to police the city and manning it with Greek gendarmes. The provinces that were lost in the Middle East that had been under Turkish rule for only 500 years, were inhabited primarily by nomadic Arabs who did not possess any kind of national feelings. Their allegiance was to the Sultan because he was the Great Caliph of Islam, and they were bound by religion and race, not nationalism, which was to them a foreign concept then as much as now.

Germany was stripped of all her overseas colonies, the British taking the lion's share, with France and Japan taking the leftovers. The war reparations imposed upon her were impossible. She was condemned to pay installments to France until 1999. Furthermore, she was to be ruled henceforth as a Democracy under a theoretically good, but in reality, absurd, Constitution conceived by the French. The reparations were so exaggerated that in one year after the war was over, and Germany had turned into the Weimar Republic, her already weak economy collapsed totally, and the German mark was so worthless that it wasn't matching the value of the paper on which it was printed.

The Weimar Republic, the period of German history between 1919 and 1933, marks the lowest ebb into which Germany had ever fallen. It was decadent and very perverse. It was during the Weimar Republic that the government legislated marriage between homosexuals.

The biggest disappointment for President Wilson though, came from his own country when the U.S. Senate rejected American membership in the League of Nations. It was Wilson's brainchild, his idea of an international congress where each country, large or small, would have an equal vote in a forum of democratic principles that would safeguard eternal peace. His own country denied him participation. The League of Nations was inaugurated in Geneva, Switzerland without its founder being even a member. The other major powers had already achieved, through the various peace treaties, so much more than they had ever anticipated, that in this respect they could afford to oblige Wilson and accept his idea of the League. They stood nothing to lose by their membership, and the theory behind the principles of the League of Nations was noble, and harmless.

The end of World War I found Takis in Bulgaria. He was now promoted to second lieutenant and ordered to go to Athens and attend the last year of the Military Academy. Since he had decided to make the Army his career, it was considered by his superiors that he needed to complete his education prior to any new assignments. This constituted a rather unorthodox procedure, since Takis by now was a commissioned officer with three years of almost continuous front-line service, and he had proven himself absolutely worthy of the commission, but he accepted his orders with good humor. He was the most highly decorated low-ranking officer in the Greek army. His fame as such had generated a sort of legend about his person, and he looked forward to returning to Athens after three years of absence. He was now nineteen years old, but the war had galvanized him, and he felt much older.

He arrived in Athens in late November 1918, his pockets again full of money, and after a very brief visit with his family he reported to the Military Academy. He was given a room of his own, not a bench in the dormitory, and was treated with great respect by both the teachers who were mostly high-ranking officers, and the students who idolized him and thought of him as an example to be followed. Most of his colleagues were older than he, but his strong personality and his war record asserted him as their leader immediately.

During classes on military theory or related subjects, the instructors would invite him to address the class and give them his own opinions on the subject matter based on his practical experiences at the front. Indeed, he was treated with such reverence that sometimes he felt a little embarrassed, but he enjoyed it. His classmates were the same ones that he had started with in the academy three years ago but the ones who had offended him in the past were now behaving with utmost respect and pretended that they had forgotten. Takis, of course remembered, but his was not a petty character and he mostly ignored them.

He was not subjected to the normal curriculum of the academy; he had no guard duty, or other menial tasks, and he did not have to participate in maneuvers or physical exercises unless he chose to. That gave him a lot of spare time that he was using to catch up with the theoretical subjects he had missed. He was also allowed leave of absence twice a week.

He had been in Athens only ten days when he received an invitation to the Royal Palace, by King Alexander who wanted to meet the most decorated officer in the Army. This triggered an avalanche of invitations, and in no time Takis was the toast of Athenian society. He was very surprised, but equally pleased, when he was invited for a reception at the French Embassy. He was immensely pleased to see David Townsend there, who now was a captain in the Australian Army on leave waiting for his demobilization and spending his time sailing and enjoying the Mediterranean Sea.

Both young men were happy to be rejoined and agreed to stay in close touch. The reception was over at eleven o'clock, so they decided to spend the rest of the night together in some mixed company. They went to the most exclusive bordello in Athens and Takis asked the 'mama' how many girls she employed in the establishment. She said she had six and Takis asked her if he would get any discount for all six of them, one after the other with no interval. The 'mama' knew who he was and told him not to be ridiculous and brag.

"The bed," she said, "is different from the trenches. The girls will be too much for you."

Takis persisted and the 'mama' became irritated by his vanity and decided to give him a lesson. She said that one hour with any of her girls cost ten drachmae, which was one gold coin equivalent to $150, and she was willing to wager that Takis could not copulate with all six in a row. The bet was that if he succeeded, the whole thing would cost him nothing, but if he failed then he would have to pay double—six times ten drachmae—that is 120 drachmae, equivalent to $1,800.

"That will teach you an expensive lesson," the 'mama' said. Takis accepted the bet and, choosing one of the girls went upstairs with her to her room. Most of the girls at the time were entertaining other patrons of the establishment so they had no way of knowing about the bet. The two that were in the salon while the bet was made were quite pleased, because they liked that flamboyant and handsome officer whose reputation both as war hero and lover had not escaped them.

A few minutes after he disappeared with the first girl, Takis shouted, "Who is next?"

So, the 'mama' sent another girl upstairs. Ten minutes later, Takis' baritone echoed in the brothel, "Who is next?"

So, the third girl was dispatched. A quarter of an hour later Takis' voice once again called out, "Who is next?"

The fourth girl followed and by now everybody in the establishment, customer as well as occupant, were enjoying the proceedings and teasing the 'mama.' After the fifth girl had joined Takis, the 'mama' felt some relief because the minutes were passing and then the quarter hour, but after almost an hour, Takis voice, "Who's next?" shouted again, putting 'mama' in a state of amazed anxiety.

Before she sent the sixth and last girl, she instructed her to be as complacent and uncooperative as possible.

"This is business, you silly geese," she told the giggling girls, "You are not supposed to enjoy it." It was a moment of hilarity when Takis' voice, after only ten minutes, broke the anticipatory silence. At this point all five girls rushed to his room. Everybody was laughing except for the 'mama' who was saying, "I have been fifteen years a 'mama' and before that I was for thirty years a prostitute and in all my life, I have never experienced anything like that."

It was by then three o'clock in the morning, so Takis invited Townsend to the room he was sharing with the girls, and they spent the rest of the night and next day with them and drinking themselves to a stupor in a bath of champagne. Late in the afternoon they were ready to go after they had tipped most generously the six girls. The 'mama' took her loss in grudging good humor, but her parting words were, "Please don't come back."

CHAPTER 10

Greece's Due, Lost

VENIZELOS WAS THE head of the Greek delegation to the peace negotiations in Paris and he was trying very hard to obtain as much as he felt Greece was due. Italy's Orlando was giving him some hard times, but he had succeeded in gaining President Wilson's friendship and confidence, and the support of Lloyd George, the Prime Minister of Great Britain. Unlike the other Allies, Greece was not behaving like a predator, she was only demanding what was rightly, historically and ethnically hers: the vast regions of the Ottoman Empire in Asia Minor that were inhabited for millennia by Greeks; the region of north Epirus which had a ninety percent Greek population and was now a part of Albania; the island of Cyprus with an eighty-seven percent Greek population; and the parts of Macedonia that had a Greek ethnic majority.

Except for the United States, that had no territorial claims whatsoever, the common characteristic of all the other Allies was their voracious greed to acquire as much land as possible, to collect as many reparations from Germany as possible, and their apprehension that no other ally gets more than themselves.

Russia was not invited to the peace negotiations for two reasons: one, as the Soviet Union, she had not been recognized by the Allies and two, the Allies were waging war against the Bolsheviks in the hope of restoring the monarchy in Russia. When Lenin came to power in the Soviet Union, he exposed the duplicity and dishonesty of the Allies by publishing the text of the various secret treaties signed while the war was still going on, whereby the same area promised to one ally in one such treaty was also offered to someone else in another treaty.

Venizelos was to be subjected to this duplicity, especially on the part of Italy and France who were not pleased with the idea of Greece becoming too strong and a future antagonist. So the demands of Greece were met with opposition based on the notions that Greece had not joined the conflict when it first started; that Greece had not honored her obligation toward Serbia when that country was attacked by the Austro-Hungarian Empire; that Greece was practically dragged into the war by the double breach of her neutrality—and the most decisive factor was that the French were very resentful of the losses they had suffered when they tried to invade Athens and arrest the former king, Constantine. In other words, Venizelos was being held responsible for a policy that he had opposed all the way. The whole thing did not stand to reason or logic, but it was the means for diminishing the Greek claims, and a fraudulent effort to belittle the contribution of Greece in winning the war.

The negotiations took all of 1919 and a good part of 1920 until the final treaties with the defeated Central Powers were signed. The first treaty to be signed was the one in Versailles with Germany. Here Greece was only involved in true and undisputable claims for cash reparations concerning the hundreds of Greek ships sunk during the war by German submarines. The next treaty was signed in Trianon and dealt with the Austro-Hungarian Empire, which was dissolved into three different countries: Austria, Hungary, and Czechoslovakia, in addition to the vast regions that went toward the creation of Poland and Yugoslavia. Here again, Greece had only moderate cash claims deriving from destruction of property due to the Balkan Front.

The treaty with Bulgaria was signed in St. Germain, and there Greece was treated very unjustly in that considerable regions of Macedonia that were populated by Greeks, regions that Greek troops had spilled their blood liberating, were either ceded to Yugoslavia or left to Bulgaria. Less than one third of the Greek claims *vis à vis* Bulgaria was satisfied. Serbia, now Yugoslavia, was the big winner in that treaty and obviously sided with the other Allies, notable Italy, against the Greek claims. The treaty with the Ottoman Empire, was signed in Sevres. In this one, Venizelos fought like a lion and registered the largest gains: all of Thrace, with the exception of Constantinople and a small periphery surrounding the city, was ceded to Greece. Constantinople was to remain the capital of Turkey and the seat of the Sultan but was to acquire international status.

Smyrna and the regions directly to the north and south of the city were also ceded to Greece. This was an area almost equal to one quarter of the then size of Greece and had a solid Greek population of over 1,000,000. But there were vast areas in Asia Minor, farther to the interior, which had Greek populations and were left to Turkey. Further south of Smyrna, a province which had a Greek majority was ceded to Italy, and one to the southeast, also populated by a Greek majority, was ceded to France. Still, the gains for Greece were considerable and Venizelos and the people in Greece had reason to rejoice.

Britain reneged and did not even discuss the release of Cyprus. Upon Italy's insistence on the ratification of the state of Albania that encompassed the Greek province of North Epirus, 100,000 Greeks were ceded to Albania. It left a very bitter taste, but the gains in Asia Minor somehow compensated for these injustices. After the treaties were signed and

Venizelos came back home, the Greece of 1912 had almost quadrupled in land area and the population of 4,000,000 was now almost 6,000,000. The people seemed happy and united, and Greece had sent adequate troops to occupy and incorporate the newly acquired land in Asia Minor to the Kingdom of Greece.

The future looked bright and prosperous, and then a tragic event happened that was to lead Greece to a humiliating and devastating tragedy: King Alexander, the man under whose throne the Greeks were at last happily united, had a small Rhesus monkey as a pet. The monkey bit him and the bite was infected. To everybody's surprise and lament, so superficial a wound led to the King's rapid deterioration of health, and within two weeks, to his premature death. Unfortunately for Greece, the king and his popular Greek wife did not have a son, so now Greece was faced with a problem of succession.

The hard-core Liberals were trying to persuade Venizelos to proclaim a plebiscite and turn Greece into a republic. The Royalists, who still entertained very strong feelings toward the ex-king Constantine I, were very suspicious of the Venizelists and feared that they were conspiring to reverse, or even worse, invalidate the Constitution and usurp all power in Greece. The dreadful phasma of discord and political unrest, the implacable fate of Greece through her history, was almost palpable. Venizelos, in order to placate the suspicions of the Royalists, invited the Queen Mother and grandmother, Olga, now in her eighties, to come to Athens and serve as Vice Regina, until the problem of succession was solved. Her Royal Highness Queen Olga was eager to comply, cognizant of the fact that she was serving both the interests of the country as well as those of her son, ex-King Constantine. The Royalists thought that this was another Venizelist ruse and challenged the constitutionality of Olga's tenure of Regency since Greece had never in modern times been ruled by a female.

Venizelos felt compelled to proclaim general elections, and once he renewed his confidence with the people, he believed that he would be able to solve the problem of succession. The elections were held in September 1920 and to the world's surprise, Venizelos suffered a decisive and humiliating defeat. He didn't even carry his own district in Athens. It was a landslide victory for the Royalist party in all of old Greece. Venizelos did carry the islands and all the newly acquired provinces, but out of 300 deputies in Parliament, the Liberals held only eighty-seven. Why did the Greek people show such ingratitude to the architect of their victory and glory? How could they be so foolishly immature in their political thinking and deprive Greece of the services of her most talented and prestigious statesman? How could they expect that anybody would be able to pursue the policies of expansion and consolidation of the aftermath of the war without the prestige of international scale that Venizelos commanded?

No logical explanation is found to the questions. The only parallel in modern history is the defeat of Winston Churchill in the elections held in the fall of 1945 when the British people rejected the architect of the World War II victory, the foremost man in their country and perhaps in the whole world, for a dubious, and as it turned out, devastating experiment in Socialism. The Greek people in their folly of rejecting Venizelos did not have any such alternative. They knew that Venizelos would be replaced in the helm of the country by Constantine, a man whose shortsighted policy had alienated him from Greece's friends, and in fact had earned himself the unmitigated hatred of France. How could he, under the present circumstances be of any use to Greece?

After the overwhelming electoral victory of the Royalists, Venizelos left the country in utter disappointment and disgust to a self-imposed exile in Paris. As a mere episode of constitutionality, a plebiscite was held in Greece which returned Constantine as the lawful king with a sixty-eight percent majority. His homecoming was greeted with a frenzy of jubilations by the enthusiastic Royalists who maintained that now, under a Constantine, the old legend would be fulfilled. They dreamed that Constantinople would again be theirs, and that in a ceremony full of pomp and glory, the Patriarch would crown him Emperor of Byzantium within the sacred walls of the Hagia Sophia.

Dark clouds were gathering on the political horizon of Greece even before Constantine's restoration to the throne. Now it looked like a storm was about to erupt. Greece had become engaged in a full-fledged war against Turkey, and the more the Greek Army was advancing into the interior of Asia Minor, the more the logistic and economic and financial problems of Greece were increasing. This turn of affairs had been brought about by Venizelos expansionist policy and his endeavor to liberate all the Greeks in Asia Minor.

After the Greeks disembarked in Smyrna, right after the signing of the Treaty of Sevres, and occupied the lands ceded to Greece, there had been numerous border incidents with Turkish irregulars. Greek towns and villages in the interior were feeling more secure with the presence of a Greek Army in Smyrna and were revolting against Turkish rule. That was bringing severe and frequently atrocious reprisals on the part of the Turks, so Venizelos, with the silent consent of the British government, decided to expand the border of the Greek territory further to the east and liberate all the areas that had a Greek population. Inevitably, that would incur the reaction of the remnants of the Turkish army under Kemal Pasha which was stationed north of the Syrian border. But Venizelos, assured of British assistance, looked forward to a final and decisive clash with Turkey now that Greece was at her pinnacle of modern glory. Her people were united and her army in the best of morale after the victorious conclusion of the war. It was well equipped, well trained, and larger than what Kemal had under his command.

What Kemal had under his command were the dispersed, demoralized, defeated, disorganized and isolated remnants of the Turkish Armies that had fought the British in the Middle East and the Russians in Armenia and on the Black Sea coast. The trouncing those armies had suffered was such that they hardly existed, even on paper, so when the government of the Sultan sued for peace, the Allies failed to demand disarmament and demobilization of the Turkish Army because they did not think that such an army existed anymore.

Kemal was in command, at the time, of a Turkish division that had taken its share of the beating in the decisive and conclusive Battle of Aleppo that sealed the fate of the Ottoman Empire, but his division was not obliterated. It still maintained some form of organization and discipline and Kemal used it as a rallying point for other formations of the Turkish Army that still existed, wandering in the semi-desert of the Turkish interior. Kemal was not only a great leader but also a very capable administrator, and a hero of the Battle of Gallipolis that had shattered the British plan to force a way across the straits.

To the disappointed and demoralized Turkish soldiers, he represented the only hope for a future in their country. His charismatic personality was a beacon of inspiration to all patriotic Turks. They resented the dismemberment of their country and the puppet government in Constantinople that had signed all those humiliating treaties. Kemal formed a provisional government in Ankara, which at that time, was a primitive settlement of 10,000 inhabitants, denounced the Sultan and his government and declared the peace Treaty of Sevres null and void.

His actions, of course, did not meet with the approval of the Allies—far from it—and the determination of Greece to enforce the treaty with her army came as a relief. As long as this policy was planned and executed by Venizelos the French—however reluctantly—offered him their moral support, and the Italians had to remain passively neutral. They could not offend the other Allies, and they were also the beneficiaries of the Treaty of Sevres. Once, though, King Constantine, the proven enemy of France, took over the leadership of Greece, France turned instantly hostile and so did Italy.

In the beginning that hostility did not change the picture on the front in Asia Minor. The Greek Army was advancing and wherever the Kemal forces stood and gave battle they were always defeated and chased further east. There was definite purpose in advancing toward Ankara. There were Greek settlements and communities throughout Asia Minor that needed to be liberated, and King Constantine, reminiscent of his triumphs during the Balkan War, had a strong desire to renew them and add the aura of conqueror to his crown. He was determined to crush Kemal and efface Turkey from the map once and for all. The Turks were now fighting for their very national existence and even though a barbarous and primitive nation, they possessed pride and a celebrated history of bloodshed and conquest. The deeper into the heart of their country the hated Greeks were advancing, the more stubborn and resolute was their resistance and the more volunteers were rushing to join Kemal's ranks.

On the other hand, the Greek army was not prepared nor equipped for so extended and distant a front, so the more it advanced the more weakened became its position. The Turkish railroads were antiquated and in poor condition, and the roads were all but non-existent. It had become a war of attrition, with many Turkish irregulars operating behind the lines. Supplies were reaching the front at a snail's pace and quite often they did not reach it at all. The rugged mountainous terrain added to the difficulties and the weariness of the Greek soldiers. Most of them had been in uniform since 1911. Ten years in the Army, especially an Army that has been fighting almost non-stop, puts relentless strain even on the most disciplined and dedicated soldiers.

The Greek Army had covered over 400 miles of conquered enemy territory, and still there was no end appearing on the horizon. But the worst enemy of all was that the Greek people were not united anymore. The feuding political factions of Royalists and Venizelos existed also in the Army, and that was the most troubling factor of all.

The first country to acknowledge Kemal and his government was the Soviet Union. Lenin offered Kemal not only moral, but also actual support in the form of desperately needed munitions and artillery pieces. Once the Bolsheviks had won their civil war they could spare such equipment, and they reflected that if Kemal were to establish himself as the leader of

Turkey he would be obligated to the Soviet Union and the straits would remain open for Soviet navigation.

The British leadership at the time, Prime Minister David Lloyd George, and Winston Churchill, were ardent opponents of Communism and had done their best to oppose the Bolsheviks from taking over in Russia. Great Britain and her allies had even sent troops to fight along with the White Russians and the Tsarists during the civil war, but consecutive general strikes called by the British trade unions and the Labor Party who sympathized with the 'cause' of Lenin forced the British government to withdraw the support. Now both British leaders were enraged with Kemal for becoming an ally of Lenin and wanted him destroyed. They decided that Great Britain should support the Greek effort with all conceivable means and were even considering actual participation in combat by British troops.

That would constitute a remarkable switch in official British policy of strict neutrality ever since Constantine had returned to Greece and taken over the rule of the country. The British were not as inimical to Constantine as the French, and besides, he was their own king's first cousin. To Churchill in particular, Communism was anathema and any move on the part of Great Britain to bar further expansion of the Communist miasma was absolutely justifiable. It did not take him too much of an effort to convince the Cabinet Ministers of Lloyd George that Great Britain should, with all dispatch, prepare an expedition to be sent to Asia Minor and fight alongside the Greeks.

The British government was comprised of Liberal personalities under Lloyd George, who enjoyed a Conservative support in the House of Commons and thus could maintain power. It was a rather precarious condition because the Tories could at any moment withdraw their support, since that was not a Tory government, and Lloyd George would have to resign. Once Churchill's idea came for debate in the House of Commons, the Conservatives indeed did withdraw their support and the Lloyd George government was toppled. The instigator of the withdrawal was Lord Beaverbrook, but his motives were much more personal than political.

The source is Queen Frederica of Greece, or more accurately, a Lady-in-Waiting to the queen, who told it to me, and I have every reason to believe that my informer was conveying what the queen had said accurately.

The Lady, Mrs. Maltsiniosis, related that Lord Beaverbrook held great animosity toward King Constantine that stemmed from an incident at the royal regatta, which was held every year on the Isle of Wight, and attended by all crowned heads, their relatives, and the international aristocracy. The newly elevated, hereditary peer, Lord Beaverbrook also attended. The 'real' aristocrats, knowing his very humble origin, saw him as an intruder and resented his very common and unattractive presence. He was short, bespectacled, potbellied, inelegant, in short, he didn't look or behave like an aristocrat.

While Beaverbrook was on the island of Wight, one day he went and watched the two cousins, the Duke of Gloucester and the Crown Prince of Greece, Constantine, playing golf. Neither of them appreciated the presence of Lord Beaverbrook. The two princes did not suspect that he understood the German language, and they were jeering, using the mother tongue of most of the European royalty, "Look at that miserable ape gawking at us." Beaverbrook understood German, and thereafter hated both the Sachs-Coburg's and Constantine.

Lord Beaverbrook was a native of Canada, of humble origins and background, but with great talent, determination, and drive. He became a stockbroker and made a fortune in Canadian cement mills, He eventually moved to London where he purchased the almost defunct Daily Express and practically overnight, utilizing his talents that had made him a millionaire in Canada, changed the paper into both a financial success and the most powerful political organ of the Conservative Party. The daily circulation of the Express soared to the millions and the self-made Canadian, Max Aitken, son of a Presbyterian preacher, was elevated by King George V in 1908 to the peerage, as Lord Beaverbrook, named aptly for the beavers and brooks of his Canadian origin. Now he was a full-fledged British aristocrat, albeit failing the noble upbringing and background of his newly found peers.

His press usually didn't directly attack the sovereigns of Great Britain—but he never missed a chance to criticize Prince Philip. As for the Greek royal family, that he hated with a passion, and because of that hatred, Greece suffered the worst defeat in her history. Lord Beaverbrook was able to avert British support for Constantine, which would most probably result in his winning the war and increase his prestige and glory. This hatred of the King of Greece changed the course of world history.

In August 1922, one and a half million Greeks were slaughtered by the Turks, and another million came as refugees to mainland Greece. Whereas World War I ended on November 11, 1918, as far as Greece was concerned, it didn't end, because Greece had to send her troops to claim what was given to her by the Treaty of Sevres. Kemal Ataturk did not acknowledge the Treaty of Sevres, so Greece had to fight to occupy the areas granted to Greece. This was territory approximately the size of New Jersey, on the coast where Izmir, that was called Smyrna, is today, and the ancient towns of Ephesus, Miletus, and Troy, and the rest of Ionia.

This campaign started toward the end of 1919, and by 1922 the Greek Army was at the Sangarius River, also known as the Sakarya, a few miles west of Ankara, and most of what is today Turkey, was occupied. However, the Greek lines were overextended. Greece was running out of money, Greece was running out of munitions, and she needed help. So, a delegation of the Greek government went to Great Britain to beg the British for help. At that time the British government was comprised of Liberal ministers under Lloyd George and Winston Churchill, but they had split from the rest of the Whig Party, so they were governing Great Britain with a vote of tolerance, or a vote of confidence, from the Tories.

The problem Great Britain had at the time was the Irish—to the point that King George V had asked Lloyd George to Buckingham Palace, and queried, "Mr. Prime Minister, do you intend to slaughter all my Irish subjects?" The genocide of the Irish was creating very unpleasant press for the ruling government of Great Britain, and that's why they had split from the rest of the Liberal Party: because the Liberals were in favor of home rule, and Lloyd George and Winston Churchill apparently were not anymore.

Winston Churchill very much favored the idea of helping Greece, not only financially and materially, but even to extend it to the dispatch of British troops to fight along with Greek troops in Anatolia. Lloyd George agreed with Churchill that Britain should send troops primarily to defray the interest of the British public from Ireland, and they would start wondering what's going on in Ankara. It was a Friday when it was agreed that Great Britain would assist Greece not only financially and materially, but also with the British Army.

Lord Beaverbrook found out on Friday afternoon, and he called his close friend, Andrew Bonar Law, the head of the Tory Party. He told him that, on Monday, Lloyd George would ask Parliament for the appropriation to send troops to fight the Turks. "I want you to withdraw the vote of confidence to the Lloyd George government," he declared. Andrew Bonar Law could not argue with Lord Beaverbrook because Lord Beaverbrook was in essence the head of the Tory Party, even though not holding any office. On Monday, the Tories withdrew their vote of confidence to the Lloyd George government, the government collapsed, the elections ensued, and Ramsey McDonald and the Labor Party won their first election in Great Britain. To the detrimental effect ever since.

Greece did not receive any help. On August 17 the Greek Front collapsed and what the Greeks had managed to gain in three years was lost in a few weeks. Ionia, which is the cradle of Hellenic civilization, was lost permanently. Of the 100,000 Greek inhabitants of Smyrna, only 20,000 survived. The slaughter included the Archbishop of Smyrna who was standing on the steps of his cathedral when the Turks massacred him, along with the flock that had sought refuge in the cathedral. That is known as the 'Small Asia Catastrophe.' Greeks call Anatolia, 'small Asia,' or Asia Minor, so this is the Asia Minor Catastrophe. Never in all the years of Greek history has she suffered so humiliating and so total a defeat. Of course, Kamal Ataturk became the father of Turkey and the most glorious field marshal. If it weren't for Beaverbrook, Turkey wouldn't exist today.

Everybody blamed the Asia Minor Catastrophe on Greece's Prince Andrew—the father of Prince Philip, who became the consort of Queen Elizabeth II. Prince Andrew was married to Alice, Princess Mountbatten, sister of Queen Frederica. The Mountbatten's, on the same day in 1916 that the Saxe-Coburg-Gothe's changed their name to Windsor, changed their German name, Battenberg, to Mountbatten. Great Britain was distancing herself from all Germanic relationships. In fact, in 1916, Covent Garden refused to play Wagnerian operas anymore. Even the music was not acceptable.

Prince Andrew did commit a major blunder, because at the time he was the commander of an army corps. An army corps comprises three divisions and his corps retreated, and eventually that retreat turned into a panic. His corps was holding the center position in the front, so when his corps retreated and then ran in panic, the other two, afraid they might be encircled by the Turks, also ran, and it was the start of the rout.

But Queen Frederica had a different point of view. She acknowledged that, "Perhaps my brother-in-law did make a strategic mistake, but the reason we lost Asia Minor is Lord Beaverbrook," and she told the story, starting with the Isle of Wight.

There is a parallel between Lord Beaverbrook's pique and Greece's catastrophe, and the defeat of the French in Viet Nam. The French committed a strategic blunder when they sent French troops, the French Foreign Legion, to Dien Bien Phu, which was the most northeastern spot in North Vietnam, hoping to attract the guerrillas to expose themselves and defeat them in a pitched battle. That didn't occur, and eventually Dien Bien Phu was encircled by the Viet Minh. France begged America to help, with the airplanes of the Seventh American Fleet which was in Tonkin Bay at the time. They didn't ask the Americans to fight in Vietnam on their side. They begged them to surprise the belligerents in Dien Bien Phu with the planes of the American Fleet. General Eisenhower, who was president at the time, refused the French request, and the French suffered a humiliating defeat, when the Foreign Legion, having spent every round of ammunition they had, and having eaten the last bite of food they had, had to surrender to the Vietnamese. And France lost Vietnam.

The reason Eisenhower refused to help the French was because he despised De Gaulle. De Gaulle was not the head of state at the time, in fact he was retired, but apparently Eisenhower extended his feeling to the rest of France. During World War II when Eisenhower was the Supreme Commander of all the Allied Forces in Europe, he had forty-one major generals under his command. One of those major generals was General Charles de Gaulle, but De Gaulle did not see himself as an ordinary major general. He saw himself as the head of the Free French and the personification of France. Whenever he demanded something of Eisenhower and Eisenhower correctly would refuse him—because Eisenhower did not see him as a head of state, he saw him as one of his forty-one major generals under his command—De Gaulle would complain to Churchill. Churchill, in order to get rid of him, would call President Roosevelt, and convey the complaints of De Gaulle. Roosevelt would call General Marshall, the Chairman of Joint Chiefs of Staff—Marshall was Eisenhower's boss—so Marshall would call Eisenhower, and in this way De Gaulle would get his way. And Eisenhower resented that. For that the French lost Vietnam.

Two books show the idiocy and futility of the mass killings of a nation's soldiers when they are actually the flip sides of the same coin. The book, *Von Westen Nichts*, or *No News from the Western Front*, It is possibly the best anti-war book ever written. The daily bulletin for the German Army during the lull of mid-1917 after the bloodbath of Verdun and the Somme, is the title of Remarque's best seller. In it he describes the horror and suffering, the killing and maiming of Frenchmen and Germans that occurred in a typical day that the daily bulletin dismissed with '*von western nichts.*'

With his uniform torn to pieces after a shell explosion and covered with blood, Erich Kramer was taken to a French hospital for treatment. When he recovered his senses, and realized he was in a French hospital, he said "*de l'eau c'il vous plais*, water, please." The nurse that brought him the water assumed he was French, and he was treated as such, and not as a prisoner of war. When asked what his name was, he pronounced his name in reverse, and it sounded like a perfect French name: from Kramer came Remarque. He had a love affair with Marlene Dietrich, the famous and blatantly promiscuous film star, but only by letters, in which he used the name 'Alfred' to communicate with her.

Stratis Myrivilis, a Greek novelist, wrote a book, *I Zoe en Tapho*, which means 'life in the grave,' describing his experiences of a day typical at the Balkan Front. Almost a word for word translation of the Remarque's German book, with only the geographic locations being different, it was first published in 1919 at his native island of Lesbos—home of the famous poetess, Sappho, best known for glorifying love among women, 'lesbianism.' It was then published in Athens in 1921.

Remarque's book was published in Dresden, also in 1921, a few weeks before the Athens publication of Myrivilis' book. Long suits and counter suits followed for copyright infringement, plagiarism, and theft of spiritual property. Since Myrivilis' book was first published in Lesbos with only 950 copies, it would appear that Kramer had stolen the idea. But the publication, out of an obscure little island in Greece, was hardly known beyond the island, and Kramer could not read Greek, even in the remote possibility that a copy of the Myrivilis book reached Germany before 1921. It was finally determined that two people of different origins and backgrounds can have inspiration simultaneously.

CHAPTER 11

The Greek and Goering

MY FATHER, TAKIS Panayotopoulos, was sent to Evangelismos, the main hospital in Athens, as Surgeon-Captain Prossas had informed him at the field hospital at Proussa, after the artillery shell took his elbow, and the arm had to be amputated, because he was very feeble, having lost most of his blood. The Royal Hospital was under the auspices of Queen Sophie of Greece, who was Princess Sophie of Prussia and sister to the German Kaiser Wilhelm.

Takis' family was Republican. They resented the king and his German wife because of his pro-German policy in the beginning of World War I. They were Anglophiles and Francophiles, liberals, and free traders.

After his arrival at the Royal Hospital, Takis was told that King Constantine himself would appear and decorate him with the gold medal, the Order of Valiance. He was twenty-one years old, and at the time the most decorated junior Greek officer and had a splendid reputation as a daring and very brave soldier. Upon hearing that the king would come and visit him, he acted with a foolhardy effrontery which was meant to offend the king. Impertinent, he attached to his stump an election button of the king's archrival, the leader of the Republican Party, Venizelos, and a garlic. The garlic, in Greek folklore, keeps the evil eye away, and the symbolism was that the king would not be able to harm Venizelos with his evil eye.

The king knew the symbolism of the garlic and was very offended, but he bestowed the decoration without commenting. When he went back to the palace, he told his wife how disappointed he was with this extremely disrespectful and audacious lieutenant. The queen said, "No, just ignore the effrontery and leave him to me. I will turn him to a staunch Royalist." The king declared, "Not him, you will be wasting your time." So, they ended making a bet.

Next day, and every day for two weeks, the Queen in her capacity as head of the hospital, would visit Takis and take a very keen interest in his recovery. When he gained enough strength to walk, a royal limousine would come from the palace to take him there for tea. He became very fond of Queen Sophie. The king avoided him.

Eventually, when he was about to be released from the hospital, Queen Sophie informed him that he was to go to Munich to be operated by the best orthopedic surgeon in the world, Dr. Sauerbruch, for a prosthesis that would enable him to move the fingers of the false limb. He would be in a semi-official capacity as Envoy to the Queen attached to the Greek Consulate in Munich, with full pay, and the army would cover all his expenses. At the same time, it was confirmed that he had been promoted to captain for his bravery in the battlefield. He was now the youngest captain in the Greek Army and had just become 22 years old.

He had never traveled so far before. He had only briefly traveled to Italy as a fifteen-year-old. He knew no German but spoke fluent French and a few phrases in English and Italian.

Takis arrived in Bavaria in the early spring of 1922, with a lot of Swiss, English, and French gold coins. He was immediately interned in Dr. Sauerbruch's clinic where a number of delicate operations were performed to connect the nerves of the stump to the prosthesis. Because the Germans had suffered so many millions of casualties during World War I, their surgeons were the best, and Sauerbruch was the best of the best. Takis was very lucky. After a few months he was released from the clinic but had to go every day as an outpatient. It was the middle of summer and apparently very hot in Munich.

Takis repaired at a suite in the *Bayerische Hof* and was ready for his day in town, after more than a year of confinement in various hospitals. The only clothes he had were uniforms since he had been in the army since 1916. The Greek uniforms, then, were identical to the French with the only difference being a crown insignia on the kepi instead of the tricolor circles of the French. Takis knew that, although Greece and Germany were on opposing sides during the war, there was no animosity in Bavaria against the Greeks. So, he donned his best all-white uniform with all his decorations, and took to the streets of Munich, happy to be free for the first time in a long while.

He had walked hardly more than a few blocks and realized that the urchins of the street had started looking at him and following him, their eyes full of hatred, and the only word he could hear and somehow understand was "*Franzoese.*" Eventually they began throwing horse manure and stones at him. He started running back to the hotel, but more people were gathering, blocking his path, and throwing all kinds of garbage at him. In desperation and panic he saw what appeared to be a *gasthaus* and rushed in. The mob that was chasing him gathered at the door, and the patrons and the waiters were about to throw him out. At that moment a deep voice from within the establishment was heard over the din and noise and everybody in the *gasthaus* paused.

A waiter showed Takis to the table of the man who had called out. He sat at the *stammtisch* alone. He wore a threadbare German uniform with captain's insignia and a decoration around his neck. The man spoke good French, and asked Takis if he was insane or just stupid to offend the people of Munich by parading himself in the hated French uniform with all those decorations, that he had probably earned for killing the fathers and brothers of the children who had tormented him on the street. Takis said that he had killed no Germans and he was unaware that Greeks were so hated in Bavaria. He showed the crown insignia on his kepi. The man started apologizing. He then shouted to the patrons that their guest was Greek, not French, and now everybody started apologizing and sending offerings of beer and *aufschnit*.

"Even if it is a Greek uniform, why are you not wearing civilian clothes? The war was over three years ago," said the man.

"I have nothing else to wear but uniforms," replied Takis. "The war is not over in Greece. We are still fighting the Turks."

And then he asked, "Why are you wearing your uniform, which seems to have seen better days?"

"I have nothing else to wear," said the man, and introduced himself as *Hauptmann* Hermann Goering. He was the most decorated officer in Bavaria and the only living Ace in Germany.

Hermann Goering had won the Blue Max, the *Pour le Merite*, the highest decoration World War II Germany could bestow. He had distinguished himself as an Air Ace, credited with shooting down twenty-two Allied aircraft. There were two other German officers that had more kills than Goering, but they were both dead. Also, he had been awarded the Iron Cross, First Class. Takis told him that he, too, was the most decorated Greek officer. It was obvious from that first encounter that there was affinity between them. Goering, like Takis, was a *bourgeois* and a war hero. They had entered their respective armies at about the same time, and both distinguished themselves. Goering had entered the German Army in 1914 as an infantry lieutenant, before being transferred to the Air Force as a combat pilot. In 1918 he was Commander of the Richthofen Fighter Squadron.

Goering was in his element in Munich, treated like royalty, but penniless. Takis was loaded but knew nothing and nobody. A perfect symbiosis was then and there established. Goering moved to Takis' suite in the *Bayerishe Hof* and provided his expertise, Takis financed all their living and entertainment expenses.

At Goering's suggestion, Takis became a student in the School of Art at the university so he could learn to use his left hand. It was also the best place to meet models and female students. Takis declared that the eight months he spent with Goering were the happiest in his life. Germany was experiencing a galloping inflation but that did not affect them because Takis had gold.

At that time, the involvement of Goering with Adolf Hitler and Eric Ludendorff did not in any way bother their friendship. Ludendorff had been leader of the German Army at the end of World War I and found Hitler's claim that the loss of the war was due to Jews, Socialists, and Communists attractive. Hermann Goering's aristocratic background and war hero prestige made him a prize recruit to the infant Nazi Party—the National Socialist German Workers Party, NSDAP.

Takis would often go to the *Bierhalle* with Goering—Hitler appointed Goering head of the *Sturmabteilung*, SA, also known as Brown Shirts, or Storm Troopers in December 1922—but was bored because his German was not enough for him to understand the discussions. He noticed that Hitler had very piercing, magnetic blue eyes, the only attribute in his drab, low class appearance.

Takis was recalled to Athens in June 1922 before Goering participated in the Munich Beer Hall Putsch of November 1923, which was Hitler's attempt to overthrow the Weimar government and establish his own. On November 8, a meeting of 3,000 Bavarian government officials had convened, and during one of the speeches, Hitler and armed storm troopers entered the building. Hitler jumped on a table, fired two shots in the air and told the audience that the National Revolution had begun. A confrontation with police during a march across town resulted in twenty-one people killed, and one hundred wounded, including Goering. Hitler was jailed for a short time, during which he wrote *Mein Kampf*, My Struggle, as a propaganda piece.

Goering fled Germany for four years, and, wounded in the *putsch*, he became a morphine addict in the course of his recovery, and was admitted to an asylum in 1925.

Goering returned to Germany in 1927, under a general amnesty, where he rejoined the Nazi Party and was elected as one of its first deputies to the Reichstag a year later. During the next five years Goering played a major part in smoothing Hitler's road to power, using his contacts with conservative circles, big business, and army officers to reconcile them to the Nazi Party and orchestrating the electoral triumph of July 31, 1932, which brought him the Presidency of the Reichstag.

Following Hitler's appointment as Chancellor only six months later, January 1933, Goering became second in command, and was made Prussian Minister of the Interior, Commander-in-Chief of the Prussian Police and Gestapo, and Commissioner for Aviation. As the creator of the secret police, Goering, together with Heinrich Himmler and Reinhard Heydrich set up the early concentration camps for political opponents. Goering exploited the Reichstag fire—which many suspected that he had engineered—to implement a series of emergency decrees that destroyed the last remnants of civil rights in Germany, to imprison Communists and Social Democrats and ban the left-wing press. He directed operations during the Blood Purge, which eliminated his rival Ernst Rohm and other SA leaders in June 1934.

In 1934, when our family business in Greece needed to renew the mechanical inventory of most of our manufacturing plants, it was decided to buy all the new equipment in Germany. My father went to Berlin to see his friend Goering and negotiate terms for the purchase and he found him in the best position to help. Goering took my father's list of requirements and ordered his subordinates to fill the orders and make sure that everything would be of top quality and shipped to Greece on credit.

Goering invited my father on hunting trips, first in East Prussia and then to Bavaria. My father reflected that that was the best time he had ever spent. Goering used his position to indulge in ostentatious luxury. He lived in a palace in Berlin, and built a hunting mansion where he organized feasts, state hunts, showed off his stolen art treasures and pursued extravagant tastes. He changed uniforms and suits five times a day, affected an archaic Germanic style of hunting dress—replete with green leather jackets, medieval peasant hats and boar spears—flouted his medals and jewelry, and enjoyed the trappings of power. He styled himself, with characteristic egomania, 'the last Renaissance man.' Despite his debauches and bribe-taking, he remained popular with the German masses who regarded him as manly, honest, and more accessible than the *Fuhrer*, mistaking his extrovert bluster for human warmth.

In March 1935 he was appointed Commander in Chief of the Air Force and organized the rapid build-up of the aircraft industry and training of pilots. In 1936 he was appointed Plenipotentiary for the implementation of the Four-Year Plan, which gave him virtually dictatorial controls to direct the German economy. The creation of the state-owned Hermann Goering Works in 1937, a gigantic industrial nexus which employed 700,000 workers and amassed a capital of 400,000,000 marks, enabled him to accumulate a huge fortune.

When my father returned to Germany in 1936, as the Military Attaché, under the auspices of the Metaxas government, at the Greek Embassy in Berlin, his friendship with the number two man in Germany, Hitler's successor, was most valuable.

Following the Crystal Night pogrom of November 9, 1938, it was Goering who fined the German Jewish community a billion marks and ordered the elimination of Jews from the German economy, the 'Aryanization' of their property and businesses, and their exclusion from schools, resorts, parks, forests, etc. On November 12, 1938, he warned of a 'final reckoning' with the Jews' should Germany come into conflict with a foreign power. It was also Goering who instructed Heydrich in July 1941 to 'carry out all preparations with regard to *Gesamtlosung*, a 'general solution,' of the Jewish question in those territories of Europe which are under German influence...'

Goering identified with Hitler's territorial aspirations, and despite his bludgeoning of the Czechs into submission, he preferred to dictate a new order in Europe by 'diplomacy' rather than war. He was appointed Reich Council Chairman for National Defense in August 1939 and officially designated as Hitler's successor on the first of September. Goering directed the Luftwaffe campaigns against Poland and France, and in June 1940 was promoted to Reich Marshal.

In August 1940 he began the offensive against Great Britain—Operation Eagle—confident that he would drive the RAF from the skies and secure the surrender of the British by means of the Luftwaffe alone. A fatal, tactical error occurred when he changed to massive night bombings of London in September 1940 just when British fighter defenses were reeling from air and ground losses. It saved the RAF sector control stations from destruction and gave the British fighter defenses time to recover.

The failure of the Luftwaffe, which Hitler never forgave, caused the planned invasion of England—Operation Sea Lion—to be abandoned, and began the political downfall of Goering. Further failures of the Luftwaffe on the Russian front and its inability to defend Germany itself from Allied bombing attacks underlined Goering's incompetence as its Supreme Commander. Technical research was ignored by a commander-in-chief who prized personal heroism above scientific innovation and whose idea of dignified combat was ramming enemy aircraft.

My father returned to Greece in 1940 and did not witness the deterioration of his friend's personality and his depression. Goering rapidly sank into lethargy and illusions, expressly forbidding reports of enemy fighters accompanying bomber squadrons deep into German territory in

1943. Goering had become bloated, discredited, isolated, and increasingly despised by Hitler, who blamed him for Germany's defeats. He was undermined by Martin Bormann's intrigues, overtaken in influence by Himmler, and Propaganda Minister Joseph Goebbels and Albert Speer. He was mentally humiliated by his servile dependence on the *Fuhrer*, and he began to disintegrate. When Hitler declared that he would remain in the Berlin bunker to the end, Goering, who had already left for Bavaria, misinterpreted it as an abdication and requested that he be allowed to take over at once; instead, he was dismissed from all his posts, expelled from the Party, and arrested.

Shortly afterwards, on May 9, 1945, Goering was captured by forces of the American Seventh Army and put on trial at Nuremburg in 1946. During his trial Goering, who had slimmed in captivity and had been taken off drugs, defended himself with aggressive vigor and skill, frequently outwitting the prosecuting counsel.

With Hitler dead, he stood out among the defendants as the dominating personality, dictating attitudes to other prisoners in the dock and adopting a pose of self-conscious heroism motivated by the belief that he would be immortalized as a German martyr. Nevertheless, Goering failed to convince the judges, who found him guilty on all four counts: conspiracy to wage war, crimes against peace, war crimes and crimes against humanity. No mitigating circumstances were found, and Goering was sentenced to death by hanging. On October 15, 1946, two hours before his execution was to happen, Hermann Goering committed suicide in his Nuremberg cell, taking a capsule of poison that he had succeeded in hiding from his guards throughout his captivity, or is rumored to have been supplied to him.

My father Takis, on right with Adolf Hitler, while a Military Attaché at Greek Embassy in Berlin.

Berghof

A chance meeting with Hermann Goering after WWI resulted in a lasting friendship despite opposing views. Takis accompanied him on hunting trips and through him became a guest at Berghof, Hitler's Bavarian retreat. Takis bigamously married an entertainer there. Hitler was best man.

CHAPTER 12

Family and Business

IN JUNE 1922 Takis was ordered to return to Greece and resume his duties in the Greek Army. He could now speak German and his prosthesis was a wonder of German engineering. He could move the elbow and the fingers and do simple chores like lighting a match. The drawback was that the artificial limb was heavy, cumbersome and in the summer, heat irritated the stump. He was given a job as instructor of machine-gun tactics in the Military Academy.

By August the situation was critical for the overextended Greek Army. An insignificant gain of the Turks resulted in the collapse of the whole Greek front, a rout and an ensuing panic that lost, in two weeks, the territory liberated in three years of fighting, and close to 2,500,000 Ionian Greeks were massacred by the Turks or went as refugees to the Greek mainland.

The culprit in this Asia Minor Catastrophe was Prince Andrew of Greece, the father of Prince Philip, who became the Duke of Edinburgh, consort to Queen Elizabeth II of England,

The few remnants of the Greek Army, led by Republican officers, undertook a *coup d'état,* and took over the government. The royal family fled Greece in a destroyer sent by the British. The wife of Prince Andrew, Princess Alice Mountbatten, mother of Prince Philip, had served Greece well; she acted as a nurse in a field hospital during the Balkan Wars, and was loved and respected by everybody. She returned to Greece and devoted herself to charity work, staying in Athens during the Second World War sheltering Jewish refugees, and founded a Greek Orthodox nursing order of nuns, going to England shortly before her death in 1970.

The Republican officers that took over the governance of Greece executed all the members of the previous government that were found guilty of treason and gross negligence for the Asia Minor disaster. They proclaimed a plebiscite that turned Greece into a republic and invited the Liberal leader Venizelos to take over.

That same year. Helen McDuff, my mother, first arrived in Greece when her father transferred from Constantinople to the British embassy in Athens. At about the same time Takis Panayotopoulos returned to Athens from his surgeries in Munich, and his position as Queen Sophia's envoy at the Greek consulate there, to resume his army duties. It didn't take long and Takis found the nurse that had soothed him at Proussa after the loss of his arm. It was love at first sight. She was a girl of five foot seven, she weighed about 120 pounds, with a sort of hourglass figure, with a very narrow waist. She had blue eyes, and blond hair that eventually turned to dark brown.

Helen McDuff had been at Proussa as a nurse because her father served as the British consul general in Constantinople. Proussa is a hundred miles away. There is no direct line. From Constantinople one can sail to a little port of Modania on the Propontis, now called the Sea of Marmara, and from Modania go about twelve miles to Proussa.

She was born in Inverness, Scotland in 1903. Her Scottish father was the fourth son of the Earl of Inverness, which means he had no chance whatsoever to ever inherit the title, so in typical British tradition he went to the consular service. Britain was then rich enough to have a separate diplomatic and a separate consular office. The Consular Office belonged to the Colonial Office, and in 1919 he was the British consul general in Constantinople.

At the time, the wife of Prince Andrew of Greece, Princess Alice Mountbatten, was setting up field hospitals for the Greek Red Cross. Helen did not have a chance to join the British Red Cross, which was what all well-born British women did during World War I, because she was too young, but since Greece kept on fighting the Turks, and with Alice Mountbatten being with the Greek Red Cross, she felt that she now would fulfill this obligation by volunteering in the Greek Red Cross.

In 1921 she joined the Greek Red Cross, and she was sent to something equivalent to a M*A*S*H, a sort of field hospital outside the town of Proussa in Asia Minor—the Turks call it Bursa. She had been in that hospital for less than six months when a young Greek officer who had lost his right arm was brought to the hospital and was taken to surgery, where she assisted the surgeon.

My mother told me that she fell instantly in love with that Greek officer when she first saw him at the field hospital, because having bled almost to death, he was white like marble, and with his right arm missing, he resembled the statue of Hermes by Praxiteles, a sculptor who also crafted the Venus d' Milo. According to my father, when he opened his eyes at the field hospital and saw my mother, a blond, blue-eyed woman in a white dress, standing next to him, he thought he had died and gone to Paradise, and that she was an angel. When the angel started speaking English to him, he was convinced that God was an Englishman. It was a mutual *coup de foudre*.

Once they met again in Athens, they immediately decided to get married. My mother, an ardent Catholic of the Royal Stuart clan, which denounces the Stuarts who renounced their faith in order to become kings of England, carried her Catholicism as a badge of honor. At that time, if a Catholic woman married outside her church she was automatically excommunicated. My mother did not want to be excommunicated, so she took my father to the Catholic bishop in Athens to see if there was an alternative. The Catholic bishop of Athens advised that there is, if he swears that the issue of the marriage will be baptized according to the Catholic rites and raised up as a Catholic. My father was so much in love, and he reluctantly gave the oath. It was rather a moot point since my Greek family married almost exclusively foreign girls. She was a great-granddaughter of the Duke of Argyll which provided even more respectability.

My father spoke very little English, so my mother perfected her French and that was the language spoken in our house. All the servants but the laundress were Francophone. Business was good in the 1920s and early 1930s for the family enterprises and we, my cousins and I, were born into great affluence. Children of privilege, the Panayotopoulos cousins, Micky, and Peter, nonetheless became criminals and thieves, while I, Michael…. Micky was the son of Alexander and Margo, Princess de Polignac, and Peter was the son of Paul and Aime, also a Princess de Polignac.

My father was still on the active-duty list, but he was not required to serve, so he could dedicate all his time in business, mainly as the traveling ambassador and trouble shooter. All the while he kept corresponding with Goering and following his German friend's rise in the ranks of his party and government. Politically they were diametrically opposed, my father being a typical liberal bourgeois, believing that the best government was the smallest and least active government while the National Socialists, the Nazi's, of Germany believed exactly the reverse: a one-party, all-powerful government with total and absolute control of all aspects of their citizens' lives, from cradle to grave.

Three of the biggest nations of Europe, Russia, Italy, and Germany, were following that path. A number of smaller nations, Austria, Hungary, Portugal, Romania, and later Spain also had Fascist regimes. Poland could hardly be considered a democracy at the time, nor could the term apply to Yugoslavia or Bulgaria.

The major theme of National Socialism is that the Germans are the *herrenfolk*, the superior race, the race destined to be ruler of the world. That obviously cannot be exported anywhere else, unless anywhere else you have a German population. On the other hand, nationalistic movements known as fascism evolved, with the Latin word *fasces* and a bundle of rods as a symbol. During the 19th century, the bundle of rods, in Latin called *fasces*, and in Italian *fascio*, came to symbolize strength through unity, the point being that while each independent rod was fragile, as a bundle they were strong. As established by Mussolini, fascism was an export item, and it had been exported successfully after the end of the civil war in Italy, to Romania, to Hungary, and to Slovakia. Poland had some kind of a fascist regime before the Germans invaded her. Austria had a fascist regime under the dictatorship of Chancellor Engelbert Dollfuss, before being annexed by Hitler. So, fascism had been exported quite successfully to quite a few countries. In America the closest to a fascist regime was the implementation of the New Deal by Franklin Roosevelt.

The city where the most fascist symbols can be seen is Washington, D.C. The Supreme Court is adorned by fascist symbols, and in the House of Representatives, the podium of the Speaker is flanked by two huge fascist symbols. At the Lincoln Memorial, where Lincoln sits on an armchair, where his arms rest, are two fascist symbols. The fascist symbols are a hatchet, or an ax, surrounded by ten rods and attached by leather straps.

The legend of fascism is that a Roman patrician was lying on his deathbed, and his ten sons were around the bed waiting to see to whom the father would give the estate, or most of the estate. The father had ten rods under his bed, and he asked each of his sons to take a rod. "Break it," he said, so they all broke the rods they held.

On the other side of the bed, he had ten more rods, and he instructed, "Take those and make a bundle out of them." They did.

"Break them," he said, but, of course, they couldn't.

"After my death, if you disburse of your heritage and divide it by ten, you will be too weak, and your neighbors are going to devour you, but if you stay united, the estate will survive."

This is *fascio*, 'strength in unity.' One to fight for preservation of the union was Lincoln. One who emulated Mussolini's example and considered Benito Mussolini the most successful leader in the world at the time, was Franklin Roosevelt. *Time* magazine had Mussolini twice as 'Man of the Year.'

Fascism took a bad name when Soviet propaganda, especially in the American universities, in order to glorify Communism, needed an evil in comparison. They concentrated their accusation on fascism and maintained that communism was fighting fascism. Communism was not really fighting fascism, because Communism *is* fascism, under a different name. The only difference is that fascism allows private enterprise, believes in the market, and does not impose its will upon what each and every individual is going to do with his life. Other than that, it has every common characteristic with communism: one party, one leader, one union, one youth organization and the nationalization of transportation, education, and utilities. That's fascism. The Tennessee Valley Authority is fascism if you don't want to consider it Soviet.

I personally do not consider being called Fascist as being something derogatory, because I can't imagine of a better governed country and a more successful country than Singapore. Think of it. Singapore is a barren rock. Nothing grows on Singapore. Even water has to be imported in Singapore because there is no water. That was the main reason why 100,000 British surrendered to 32,000 Japanese in the impregnable fortress of Singapore. Because they didn't have water. The water was on the mainland, and the mainland, Malaya, was already captured by the Japanese. On this barren rock, that nothing grows, are over 2,500,000 Chinese, and about another 1,000,000 Malays and Indians, and they have the highest per capita income in Asia. Out of that barren rock they have made a financial success and also a social success.

Compare Singapore to the Philippine Islands: the Philippine Islands is one of the most fertile regions on our globe; it has immense resources of natural treasure, yet in Manila, one the biggest cities on earth, over 10,000,000 people live among the garbage dumps. This illustrates the difference between the Fascist regime in Singapore and whatever regime arises in the Philippine Islands, and the difference between Chinese and Filipino.

Extrapolate from the Philippine Islands to Mexico. Mexico also is blessed with immense natural resources. Mexico has oil, more than it needs for its own consumption, it is one of the major exporting nations of oil and gas. Mexico has gold and silver in overabundance, Mexico has some of the best farming land, Mexico has water that teems with fish and shrimp. Yet in Mexico City, many of the 9,000,000 Mexicans, like their cousins in the Philippine Islands, live in the garbage dumps, and the rest of them dream of when they can come to America to collect lettuce in California. If Mexico were Singapore, it would probably be the greatest power on earth. Fascism is not that bad, depending on the people.

When Adolf Hitler came to power in Germany, Mussolini was one of his most severe critics, because Mussolini resented the fact that the Nazis had assassinated the Austrian Dictator Dollfuss and attempted to seize the government, in contravention of other plans that Mussolini had. Mussolini was a participant at the famous Munich conference, where the French and the British betrayed Czechoslovakia and allowed Hitler to swallow it. Mussolini initially went to Munich with the intention to oppose Hitler, but when he saw how weak-willed and gutless the French and the English Chamberlain were, it then occurred to him that he should better side with strength, and that's how eventually Mussolini became Hitler's ally. It was not meant that way, in fact England and France were hoping that they could ally themselves with Italy against Hitler.

"I'm bringing peace on earth. I have Herr Hitler's signature." The newsreel cameras rolled as Chamberlain held a piece of paper and displayed it for all to see, as he returned from Germany to England. The appeasers in England, among them Lord Darlington, and Nancy Astor, thought that that was the apotheosis of their correct policy to appease Hitler, since after all, it wasn't nice to betray Germany at Versailles. We saw the results of the appeasement policy. A year later Germany invaded Poland and we had World War II.

Today we have something similar in the Middle East. Apparently, Americans fail to realize, that no matter what the press says, if they want their country to be impervious to terrorist attacks, they have to hit terrorism at its head. And that is the so-called West Bank and Gaza Strip, where the deceased Yasser Arafat's former henchmen, suicide bombers and the rest of the Arab Islamic fundamentalist gang congregate to plot and plan. A war on terror would allow Israel to fight it with all the deterrents available in her arsenal.

Appeasement politics, "Let the poor Palestinians have a country," is historically erroneous. There can be only one solution in the Middle East, and it can only be military, not political, not diplomatic. If the Arabs had the arsenal, they would exterminate all of us, it's as simple as that. If the Arabs were so much interested in their Palestinian brethren, they could have accommodated them eighty years ago in the Sudan, which is about five times the size of Texas, and inhabited only by a few million starvation-stricken Moslems. The Sudan is transversed by the largest river on earth: the Nile. It is not arable land because of incompetence and stupidity. A hell of a lot of productive fields could be made in the Sudan. It doesn't have to be a desert.

The reason the rest of Egypt is not a desert is because there is too much water in the delta of the Nile. A good example is Iraq. Iraq is transversed by two very large rivers, the Tigris and the Euphrates, the rest of it is desert. The reason they didn't manage to turn the between-the-rivers area into a desert is because there is too much water. They managed to turn it into a swamp, and even though it's a swamp, still they had to import rice from the United States. So, they had a swamp, but they didn't produce their own rice in it. If Iraq were inhabited by Chinese, it would be exporting rice. The Sahara, when it was inhabited by Greeks and Carthaginians, was a very fertile part of the world. It took six centuries for the Arabs to turn it into the biggest desert on earth.

In spite of their political differences, it seemed that the friendship of Takis Panayotopoulos with Hermann Goering was genuine and could withstand distance and time. In 1934, our family business needed to renew the mechanical inventory of most of our manufacturing plants, and it was decided to buy all the new equipment in Germany.

My father went to Berlin to see his friend and negotiate terms for the purchase of a few million marks worth of machinery and tools. By then Goering was the Prime Minister of Prussia, and the number two man in the Nazi hierarchy. Their reunion was hearty and jovial. Goering took my father's shopping list and ordered his underlings to make sure that everything would be of top quality and shipped to Greece on credit. Then he invited my father to a long hunting vacation, first in East Prussia and then to Bavaria. They must have had a hell of a good time. Until his death my father used to say that that was the best time he had ever spent in his entire life.

The year of my birth, 1934, was a very good year for the family fortunes. Our factories were now modernized, no more Baxter, Simons, Blake, and Baldwin. We now featured Humboldt, Krupp, MAN and AEG.

CHAPTER **13**

Rescue from Exile

IN 1935 THE political scenery in Greece turned gloomy. The Royalists—right wingers, pro-fascists—were on the rise. After a disputed plebiscite in 1935, George II, son of King Constantine I, was invited to return to Greece and take the throne in 1935. Elections were to be held in 1936 and the predictions were that the Royalists would win by a landslide.

The Republican officers, in 1935, decided to stage a coup and take over the government in order to prevent the elections from happening, and avert the restoration of the monarchy in Greece. My father was among the conspirators and organizers of the *putsch*. Some organizer. The coup failed within the first week of its execution. The conspirators, my father among them, were arrested and sent into exile pending their trial for conspiracy and treason.

Eleftherios Venizelos had joined this last desperate attempt to stem the royalist tide by armed uprisings in Athens, and when the rebellion was put down, he fled to France where he died in 1936, at the age of seventy-two. From his first premiership in 1910-15, his premierships were an on-again, off-again series of recalls to office, then forced resignations.

My father had been recalled in 1922 to a Greece where support was building for Venizelos to again become premier in 1924, spurred by the Asia Minor Catastrophe—and causing King Constantine I to again abdicate—thus there was no authority for my father's position as an envoy of the queen. After an overwhelming victory, Venizelos retired from office before the plebiscite that soon declared Greece a republic. It was *déjà vu* for him, since in 1917, on Constantine's first abdication, Venizelos had become premier for the third time. He was recalled to office again in 1928, but growing Royalist opposition forced his resignation in 1932, and he returned to power briefly in 1933. Venizelos is generally regarded as the greatest Greek statesman of modern times.

The elections of 1936 produced a deadlock, but the Communist Party had made gains. Disliking the Communists and fearing a coup, King George II appointed General Ioannis Metaxas, then Minister of War, to be interim Prime Minister. With the support of the king, he dissolved Parliament and established a dictatorship.

General Metaxas, a brilliant tactician, was a career soldier, and a staunch monarchist. In 1917, when Venizelos was empowered and King Constantine I abdicated, Metaxas left Greece with the king. In 1920, following a plebiscite, when a war-weary population rejected the party of Venizelos, and King Constantine I was restored in December 1920, Metaxas returned with him. The Greek royal family of King George II was restored in a regime that was the clone of Mussolini's Italy. General Metaxas imitated and copied everything of the Italian model except the pomposity of Mussolini himself. The fundamental ideology remained conservative, and Metaxas was clearly aware that the greatest threat to Greece came from the Fascist powers.

While all this turmoil was happening, my father lived in isolation, in exile on the island of Ikaria. At the same time Goering had sent three letters to him that were unanswered, and he started worrying about his Greek friend. He knew about the coups and countercoups that had occurred in Greece and knowing Takis, he was sure that he had been involved. Goering ordered the German Ambassador in Athens to try to find out the whereabouts of Captain Takis Panayotopoulos. When the German ambassador started making his inquiries, most Greek officials were puzzled. Why would a German ambassador be interested in a Greek officer who was known to be Liberal and an anglophile?

The letters Goering had written had been held by some obscure army bureaucrat who had no idea that they were indeed letters from one of the foremost personalities in the world. The ambassador was persistent. And finally General Metaxas had to see him and explain that Goering's friend, Takis, was indicted for conspiracy to overturn the government and condemned to life in exile.

A frenzy ensued to find Goering's letters and get my father back to Athens to be presented to the German ambassador, who suspected that my father had been murdered. In 1936 the whole world was taking good notice of a revived and united Germany that was again flexing her muscles. Nobody wanted to be on her sore side, least of all General Metaxas who was a staunch Germanophile and a great admirer of Germany and the Germans. Ioannes Metaxas was a graduate of the *Kriegsakademie zu Berlin* and was a fellow cadet with the Kaiser Wilhelm at the German military academy. He had graduated near the top of his class at the

Kriegsakademie zu Berlin and his nickname was *der kleine Moltke,* 'the little Moltke'—after Helmuth Karl Bernhard Graf von Moltke, the genius German General of the nineteenth century—and because he was short.

After having spent almost a year isolated in exile, my father was in bad shape. He had lost weight, his health was troubling him, and he was depressed. After being presented to the German ambassador, he was taken to the office of the dictator, General Metaxas.

"Who do you know in Germany, and why is Goering interested in you?" the general wanted to know.

"Well, starting with Hitler, I know everybody worth knowing in Germany." He then explained to the baffled general the circumstances of his meeting Goering and through him the rest of the Nazi inner circle.

"If I promote you to major and send you to Germany as my military attaché, do you think you might convince your friends to sell us modern weapons?"

"I don't know," Takis said, "but I can give it a try."

The circumstances for Greece at the time were rather peculiar: her traditional friends and allies, France and Great Britain, would not sell her any modern military hardware because they resented her Fascist regime. Italy would not sell either, because Mussolini planned in the foreseeable future to attack Greece. Germany also would not sell Greece weapons because in spite of her Fascist regime, the Germans correctly estimated that, in case of war, Greece would in all probability fight on the side of England. So General Metaxas, who could also foresee the coming conflagration, desperately wanted to modernize the Greek armed forces, and only the Poles would sell him the PZL biplane fighter planes, manufactured by *Państwowe Zakłady Lotnicze* in Poland, but which were already obsolete. It was a fortuitous scheme of his to set aside politics and take advantage of my father's unique position as a personal friend of the top German leaders.

"If I send you to Germany, do I have your word that you will be loyal to me?" the general asked.

"No, not to you," Takis answered, "but to Hellas. If you are loyal to her, then we shall serve the same purpose."

My father thus began four years as the Military Attaché of Greece in Berlin. He obtained everything General Metaxas wanted except airplanes. The Germans had hardly enough planes for themselves and were not selling to others. The very effective German propaganda and the location of Tempelhof Airport in the middle of Berlin created the impression that the Luftwaffe had countless airplanes. In August of 1939, a few weeks before the war started, there was a very big parade of the Wehrmacht in Berlin. The parade lasted for several hours and all the while the sky was full of military airplanes passing over the awed spectators in constant and neverending formations. What most of the spectators didn't know was that the same planes would go and refuel in Tempelhof and keep flying for hours, always the same planes. At the beginning of the war, France and Great Britain had a three to two advantage over the Luftwaffe, but they didn't know it.

Both Napoleon and Hitler had the same vision or dream: a pacific and united Europe, one under the French aegis, the other with the Germans as the *Herrenvolk*. Both shed tons of blood and sacrificed the cream of their country's manhood to accomplish their vision. In both cases it was England that shattered their dream because England in her insularity felt superior to any European nation, or the whole of Europe for that matter, and would never permit anyone to become master of the whole continent. World War II with its catastrophic and devastating results, and the total misery it brought to the whole continent, was also a catharsis. It took that kind of blood, toil and sacrifice for at last both the French and the Germans to see beyond their petty rivalry and insignificant geographic disputes. It also took two great men of vision: Conrad Adenauer and Charles de Gaulle to reach each other and shake hands. Adenauer was magnificent in playing the subordinate role and feeding De Gaulle's gigantic ego, when all along he knew that Germany, as the economically superior power, would end up holding the reins.

A United Europe with Germany at the helm is not any more a dream, or a remote vision. It is reality. And as time goes by, it develops stronger bonds, until the United States of Europe is established in perhaps fifteen to twenty years from now. The fly in the ointment is again England. Only now she has neither the strength nor the determination to prevent it. The European Union is a reality and not a single drop of blood was shed. In spite of the negative aspects, we would never have reached that point without Hitler. Unbiased and objective history perhaps fifty years from now will confirm that.

My father's friendship with Herman Goering sometimes resulted in invitations to festivities hosted by Adolf Hitler. At one of these at Berghof, Hitler's favorite retreat at the peak of the mountain near Berchtesgaden, a Bavarian female choir entertained, and my father was attracted to a singer named Thilda Kopenleitner. He asked permission to meet her, and Hitler obliged. My father eventually wanted to marry her, and Hitler approved of that, too, and served as best man at their wedding. A daughter was born of their union.

It was a bigamous marriage because my father was married to my mother in Greece. However, because it was a civil marriage and not recognized in Greece, where only the Orthodox or Catholic Churches could perform or authorize marriages, it was not technically illegal. When he came to Greece, he would bring her and introduce her as his wife. My grandmother Helen accepted her. Of course, my mother was furious, but would not consider divorce.

My father liked Germany, and five years of his life were spent there: in 1921-22, and from 1936 till the end of 1940. He always said that the German women are the best.

CHAPTER **14**

Prelude to War

WHEN THE CLOUDS of war were gathering in 1939—it must have been April or May, because the weather was pleasant—and I was five years old, my mother took me to Marathon which is near Athens, in the Citroen to show me the battlefields and prepare me for the oncoming war. She described every day's battle to me. She showed me where the Persians were disembarking, and re-embarking as they fled, and because there were so many of them, they couldn't board their ships very fast, and she showed me where the Athenians had deployed. She told me how the Athenians, even though they were outnumbered greatly, 26,000 Persians to about 10,000 Athenians, decided to attack rather than to defend. She got so enthused with her description of the battle and the slaughter that ensued that she started screaming, *"Alalay!" Alalay* is the battle cry of the Athenians. Since then, I have called her Alalay. *Alalay* means whatever 'hurrah' means.

She said, after the battle was over, the general of the Athenians, Miltiades, asked a cavalryman to gallop to Athens and tell the anxious populace we have won. The Athenians knew the Persians planned an overland attack from the Bay of Marathon to Athens and would lay it to waste for its part in the Ionian Revolt that ended four years before, against Persian domination. The cavalryman had to tell General Miltiades that the horses were too exhausted to even walk. The general asked for the best runner among the Athenians. He was told it was Pheidippides, a long-distance runner. Pheidippides was presented to the General who asked him to run to Athens and tell them we have won, and to warn of an attack from the sea. Three hours later, he arrived in Athens, exhausted from his run, and exhausted from the twelve-hour battle—they had fought from sunup until sundown. Pheidippides reached the assembly of the Athenians, uttered one word *"Nenikikamen"* which means, "We have won," He then collapsed and died.

There were so many Persians dead at Marathon, that the worn-out Athenians couldn't possibly did graves and put them in. There were about 16,400 Persians killed, and one hundred ninety-two Athenians. About a thousand Persians had been captured, and the Athenians made the prisoners make a pyramid of all the dead Persians. Then they strewed dirt on top of the dead bodies and created a hill. That hill is still there. On top of the hill, the Athenians erected a memorial and a trophy at the same time, which reads, still to this day, *'Of all the Hellenes, the Athenians alone destroyed the gold bearing Medes' glory'* It was September, 490 BC. The Spartans arrived afterward, toured the battlefield at Marathon, and agreed that the Athenians had won a great victory.

The common enemy, Persia, helped provide some solidarity to the disunited Greek city-states. The victory helped solidify the view that Greeks were 'civilized' and Asians were merely 'Barbarians.' Marathon was in no way a decisive victory over the Persians. However, it was the first time the Greeks had bested the Persians on land, and their victory endowed the Greeks with a faith in their destiny which was to endure for three centuries during which western culture was born.

After this glorious battle it was agreed among all the Hellenes that to commemorate Pheidippides and his feat of running back to Athens from Marathon to proclaim that we had won, in his honor, there would be a race run every four years in the Olympics called the Marathon race, and it is run to this day. The International Olympic Committee estimates the distance from the Marathon battlefield to Athens as 21.4 miles. The story became the basis for the modern marathon athletics event. The race is run over a distance of 26.2 miles.

Herodotus, the Greek historian, was born in the year of the battle, 490 BC, and, along with Plutarch and others, he recorded its details. King Darius I of Persia planned to take Athens by means of having part of his force take Eretria, which would offer little resistance, then land at Marathon Bay, threatening an overland attack in order to draw the Greek army away from Athens. The Eritreans sent an urgent message to Athens for help, and the Athenians agreed, but realized they needed more help.

They sent a courier to Sparta and probably a messenger to the Plataeans. The courier, said to be Pheidippides, arrived in Sparta on September 9, and the Spartans agreed to help, but pointed out that they could not go to war until the Karneia festival ended on the full moon on September 19-20. Karneia occurs in the Spartan month of Karneios when warfare was prohibited for a week.

As Artaphernes, the Persian Army leader was laying siege to Eritrea with part of his army, the remainder of his army crossed with Admiral Datis, the Mede, and landed in the Bay of Marathon. The Athenian Army, about 9,000 or 10,000 men under Callimachus, the Polemarch accompanied by his ten tribal generals, marched north from Athens. When Callimachus heard that the Persians had landed in the Bay of Marathon, he wheeled right and reached the valley of Avlona and encamped his army at the Shrine of Heracles. One thousand Plataeans joined him there. Since it was obvious from the Persians' disposition that they did not intend to march to Athens, the Athenians waited for the Spartans. For eight days the armies peacefully confronted each other.

On the ninth day, it became known to the Athenians that Eretria had fallen by treachery. This meant that Artaphernes was now free to move and might attack Athens. On September 21, the Athenian army went out to face the Persians. This was probably a combined decision of the generals. Although Herodotus reports that they were rotating days of command and that Miltiades was in charge at this point, and he had a large part in persuading the others to do so. According to Herodotus, five *strategoi* voted for the move and five voted against it, with Callimachus, the Polemarch, casting the deciding vote in favor of attack.

Since the bulk of Persian infantry were archers, the Greek plan was to advance in formation until they reached the limit of the archers' effectiveness, the 'beaten zone,' or roughly two hundred yards, then advance in double time to close ranks quickly and bring their heavy infantry into play. This meant they would end up fighting in disordered ranks, but it was preferable to giving the Persian archers more time. The Greek center was reduced to possibly four ranks, from the normal eight, in order to extend the line and prevent the Persian line from overlapping the Greeks. The wings maintained their eight ranks.

The Greek heavy infantryman, or hoplite was much more heavily armored than the Persian troops, and the pike the Greeks carried gave them greater range than the short spears and swords of the Persian foot soldier. The Persian advantage came from the bow that most of them carried—the advantage was partially cancelled by the superiority of Greek armor.

As the Athenians advanced, their wings drew ahead of the center, which was under heavy fire from the archers. As they closed, some Persians broke through the resulting gaps and drove the center back in rout. The Athenian retreat in the center, besides pulling the Persians in, also brought the Athenian wings inwards, shortening the Athenian line. The inadvertent result was a double envelopment, and the battle ended when the whole Persian army, crowded into confusion, broke back in panic toward their ships and were pursued by the Athenians. Herodotus records that 16,400 Persians died for the loss of approximately 192 Athenians.

As soon as Datis had put to sea with his much-reduced transport, the Athenians marched to Athens. They arrived in time to prevent Artaphernes from securing a landing. Seeing his opportunity lost, he set about and returned to Asia.

The Athenian upset of the Persians, who had not been defeated on land for many decades, caused problems for the Persians. When they saw that the Persians were not invincible, other people subject to their rule rose up following the defeat of their overlords at Marathon, and order was not restored for several years.

As is the case with scholars, there is not complete agreement about all the storied events, and research continues. Recent analysis at Texas State University at San Marcos, of lunar records show the 490 B.C. battle occurred not on the long-accepted date of September 12, but a full month earlier.

That month could be a matter of life and death for a runner like Pheidippides. Temperatures in August can reach 102 degrees Fahrenheit (38 degrees Celsius) along the Marathon route, which could lead to heat exhaustion or heat stroke in even the hardiest of athletes. The average temperature of the route in mid-September is about 83 degrees Fahrenheit (28 degrees Celsius), a time when thousands of amateur runners successfully complete the run with non-fatal results. In the 2004 Olympic Games, where long-distance runners retraced the famous trek on Aug. 29, it started at 6:00 p.m. Local researchers believe the Greek-Persian battle occurred in August at a time after the day's peak temperatures.

Herodotus provided precise descriptions of the phase of the moon in his account of the battle, a key tool used by later investigators to time the event. But researchers now believe the September 12 date originally set by German scholar August Boeckh in the nineteenth century, based on the Athenian lunar calendar, overlooked the importance of nearby Sparta.

The time of the Marathon battle and fatal run depends heavily on an earlier recorded trek by Pheidippides when Athens' city leaders dispatched the messenger to Sparta—150 miles away—to plead for assistance in the defense of Greece. The Spartans promised help, though their army could not march until the next full moon six days away due to a religious festival.

Boeckh assumed the festival was Karneia in the Spartan month of Karneios, when warfare was prohibited for a week, then jumped to the Athenian calendar using previous connections between the two and determined the September date.

However, the analysis should have been conducted wholly in Spartan lunar calendar, which—although similar to the moon-based Athenian system—began later in the year at the first new moon after the fall equinox.

There were also ten new moons instead of the typical nine separating the fall equinox of 491 B.C. and the summer solstice of 490 B.C., which caused the Spartan calendar to run a month ahead of Athens. This led to present-day disputes.

In 1939 Greece was a Fascist dictatorship under the leadership of Prime Minister General Ioannes Metaxas. General Metaxas had established, since August 4, 1936, a Fascist dictatorship in Greece which was modeled to the Italian dictatorship of Mussolini and followed Mussolini's lead in every detail, including a blue shirted youth organization, like the Italian *Balilla*. You couldn't be a Boy Scout any more in Greece. If you wanted to participate in a youth organization, you had to join that one. In 1939, the Minister of Interior and Public Safety was General Konstantinos Maniadakis. Even though he was also a right winger and a Royalist, since he was an old politician, he had established a sort of friendship with George Papandreou, who at the time was out of office and out of influence. Papandreou was *persona non grata* to the Fascist dictatorship, however, Maniadakis liked him even though they had been political opponents.

One day in 1939, it was no later than May, he called early in the morning to George Papandreou and told him, "We have concrete information that your son Andreas is a Communist, and he has created a Communist cell at the Athens College. I give you twenty-four hours to get your son out of Greece, otherwise he will follow the procedure that we reserve for all Communists." Communists, at that time in Greece, were apprehended, and were made to sit on ice slabs and interrogated under torture. At that time George Papandreou was married to a famous Greek actress who was fairly well to do. Through the influence of his wife and her money, Andreas Papandreou was eventually ferried to the United States, and because Andreas Papandreou was apparently a top student, he obtained a scholarship at Harvard. He graduated Harvard a little before World War II and upon graduating, he joined the U.S. Navy and, in this way, he obtained American citizenship. He married an American woman of Bulgarian origin, called Margaret, and he ended up with professorships at the University of Minnesota, Berkeley in California, and then Harvard. His specialty was econometrics and economics. He figured in the 1960 election of John F. Kennedy.

By 1940, my father's elder brother by two years, my uncle Dimitri, whom I never met, had joined a Soviet organized International Brigade and was in Spain. Two decades earlier, when my father jumped over the fence of the military school to join the troops that would fight for the Republicans, Uncle Dimitri had been in Paris to study law at the Sorbonne.

Instead of returning to Greece to join the army, or volunteering to fight for France, since he was in Paris, he remained a student. When the war was over and he came back to Greece, without a law degree, they used to call him *couraigie*, which means 'cookie.' It was a derogatory term for men who, instead i going to the army, had found the sanctuary of the university. He was disturbed at being called a *couraige*, another word for coward. Dimitri, in Paris while attending the Sorbonne, apparently had been influenced by communist theory. When the Spanish Civil War started, the Soviet Union organized the International Brigades known to Americans as the 'Lincoln Brigade.' One prominent member was Earnest Hemingway. From his experiences came books and films such as *For Whom the Bell Tolls* and *The Snows of Kilimanjaro*. Dimitri, in an International Brigade, was killed in 1940 when the Germans bombed Madrid.

Uncle Alexander was also active in the Spanish Civil War. He cheated both the Spanish Republic and the Nazis. He took payment from the Spanish Republic for 200 obsolete Greek military pieces, most of them only valuable as scrap metal but with a modicum of working arms; among them were World War I French Schneider .75's. The Nazis paid him *not* to ship weapons into the Iberian conflict zone. The Greek freighter carrying the scrap metal and the few working guns arrived in Spanish territorial waters on December 7th, 1941, and it was sunk by its captain and made to look like a casualty of a German torpedo.

Uncle Alexander sank another ship in Japan. It was filled with barrels of Greek wine that were really 95 percent water.

He eventually got the European concession for SONY. But he lost that.

November 1940 was a glorious time for the Hellenic forces as they were chasing the Italians out of North Epirus, and everybody was exhilarated. Peter's mother Aime, the Princess de Polignac, and 'Aunt' Helene, Mrs. Alevras, at the time, had prepared a party at Peter's home at Nemeseos Street, to which four-year-old Peter's cousins, Micky and me, were invited. I was six years old. Cousin Micky was wearing a nice navy topcoat and refused to take it off even though the temperature in the house was quite warm. Peter's mother told him to take it off more than once, but he claimed he was cold and kept it on. Micky's father, Uncle Alexander, at the time, had the practical monopoly of all toys imported into Greece, and Micky was getting all the samples. He had a big room full of toys. However, the reason he kept the topcoat on was that he had cut out the seams of the pockets, so all the lining was a receptacle of toys he was stealing from his cousin Peter. Peter's toys were mostly bought at retail and were so very few in comparison to Micky's whole warehouse of top-quality toys. I caught him stealing that day and gave him a thrashing. He confessed to me that he had acquired a used shaving blade that his father had discarded by means of which he had turned his coat into a loot bag. He was anticipating the invitation and had prepared for the stealing of Peter's toys. At the tender age of six, I concluded that it is not environment, it is definitely heredity. The cousins—Micky, Peter and I—grew in almost the same environment, children of privilege, and Peter and Micky became criminals and thieves whereas I ....

My Greek grandmother, Helen, who was very much an Orthodox, resented the fact that her grandson was a Catholic, so behind my mother's back she would take me to the Greek church. As a child I couldn't understand either the ancient Greek, or the Byzantine Greek of the Greek church, or the Latin of the Catholic church, so it didn't make a difference into which church I was taken. But I had already taken, a number of times, communion in the Catholic church, which is very simple. You open your mouth, and the priest places the host on your tongue, and there is no contact with anything. I think I was either five or six years old, and my Greek grandmother had told me—speaking in Greek, a very purified Greek, but realizing that I didn't understand much of what she was telling me, she had to revert to French—about the Orthodox communion. Inside the Greek church was a line of people waiting to be given by the priest, a crumble of bread soaked in wine, coming out of a golden chalice. But there was one spoon, also gold, and that same spoon was going from mouth to mouth to mouth. When my turn came, I clamped my lips and wouldn't accept the communion. My grandmother felt extremely embarrassed. After she took the communion, she said, "Why did you do that to me, Michael? You can't imagine how embarrassing it was when you refused the communion."

I said, "Because I was disgusted that the woman before me was an old crone, and she had bad teeth."

Confidently, she replied, "The communion is one of the mysteries of the church, and it is done under the auspices of the Holy Ghost. Nobody has ever died by accepting communion."

Even though I was rather young, I had a good argument. I said, "Grandmother, I didn't expect that somebody would drop dead right on the spot just because he took the contaminated spoon in his mouth, but nevertheless I don't like the Greek Orthodox communion. I'll stick to the Catholic one."

That was my first good reason for being relieved not to be a Greek Orthodox. The next one came when I was sixteen and my school took us on an educational excursion to Jerusalem. At the Greek Orthodox Patriarchate of Jerusalem they had, in glass covered containers, epistles written by the various Greek Orthodox patriarchs. One of them attracted my attention because it was addressed to Martin Luther. It read, in very calligraphic Greek, "God in his magnanimity sent us the Turk because it is much more beneficial to accept the Turkish yoke rather than lower our heads to the papacy." It seems that Martin Luther was a scholar because his Greek was just as good, although not calligraphic, and he answered that, indeed, he agreed. After that I thought being a Catholic was also an act of patriotism.

CHAPTER **15**

Wartime Athens

ON APRIL 6, 1941, Germany declared war on Greece and Yugoslavia and invaded both countries. The bulk of the Greek Army, about 250,000 strong, was in Albania fighting the Italians, or more precisely kicking the Italians out of Albania. Greece had a pact with Yugoslavia, whereby the Yugoslavs, in case of German attack were supposed to resist for four days, because that's how long the Greek Army needed to withdraw from Albania and hold a defensive line on the ridge of Mt. Pindos. At the same time Mt. Olympus was occupied by British troops. The idea was that the ridge of Pindos and Olympus could preserve the rest of Greece since the Germans could not deploy large tank formations to force the defense of those two mountains. The Yugoslavs, after having resisted for four days, would also join the Greek and British troops defending that part of the Balkans.

However, on the seventh of April the spearhead of the SS tank division, 'The Lifeguard of Adolf Hitler,' at about 8 o'clock in the morning, showed up in the Greek town of Florina, in Macedonia, which was the headquarters of the Greek army fighting in Albania. The commander of that crack German tank division was Sepp Dietrich, who had once been Hitler's chauffeur and bodyguard. The Commander in Chief of the Greek forces fighting in Albania was General Tsolakoglu, he had a Turkish name, but he was Greek. General Tsolakoglu was very fluent in German. Of course, he was taken totally by surprise, because it is practically impossible to cross Yugoslavia in less than forty-eight hours. How did the Germans manage to do so and be in the town of Florina on the morning of April 7—it didn't make sense. Dietrich told him that they had come from Bulgaria. The Greek-Bulgarian border was fortified, but the Greek-Yugoslav border was not, because we were always allies and friends with the Serbs. Dietrich told him, "We started in Bulgaria, there was no resistance anywhere, and that's how we came here." Dietrich demanded that all Greek forces in Albania surrender to the Germans. He guaranteed that they would not be made prisoners, that the soldiers would be disarmed, and sent home, and that's what happened.

Coincidentally, my landlord in Bad Godesberg, when I was at the Greek Embassy in Bonn, in Germany in 1969, Horst Schutz, had been a young lieutenant on board one of the tanks of that elite SS armor division that crossed Yugoslavia and reached Greece. He told me that all the day that they had crossed Yugoslavia and entered Greece, they had not fired one single shot. He told me that Dietrich made his arrangements with General Tsolakoglu about the surrender of the entire Greek army in Albania, and that they stayed there to collect the Greeks as they were returning from Albania.

He said, "We were there for about a week, and then the Italians showed up. The Italians demanded that we give them the Greeks, but our deal was that the Greeks would be disarmed and sent home. Dietrich was not about to break his word, and told the Italians, 'There are no prisoners for you.'" The Italians insisted, and Schutz assured me that the first shell fired by the German tanks was at the Italians who did not want to agree with the terms that the Germans had offered. "For a whole week, we never fired at either Serb or Greek, but we fired at our allies, the Italians."

It was different story at the Greek-Bulgarian border. There the Greek position was fortified. They called it the Metaxas Line. Of course, the Metaxas Line was no comparison to the Maginot Line in France, but it was something similar. It was a succession of fortifications meant to defend Greece from a Bulgarian attack. The Germans did attempt to breach that line, but they suffered heavy casualties, so since their troops already were in Greece, they refrained from putting a very big effort to break that line, and on the 21st of April when the Germans captured Athens, they communicated with the forts of the Metaxas Line using the radio and the frequencies of the Greek general staff. They said, "It is needless for you to fight any further, we are in Athens, we are in your headquarters," and they were asked to surrender, which they did.

My father was the commander of the Fort Rupel, part of the Metaxas Line. He was a major. There were fifty-seven living defenders in that fort, all of whom were wounded. There were probably a couple of hundred who were already killed. When my father and his troops came out of the fort, what they saw was German soldiers standing in two rows and presenting arms. The general commander, General List, or Von List, told my father—they knew each other, — "I am authorized by the Fuehrer to tell you that you, the soldiers of the Metaxas Line, are the bravest soldiers that the German army has encountered so far." He told him, "We are not taking prisoners, we honor you Greeks, and you are free to go wherever you want."

After Greece was occupied by the German armed forces, the first thing the Germans did was usurp, or confiscate, all our factories which were related to the war effort of Germany. That meant the emery factory and the munitions factory, and since trade was now impossible, there was not much for the members of the family to do.

My father had, at that time, four tugboats. Those four tugboats belonged to him; they were not an asset of the family company. He also had a number of hulls, that is, unfinished ships, which could be loaded with merchandise and the tugs could tow them to a destination. He decided, in view of the fact that there was famine in Athens and Piraeus, to use his tugs and send them to parts of Greece that had a surplus of foodstuffs. The famine in Athens was not primarily because of the Germans stealing the foodstuffs and sending them to the Eastern Front. It was because Athens, due to the blow up of most of the bridges and the railroad connections, didn't have the means of proper transportation to bring in the foodstuffs necessary to feed the population. Whereas Athens was starving, many parts of the province had surplus food that they didn't know what to do with. He would send his tugboats, load them with foodstuffs, bring them to Piraeus and distribute them for free to the population, hoping that when the war was over, the bastards would remember who fed them and they would vote him as mayor of Piraeus. Which the Panayotopoulos clan thought was their domain, that they should always permanently be the mayors of Piraeus. He didn't think that his career in the army would have any future.

In order to be able to operate the tugboats and send them wherever you pleased, one needed permissions and licenses from both German and Italian military authorities. My father had established some connections with Italian officers, and one in particular became a family friend. My mother considered him civilized because he spoke good French. And he was definitely not a Fascist. His name was Creton—at least that's how my mother insisted we pronounce it, although it was actually Cretone. She called him always, 'Capitan Creton' Eventually he came to be often invited to our home for dinner, and he taught my mother how to make spaghetti sauce with basil that reminded him of his native Naples. Through him, other equally civilized and acceptable Italian officers became friends of the family.

My father—and I think, naively, or stupidly—on occasion would discuss the war with his Italian guests. And he always was very well informed, to the surprise of the Italians because the radio in Athens would only broadcast news that was approved by the Germans. The Germans would never divulge any defeats whether they were in Russia or in Atlantic, they were only broadcasting victories: how many millions of tons of shipping they had sunk in the Atlantic, how they were driving the Russians back to the steppes, and such. But occasionally they had some setbacks, and my father knew about them. The Italians were curious how he could know, so he told Creton that he was listening to the British Broadcasting Company, the Greek broadcast of BBC, which always started, *pah-pah, pah-pom*, the first notes of Beethoven's Fifth Symphony. Telling that to an Italian occupation officer was like putting your head in the lion's mouth because if you had a radio back then, you were only allowed to listen to the Athens radio station. All the radios were sealed so you couldn't turn the dial to any other station. Listening to BBC was definitely punishable by death. But the Italian was so intrigued that he wanted to listen to the Italian broadcast from BBC, so the two, now like conspirators, would go and listen, the one to the Greek broadcast, and the other to the Italian broadcast. Because part of British propaganda was to tell the truth, no matter how painful the truth was, you knew that BBC would not conceal the defeats and they would not exaggerate the few victories we had in 1942.

The Italians brought my father into contact with two German officers who were also important for his business, and one day in the summer of 1942, three Italian officers and two German naval officers were invited for a banquet. One of the Italians we knew was a Black Shirt, which means he was a Fascist, therefore, not to be trusted, and of course, the two Germans were certainly Germans.

We awaited their arrival, and my mother was in the kitchen preparing the banquet. When the telephone rang and rang and rang, and nobody answered, I decided to go and answer it. It was Capitan Creton, and he said something has happened that we have to postpone the dinner party, so please tell your mother and your father that we won't be coming. I went to tell my mother, and she said, "What do you mean, they won't be coming. We have been preparing all day." She called my father, and asked him why are they not coming? My father didn't know, because any news from the broadcast of the BBC was late in the evening, but he said, "I'll call and tell them that we insist that they come." So, they came, and by the time the banquet started, my father had already listened to BBC, and he knew why Capitan Creton did not wish to come.

That day, Tobruk had fallen. That was a major defeat for us. Apart from losing 30,000 troops which were captured in Tobruk, Tobruk was a major fortress in Libya, and the fall of Tobruk predicated the possible fall of the whole of Egypt, and the Germans would be at the Suez Canal. It was a major victory for the Axis powers.

Still the banquet took place, and of course the Italians and the Germans were jubilant and very happy, and the Greek guests were silent and gloomy because that meant that the German occupation would last forever. The German officer, who was not an intimate friend of the family, stood up—he was the highest ranking of all the officers, he was a naval commander—raised his wine glass to make a toast and said, "Here I drink to the glorious forces of the Axis, and I express a wish that you will all participate in the new world order that our glorious fuehrer has in mind." The Italians rose to accept the toast, but the Greeks remained silent, and none drank, so it was a very unpleasant moment.

My father, angered, stood up and said, "I shall also make a toast. There is an old English Army song, called 'It's a long way to Tipperary,' and as long as nobody has taken Tipperary (which of course, is in Ireland) don't take it for granted that you won the war. You haven't. Tobruk is definitely a setback, but England is extremely resilient, and bear in mind that since the year 1066 Great Britain has never lost a war."

Now it was really very, very tense, you could feel the atmosphere, like a drawn cable ready to snap. What my Uncle Euripides would call the *deus ex michina*—the mechanical god, showed up. When Euripides would twist his tragedy to the point there would be no solution, a god would come and give the solution. Suddenly a siren started blowing. There was a British air raid.

All the Greeks disappeared. The five Axis officers were still sitting at the table—I was not at the table, at eight years old, I was too young to sit at the table—I and my nanny were outside the dining room, but I could follow what was going on. Because the Germans were asking what happened, Creton came to me and asked—we spoke French to each other—Where is everybody?"

I said, "Up at the terrace," and Creton explained to the Germans—I don't know if he knew German, or if the Germans knew Italian, that they were up on the terrace. The Germans wanted to know if we had an air raid shelter, so Creton asked me. I said, "Yes, we do, but they all go up on the roof."

"Alright," they said, "let's go to the roof." When we reached the roof, they saw that my mother and the other Greek women were all on their knees praying, because the spotlights were directed on the British airplane and the women were praying for the plane to be saved. The Italians and the Germans wondered, that instead of going to the shelter, they were there to pray that God would protect the British planes.

In 1942, lacking fuel for the Citroen, for the first time my mother decided to take me to the municipal swimming pool of Athens to swim, even though that went against her grain of exposing her child to so much of an undesirable humanity. She took me to the swimming pool. The result was that I had a terrible ear infection after having swum there, with very high fever and excruciating pain in my ear. My mother was extremely frustrated. She didn't know how to handle the situation, but she had heard that the Germans had a miracle drug called sulfonamide, which was the German equivalent to the Allies' penicillin. I was a big boy, much bigger than an average eight-year-old. But my mother in her frustration, not knowing how to manage my 103-degree temperature and my terrible pain, took me in her arms—and as I said, I was a heavy child—to carry me. Often there was no electricity for hours in Athens, so our elevator didn't function. She climbed down the three flights of steps to the ground floor, carrying me. And then she carried me as she walked two miles to a hospital which had been appropriated by the German occupying authority and was turned into a German military hospital. There was a hospital about 400 yards away from where we lived, but she had heard that the Germans had the drug, so she carried me to that hospital.

We entered the hospital after climbing a number of steps again. In the main lobby of the hospital, she shouted in English. She could scream in French, which would be less offensive to German ears, but she was screaming in English, the language of the enemy. "Anybody speaks English here?" A sort of corpulent woman, red faced, a German nurse, about forty years, approached and asked, of course in German, something like, "What the hell do you want?"

My mother kept on yelling, "I need someone who speaks English. My son has an ear infection and I want him treated." A woman having the bravado to go in there carrying a child and screaming in English apparently was too much even for the Germans to react, so the nurse, realizing that the woman with the child didn't speak any German, said, "Wait here," pointing on the floor, "I'll go find someone who speaks English."

The one who spoke English was a German officer, a doctor in the medical service. He had earned his medical degree in Cambridge, England and spoke fluent English. With remarkable coincidence he was an operating otolaryngologist, an ear, nose, and throat doctor. He took me, with my mother, to his part of the hospital where he was treating ear, nose, and throat ailments. He was holding a huge syringe in his hand—at least it looked huge to me—and he put it into my ear. The pain was insufferable. I think I fainted. But then after I recovered the pain was not as acute as it used to be, and he gave my mother a box containing those famous German sulfonamides which were big gray pills about the size of half a dollar. He said, "He has to eat those ten and he'll be okay." And I was.

When, later, I asked my mother, "Why did you speak English, why didn't you scream in French?" She didn't have an answer. It was purely an act of defiance. She was begging the Germans to help her, but still asserting her British superiority *vis a vis* the German officer. Apparently, a Scotch woman is defiant no matter what the circumstances are.

In 1942, a few months before my mother and I eventually left Greece, I had a governess, not a nanny anymore, a governess, who was not living with us. She was happy to be with us because she was assured of three meals a day and that was the important thing at that time. Her name was Madame Tivoli, and she was teaching me French. Madame Tivoli and my mother often would sit and discuss things, and my mother would say, "No matter how much I hate the Germans, I must admit that Hitler is doing a good job cleansing Europe of the Jews." We assumed that Madame Tivoli had told the truth, when she told us she was a Parisian, that she was French and that she was Catholic. My mother didn't just once say that we owed Hitler some kind of gratitude for cleansing Europe of the Jews but said it repeatedly.

At one point Madame Tivoli didn't come for work. A week went by, so my mother decided to go and see what's wrong with her, because we had the address. When my mother came back, she looked terrible. "What's wrong, Mother?"

"As I had suspected, Madame Tivoli is dead. It is a pity because I liked her. But worst of all is not just that she is dead, but that she is Jewish."

"How do you know? I asked, surprised.

"She had the menorah over her bed. All those nasty things that I was telling her about the Jews, had I known, I at least would not have said."

I said, "Had you known you probably wouldn't have hired her."

Madame Tivoli was in her forties. When my mother found her dead, she undertook all the necessary steps for Madame Tivoli to be buried, and even found a rabbi.

In Athens, there were about 6,000 Jews, the Jews lived among and with the Christians. There was no such thing as a Jewish ghetto or a Jewish neighborhood in Athens. The Germans first went after the Jews of Thessalonica, and there was an interval before they went after the Jews of Athens. During that interval, the then-prefect of the Athens police, Avramopoulos, in coordination with the various rabbis in Athens, asked that all the Jews would go to the various police precincts and get new identification cards with Greek sounding names and where it says 'religion' it would say 'Greek Orthodox' so at least the Germans wouldn't find it obvious on identification cards that said 'Israelites.'

The Jews in Thessalonica, about 96,000 of them, lived in their own part of the town, which was the better part of the town. When the Germans went to pick up the Jews of Thessalonica, they had no difficulty in picking up practically every single one of them because they lived in their own part of the town. Thessalonica had always had a Jewish presence, much bigger than what you would call a minority, since times immemorial. The epistle of Paul to the Thessalonians was addressed to Jews in Thessalonica, not to Greeks. They had a big synagogue 2,000 years ago. The Germans collected all 96,000 of them in one night.

One Jew with whom my Uncle Alexander had done business before, approached him and said, "I have a cousin who is not from Athens and he doesn't know anybody, and this cousin of mine needs some kind of shelter. Could you please help him?" My uncle said, "Why are you interested about your cousin, and not about yourself?" He answered, "I have made arrangements and I'm safe, but my cousin doesn't know anybody in Athens". So, my uncle hired the Jew who had graduated from the University, and who had a civil engineering degree. He hired him at our emery factory

'Marcopoulos' had obtained from the precinct an identity card that showed that name instead of Levi, his actual name. You can't imagine how petrified that Jew was when he went to live and work at the factory where German cooks were preparing the food every day. But my uncle always said that was a feather in his cap because he had the Germans feed a Jew. This man showed his gratitude at a later date when he became the chief engineer of a large banking concern, a conglomerate of banks that was constructing many buildings in Athens and elsewhere.

Uncle Alexander had acquiesced to resume the management of our emery factories on behalf of the German occupiers on the condition that the Germans would feed our workers. This was considered or construed by the Communists in Greece, the so-called 'resistance,' as being a collaborator with the enemy. Our workers obviously saw it differently because now they were being fed. Initially they didn't like the food, because the German Army eats goulash with a black pumpernickel bread with high nutritional value, but they adjusted, and it saved them from the famine. In the first fifteen months of German occupation, over 100,000 people in Athens died of starvation.

Alexander undoubtedly did make money out of the Germans. However, he used much of that money to create a gaming casino in the heart of Athens, and he used it for garnering information and transmitting that information to the Allies in Cairo, in the Middle East. In 1941, in the gaming casino that Alexander and Takis, my father, now back from

Berlin, had opened together in Athens, one of the frequent guests was the Bulgarian ambassador. He was a fairly handsome man. What I really admired about him was his Packard. He had a beautiful black Packard with a white cloth top, with big white tires. Because he had access to gasoline, he would invite us children to go swimming at the seashores of Athens, and that Packard could really run. At that time my uncle Alexander was using the car that was burning the least gasoline: a Morris Minor, a four-cylinder, ugly little thing. Because of the gaming casino, Alexander's wife, my Aunt Margo, met the Bulgarian ambassador. Apparently, they fell in love, and she absconded with him, they in the Packard, and my uncle, upon finding out immediately, chasing them with the little Morris Minor.

The Bulgarian had diplomatic plates which meant he didn't have to stop at German control posts. But my uncle was chasing them with the Morris Minor, and ignoring the control points, never stopping, breaking through the barriers, and firing at them with a very inaccurate .45 caliber Webley, a British service pistol of the First World War. He stopped the chase when the Morris Minor ran out of gas. In occupied Greece under German occupation, if caught with a weapon it was instant death, no trial. My uncle had the effrontery to chase the Bulgarian ambassador, who is an ally of Germany, and shoot at him.

The Bulgarian, with my aunt Margo, ended up in Brazil. The Bulgarian eventually died of brain cancer, at which point Margo asked her ex-husband's help to come back to Greece to be with her children, my cousin Micky among them. She had abandoned her children to go with the Bulgarian.

Alexander was a very devoted husband, but he was also a workaholic. As far as he was concerned, Margo, or Margrite, Princess de Polignac, who was his second wife, was the epitome of womanhood. She was the ideal woman. But being a workaholic is not conducive to a happy marriage. When the wife feels neglected and alone, and obviously, depending on her character and temperament, sooner or later, she will get herself a lover, which was always the case with my uncle Alexander with his various wives, because he married quite often.

It was winter, the beginning of 1942, and I was with my uncle Alexander and two others, when he was driving that black, ugly, Morris Minor on the road leading to the Thesion temple in Athens, which is almost a kilometer of straight stretch. For unknown reasons, the Morris Minor stopped—right on the tramway tracks. The tram was coming, and the tram driver was ringing the bell, but no matter how much he was ringing the bell, the Morris refused to start. It was stuck there on the tracks of the tram, and the tram smashed into it. The Morris Minor was a total loss, but it was now out of the tracks after being hit. None of us was injured, but the Morris Minor died, impaled by a tramway. Then, Alexander chased the tram, boarded it, grabbed the tram driver, and started beating him and crying, "I needed it so much!" He might have killed the tram driver, but the passengers rescued him. That was the end of the Morris Minor, and after that, my uncle had to use a Dodge eight-cylinder which used so much scarce gas.

That's when my uncle married Theodosia, who wanted to be called Dorette. She was Greek and very, very rich. Alexander married her in 1943 before he had to flee Greece and go to Italy. The income of that very rich aunt derived from flour mills that her family owned both in Greece and in Nigeria. The flour in each loaf of bread in Nigeria and half the bread sold in Greece came from their mills. Nigeria had a population of about 60,000,000 and that's where the real money was coming from.

Dorette also had a daughter. Her daughter and I, the same age, were a puppy love case. We met when I was sent by my mother to an Athenian school that determined after a week that I was retarded. Our meeting was opportune because Dorette's family and my family thought it would be the ideal marriage to combine the fortunes. She became a very successful actress despite having started her acting career at the age of forty-one, very late.

The year 1942 was a very eventful year. The year started well because the Germans had suffered their first defeat outside of Moscow. But then as the year was progressing, it seemed that we were about to lose. The Americans had lost their fleet and had lost the Philippine Islands; the British had lost Hong Kong and Singapore; the French had lost Indo China; the Dutch had lost the East Indies, and the Japanese were the conquerors in Malaya and in Burma. Things looked terrible. We were losing in Africa, we were losing in Russia, and we were losing in the Atlantic.

CHAPTER 16

Escape to Scotland

WHEN MY FATHER sued for divorce in order to legalize his bigamy with the German girl, my mother fought like a tigress and the Greek court denied him the divorce. That was 1937 to 1939—they fought for two years in the Greek courts, but my mother prevailed because she had an assembly of very important personalities who appeared as character witnesses on her behalf, and who said that she was a magnificent wife and mother. One of the best witnesses, I think, was the abbot of the richest monastery in Greece, the monastery that owns the quarries on Mt. Pendelikon where the marble of the Acropolis was quarried. He was a very tall, very impressive man with a white beard. My father's star witness was a gynecologist who never examined my mother. The gynecologist claimed that my mother was sexually deficient, and unable to satisfy her husband in this respect. He was asked if he had ever examined her, and replied, "No." When asked how he could know, he said, "Her husband told me." So that was my father's best witness. Among my mother's witnesses were the minister of the merchant navy of Greece, the abbot of the most prestigious monastery, and the governor of the Bank of Greece.

I have a scar from our visit to the house of the governor of the Bank of Greece, whom she knew, when my mother was trying to get him to come as her witness in the divorce case. He and his wife didn't have children. They had, however, a big Macaw parrot, and to them that was their child. The parrot was on a sort of pedestal with chain hanging from his leg so, I suppose, he couldn't fly away. I had never seen a Macaw parrot until that time, and I was probably six years old. I decided to go and pet the parrot while my mother was talking to the governor and his wife. I had seen a white parrot, the Australian type, before but I had never seen one with so many nice colors, and big. So, I approached, and the parrot was very unfriendly, and he bit me and cut off a piece of flesh from the end of my thumb. I was bleeding quite profusely, it hurt, and I was mad because my intentions were friendly. The damn parrot bit me with no provocation, so I grabbed a brass rod that was hanging from a chain nearby and hit him on the head. The parrot dropped dead.

My mother, instead of seeing my bleeding and realizing that I had some good reason to take that action against the parrot, kicked me, and I tumbled down the steps of a long staircase. The governor and his wife were crying grievously because that parrot was like a son to them. Still, they came as witnesses for my mother, to say she was a good mother—despite she had knocked me down the stairs with a vicious kick. Her left hook was not too bad, either.

She told me that she fought the divorce for my behalf, because, she said, those German women procreate like rabbits. "If I were to allow your father to marry that German woman legally, she would fill the place with little Germans, all over. So, that's why I didn't grant the divorce."

In the summer of 1942, my father again demanded a divorce. I was now eight years old. I thought, *Oh, hell, not all over again*. The first attempt at divorce did traumatize me because I was quite frequently dragged to the courthouse, and I hated it. So, I thought, not again, the same ordeal.

My father and his mother, my widowed Greek grandmother, Helen had moved to the second floor of the house. The ground floor where the Chancery of the Polish Embassy used to be was now vacant, because at that time there was no Polish Embassy; Greece was under German occupation. My mother and I were on the third floor. I was used as a messenger because they were not on speaking terms. If they wanted to communicate, they would either write notes or tell me what to tell.

So, my father told me, "Tell your mother I want a divorce."

After a week or perhaps ten days, my mother said, "Go tell your father he can have a divorce under certain conditions."

"Fine, what are the conditions?" I was the messenger running up and down, because by the summer of 1942 there were blackouts in Athens. There was not enough electricity, and the elevator was not functioning.

My mother said, in essence, "I want 20,000 gold sovereigns, I want full title to the house in my name, I want all the accounts that you have abroad in England, in Switzerland, in Hong Kong, and elsewhere, and I want a sailboat to take us to Turkey." At that time, you couldn't travel anywhere unless you had permission from the occupying forces, the Germans and the Italians, and there was a curfew imposed on all of the Greeks from 8 o'clock at night. Traveling at night was forbidden, and that's why she wanted a competent vessel with a reliable crew.

My father read the terms and he said, "Tell your mother I don't have

20,000 pounds, everything else is ok."

So, I went upstairs and told my mother, "He says he doesn't have 20,000 pounds."

She told me, "Ask him how many he has."

"I might, I might, collect 5,000, tops 6,000." We were talking about gold coins.

My mother said, "He's lying, he has more." That went on for three or four days, till my father came up with 12,000 gold sovereigns. Those gold sovereigns were either Victorias, or Edwards, or George V. Most of them were one-pound coins, but some were five-pound coins. When my mother got hold of all this gold, she made, out of canvas, money belts with pockets. You could put in each pocket ten coins. She and I had those belts around our torsos and our thighs, and that is how we transported the gold out of Greece.

I was asking my mother why, after she acquiesced to give my father a divorce, and I had found out that the woman he wanted to marry was a Greek whore, or what you would call in America, a call girl, only back then they didn't have too many telephones. She was a luxury whore, but nevertheless a whore. You didn't need to marry her, you could have her for a certain fee. But my father decided to marry her, and to my very great surprise, my mother acquiesced to the divorce, and fleecing him pretty much like skinning him alive. I was curious, I said, "You fought like a tigress not to give him a divorce when he wanted to marry a decent woman, and now you give him a divorce without even blinking an eye. Why?" She said, "I can't tell you that, but I did it in your own interest."

My mother would never divulge the reasons why she acquiesced to the divorce, and after many years, I stopped asking. But sometime in the early 1960s, we were in Greece, and we were attending the funeral of Dr. Prossas. Dr. Prossas had been the young army surgeon in 1921 when my father had been amputated, where my mother had served as his nurse. Dr. Prossas, after his military duty was over, specialized in urology, and he became a practicing urologist in Athens. But urologists usually cure, or attempt to cure, venereal diseases. So, Dr. Prossas had as his patient, the Greek woman that my father wanted to marry. He told my mother that due to an advanced stage of gonorrhea she had no functioning ovaries, which means she couldn't have any children. Dr. Prossas, by telling that to my mother obviously violated his Hippocratic oath, and my mother gave him her word of honor that she would never tell anybody about it. So, during the funeral, she said, "Now, Michael, if you want to know why I gave your father the divorce, back then, to marry the Greek whore, you may ask me." So, I asked her. She said, "I knew she didn't have ovaries, therefore she couldn't have any children, therefore there was no threat for you."

Eventually my father married that whore and sure enough, to his disappointment—he always wanted children—she couldn't get pregnant. She didn't know exactly why she couldn't get pregnant, so she thought because she was at least twenty-five years younger than my father, that my father was not potent enough for her, and she began an affair with a captain of one of our ships—a small ship, because the big ones were already sunk: sunk by the Germans, by the British bombarding Piraeus, by the convoys in the Atlantic. Eventually my father found out about the young, handsome captain, and he turned her out and he got a divorce.

After he got a divorce, at about the end of 1943 or the beginning of 1944—by that time I was in Scotland—when all his tugs had been sunk by the British bombardment of Piraeus, he escaped Greece also. He went to join the Allies in the Middle East, in Egypt. He began an active-duty position in the Greek contingent of the British Eighth Army after the invasion of Sicily. He obtained the command as a lieutenant colonel in Italy when the Allies were pushing up the boot of Italy in 1944.

Without the divorce we would not be going to England, it was the money that talks.

The vessel was really a very good vessel, it was what in America would be considered a sloop, a one-masted vessel. The crew indeed was very competent because they sailed at night, preferably when there was no moon, and the sea in August in Greece is very unruly because of the seasonal north westerlies that blow. When those north westerlies blow, the occupying Italian Coast Guard was not willing to patrol the islands. So, we hopped from one island to the other at night until we reached the little island of Kastelorizo which is only about a mile away from the Turkish coast. From there we reached Turkey.

I was actually petrified. With all that gold around me, I would go down like a stone. I was still not in a very good condition when we actually landed in Turkey. There was a small village near where we landed. My mother spoke some sentences in Turkish. And she had gold in hand. The first Turk we met she gave a sovereign and told him we wanted to get a taxi—taxi, thank the gods, is an international word, it's the same in every country on earth. The Turk understood what we wanted, and he showed us the way to that little village. There was no taxi, however there was someone who had a motorcycle with a sidecar. He agreed to take us to the nearest town where we could get a taxi. We had luggage but we couldn't carry luggage on a motorcycle with a sidecar. Besides, who needs luggage when he has 12,000 gold sovereigns? We didn't take much with us to start with, but we had to leave some things on board the sloop. Eventually we obtained a taxi, it was a very dilapidated thing, some kind of a Ford, but not a Model T, it was a newer version of a Ford. That poor thing managed to take us to the Syrian border.

Syria now was under British occupation; the British had expelled the Vichy French from both Syria and Lebanon. When we reached the British sentries, my mother started dropping names, which of course had no resonance to the soldiers who stood sentry at the Turkish border. The highest-ranking person we saw was a sergeant who thought that she was a crazy woman.

He said, "What do you want?"

"We want passage to Alexandria in Egypt."

"Well," he said, "We have a lorry here that could take you to Damascus." They loaded us with potatoes and other vegetables on board that army lorry, and it took the better part of six hours to get to Damascus.

In Damascus we found a few British officers. They were also quite doubtful as to whether that woman was indeed who she claimed to be, but they had another truck going to Jerusalem, so they loaded us on that truck. We had no papers of any kind, but I suppose if your English was convincing enough that you were British, that was a good enough thing as a passport. It reminds me of the apostle Paul, who used the Latin phrase, *"Romus civis sum"* which means "I am a Roman citizen" to go anywhere he pleased, which apparently also applied to the British Empire.

Once we were in Jerusalem, we went to the King David hotel—which Menachem Begin and the Irgun, the Jewish terrorist organization, blew up in 1947—the headquarters of the British Army in Palestine. There we found high ranking officers who might recognize my mother's connections. Imagine how we looked, having been driven in lorries, and not in the passenger compartment, all the way from Turkey to Jerusalem, but there we found officers who knew people whom my mother was claiming to be her relatives. We were given a suite at the King David Hotel to bathe, and servants were sent to bring us clothes. My mother got a British outfit, a kind of red uniform of the Women's Auxiliary Force, the WAF. They got me also some kind of a khaki thing to wear. And a staff car, with a British soldier as chauffeur, was given to us to take us to Alexandria. General Allenby had made sure there were roads. It took two days and two nights to reach Alexandria. On the way to Alexandria, we slept at the magnificent Shepheard Hotel in Cairo, which still exists as a five-star hotel along the Nile, in the Garden District.

The Shepheard Hotel was also headquarters of the British Army at the time. A story was told of a young officer, probably a captain or possibly a lieutenant, who was caught there in *flagrante delicto* with a brigadier's wife. When the brigadier entered the room, the young officer jumped out of the bed and ran stark naked in the corridors of the Shepheard Hotel. Of course, military police were available to stop him and arrest him. He faced court martial, and he was acquitted. Because, according to British Army regulations, a British officer has to always be in uniform or dressed in the appropriate accoutrements of the sport in which he engages. And he was.

We arrived in Alexandria, and Alexandria looked to me like a fabulous city. Beautiful. At night it was fully illuminated, there was music, happy faces, exactly the opposite of Athens under German occupation where we had the 8 o'clock curfew and you were not allowed to have lights showing under penalty of death. So, it didn't look like Alexandria was a city under British occupation. Or any kind of occupation. The Greek part of the city, which was most of it, was affluent, very clean. I was extremely impressed with Alexandria. There was barbed wire on the beach separating the European sand from where the Arabs were allowed to go. You could see them peering through the barbed wire to where the Europeans were swimming. The thing that impressed me the most was that in the bazaar the Arabs were freely selling pictures of Rommel, Mussolini, and Hitler as well as German and Italian flags. Arabs were buying them to decorate their houses to welcome their liberator, Rommel, who had acquired by then, legendary proportions. I asked my mother, "How do they dare?"

She said, "Why shouldn't they?"

I asked, "But why are the British tolerating it?"

"Oh," she answered, "who cares about it? They are just providing the cacophony, the dirt, and the squalor, otherwise they are totally insignificant."

About a week later, we knew, since the sound carries in the desert, when the bombarding started, from the thousand guns that Montgomery had assembled outside El Alamein, which is only forty-five miles outside Alexandria. You could hear the roar of the guns, and that lasted for about forty-eight hours. The sound of guns stopped, but machine gun fire doesn't carry that well. Then the lorries with the wounded started coming, hundreds of them. We started wondering, thinking "Oh, damn, we lost the battle." There were no announcements, only negative reports about how the battle was progressing. Then a few days later, thousands of trucks started arriving with the prisoners. The trucks were covered with canvas, but if the trucks were carrying Italians, you knew because the Italians were singing. If they were carrying German prisoners, you knew they were German because they were silent. So, we knew we won the battle. The official announcement came: the Germans and Italians were routed, and they were fleeing, and very soon North Africa will be free of all Axis troops.

Instead of Rommel, it was General Montgomery who was now reaching heroic proportions. "I don't count them, and I don't count on them," said Rommel of the Italians. There were probably three times as many Italians as German prisoners.

Since there were quite a number of heavy casualties that needed treatment in Great Britain, there were Red Cross ships, which were all white with a lot of red crosses painted all over those ships. There was one named the *Calpurnia*, a fairly large one that was a Pacific and Orient Line ship that used to go to Australia. My mother offered her services as a Red Cross nurse to serve on board that ship if it would take us to its final destination which was Portsmouth in England. Finally, she succeeded, with whomever she approached, in convincing them she had credentials. She had served with the Greek Red Cross and she had even been commissioned with the Greek Red Cross. She dropped the name of her patron, Princess Alice of Mountbatten, the British princess married to the Greek king's uncle.

We boarded the *Calpurnia* and we were given a berth for just the two of us. My mother was doing her best to serve as a nurse aboard the ship for the very badly wounded that they didn't want to treat in Egypt. As we approached Malta, we saw that Malta was burning. We could see the flames from five miles away. Malta was constantly under bombardment. At one point I heard the intercom, the captain was speaking. But I didn't understand what he said, so I went and found my mother to ask, "What did the captain say?" She told me he announced that he had communicated by radio with the squadron leader of the German bombers, and the German gave him one hour to dock in Malta, and after that they will resume the bombardment regardless of whether the ship is in Malta or not. I thought it was decent on the part of the Germans to observe the Red Cross. But she said, "He doesn't have much of a choice in view of the Geneva Convention."

It didn't make much sense to me since my mother had convinced me that the Germans were monsters, Huns, totally uncivilized Barbarians, but I got a different impression with the officer of the Luftwaffe agreeing to stop the bombardment. We couldn't dock in Malta because it was burning. There was no point. So, we left, and as we were leaving, we saw the German bombers returning. They had gone back to Italy, refueled, rearmed, and returned to continue the bombardment.

Our next destination was Gibraltar, and from there the next stop was Lisbon, Portugal, which was neutral at the time. Apparently Red Cross ships were not considered belligerent ships and could dock in neutral ports. The next stop was Portsmouth, England.

I was not particularly impressed by Portsmouth, but my big disappointment was London. The way London had been described to me, I expected to see something extremely grandiose, I expected to see Shangri La, a fantasy town. London was big, no doubt about it, but to my eyes, there was nothing so impressive that I hadn't seen in Athens. And it was full of ruins because of the German bombardment. We arrived in Victoria Station which had been bombed. Euston Station had also been bombed— the one that goes north with 'The Flying Scotsman.' London has a lot of railroad stations depending on which way you are going. I was not the least impressed with London. I liked Trafalgar Square a little bit because of those big lions, and the column of Admiral Lord Nelson, but nothing compared with the Acropolis.

We boarded The Flying Scotsman, the crack train that took us in eleven hours to Inverness. I expected, again, to see something else of magnitude to impress me, and what I saw was a ruin.

CHAPTER **17**

The Keep at Urquhart Castle, and Gordonstoun

I ASKED MY mother, "Is that is where we are going to live?"

"Yes, this is a famous castle." I wondered, what is it famous for. That was Urquhart Castle, on the shore of Loch Ness. There were some living quarters available.

On the form which was once required to apply to get a federal job in the United States, where you have to provide addresses since 1937, I wrote '1942 to 1948, Urquhart Castle' and they questioned that. They said, "Urquhart Castle is not inhabited," and I said it was back then.

I had a room at the keep—the tower, which is part of all fortified castles—I had to climb three flights of circular steps without a banister and without illumination except torches stuck in the wall. My room had no running water. It had a fireplace, but I had to climb the three flights down and another two to the dungeon to get coal to light the fireplace. Worst of all, the window didn't have glass. It had only a shutter. Life at Urquhart Castle was Spartan, if not worse. My mother, on the other hand, had a fairly large room in the basement with running hot and cold water and heat. She didn't have to depend on a fireplace. She had a radiator. So, there were different ways of life at Urquhart Castle. But most of it was a ruin, no doubt about it. I didn't really stay all the time in the castle because my mother did me the worst disservice by sending me to school at Gordonstoun. I stayed at the school except on weekends and in the summers.

The nearby Inverness Castle at that time was used as a hospital for military purposes. My grandfather was living there, as overseer and manager. My grandfather lived in Urquhart castle because his nephew, the heir, the Lord, asked him to do so because he was serving in the army. Otherwise, my grandfather probably would have lived on his pension somewhere in

Scotland. He had been in the consular service of Great Britain and had served in Constantinople and Greece. Though he was descended from the Earl of Inverness, he was the fourth son, and he had no chance whatsoever of an interest in the property, so he had entered the consular service.

On a very pleasant day, I think it was May 1943, about 7 o'clock in the morning, and it was a Saturday, I was waiting in the rare sunshine in Scotland, for the chauffeur to come and pick me up from the school. But it was a pleasant day, sunshine, no rain, no cold, so I decided rather than wait for the chauffeur, because there was no designated time when he was supposed to pick me up, that I would walk the five miles home to the castle. And as I was walking, taking short cuts through the glens, all of a sudden, my nostrils were aroused by a most beguiling aroma. I thought I had some memory of what that was, but I had forgotten, so I let my nostrils lead me, and they led me to a chicken wire fence, not barbed wire. The fence was tall, about eight feet, but very large gauge, and I could see clearly what was behind that fence, so I went there and stuck my nose through, to enjoy the aroma.

I saw a fairly large gathering of German officers, singing and having a hell of a good time, and eating ham and eggs. I had forgotten ham and eggs since eggs were scarce and the ration then in Great Britain was one egg per person per week. Usually, you ate it boiled or poached. No ham. I hadn't seen ham since Greece. The Germans were an agreeable group to watch because they were picturesque: the naval officers in the black uniforms, the air force officers in their blue gray uniforms and the Wehrmacht officers in their gray uniforms. They seemed to be very happy, and I thought it was incredible that the Germans were eating much better than we do. I rushed to go home, which I reached at about 8:30 a.m., the time of day on Saturdays when we always had late breakfast, which comprised most of the time of porridge made with water and the same oats the horses were eating, and haddock.

When we started breakfast, I asked my mother—we still spoke French, my English was not adequate, "Mother, are you sure we are winning the war?"

"Of course, we are winning the war. What makes you wonder?" "Well, I thought since the Germans eat better than we do, we must be losing the war." My mother never had any doubt that the Germans would lose the war. Even in the worst times, and now it looked much better, in 1943, after their terrible defeat in Stalingrad. Possibly, arguably, the worst defeat the Germanic race has ever had suffered in their history.

"No, the Germans don't' eat better than we do, their rations are not half as good as ours."

I insisted, "I saw them with my own eyes. In the glen, before Glen Cove. They eat ham and eggs."

"Ah," she said, "What you saw were German prisoners of war—officers. According to the Geneva Convention we have to feed them the same as we feed our own officers."

I asked, "Our own officers are not subjected to rations?"

She answered, "No. Our own officers are supposed to eat well so they can fight well." Apparently, she was going according to the Napoleonic dictum that if you want a successful army, make sure the stomachs are full.

I wanted to know if our own officers who were prisoners of war in Germany ate as well. She answered, "According to the Geneva convention they have to feed them the same they feed their own officers."

I knew that the estate my grandfather managed was contributing to the war effort by producing eggs, and everyday my grandfather was delivering eggs to the Ministry of Supply. Eggs were scarce and people were rationed only one egg per week per person. I don't know exactly how many chickens he had, but about 3,000 Leghorns. Those are good chickens; they lay an egg a day. So perhaps he was delivering close to 3,000 eggs a day.

So, I asked, "Couldn't we keep a few of our eggs for our own consumption, when the Germans eat two each, couldn't we have at least one each every day?"

My mother said, "No, everything has to go to the Ministry of Supply. The people in London don't have chickens laying eggs for them and there are 8,000,000 of them."

I pursued, "What about a few?"

At which point, my grandfather said, "You are Greek, after all." I didn't realize that he was insulting me. My grandfather refused to speak anything other than English or Gaelic, and I spoke in French, but he understood.

So that was the explanation of why we didn't have more than one egg per week, but I thought, *if you two insist on giving everything to the Ministry of Supply, I don't agree when I see the Germans eating better than I do.* I found a needle, and since chickens, unlike all the other birds, are the only ones that advertise their product, I was waiting, and the moment I would hear a hen cackle, I would go, find the egg fresh and still steaming, drill two holes in it, and suck it. The Ministry of Supply could be damned. I couldn't resist when I saw the enemy eating eggs, probably eggs that came from my grandfather's farm.

I was wondering why we were living out in the wilderness next to the loch and not in Inverness proper. My mother explained that Mary, Queen of Scots, some five hundred years ago, had given to my mother's ancestor the title, but not the possession of Inverness castle. Sometime before 1528,

Mary, Queen of Scots, was visiting Inverness, and the Earl of Inverness, who lived in Inverness Castle, refused to greet her. Angered at the earl's insult, she ordered him arrested and hanged, not beheaded. Then she gave to my mother's ancestor the title, but the Inverness Castle remained the possession of the crown, the Scottish crown.

The heir to the title, my grandfather's nephew, for whom he was managing the estate, was later killed during the invasion of Normandy on June 6, 1944. His son was born that very same day in Urquhart Castle. When the place had been made habitable, the lady had moved also to the Urquhart Castle, while the lord was fighting. He had been the only male alive other than my grandfather, and he was the lord, he was the heir. British nobility is marked with being the first in battle, not hiding behind boulders, but leading the troops.

More than any other aristocracy, the British aristocracy takes *noblesse oblige* very seriously and it is always British aristocrats who are first in battle. You can't say that about the Italians, or the French, and to a lesser degree about the Germans. There was nobility that followed that same pattern, but that nobility unfortunately has ceased existing, and that was the Russian nobility. The first casualty in World War I, the very first Russian to be killed in 1914, was Prince Seremetiev in a cavalry charge against the Austrians. In Germany, the mentality was, let's prevent the *junkers* from being killed by making them staff officers so that they won't be in the front line of battle. In America we know that the very rich usually bought a deferment. All during the Civil War the rich would pay someone else to go and enlist instead of them.

The death in 1944 of the lord, my grandfather's nephew, and my mother's cousin, was before the Socialists took over so the estate was not subjected to the destruction of inheritance taxes. The present lord, Lord Osborne, my second cousin, has it all. Nobody lives there now, but scorpions, or spiders.

There were only two male survivors on my mother's side that survived the First World War. There were about six that were killed in the battles of Somme, Ypres, and Passchendaele. Two were killed with the Sutherland Argylls at the retreat of Dunkirk, and another one was killed in the invasion of Normandy on June 6, 1944. That dying was one of the reasons why my mother hated the Germans with such a passion.

Ariston means 'the best;' *kiratos* means 'power' or 'authority,' so aristocracy is where the power and authority lie among the best. That's aristocracy, as opposed to democracy, where the power and the authority lie among the municipalities, the municipality representing the people. The preamble to the existence of independent colonies, declares 'We, the people.' The people usually are wrong. They elected Clinton twice, didn't they? And they elected Roosevelt four times. The Scot aristocracy, like any aristocracy derived from the warrior class. In every society regardless how primitive that society is, and regardless how far back you go, you will find the warrior class. You will have on the top of the societal pyramid, the priestly class, like the Brahmins in India; underneath you will have the warrior class; and beneath that you will have the trading class; then the artisans and last the slaves. The most powerful, the most able, the bravest, of the warriors were the ones who obtained the most of the land, either conquered or acquired. Or stolen. And land is what created the aristocracy, or landholders.

Not only in Scotland, but throughout Europe, the distinctions and the classes of the aristocracy were a direct proportion of the land you owned. No god descended and said, 'you shall be a duke and you shall be a marquis, and you shall be a count.' If you owned, in England more so than in Scotland, at least 20,000 acres, that was a county, so you were a count or an earl (earl and count meaning the same thing). If your county was on a border, on a part of the border where your country bordered another country, you would be a marquis because that would be the mark. Of course, you had more responsibility because if the enemy invaded you would be the first one to have to defend. Therefore, the marquis ranked higher than the earl. If you were of royal blood, you would be a grand duke, or in England just a duke, and of course, most dukes in England were royal bastards. In France the royal bastards had the prefix *Fitz* meaning 'son of.' Fitzalois, Fitzpatrick, Fitzwilliam…. which the Normans brought over to the British Isles. If you had an area between 5,000 to 10,000 acres you were a baron, and your order was called a barony. If you had less than 5,000 acres, and of course this is relative, you were a baronet. If you did not own land, but you were a free man, and owned your horse and your armor, you were a knight. In Germany, if you were of royal blood and in direct ascendance to the throne you were a prince and you owned a principality. The only principality in England is Wales. That's why the heir to the throne is always the Prince of Wales. The principality of Wales at one time was usurped by the crown and given to the firstborn.

In Scotland the distinctions of the classes were not as pronounced as the classes in Germany, or Portugal, or in Spain, or in Italy. In Scotland, unlike any other feudal country of Europe, since almost all Scots would be, at one time or another, soldiers, or warriors, there was the development of clans. Clans would have their leader, who would be the greatest landowner. But even in a clan's member who was not a landowner, you would see a certain degree of affinity in kinship to the laird because they belonged to the same clan, and they wore the same tartan. Scottish aristocracy is differentiated from all other aristocracies of Europe because of the clan. That doesn't mean that the laws of Scotland were any more humane than those of England. I have my own example: my mother's great-great grandfather, in 1830, determined that he would be better off with sheep than humans, so he evicted all his tenants and sent them to Nova Scotia and exchanged them with 30,000 sheep. The clan is Stuart.

The Stuart clan split because the son of the martyred Queen Mary—who was beheaded by her cousin, Queen Elizabeth—succeeded her on the throne of Scotland as James VI. Since Queen Elizabeth, the alleged 'virgin queen' of England died without heir, the line was finished. The English throne would go to the Stuarts, so King James VI of Scotland ascended the English throne as King James I of England. At that time in England, because of King Henry VIII, the king of England was at the same time the head of the Church of England. The Church of England was a Protestant church so one couldn't possibly ascend the English throne as a Catholic. So, James VI of Scotland, or James I of England, in order to ascend the English throne, converted himself to Protestantism so he could be the head of the Church of England, or the Episcopalian Church as it is called in America. To prove that he was indeed a good Protestant, he spent his own money to translate the Bible into English, thence you have the King James Version of the Bible.

The rest of the Stuart clan remained Catholic and wanted that, should there be union of the two crowns, it should be under a Catholic Stuart. Eventually, in 1745, they brought Prince Charles Edward Stuart, the 'Bonnie Prince Charlie' from France where he was in exile and staged a rebellion. The English crushed the rebels at a place called Culloden which is within walking distance from where I grew up. That was the end of aspirations of Scotland to be fully independent.

My mother was of the part of the clan that remained staunch Catholic and denounced the Stuarts who renounced their faith in order to become kings of England, so when Cromwell chopped off the head of King Charles no one in the Stuart clan in Scotland shed a tear for that. The royal history of England is extremely bloody.

The aristocracy of Scotland exists as long as there is the House of Lords in London where all British peers, through heredity, have a seat. The aristocracy of Great Britain not only exists but has a say in the political process of Great Britain. It does not exist anymore as a vast landholding and the wealth which derived from the vast landholdings. That was a result of the landslide victory of the Socialist Party in 1945 which imposed 96 percent inheritance taxes. When the ancestor died and one inherited the county, it was required to pay 96 percent taxes, and that's what killed financially the British aristocracy.

If the heirs were not able to pay the tax, the landholding went to the state. Only a few of the British aristocrats were able to withstand financially or economically the onslaughts perpetrated on them by the Socialist Party after 1945. After the aristocracy, the tax went down to almost every aspiring Briton who wanted to excel in something. The Socialist Party also imposed the surtax on earnings over 6,000 pounds a year, which at that time was a little less than $30,000; then everything earned in excess of 6,000 pounds was taxed at nineteen shillings and six pence per pound, which meant something close to ninety percent. Not that the amount earned before 6,000 pounds was tax free, but it was taxed reasonably, and after 6,000 pounds the surtax applied. That killed every incentive because there was no point in trying to make more money when the government would take all of it and one would be left with sixpence.

For six years, beginning in 1942 when I was eight years old, until 1948, when I was fourteen, I lived at a school in Scotland, called Gordonstoun. Prince Philip, son of Prince Andrew of Greece, who became the Consort of Queen Elizabeth of England, preceded me at Gordonstoun. His father could not afford to send him to Eton. Later, Prince Charles, the future king of England, attended Gordonstoun, and there were no concessions made for Prince Charles. Although Prince Philip was not particularly happy there, he sent his son there also because he thought his son was unruly and undisciplined. The other British princes didn't go to Gordonstoun.

One story told about Prince Philip concerns his return visit to the school to open a school fete in 1951. The grounds were tidied in anticipation of his arrival, and students went over the terrain so minutely that not a speck of cotton wool, let alone a slither of paper or matchstick, could be found. When the Duke arrived, he headed straight for the pigsties, which he had helped to build. To his evident delight, he found them in precisely the same primordial state as when he had left.Flogging was a way of life at the school, and I got much more proportion of flogging than anybody else because I couldn't speak English. That was my problem: I was being flogged because I didn't know that I was to answer "Sir, yes sir," or "Sir, no sir," and because I was addressing members of the faculty in French, without being spoken to. The inordinate amount of punishment I received dropped quite considerably once I spoke English, which I tried to do as fast as possible. If more than ten words were misspelled, you got flogged. A word you spelled wrong, you had to rewrite one hundred times and also use it in a sentence, once. If you misspelled that same word again you got flogged. If it was a minor infraction, you got caned by a monitor, a fellow student who was older than you. If the infraction was considered of a higher degree you were going to be hit with a cricket bat, the next offense you were going to be whipped with a whip.

At that school I was a nobody, even though I am the great-great grandson of Duke of Argyll and descended from the Earl of Inverness. There were too many somebodies.

The English, at that time, had a very good system: a youngster had to take a test called Eleven Plus. If your brains, your intellect, your capability of absorbing knowledge and using it to solve problems, was beyond that of a ten-year-old, you passed the Eleven Plus. That meant you were eligible to go to a grammar school. If you didn't pass the Eleven Plus, that meant you were not good enough to go to grammar school, and you would go to the secondary school and then to either a trade school or some other school, but not a university. They appreciated the children regardless of birth or wealth, and whether they would be eligible for higher education.

I liked that system, which the Socialists abolished, because the Eleven Plus was not easy. However, I passed it with flying colors. When I was ten, I spoke *very* good English—motivated by flogging. Gordonstoun was a very unhappy period of my life, and I will never forgive my mother. I had begged her to send me to Rugby, a public school (equivalent to a private school in America) in England, synonymous to the town of Rugby where it is located. I wanted to be away from the torture chamber of Gordonstoun, but she insisted that Gordonstoun was right for me, that Gordonstoun would make a man out of me—as if Rugby would make a girl out of me.

The game known in America as football is derivative of a game played in England and the rest of the world known as rugby. Rugby was born sometime in the 1700s, when the children of Rugby were playing soccer, and because it is played with your foot, it is also known the world over as football. You are not allowed to touch it with hands. If the ball touches your hand, it's a foul. The football was comprised of the bladder of a pig, inflated, and protected by an outer skin made of strips of pig hide. While the children were playing with it, the stitches connecting two of the strips broke and the ball lost its spherical shape, so it was very difficult to pass it with a foot. The thing which then looked more like a melon than a ball, wouldn't go straight, where it was kicked to go. But there was no other ball in Rugby, so the coach conceived then and there that the game should not be interrupted, and that the children could pass the ball by hand, and the ball would be scored if a player holding the ball would go through the goal post. The end of the war was announced on May 8, 1945, and it brought immense jubilation all over the British Isles, and when our prisoners started returning from Germany, they looked quite well: red cheeks, nice well-pressed uniforms, and they were not skeletal. They seemed to have eaten fairly well. We were all very happy and rejoiced to see the men return.

About eight months later when the prisoners started returning from the Japanese concentration camps, it was an entirely different story. They were skeletons wrapped in sore skin, hardly alive, and they all had horror stories to tell. So, my hatred for the Japanese was augmented by seeing the difference of how our prisoners were treated by the Germans as opposed to how our prisoners were treated that were captured by the Japanese. After all, there were too many British prisoners caught by the Japanese, because in Singapore where 100,000 British and Indian troops surrendered to 32,000 Japanese troops. That was not only lopsided, but an extremely humiliating defeat. It took me many, many years, and the reading of the book, *Shogun*, to understand that the treatment of the prisoners was not a matter of cruelty or barbarism on the part of the Japanese, but it was part of *bushido*, their idea of a warrior.

The Japanese do not understand surrender. It is not part of their warrior culture or their philosophy of life, and if a warrior allows himself to be captured, he has degraded himself to such an extent that he does not deserve to be considered a human being. He is treated worse than a cockroach. Worse than a rat. So, to the Japanese it made absolute sense to mistreat our prisoners of war because they had degraded themselves for having surrendered.

It was 1947, in early spring, when I was twelve years old, and the rations for gasoline were over, you could now buy gasoline in Great Britain, that my mother told me, tomorrow, Monday, you don't go to school, and we go to Edinburgh to buy a new car. Good, I was looking forward to going to Edinburgh. It was a town that in some degree reminded me of home because it had a replica of the Parthenon, and the Scots used to call Edinburgh, 'the Athens of Scotland.'

My grandfather had an antiquated car, probably a 1931 model, a Humber, which looked just as bad as it sounded and appeared. We drove to Edinburgh, to the Rolls Royce dealership. I knew that Rolls Royce was an expensive car and I wondered what business we had at the Rolls Royce dealership, because I doubted we had that kind of money. The dealer showed us the newest model that had arrived from Crewe, in Staffordshire where they made Rolls Royce's. He lifted both sides of the bonnet, exposed the engine, and an employee started the car. The dealer placed two wine glasses on the top of the block of the engine, and he poured— I still remember it was a bottle of Bollinger champagne—and filled the glasses, the employee accelerated, and there was no ripple. Not a sign of movement on the wine. So that was the proof of the pudding that the Rolls Royce was up to her reputation, she didn't wiggle, or jump up and down. They drank the wine, they broke the glasses, and the transaction was completed. My grandfather bought the Rolls Royce, and the same chauffeur that had brought us in that antiquated Humber drove us back in the Rolls Royce. Apparently, he had the necessary credentials to drive the Rolls Royce.

I was intrigued, and I asked my mother if we had the money to afford such an expensive car. She said, "Of course we can, what makes you wonder?"

"The way we live, like Troglodytes." We were still living in the Urquhart castle, I in the keep—the round tower where the soldiers used to stay to defend the ramparts. All castles had keeps if they were meant to be a defensive fortress. All castles are not meant to be used in war but the ones which were meant for war have keeps.

The first national strike occurred, I think, in 1947. A national strike is when all unions agree to go on strike, which paralyzes the whole nation and since England is an island, she is very much dependent on certain unions, especially the dockers, which in America are called longshoremen. Because if the dockers go on strike, nothing is unloaded, so when you have a national strike which means all the unions strike simultaneously, the railroads don't run, the busses don't run, there is no electricity, there is no gas, there is no merchandise being unloaded from the ships—the island sinks. If you have a national strike during a Tory government, it's understandable. But to have a national strike when you have a Labour government, that's totally incomprehensible. The workers are supposed to be the ones who are governing now, it's their party. The Labour government did something which a true Marxist would consider absolute heresy. The Labour government sent the troops to take over the jobs of the striking workers. Imagine if the Tories were to do that.

Everybody suffered under that strike, but in 1948, a second national strike was called, and this one was even worse than the first one, because this time Britain had fewer troops in the army demobilized by quite a few hundred thousand, so they didn't have enough troops to replace the workers. The island was really plunged into total chaos.

I was finished at Gordonstoun in 1948, and my mother decided to leave Scotland.

She announced to me, "Michael, I've had it. Great Britain under the Socialists is worse than Greece was under German occupation. I can't stand it one minute longer. Get ready. We are going back to Greece."

I said, "Greece is plunged in civil war." I knew that much.

"We are going back to Greece, and I don't care if there's a civil war or not, there's a worse civil war here in Britain. If I stay a minute longer, I shall kill the first Socialist I see."

So, we went by Rolls Royce to Doddlespool which is south of Newcastle. It was a fishing town. My mother negotiated with a captain of a herring boat to take us to London because there were no trains running, thus we went by trawler to London. We went to London, and we went to the airport, hoping that a foreign airline might be attempting to break the strike, and sure enough, Air France defied the British strike, and she was running her airplanes, so we boarded Air France. We went to Paris and from Paris we flew to Athens.

Gordonstoun, the school in Scotland where I was unhappily a student for six years. Three generations of British Royals also suffered there. I will never forgive my mother.

Urquhart Castle, and the keep. We lived in the ruins of my mother's ancestral estate overlooking Loch Ness during World War II after escaping from Nazi-occupied Greece.

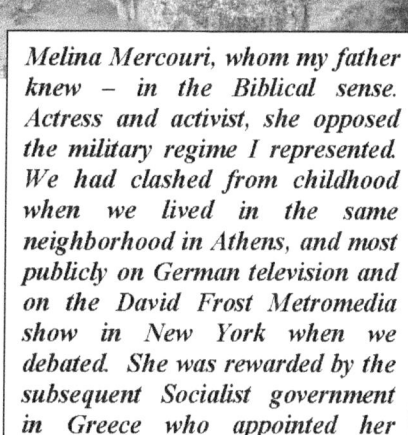

Melina Mercouri, whom my father knew – in the Biblical sense. Actress and activist, she opposed the military regime I represented. We had clashed from childhood when we lived in the same neighborhood in Athens, and most publicly on German television and on the David Frost Metromedia show in New York when we debated. She was rewarded by the subsequent Socialist government in Greece who appointed her Minister of Culture.

CHAPTER **18**

Return to Athens

IN ATHENS, A small periphery, perhaps a radius of 20 kilometers, was still in the hands of the national government. Most of the rest of Greece had been taken over by the Communists. We were losing the civil war. My father now was a brigadier, and he was fighting the civil war with his brigade.

My mother and I went to our home—it was *her* house, following the divorce, she had the deed and the keys. What really surprised me was the car. Before we left Greece, my mother had a Citroen which my father had bought her in 1934 as a gift when I was born, for giving him a son. When we left in 1942, the car was lifted and put on top of wooden blocks, but that was it. When we came back, that car had not been moved for six years. My mother called a mechanic at a garage not too far from our home—the telephone functioned to my great surprise—it was still the same number it was before we left. They removed the blocks, they lowered the car—it's a very low car, that Citroen—and since most of the asphalt roads of Athens had a lot of holes, which were hardly ever repaired, it was hazardous to drive that car on them because it was so low. If you hit a pothole, you might destroy the car. I was surprised the Michelin tires were still inflated, and the moment my mother put the key in the ignition, the car started. It didn't need a new battery or anything else. It needed gasoline, however. There was not a drop of it because it started and stopped immediately. That astonished me, and ever since, I have a very high opinion of Citroen. It's a very ugly car, but it's a helluva good car. My father learned that we were back in Greece, so we had a reunion. But now what bothered me was that I am Panayotopoulos, and my mother is McDuff. And for some reason, I don't know why, it bothered me. So, I suggested to my father, "Father, would it be possible for you to remarry my mother?" He said, "I have no objection. Ask her."

of heroism, primarily that he warned the other soldiers.

The soldiers, upon seeing their commander, their brigadier, being badly wounded while leading the assault, got more enthusiastic and with the bayonet, they rushed. They reached the Communist positions, and they took the hill. As a result of that my father became a full general. Brigadiers in the Greek army were not generals, they were not called 'general,' they were called 'brigadier,' and they were like super colonels. They didn't have a star. The general star he got after he lost the foot.

We were discussing my future, and my father was adamant that I should stay away from the army, and when I asked why, he said, "You'll never make it to general. You don't have the proper character to become a general,"

That bothered me, and I said, "Well, how about you?"

"Don't forget that both of my promotions were a result of losing a limb," he reminded me.

"But, why don't I have the character?" I persevered.

"Consider that in order to become a general, first and foremost, you have to be a boot licker, and you are not. Second, if your wife screws around with a superior officer, you have to look the other way and ignore it. This way you get the promotions."

My father discouraged me, and my mother encouraged me in a military career. My mother felt that there were only very few things a man was destined to do if he belonged to the British nobility. One was serve the crown and the country. The other one was to become a priest. She certainly despised trades people and she didn't have any respect for professional people. That, I suppose, she inherited from her father, because at the Urquhart Castle in Scotland the physician was only allowed from the servants' door, but the veterinary was considered to be a gentleman, and he was admitted from the main gate. There was a tremendous discrimination.

I graduated from the Athens College, which was a very successful combination of an English public school, an American school and an Athenian gymnasium. It was like an English public school because it was exclusively for boys, and because if you collected four demerits—that was American—you were given a note to present to your parents and have them sign it, which said, 'Your son has already collected four demerits and if within the next ten days, he collects two more, he will be subject to corporal punishment.' I never collected four demerits. In this respect it followed the path of an English public school. The American part was that there was a student council and the students had representation in the administration of the school and in the faculty meetings. The school was run in a democratic manner pretty much like an American high school.

So, I asked her, and she mused, "Well, I don't have any particular strong inclination…"—but she was lying, because why else to go back to Greece? "I don't have any strong inclination to remarry your father, but if that's what you wish, I have no objection."

My father said if he were to remarry my mother it would be in the Greek Church. So, I went to the Greek church near our home, and I spoke to the priest. "I want my father and my mother to remarry, and now since I'm born, and reared, I want them to marry in the Greek church. Is it ok?" He was a man of humor, and he said, yes, it is ok. We arranged that I was the best man. The priest came to our house to marry my father and mother. In the Greek ritual of marriage at one point, the priest says, "…and give her fruit of the womb," he paused and looked at me, "It's alright," he said, "you already have." So, they remarried according to the Orthodox ritual this time, and my mother now was also Panayotopoulos. So, whenever we went anywhere, we had the same name, and I felt at ease.

At the beginning of 1949 occurred the Battle of Gramos, in Epirus, very near Macedonia, which was the most decisive battle of the Greek civil war between the Nationalists and the Communists. My father was the commander of a brigade, which means he had two and half regiments, that is two full complements and one lesser regiment, a reserve, and he was ordered to take a specific hill. He sent the first regiment and they failed in their assault. He sent the second regiment and they also failed, and they sustained some very heavy casualties. So, then my father placed himself in charge of the auxiliary regiment and led the assault himself.

At one point, he walked on a Teller mine. They were German mines, but all the combatants eventually adopted them. A German seized the invention. That mine actually looked like a food can. Less than a foot tall, it was buried and if you walked on it, you triggered it and it would jump about three feet off the ground and explode, so it was meant to kill as many people as possible. But if you had the presence of mind and realized that you had walked on one of those, and kept your foot on the spot, the mine would explode underground. It was buried about three inches below ground, which means it would kill only you, it probably wouldn't kill anybody else. So, my father walked on a Teller mine, and he realized he walked on a Teller mine, because when you walked on the igniting cut, it was like a nail protruding from the earth, you felt it. He told the soldiers, "Spread away! I walked on it!" It exploded, but it only took off part of his left foot. Of course, he had some more wounds, one of the testicles was damaged, which is just as well, because he was overusing them, as it is. He had a splinter in his buttocks and his thigh, but the real damage was part of the left foot, all the toes were gone. But that was considered an act

Even though that school attracted the richest, it operated under a strict scholarship basis, in other words it didn't make so much difference how much money your parents had, you were subjected to both intelligence and knowledge tests, depending on your age, and that determined whether you would be admitted or not. The rich were paying through the nose. The fees were exorbitant. The poor were paying very little or nothing depending on what percent of scholarship you had, but if the poor did not maintain a high standard and obtain top grades, the scholarship was reduced until there would be no scholarship, in which case they would be expelled because they couldn't afford it. So, you had the son of the street sweeper and the son of the prime minister sitting at one desk, next to the other and they were treated as equals, and they were supposed to acknowledge this equality. Those were the American characteristics of the Athens College: democracy, equality, participation, and elections.

That was a high school that you had to attend for one extra year, which was a collegiate year in order to prepare you for further study in America. The Athens College was the sister school of Choate, a rather exclusive boys' school in New York, and it was under the umbrella of Columbia University. Anytime we competed with Choate in either academic or intelligence tests, we blew them out of the water. It was an elite of elite school. I loved it, and I never collected more than one demerit. Considering Gordonstoun, it looked like Paradise. Most of our professors were Fulbright scholars. Athens College and Athens University are not the same. Athens College is an American institution.

We had an American female professor whose name was Mrs. McClean. Her husband was a marine fighting in Korea, and Mrs. McClean at one time bore the obvious signs of pregnancy and she hadn't seen her husband for about six months, and this was in 1951, so I was not old enough to be among the suspects, but I remember they wanted to determine who was responsible for Mrs. McClean's pregnancy. There was a big investigation in the Athens College because they suspected it was a student. She had said that one of her students impregnated her, but she wouldn't say which one, and she was teaching English, so she had students from various classes, from the sophomore through the senior year. As it turns out it was a member of the faculty. I was a freshman at the time, and I wouldn't even look at a woman, I was totally disinterested in the female sex. I was concentrating on boxing and fencing.

The motto of Athens College was the Athenian motto, 'A Healthy Brain in a Sound Body' and the American motto was, 'We Breed Men,' as if the Athens College was giving birth to them. We were the only school in the whole of Greece which had its own stadia. We excelled in all sports, especially track and field, and it was humiliating for all the other high schools in Greece to compete with us. It was a magnificent school.

When we had rejoined my father, when I was fifteen, my father decided to make a man of me. He became concerned that I was apparently not so interested in girls as he had been. He devoted several weeks to this, introducing me to various opportunities.

One such place was a Turkish *tekey*. An interesting aspect of the Turkish *tekey*, were the *choglan*, the *tgibuk choglan*, "*Tgibuk* in Turkish means 'pipe.' There were boys, anywhere between eight to twelve years old, running around, half naked, that were servicing the water pipes, adding layers of tobacco and hashish, and bringing fresh charcoal. If anyone wanted to fornicate with the boys, they were free to do so. It was part of the arrangement of being a guest there and it was incorporated into the bill. My father said, "If any of those boys meet your fancy, help yourself." I was not a faggot, and I was not interested in the boys either.

But my father would not yet give up. The next Friday he had arranged a *paktouge*. We went to a good restaurant, where we had a good meal. We had a hostess who was a lesbian, in her forties. Before she became a hostess, she used to be a madam in a brothel. That's how my father knew her. She was a lesbian like most prostitutes are, and she had two young prostitutes with her. We were shown to a sort of pool, but not with a lot of water, like a Jacuzzi but without the bubbles. The two young girls were playing nude in the pool. My father was hoping that watching them might entice me. It didn't entice me, it enticed him. He took off his clothes and joined them. I had the pleasure or, depending how you see, the misfortune of watching my father fornicating with the three lesbians. It didn't work.

My mother, on the other hand—because I was reporting everything to her—told me, "The less you have to do with girls, the better off you are." Meanwhile, she was giving orders to the coaches at the Athens College to make sure that I was getting extra training in order to drain my energy.

The last attempt of my father was a time that we went to another very nice restaurant. I saw him take out of his watch pocket—a very small pocket at the waist of his trousers—an envelope of powder. He also had little straws. He said, "See what I'm doing," and he sniffed a little bit with the straw. Extending it to me, he said, "Try it."

When I went to my mother—and of course I gave her full account—she asked how did it taste. I told her I didn't taste it. I only sniffed it, and it actually disturbed my nose. It made me sneeze. She said, "That might have been cocaine."

I said, "It might, I don't know." It was.

A few weeks later, I was at the Argentin, a cabaret, in Athens. There was a mulatto dancing there, and she was half naked, topless. She introduced the mambo in Athens. She was a half French-half Negress from Martinique, and her name was Josefine. That reminded me of Josephine, the wife of Napoleon, only this one was much prettier. She was the first woman that ever attracted me, and she did it topless. That was it, I wanted her.

My mother learned of it because the school started complaining that I was not attending school, that I was not paying attention to training, that I was not diligent with my duties, and I was always very tired, very sleepy, so my mother eventually found out that I was spending all my time at the nightclub, the cabaret, and she also found out that I was infatuated with a mulatto girl. But, unfortunately, the mulatto girl, even though she had fun with me, wouldn't go to bed with me. She had attached herself to the governor of the Bank of Greece, who was a short, fat, bald, pot-bellied, unattractive man in his late fifties I was so frustrated that she wouldn't go to bed with me, and I was straightforward with her. I told her, "You are the first woman I've ever seen that I liked. In fact, I like you very much and I would like to go to bed with you. Forgive me for being so direct. I don't know how to flirt with women because I've never done it before."

"Oh, no," she said, "you are a very sweet boy and I like you, but unfortunately I'm engaged." Of course, she was not engaged, she was being paid by the old man. One time I went to that nightclub, and I saw her with the banker, and I got very mad. The banker was eating soup, vichyssoise, which is a cold, red soup, and I took hold of his head and pushed it into the plate. Of course, they threw me out of the nightclub, and my mother heard about it and convinced the banker not to sue me. She also demanded from the Greek authorities to deport the mulatto girl as an undesirable alien. When the news reached my father, who was at his farm in Macedonia at the time, that at last his son had found a woman that he wanted, he rushed to Athens to find her, but she was gone.

In 1949, my father decided to become a gentleman farmer, not that he had any idea of farming, but it seemed to him the opportune thing to do at the time. He purchased, in Macedonia, about 700 acres, considered in Greece to be an enormous amount of ground. He leased an equally large amount of ground and decided to become a big-time farmer, at least big-time as far as Greece goes.

It was the time of the ending of the Marshal Plan. The Marshal Plan in Greece was mostly wasted on ammunition and weaponry to fight the civil war, unlike other countries which benefited fully. The Marshal Plan in their case was used to rebuild and modernize their industrial infrastructure which had been demolished during the Second World War. That was unfortunately not the case with Greece. Between 1947 and 1951 Greece received $1,491,000,000 in aid, of which $1,150,000,000 was in military aid. Although corruption was rife, and there was some trickle-down effect, little remained for any kind of aid that would directly benefit ordinary people.

However, by the Marshal Plan, my father obtained tractors, harvesters, incubating machines for thousands of eggs, five Jersey dairy cows and a bull, twenty Swiss Saanen goats and two rams, and a few other items. My father named the Saanen goats after his wife and paramours. One of them had horns, and her he named 'Lilly,' after my mother—my mother's name was Helen, but everybody called her Lilly. My father engaged in farming and animal husbandry and chicken husbandry at the same time. He lost pretty much everything he invested except for one endeavor.

We had a seventy-acre field which was given over to a landless cultivator who was an expert on tobacco. He knew how to grow and cure tobacco. The agreement at that time was that the landowner provided the field and plowed and fertilized according to the requirements of tobacco. The cultivator and his family would work the field and would get seventy-five percent of the crop. As it turned out, our tobacco was the best in the region. The man was a splendid expert on production of tobacco, and he had three daughters and a wife who all worked the field. It's demanding and hard work. Very demanding and variable, because you need a certain amount of sunshine, but not too much, you can't afford any rain when you hang the tobacco leaves to dry. So, it's really an extremely demanding and terrible job.

It was a good crop, and the representatives of Reynolds Tobacco Company came to buy Greece-specific tobacco. I asked one of the Reynolds buyers, "Since you buy your tobacco in Greece, why do you write on the package, 'Turkish and Domestic Blend'?" He said, "When we started buying tobacco, this part of the world was still Turkey. If we were to change the wording our customers might think we changed the blend. Even though it's no longer a province of Turkey we call it Turkish tobacco." Thus, 'Turkish and Domestic Blend' in Camels, or others, is a misnomer, not necessarily a false advertisement.

Our tobacco farmhand emigrated to Australia. He was one of the pioneers in Australia. There are two things that Greek emigrants to Australia did that inadvertently damaged the mother country. Before the Greeks went to Australia, there was no tobacco production in Australia and Australia was importing cigarettes and tobacco. Now Australia is exporting tobacco. Before the Greeks went to Australia, there was no Australian wine. Now Australia is exporting wines. Inadvertently our compatriots had reduced Greece's export business, to Australia's advantage.

There are way too many varieties of Greek wines, so there were no standardized names like Cabernet Sauvignon or Pinot Noir. The Retsina wine is made of grapes, but they predominately grow in Attica, which is the valley of Athens. Retsina is an acquired taste. They used to say that there were three major equalizers in Greece: Retsina, the khaki uniform of the army, and backgammon, because those three transcended all social classes and all income brackets. It didn't make a damn difference if you were rich or poor, you couldn't avoid the military draft, so you had to wear the khaki uniform. Regardless of whether you were rich or poor, you equally liked Retsina. At backgammon you would have the mix of rich or poor playing the same game at the same coffee shop. So Retsina is a major equalizer or was. But now, the draft is not compulsory, most Greeks don't drink Retsina, and I doubt that a rich Greek like Onassis, will search around the villages to find challengers who claim they are better than he in backgammon.

Not far from my father's farm, in a village in Macedonia, I saw, with my father, on the commemorative day of St. Catherine, the firewalking faithful. It only happened on St. Catherine's commemorative day in November. On that day the people made long—about thirty feet—strips of burning charcoal, then took off their shoes and their stockings and danced on the burning charcoal. They said that St. Catherine is their protective saint, and she wouldn't allow them to be injured or to have their feet burn. They invited tourists. They said, "Come! If you believe that St. Catherine is going to protect you, you won't get burned." I wanted to, but I was unbelieving.

Before our return to Athens, while still in Scotland, I had begun the sport of boxing. My mother had noticed that I was all bruised from playing rugby and didn't like this, so she wanted my sport changed to boxing. This continued when I was in Athens. Boxing was not a big sport in Greece. Competitive wrestling was probably born in ancient Greece, and wrestling remained the big military combat sport, along with fencing for the upper classes training to be officers. They didn't have boxing as a program sport at Athens College, so my mother hired a tutor and set up a gymnasium with a boxing ring for me at home. With my intensive training, it was not hard to qualify for a spot on the Greek Olympic boxing team. In those days poor nations like Greece had very limited funds to support their teams, and anyone who could afford our own way, did. My parents paid not only for my training, but for the entire costs of sending me to Helsinki, housing, meals, and expenses.

In 1952, I was honored to carry the flag for Greece in the 15th Olympics in Helsinki when I was on the Greek Olympic Boxing Team, after having won the Golden Gloves in Athens twice.

There were eighteen Olympic athletes for Greece. The idiotic coach of the Greek team, who didn't know much about boxing anyway, considered that I was a light heavyweight. That means I was 180 pounds. He said, "You are so tall, and you have a tremendous reach. With light heavyweights it's touch-and-go, but if you fight as a middleweight, you are assured of a medal because you are much stronger than the middleweights."

But in order to be a middleweight, you have to be 168 pounds, so I had to lose twelve pounds. To lose twelve pounds when you are eighteen years old and still growing—because I kept growing until I was twenty—is not an easy thing. And when you train, you have a hell of an appetite. So, I was having a hearty breakfast and then he had me run all the time to sweat it out. I made the scale at 170 pounds which was not good enough and then I started fasting to hit the scale at 168 to 167—some of them were 165, so it was easy going, but I would gain a couple of pounds every day and I had to lose it. Even if I drank a glass of water, it made a difference.

I had reached the semifinals. I had defeated three others. In my preliminary bouts, I defeated middleweights from Poland, Ireland, and Iraq. There were eight of us left. Of the first eight, four were assured of a medal because back then they were giving two bronze medals. You had the semifinals—eight people, because they were paired. The winners would then contest for the gold, the silver, and the bronze. The two losers would end up with the bronze medals. They didn't have the two losers fight it out to see who would win the bronze medal, they were giving two, so as one of the eight semi-finalists, if I won the next bout, I was assured of a medal.

So, I looked over the other seven, and there was one who concerned me. He was about as tall as I was—I was tallest of all. One of them was a South African, and he was a well-built boy, about twenty-three years old, and I thought I wouldn't want him, and there was a skinny little Negro. He was about an inch shorter than I, he was four pounds lighter, I outreached him by three inches, and I was a year older. So, I thought, *God, give me that skinny little Negro, I'll beat the s—t out of him.* So, sure enough, 'beware of what you pray for, your prayers might be answered' —back then I was a very pious Catholic, and I was praying to the Jewish God. I was a very pious Catholic because in essence I didn't know what I believed in. I got—it was a matter of lottery among the eight semi-finalists who was going to meet whom—I got the little Negro kid.

I entered the ring with absolute self-assurance that I would probably demolish him. But I just couldn't connect. The little fellow was so fast, I just couldn't touch him. None of his punches hurt, but he was scoring points. In amateur boxing, whether you knock someone out, or you just touch him with the glove, it's the same point, it makes no difference how hard the punch is, just touch him and you gain a point. After the first round, I was told, because I had no idea, that I never connected once, and he hit me sixteen times. So, the coach said, "Michael, you have to connect. Try to hit him from the left,"—because he was always starting from the left side. "The only hope you have to win is by knocking him out, otherwise, you are done."

But I couldn't connect, and I realized that, now he saw that I was an easy opponent, he started boxing like an American professional—he wanted to draw blood. So, he was hitting me with the lower part of the glove where the laces are, because if you hit someone with that, it might break the skin and draw blood, and when the referee was not particularly observant, he would walk on my toes. Well, he didn't need all that, because I didn't connect. He was too fast for me, too well trained—now, I'm sure that had I connected he would probably become ballistic and gone out of the ring, but I never touched him. He won easily, and I was out of the semi-final. In the finals he and the South African met for the gold medal, and the little Negro won, and when he gained some weight and he got a Sunday punch, in 1956 he became the first Olympic champion to win the world heavyweight boxing championship. His name was Floyd Patterson.

When I didn't bring home a medal, my mother didn't speak to me for two months.

After I graduated Athens College in 1953, at nineteen years old, I did attempt, but didn't spend any particular effort, to see if I could get to the MIT, the Massachusetts Institute of Technology, because that was one school that everybody had heard of that was worth going to in America. The MIT didn't think I was good enough for them. The only American school that admitted me on a scholarship was the University of Texas, but from what I had seen in cowboy movies, I had no desire at all to go to Texas, so I decided to be a rich father's son, and reap whatever I pleased.

CHAPTER 19

With the Argyll and Sutherland Highlanders

WHEN MY MOTHER realized that I was not making any particular effort to go to any school of higher learning, she demanded to know, "What's wrong with you, why aren't you writing to the schools?" I said, "I wrote to them, but only the University of Texas was interested in me, and I couldn't care less." She retorted, "Well! I can't have a wastrel being here, so I will look to it." "Alright," I said.

About a month later, she announced, "Michael, get ready, you are going to Scotland." And I said, "Oh, no!"

"You are going back to Scotland. I have made all the necessary arrangements. You are going to serve with the Argyll and Sutherland Highlanders." She said that for seven hundred years a member of our clan, and sometimes many more than one, has served with the Sutherland Argylls, because the Argyll were not always Protestants. They were Catholic until the Duke of Argyll, who was friends with that horrible English murderer, Cromwell, turned. He was the one who instigated the intrusion of Protestantism in Scotland. So, my mother, following the Clan tradition, more than the religious affiliation, made the arrangements.

"You will be," she continued, "part of a newly initiated program in the British Army which is called the Eight-Year Short Commission. You will start as a private, you will go through the ranks, and get a commission, and you will remain in the British Army for eight years." She told me, "If you then want to get out of the army, you will get a lump sum, or if you want to remain in the army, you will be at the bottom of the list of the Sandhurst graduates of that particular year." Sandhurst is the British equivalent of West Point. The Eight Year Short Commission was established by Queen Elizabeth II when she first became queen. "You will be a British soldier.

And you will call yourself Angus McDuff. You can't be a Scottish soldier calling yourself Panayotopoulos."

So, as Angus Michael McDuff, and to continue the family tradition, I was admitted to the Sutherland and Argyll Highlanders. Now the Argyll and Sutherland Highlanders consider themselves the best and foremost regiment of Great Britain. The Argyll and Sutherland Highlanders were not in Culloden—a small village outside Inverness—where the Scots suffered their worst defeat, because the Duke of Argyll was on the other side. My mother's people were massacred in Culloden. The Argyll's were Protestant by that time.

The Argyll and Sutherland Highlanders have never been defeated in their whole history. Considered one of the biggest feats of the Argyll and Sutherland Highlanders was their role in taking Quebec. There, they cut strips off their kilts, tied them around their boots so they wouldn't make any noise, climbed up the cliff of the Citadel of Quebec, lowered the French flag, and flew the Union Jack. The next day the French looked and saw the Union flag, and thought they had lost the citadel, so they were demoralized, and Major General Wolfe attacked them and quickly defeated Montcalm's troops.

The other, the biggest, accomplishment was in 1857, in the Kali rebellion in India. Kali is named for the Hindu goddess with the six arms. This was the first time that both Moslems and Hindu united, due to clever lies of Russian agents. Russia always resented the fact that India was British because they wanted it for themselves.

About 1854, the Maitland Enfield rifle was introduced into the British Army and eventually replaced the 'Brown Bess' which was the musket with which they fought the Napoleonic wars, and even before, and it had been the main weapon of the British infantry, the Red Coats for over 200 years. The Maitland Enfield was also a front-loading rifle, but it had cartridges made of paper, which was coated with paraffin. That's why it was a prerequisite, in order to be accepted into the British army, to have seven front teeth—either three up and four down, or four up and three down—so that you could bite that cartridge and have holes in it, so that the powder would be exposed. You took the cartridge, stuck it into the barrel, lifted the cock, and put in a percussion cup so that it would ignite the powder. But the only way it could ignite the powder was if the powder was exposed, and that's why you needed the seven teeth. Otherwise, you couldn't get the king's schilling, and become an English soldier. You had to have seven teeth to bite the paraffin-coated cartridge. Before that it didn't make a damn difference whether you had teeth or not.

When the Maitland was introduced into the Indian Army, the Indian Army had units which were exclusively Moslem and units which were exclusively Hindu. There was not any unit of the Indian Army with mixed Hindus and Moslems. So Russian agents went to the Hindus and said, "See how your British masters are treating you? Now they make you bite into cow fat and humiliate you in such a manner." They went to the Moslems and said, "See how your British masters are mistreating you? Now they have you bite into pig fat, in order to bite that cartridge," and both the Hindus and the Moslems believed it. So, they threw away the Maitland Enfield rifles, and they rebelled against British rule.

That was the first time that there was a combination of both groups fighting. Until then when the Moslems rebelled, there were Hindus to fight them, and when the Hindus rebelled, you had the Moslems fighting them. That's why they said, 'Perfidious Albion, divide and rule and conquer,' because she was using either the Moslems or the Hindus against each other. 'Perfidious Albion' is what England was called by those who hated her. But England always said, we don't have friends and enemies, we only have interests.

This time England had to send metropolitan troops to subdue the Kali rebellion, and the metropolitan troops didn't fare very well. Things looked pretty bad, especially after the massacre in Delhi and in Madras where the Indians would kill every European they found. Things looked pretty damn bad. We were about to lose India. That's when they sent the Sutherland Argylls. All 3,000 of them. And when they arrived, they were singing a song, which was:

> We are the Sutherland Army,
> The Argyll Infantry.
> We cannot fight, we cannot sing,
> But bloody good are we.
> And when we go to India,
> The Viceroy there will say
> *Hoch Loch, Mein Gott!*
> What a bloody fine lot,
> To fight for six pence a day.
> A day, a day!

The Viceroy was a German, an uncle of Queen Victoria, a Sax-Coburg-Gothe, and spoke with a German idiom. Another in which Queen Victoria is 'the widow,' was:

> Hands off the widow at Windsor,
> For half the creation she owns.
> We have bought her the same
> With the sword and the flame,
> And we salted it down with our bones.

The Sutherland Argylls engaged the combined forces of the Indians with bloody battles all over the northern part of India, and in each battle, obviously a number of Argylls are killed. But they did a lot of damage to the Indians. They killed a hell of a lot. And because they were Highlanders, they went to fight them where the Indians felt they themselves had the advantage: up in the mountains.

That was the battle of Mensore. The Indians, the combined forces of Moslems and Hindus, saw that they were not up to par to fight the Highlanders in the mountains, their own terrain. Because they had tremendous numerical superiority, they thought that if they could lure the Scots into a battle on an open plain, obviously the fact that they had cavalry, the Scots didn't, the fact they were hundreds of thousands, the Scots were less than 3,000, that they might be able to exterminate them, so they did lure them to a battle at Mensore.

If it had been another Saxon regiment, upon seeing so many Indians, and all those horses, it would certainly have turned tail and got the hell out of there, but the Scots stood their ground. Their advantage was that they had the Maitland Enfield rifle, which if you were good, and they were all good, you could load and fire six times a minute. Very fast. So, when the Indians attacked, the fire they received was lethal, because the Enfield, a very accurate rifle, was like firing at them with machine guns, and they started dropping like a scythe going through a wheat field. Their cavalry attacks were repelled by bayonets. And then the most incredible thing happened.

The Scots counterattacked. And the Indians ran away. But still there were so many of them. And there were only one hundred, exactly one hundred wounded Argylls. All the rest were dead. Out of 3,000. But they still had ox carts, so they took the dead, they sat them in the oxcarts, and they stuck the bayonets through their necks, and had the hands on the rifle, so they could sit upright with the bayonet holding the body so it couldn't topple and fall down. They placed the dead in those oxcarts, and the hundred who were able to walk took the bagpipes and marched toward the Indians. Any Scot is supposed to be able to play a bagpipe, because if the bagpipe, which goes to battle with them, is shot, somebody is supposed to be able to pick it up and play. Of course, they played 'Scotland the Brave.'

The Indians looked at all those carts approaching, and they thought they hadn't killed enough, and they didn't want to fight any more, so they surrendered. When they surrendered, they realized they surrendered to a dead regiment. This is the most glorious chapter of the long history of the Sutherland Argylls. But the Saxons, the English, said it was not the bravery of the Scots that subdued the Indians, or the fact that the Indians had enough and didn't want to fight any longer, but it was that the shrill of the bagpipe was so offensive to their ears that they decided to surrender so they didn't have to endure those bagpipes any longer.

I was stationed in Germany, outside Dortmund, which is in the north of Germany. I marveled how much faster Germany had recovered from the total annihilation of the war compared to Great Britain. A lot was due to the Marshal Plan, but nobody in Europe performed *Wirtsschaftswunder* to come close to the accomplishment of the German people.

We were being trained and learning the usage of the 81 mm mortars. Our maneuvers involved target practice. We located a field that was empty, and large enough to harmlessly explode 81 mm mortars, so we placed the target, and we fired the mortars. It is quite a powerful weapon and since we hit most of the time, we were quite happy that we had learned how to use the 81 mm mortar effectively.

Next day a delegation of German peasants showed up to complain to our commander, Lt. Colonel Mitchell, also known as 'Mad Mitch.' We didn't understand a word of German, but through the interpreter, we knew that I had to be in his office because I was part of the detail that had fired the mortars. We found out that the Germans were complaining that where we placed the target was their potato field, and we had ruined their crop of potatoes. The mortars, of course hit the ground, burrow for about half a foot, and then explode, and that's where the potatoes are. None of us had ever seen a potato field, none of us knew that those scrawny bushes were of any worth, and we had never seen potatoes growing underground before, so we were ignorant, we didn't do it deliberately. But the Germans were insisting and one of them was quite animated and was shouting. Mitchell stood up, touched him with his little crop on the shoulder and said, "You bloody jerries lost the war, didn't you? Get the hell out of here."

After the Germans were kicked out of the office, I said to Lt. Colonel Mitchell, "I lived through the German occupation of Greece, and I can assure that no Greek peasant, no matter what damage had been perpetrated on him, would ever dare look at a German, forget about going and complaining. Had we been Soviet instead of British, do you think the Germans would dare come and complain?" He averred, "No, we are civilized."

I had a mate, a colleague, a very insular Scotsman, who would watch the German children play soccer on the street. He said, "Michael, those kids are quite intelligent, so young, and they already speak a foreign language." I was with the same fellow again when we were in the big football stadium of Dortmund, where a select eleven of the British Rhine Army, as we were called at the time, were playing a professional football team of Dortmund. The stadium was full, and that same Scotsman turned to me and said, "Michael, I've never seen so many foreigners gathered in one place in all my life." That was so typical of the mentality: we were in Germany, but all the Germans were foreigners.

I served during six months in Kenya in 1953. The British still held Kenya as a colony, but anti-colonial insurrections were beginning there as elsewhere throughout the Empire. Among the Kikuyu people a group of insurgents who called themselves Mau-Maus were attacking colonial farms. Not every Kikuyu was a Mau-Mau, but all the Mau-Maus were Kikuyu. The insurgents were poorly equipped and hardly trained at all, but they fought with determined ferocity and used any tactic to terrorize British colonists, and Kenyans loyal to them.

Our assignment was to clear out Kikuyu settlements targeted for their support of the Mau-Mau Rebellion. Support was defined as harboring even one suspected Mau-Mau, and none of us soldiers was privileged to know how the determinations were made. The strategy was straightforward and paved the way for similar American campaigns later in Vietnam. The Royal Air Force bombed villages with burning napalm, and we shot any villagers trying to escape. It was more like target practice than combat. In 1953 the Argyle and Sutherland Highlander companies in Kenya completed our mission and my company was transferred to Cyprus.

I felt some concern. I was Greek, the only Greek in the regiment, and probably the only Greek who had ever served in it, and there was a Greek uprising against the British on Cyprus.

Cyprus was a British colony and had been under British rule since 1878, when it was awarded by treaty to Britain from the Ottoman Empire. Since ancient times, the island's strategic position in the eastern Mediterranean had been ruled by nearly every empire or army in the vicinity. Rebellions against Ottoman rule were frequent, and at one point there were almost thirty recorded within a century. In many of these rebellions Greek and Turkish settlers united against their foreign oppressor. By the nineteenth century, Greeks constituted the majority ethnic group when many Turks emigrated after the end of Ottoman rule in 1878.

In 1953 Greeks comprised about eighty percent of the population, and Turks about eighteen percent. The communities lived side by side throughout most of the island, culturally separate by language and religion, but without conflict. Like most colonies after World War II, Cyprus had a vocal number of people who wanted freedom from British rule, but freedom did not mean independence because the Greek majority wanted unification with Greece, *Enosis*. They wanted to be part of the larger Greek culture, politics, and governance, and to govern themselves like any other Greek province, controlling their own schools and local budgets.

However, centuries of authorizations from the Byzantine and Ottoman empires had resulted in seventy percent of Cyprus' land being owned by the Greek Orthodox Church. If Cyprus became part of Greece, the Church stood to lose its lands. The political leader of Cyprus was the Greek Archbishop of Cyprus Makarios III, and while Makarios publicly supported *Enosis,* he had no interest in losing title to all church lands. He was ambivalent about unification, but he was the political leader for Cypriot *Enosis*, and eventually became the first President of an independent Republic of Cypress in 1963,

Makarios was known to our family, and I remembered him from my youth. I knew Cyprus' history and the story of Cypriot independence and in some measure sympathized with the Cypriots. By the time our regiment was posted to Cyprus, the island was caught up in the movement for *Enosis*, and our assignment was to keep the peace, which largely meant dispersing crowds, most of whom were young people and children.

When I arrived on the island, I caught the attention of Lieutenant Colonel Richardson who was in charge of British intelligence, the famed M6.

"You're Greek, aren't you?" he demanded.

"Yes, sir."

"And you speak Greek?"

"Yes, sir. A Cypriot would recognize me as a Greek from the mainland."

He wanted me to take on a special intelligence assignment, to dress in civilian clothes, loiter among the Cypriots, and gather any intelligence that might lead to the capture of Rivas, a rebel leader.

I declined, saying I had no training or background in intelligence, and that I had joined the Highlanders only to fight. He was annoyed. As a lance corporal, I rejoined my company which spent most of our time in peace-keeping patrols and generally presenting the visible face of British authority and rule.

Our job was basically to break up any assemblies or demonstrations for independence from Britain and unification with Greece. The Greeks gathered and chanted *Enosis* — Union. The demonstrations were generally peaceful, except for the bricks they threw at us when we ran toward them to disperse them. They didn't throw too many stones because all the loose stones in Cyprus have long ago been used for buildings. Most of the demonstrators comprised of young people and children.

I was reported for the first time in my career. I was reported for failure to beat the children who were demonstrating for reunion with Greece with adequate enthusiasm. It was true: I was willing to break up the demonstrations, but not to beat up young children.

A few weeks later, Richardson called me in and repeated the request to work as an agent for M6. Again, I resisted.

He announced, with finality. "This time I'm not asking you. I've had you transferred from the Argyll and Sutherland Highlanders to M6. You're under my command now, and it is no longer a request but an order."

I was dismayed. I knew that disobeying military commands is the nadir of insubordination, and insubordination is military discipline's worst offense. But I also knew that Britain was in the process of freeing most of its colonies, and I could not help wondering why its Greek colony was an exception. There was also something unsavory about spying on my own countrymen. I didn't think I would be any good at it. But mainly I was a nineteen-year-old and did not like being ordered to do something that felt dishonorable and objectionable on all possible grounds.

"Sir," I said, "I did not join the British Army to become a spy." He eyed me, "Very well, Michael. You are confined to quarters and can expect discipline. This is grounds for court martial. If found guilty, you could be shot for disobeying orders in front of the enemy."

"What enemy?" I asked. "The Cypriots are British subjects. They carry British passports."

I was confined to quarters, largely because there was no military jail, while my fate was considered. The moment I arrived at my quarters, I submitted an application for transfer, either back to my regiment which was fighting in the jungles of Malaysia; or to a Gurkha regiment fighting in the jungles of North Borneo. Those were the only two spots in the fading British empire where you could still be shot and killed, and I wanted to make it clear that I was not shirking combat duty or assignments.

The application went through channels. I was afraid that Richardson, Lieutenant *Sasnach*—Greek for Saxon, of whom there were none in Scotland—would obstruct the application. It is possible that the application saved me from a court martial because I was presented only with a disciplinary action.

They stripped the buttons off my jacket. There were not too many buttons on my Scottish jacket—two. They broke my ceremonial sword, for which I had paid twenty-five pounds only two weeks before.

"I'm sorry, Michael," my commanding officer told me, "but there is a tradition in discharges like this. I'm afraid I am obliged to kick you out." He planted his left foot on my backside and literally kicked me out of the room and regiment.

So, I left the proud regiment, not feeling triumphant or very much like a hero; but not at the time regretting, either, my refusal to spy on my countrymen. My name was expunged from the roster of British officers, as if I had never enlisted or existed

My mother was disgraced and would not talk to me for months.

My first commanding officer was Lt. Colonel Colin C. 'Mad Mitch' Mitchell. A dozen years after I met him, there was trouble in the Crown Colony of Aden. It is now called Yemen, and it is where the Arabs attacked and almost sank the USS Cole in 2000.

In the 1960s the policy of the Socialist government in Britain was to gradually withdraw from every base or holding east of Suez. Aden was a Crown Colony, a main port on the Gulf of Aden. A treaty with Turkey had allowed the British to establish an administration there until it later became a Crown Colony. Its economy is supported by its suitability as a refueling stop for ships enroute through the Arabian Sea, the Red Sea, and around the Horn of Africa. A move to partial self-government in 1962 created tension between rival political groups which erupted into violence in 1967 when Arabs started a rebellion in Aden. When British troops were sent there to restore order between the warring factions, they became a target for terrorism. They were allocated the security role in the city's main commercial district, called the Crater. The terrorists had established themselves in the Crater, set-up their enclaves and made it difficult for British troops to enter and maintain good order. The local garrison proved not enough to contain the rebellious Arabs.

Against that backcloth, the Argylls, just returned from service in Borneo, were selected to serve in Aden where their task was to keep rival Arab factions from interfering with the British plans for granting independence to the inhabitants of Aden. A small contingent of Argyll and Sutherland Highlanders was flown there to prepare for the arrival of the rest of the regiment. They were ambushed and massacred.

Following the violent and gruesome deaths of Highlanders at the hands of the terrorists in the Crater, Lt. Colonel C.C. Mitchell, in command of the regiment, was livid. His orders were not to desecrate the mosques, not to kill any 'innocent' civilians and not to interfere with the everyday flow of life in the colony. Mitchell disregarded all that. He blew up all the machine gun nests which were in the minarets, he ordered his troops into the mosques—without removing their boots at the entrance—and killed the ones he found hiding with their arsenals, which also served as their sanctuaries. In short, within hours of the arrival of the Argyll and Sutherland Highlanders, insurgents were routed, all their hiding places in the mosques and their minarets were reduced into rubble, the Crater, the center of the city was re-taken, and quiet prevailed throughout the colony.

Colonel Mitchell had re-occupied the Crater district and reasserted control over the Arab stronghold that had seen some of the most serious conflict between Arab terrorists and British troops. Regimental bagpipers had accompanied him into the fiery heart of the Crater. Military strategists around the world acclaimed Colonel Mitchell's actions as well-planned, well-executed and very courageous. In 1968, Aden became the national capital of the independent Republic of South Arabia—it was later called Yemen—and the Argylls went home to Plymouth, England.

But the Socialist government in Britain perpetrated a bitter calumny against the Argyll and Sutherland Highlanders. In 1968 the 'appalled' Socialist government in London censured Mitchell and discharged him out of the army. They also disbanded the Argyll and Sutherland Highlanders Regiment which, in its nearly 300 years of existence, had the most glorious history of victories and successes. It was the Argyll and Sutherland Highlanders who took Quebec in 1761 and turned Canada into a British possession. It was the Argyll and Sutherland Highlanders who in 1857 quenched the Kali rebellion in India and maintained the Raj intact. The same Argyll and Sutherland Highlanders covered the defense of Dunkirk and enabled the bulk of the British Expeditionary Corps, some 300,000 British, French, and Belgian troops, to escape to England.

The astonishing decision to disband the Argylls was met with a worldwide campaign to 'Save the Argylls' and more than a million signatures on petitions were submitted to Parliament. The decision was rescinded. The battalion was reduced to company strength, but in 1972 was re-formed.

The Regiment has undergone many changes of name, structural organization and complement in its long history. In war time it expanded to as many as twenty-seven battalions; at one time it contracted in strength to a single company; at another time it faced extinction. In 2006, the First Battalion of the Argyll and Sutherland Highlanders was renamed the Argyll and Sutherland Highlanders, Fifth Battalion, Royal Regiment of Scotland. Through all these organizational changes and political pressures, the Regiment has survived. It is still proudly played an effective role in the service of its country in Iraq.

From 1952 to 1954, I was part of them.

CHAPTER **20**

Becoming a Mining Engineer

THE PANAYOTOPOULOS FAMILY business, with its extensive mining interests, dictated that I should become a mining engineer to make a contribution to the family fortunes.

The structure of our companies had changed, but the wealth originated from my great grandfather Michael Rapitis, who became Michael Panayotopoulos. There were also a number of shareholders who were not members of the family, but they were not participating in the council. Our factotum in Milan was a shareholder. Our business representative and associate in Salonika was a shareholder, and the elected representative of our workers voted the shares which had been allotted to the workers. Ours was a paternalistic type of enterprise and we had a union, not a union related to anybody outside the factory. The workers, every Christmas, apart from the Christmas bonus, received one share of the company, but they had to elect among themselves a president who would vote for them. Uncle Alexander believed in running his business in the nineteenth century mode. He believed in Adam Smith and Malthus.

Preparatory to going to study mining engineering, I was a student at Athens College. So was my cousin, Peter. In 1952—I was probably eighteen at the time, and Peter was sixteen—I attempted to teach Peter how to fence with two matching swords my father had given me. Because they were real swords, they had rubber stops at the edge so we wouldn't injure each other. By then, I had taught Peter only the equivalent of fencing the *floret*, where you only stab, you don't attempt to cut, because the *floret* doesn't have a cutting edge.

One time we were fencing—my mother was watching at her veranda in Athens—when the swords crossed and Peter's stopper broke. I put my sword down, and said, "Peter, your stopper is broken, so we stop here." But he attempted to stab me. If I had not parried that stab, he probably would have pierced through me. Suddenly I had to fight for life. Fortunately, I had not yet taught him how to exercise the Italian saber fencing, so when the opportunity came, I aimed and hit his wrist so he would lose the sword. To this day, whenever I see him, he shows me the scar on his wrist and says, "See? You did this to me!" And I am always asking, what would have been the alternative?

When Peter left the Athens College in 1951, he was not eligible to work for the family's companies because on a number of occasions, he had stolen from the family's company. Peter's misbehaviors were both an embarrassment and a source of some amusement. I could not escape their consequences because our family councils would be called to determine what to do with various incidents.

Peter had a peculiar talent, he, for a short period of time, could be the ideal employee, in fact the employee you had been dreaming of. He obtained his first job, at the age of nineteen, at BEA, which was then British European Airways. His dedication to work, his loyalty to the company, the fact that he would stay long hours without asking overtime, and the fact that he outperformed every employee of BEA in Athens, resulted in his being given the post of BEA's ticket counter manager at the airport. It was a very high post.

As ticket manager at the airport, he had authority for whatever BEA had at the airport. He had access to the manifest and knew what cargo each and every plane was carrying apart from the luggage of the passengers. He found that an airplane of BEA was carrying four gold bars that belonged to the Sheik of Kuwait which were being flown to London to become weighted gold coins. Peter entered the cargo bay of the airplane and attempted to steal the four gold bars. Gold bars weigh a lot, each one thirty-five kilos, about eighty-five pounds. Not only are they heavy, but they are relatively small, so they are very difficult to hold. Peter, instead of trying to steal one or two, attempted to steal all four, and while leaving the airplane the gold bars fell out of his hands. A policeman in the area saw him having difficulty with the gold bars and approached to help. Peter was known to be the BEA ticket counter manager at the airport, and he was wearing the BEA uniform. The policeman had no idea that the gold bars were being stolen, but Peter, upon seeing the policeman approaching, ran away. So, he was fired from BEA. Because he was young—only twenty— the family decided to protect him. That was all the reprimand that he got: being fired by BEA.

Peter's father was my father's youngest brother, Paul Panayotopoulos, who was killed in 1941 when the Germans attempted, and succeeded, in taking Crete. Peter and his mother were getting, every Friday, a stipendium from the company in the form of dividends to his late father's shares. Peter used to come every Friday to the office where my father was, and collect that money, which was not very much, but he and his mother could live comfortably on it.

One particular Friday, Peter saw that my father was not at his desk, and he opened my father's desk drawer where he knew the petty cash was kept, less than two hundred dollars, and took it together with the stipendium for himself and his mother. When my father discovered that the petty cash was missing, he never suspected that his nephew would be the thief. The suspicion fell on a young girl named Elsa. She had just graduated high school, and it was her first job to be assistant cashier at the company. She was questioned by the police because she was the newest employee, nobody knew her, and all the suspicion fell on her. Three days later, the following Monday, Peter's mother, my aunt Aime, the other Princess de Polignac in the family, complained that she hadn't received her weekly payment. She was told that her son had taken it. She said, "I haven't seen my son either." Peter was gone. Where did he go?

A few weeks later we found out that Peter was incarcerated in Nice, France, where he was standing trial for having stabbed, almost to death, a policeman. With the money Peter had stolen, which was not very much, probably about five hundred dollars, he went to Venice, Italy. He went to the casino in Venice and, probably with beginners' luck, won big, so he decided to go to Monte Carlo. In about a week's time, he lost everything. He went into a boutique in Nice with a knife and told the employee of the boutique to give him all the money in the cash register. Without his knowing, the employee pressed a button that alarmed the police. While Peter was helping himself to the small sum in the cash register—equivalent to seventy dollars—a policeman shows up. He stabbed the policeman. The policeman's guts fell on the floor. Peter didn't run too far before he was apprehended, so now he's standing trial, and the verdict of the trial depends on whether the policeman survives. If the policeman dies, automatically the death penalty applies, and in France, even then, the head rolled on the guillotine.

The family council met to determine what to do. I don't know whether they thought he was worth it, but the rest of them, including my father, thought that we couldn't let a member of the family rot in the French jail. I was the only dissenting vote. My mother abstained. There were eleven members of the family council: myself, my mother, my father, my uncle Alexander, his current wife Dorette, Alexander's two children: my cousin Micky and my cousin Helen, and her husband. Peter's mother was also a member of the council, and she tearfully implored everybody to help her son. Peter did not have shares; his mother did.

At that time, I only had a vote in the family council, not a decisive say in what should be done. Against my objection, because that was by far not the first time that Peter had done something hideously illegal—his career had started at the age of sixteen to be a thief and a stabber. I am on record saying that we should not assist Peter because this way we shall only encourage him to commit even worse crimes. If you can imagine a worse crime than stabbing a policeman. The family, I being the only dissenting vote, decided to assist. What evolved in assisting Peter was beyond what our company could spend. So, very rich Aunt Dorette pawned her jewels. It took 200,000 dollars. We hired a professor of psychiatry to testify, and of course to produce documentation, that Peter was a patient of his in his clinic in Paris and that he had escaped. He testified that Peter was a certified insane person, maniacally insane, and that he was not accountable for his actions.

The policeman survived. Peter had remained a total of eight months incarcerated in Nice. When he was released from custody, he was extradited from France and ordered never to return. But he now lives in Paris under a different name.

Peter had been placed in the same cell with a Yugoslav, who after winning the European chess championship in Nice, got drunk and killed someone with his car, which in his case was vehicular homicide. The authorities thought they should put the two foreigners together. Peter had spent eight months in the same cell with the European chess champion, so when he came back to Greece, he asked me if I wanted to play chess with him. I had played chess with him before, and I knew he was not a particularly difficult opponent. I was absolutely surprised, dumbfounded, how easily he beat me. He said, "Michael, for the next match I will give you the advantage of a rook, and let's make it interesting, we will play for a hundred drachmas."

I fell in the trap. Then he offered me the advantage of a rook and a knight for two hundred drachmas. After I lost a couple of thousand drachmas, I said, "It's incredible how your chess has improved. What happened?"

He said, "I could easily be champion of Europe now." Apparently, he had learned well from the Yugoslav in their jail cell and had also beaten him. It was 1958. By then I was a student in Austria.

My very rich Aunt Dorette—her name was Theodosia, but she wanted to be called Dorette—was a Greek woman whom my uncle Alexander had married in 1943 after his first wife Margo, mother of Micky and Helen, left him for the Bulgarian ambassador. The woman was exceedingly rich. She had peculiarities like all rich people do. We were rich, but she was richer.

Dorette wanted to be surrounded by foreign personnel. She always had an Italian chauffeur; she had Italian chambermaids; she had French cooks; and for her son she had with my uncle Alexander that was born in Rome, she wanted British nannies. Around 1956, the nanny was an Irish girl named Ann Quigley. She was from a place in Ireland called Dun Leary, which is the seaport of Dublin. Ann Quigley was a typical Irish beauty. She looked like the twin of the actress, Maureen O'Hara: red hair, green eyes, white skin. Strikingly beautiful. When my cousin Micky saw Ann Quigley, that was it. It was an infatuation of magnitude and he wanted to marry her. My aunt Dorette encouraged her personnel to offer their sexual services, but marriage to them was absolutely prohibited.

We had a family council about what to do about the situation. The problem was solved when my father pulled some strings and Micky was inducted into the Greek Army and sent to the most remote part of Greece to serve.

Peter was given the task to court Ann Quigley and if he managed to take her mind away from Micky—because obviously Micky, as Alexander's son, was a big catch—he would be rewarded. Peter took the assignment very seriously and within months he and Ann Quigley went back to her father's pub in Dun Leary. Aunt Dorette compensated him with about 10,000 pounds. He then lived in Ireland with Ann Quigley at her fathers' pub, and worked at the pub. He assumed Irish citizenship as O'Hara and obtained an Irish passport. A few years later, as O'Hara, he came back to Greece. He said he had obtained a divorce based on mental cruelty: the family was cruel to him in that he had to sweep the floor of the pub. However, divorce in Ireland was not legalized until 1997, and mental cruelty was not a ground for divorce, so there may not have been a marriage or a divorce. But there was a passport. And Peter began to collect them.

I was sent to study in Austria at the *Montanistische Hochschule*, which was located in a town called Leoben.

In the summer of 1958, during my studies, I was a *Ferialpraktikant*, an intern gaining experience working in a coalmine in Staffordshire, England. I had become acquainted with a man named Tom Simpson who owned one of the biggest earthenware potteries in Stoke-on-Trent, and he often invited me to a most exclusive club of his. There I met someone who had a 1939, three-liter, two seat SS Jaguar for sale. It had always been a dream of mine—up to that time—to own a car like that. The year 1939 model was quite an attraction because the war brought gasoline rationing and cars made in that year had been driven very sparingly. In fact, gasoline was rationed into the British Isles until 1948. The car had a very good motor, with less than 40,000 miles on the odometer, and ran perfectly, but needed a lot of cosmetic work. His asking price was three hundred pounds, which at the time was less than nine hundred dollars. I had saved just about that much. But I had also promised my wife-to-be, in Leoben, whom I married in February 1959, that I would bring her a fur coat from England. I tossed and tortured myself for a week, but finally I bought a Persian Lamb coat for two hundred eighty-five pounds.

At the *Montanistische Hochschule*, sixty percent of my colleagues were from Germany. One with whom I developed a great friendship was Dieter von Hoeppner from Mecklenburg. He was the son of the general whom Hitler had demoted to private for disobeying a direct *Fuehrerbefehl*. Another was Gert Gross from Berlin, who induced me to learn more about the people who, during the war, we loved to hate. Having joined a *hochschlagende, Verbindung* introduced me to *Grossdeutsch nazional denken*.

My studies at the *Montanistische Hochschule* in Austria, also qualified me to spend two months as an exchange student in the Soviet Union in 1959. I had ridden the railroad from Breslitosk in Poland, all the way to Moscow. I observed that, up to Breslitosk the gauge was the European gauge; in Breslitosk the whole train was lifted and fitted with new axles to fit the wider Russian gauge, and it was done very fast. Then from Moscow, by train again, we were taken to Rostov in south Russia. On the way, I was struck by the amount of agrarian equipment abandoned in the fields.

By the time I graduated from the *Montanistische Hochschule zu Leoben* in 1960, the mining holdings of my family had evaporated into thin air. And I was married to an Austrian.

I met my wife, Linde, while I was a student, and when we were fortuitously at a hospital in Leoben at the same time. When I first met her, she was only fourteen. When I saw her again, she was sixteen, and she was working as an apprentice at a photo and radio shop, earning the equivalent of ten dollars a month. She was extremely poor.

I realized that she was developing into an exceptional beauty. When I first saw her, she looked like a filly, all legs, like a colt. But, at sixteen, one could tell that she would become striking, so I got slightly interested in her. Eventually, when she was seventeen, I dated her. I asked her, for our first date, where she would like to go. She said, "I would like to go to watch an ice hockey game."

I wore a three-piece suit and my best topcoat with a silk muffler and thin-soled Italian shoes. I went to pick her up at the tenement where she lived with her grandmother, and she was wearing skiing clothes. I wondered, what type of date is that? I took her to the only good restaurant that existed at the time in Leoben. "Where is the ice hockey game?" I asked.

She replied, "At the tennis court." The tennis court didn't have any bleachers or any stands. People were standing on the ice watching the game. My thin-soled feet were frozen. I hated every moment of it.

I learned that she was saving money out of her small earnings of ten dollars a month to buy an overcoat, but she was too proud to let me buy it for her. Eventually she bought the most expensive coat she could buy. "Why are you buying so expensive a coat?" I asked.

She said, "I am too poor to afford anything cheaper."

I saw once my wife's family tree. She is of aristocratic origin, so the family tree is known back to the twelfth century. One had to prove ancestry In Hitler's Germany. Everybody, in order to obtain a marriage license, had to prove that none of the four grandparents were Jewish. You had to prove that, otherwise you couldn't get a marriage license. Her pedigree is longer that my mother's. She is entitled to be called *Durchlaucht*, which is the way one addresses the highest members of the Austro-Hungarian Empire, who are not of royal blood.

My wife's ancestral estate was Durenstein, outside Vienna, which was lost when a Socialist regime took over the governing of Austria after the Second World War. The Socialists disallowed aristocrats from calling themselves by their traditional names, which have the prefix 'von,' which means 'from.' It is equivalent to the French 'de.' If they wanted to keep their ancestral castles they had to pay for the maintenance and the upkeep which, of course, entailed many servants. Most of them could not afford to do so, and the castle and the estate reverted to the state. My wife's ancestral castle needed at least twenty servants to be maintained, and since she couldn't possibly afford that, it became property of the state.

I would beat my wife every Sunday. On Sunday, we both had time. It's in the Koran: 'Even if you don't know, she does,' and needs to be punished for it. I would seize her by the neck, hold her across my lap and smack her bottom four or five times. She didn't like it. She would try to run away. Sometimes she bit me. She knew that Sunday would come, and she would get her thrashing. She became the perfect wife, the perfect consort, the perfect companion.

My mother hated all the Germans regardless of class. Eventually—it took years—my mother did acknowledge that her universal hatred of the Germans was ill-placed. My wife by example and by strength of personality proved to her that all Germans are not the same and all Germans are not to be hated. My mother listened again to Beethoven, to Brahms, to Handel, to Haydn, even to Mendelssohn and Strauss, until she eventually realized what a genius Wagner was.

For Greece, the election of 1960 in the United States was notable, and the election of 1961 in Greece was pivotal. When President John F. Kennedy won the election in 1960, Andreas Papandreou, who as a Communist had once fled Greece, was invited by the Kennedy transition team to become a member of it. At the same time, his father, George Papandreou, leader of the Greek Centrist Party, told his son, "Within a year we shall have elections in Greece, and in all probability my party will win a substantial majority. So, instead of accepting whatever position Kennedy has in mind for you, and being a small fish in a huge pond, wait until I become Prime Minister of Greece, in which case you will be a very big fish in a small pond."

Andreas followed his father's advice. His father won a landslide victory in 1961 and Andreas returned to Greece. At that time Andreas Papandreou was an American citizen. His father, in order to make sure that his son would become a member of Parliament, resigned from his seat so that there would be a bi-election and his son would run in his father's Parliamentary seat. He did, and, as expected, he won by a vast majority. The opposition, the right-wing parties of Greece, said that it was unconstitutional. The Greek constitution does not allow foreigners to be members of Parliament. So, after the election of Andreas Papandreou, he obtained also the Greek citizenship without renouncing the American one.

Some of us knew that Andreas was a Communist, but his father assured the American ambassador by saying, "What better can you have than grooming a successor of mine who happens to be an American?" Andreas Papandreou may have been an American citizen, his children may have been born in America, to an American woman of Bulgarian origin—I emphasize Bulgaria, since Bulgaria has been a traditional enemy of Greece—however, Andreas Papandreou did not have the interest of America in mind.

I had returned to Greece with my wife, Linde. My mother found my marriage to an Austrian intolerable. She hated Germans and everything Germanic with a passion. She made no exception for Austrians, and in this respect she was right. Many of the war criminals, beginning with Adolf Hitler, were Austrians. Her own husband had embarrassed her by making an illegitimate and bigamous marriage to a German woman, and fathered a child, while he was attached to the Greek Embassy in Berlin from 1936 to 1940. My mother made life practically impossible in Athens, so I decided to go to England. I was, and still am, a British subject.

I went to work for the National Coal Board which was the umbrella organization of the nationalized coal mining industry of Great Britain. Even though I had a degree in mining engineering, it did not make a difference.

I had to start from the bottom and work my way to higher levels of position and pay. My wife, because of previous dealings with Viennaline, an eyewear fashion house, obtained employment as a photo model in London. She eventually became a fashion model for the large sizes, size twelve to fourteen. That meant she was independently well off in London, and I didn't have to worry about her.

When I received my first pay envelope, I saw that there was a two-shilling deduction for union dues. Since I had not joined the union, I questioned the deduction. I was told, in no uncertain terms, that if I wanted the job, I had to be a member or else, leave. That was my first encounter with Socialism in England. In view of the fact that I had no choice I decided to be an active member and participate in their meetings. In that particular colliery, north of Nottingham, there were about 3,000 members of the National Union of Mineworkers. In the meeting I attended there were only seventeen participants, the only seventeen Communists in the area. They greeted me, "Welcome Comrade." Little did they know. The subject they discussed was unilateral disarmament and the banning of nuclear bombs in Great Britain. I asked them what that had to do with the interests of us mineworkers. Soon they realized I was not one of them, but I continued to attend the meetings. I realized that to be a good union member means 'work as little as possible, complain as much as possible, and always demand more pay.'

I found a job in the coalmine in Nottingham, washing the coal on weekends, meaning you are being paid time and a half on Saturday and twice on Sunday. There was a small man-made lake where the coal would come to be washed. The job was to make sure that the water was circulating and add the various detergents and the various additives to the water to wash the coal. I was trying to find ways to beat the clock—the timecard. I tried all kinds of ruses. I even tried adding extra cardboard to make the card longer. I never managed. My brain was not inventive enough to find a way to cheat the clock. But it was so boring that I was watching mushrooms grow. Every weekend I did it, for a couple of months.

In the union spirit, I got myself the ideal job: a permanent night shift job whereby I pretended to work the first fifteen minutes, or until the foreman has passed by, and then found myself a big piece of wood and a warm corner and slept until it was time for the foreman to show up again in the morning, and for me to pretend that I worked. Since I slept for at least five hours at work, I did not need much sleep at home, so every afternoon I had a lot of time to watch television. There were only three channels then: BBC-1, BBC-2, and the commercial channel, Grenada. On the commercial channel was a quiz show called *Criss-Cross Quiz*. It was a facsimile of the American tic-tac-toe. While watching, I thought I knew all the answers, so, I decided to participate. My application was accepted, because a coalminer that was not a total ignorant was something rare in England.

The show was a big success, with me as challenger against an elderly schoolteacher. I had an *O* in both corners, and my opponent had a cross, an *X*, in the other two corners. Whoever answered correctly the middle box would be the winner and collect the accumulated money which was 2,500 pounds. My rival missed, and the subjects changed. Now the subject in the middle box was Greek mythology! The quiz master said, "Michael, the gods are with you."

But I had a foreboding. Greek mythology is a vast subject, and nobody knows or has committed to memory, all the names. The question was, "What was the name of Odysseus' mother?" I knew that she appears only once in the whole Odyssey, in Rhapsody P when Odysseus is in Hades, sent there by Circe to see the plight of his fellow combatants and be convinced to stay with Circe and become immortal. At that point, the mother appears, uninvited, and reminds him of Ithaca, and tells him that Penelope is waiting. I knew the names of Odysseus' father, his son, his dog, and his nanny, but I couldn't remember the mother. I protested that as far as we Hellenes are concerned the Trojan War is part of our history, not mythology. Still, I had to answer the question. The nanny's name was Euryclia. Had I tried that, it might have worked. The mother's name was Anticlea. I missed by not knowing, and the subject changed. The subject was 'rare English birds' and even I knew that one. So did my rival, and he trousered the money. I was livid.

After having lost at *Criss-Cross Quiz*, I was angry and frustrated for a while because I thought I deserved to win. There was another quiz show at BBC similar the American *$64,000 Question*, but it appeared to be quite difficult. It was called *Double or Quits*. With every correct answer you doubled your money, but one wrong answer and you lost everything. The show was in London in front of a live audience and that was an inconvenience for me, since I lived and worked in the midlands and Grenada TV was in nearby Manchester. However, I applied for the show and was invited for an interview at BBC. They wanted to determine how articulate I was and how I appeared on television. Apparently, the BBC people did not watch Grenada where I had been on the show for three weeks. I met with their approval, and I was given a list of fourteen subjects to select the one upon which I would be questioned for the show. It had to be a subject that had nothing to do with my vocation, or studies, or business.

One of the fourteen subjects was the Bible. As a good Catholic, I had never read the Bible. I knew some parts of the Gospels and had learned at school in Athens the ancient Hebrew history based on the Old Testament, but other than that, my knowledge of the Bible was non-existent. *But, I thought, the Bible is one book; I will try and memorize it*—I had, at the time, a remarkable, sponge-like memory, unhampered by smoking—a*nd even if I don't absorb all of it, I will retain enough to make a killing on the show*. So, I chose the Bible.

The BBC people gave me eight weeks to prepare and scheduled my appearance accordingly. Since I didn't own a Bible, I went to Earl's Court, where I knew there were a number of cheap hotels, sneaked into one of them and stole a Gideon Bible. I started the study that same afternoon on the train on my way back to Nottingham. I didn't take the Bible with me at work because there is not enough light for reading in coal mines. But I dedicated every other moment of my time in my quest to memorize it. The more I read, the more frustrated I became. All those ridiculous genealogies, who begat whom and how many centuries he lived, turned me almost insane. The thing seemed to have no literary value whatsoever and all the characters were so unreal. The only character that attracted me was the Jewish God YHVH. He is a most vindictive, capricious, cantankerous, and cruel chap who takes pleasure in tormenting his 'chosen people.'

The more I read, the more distant I felt from a religion based on Babylonian and Egyptian mythology. I couldn't help noticing the dozens of antinomies and contradictions and the questionable historical accuracy. According to the Bible 'pi' is not 3.1416, but just 3. Where my frustration reached is apogee was the last chapter of the New Testament, the Book of Revelation. It is so absurd, baseless, and incomprehensible that it must take an enormous quantum of faith for Christians to accept it as something inspired by divinity. By the time eight weeks were over, I had renounced Christianity as my religion. Hellenic mythology was so much more fascinating compared to Babylonian: the winged stallion Pegasus as opposed to Balaam's Hebrew speaking donkey Burak. I was smoking like a chimney, and I was very dubious of my chances of winning any money.

A contestant could start with one pound, or five, or ten. I unfortunately started with five. The first seven questions were so simple and easy I would have answered them without having gone through the recent ordeal. By the time I had answered the eleventh or twelfth question, the audience was screaming, "Quit! Quit!" Now came question thirteen. There is a superstitious jinx attached to the number thirteen. By now I had accumulated enough money to last me a few years. At that moment I decided to combat and defy superstition and proceed.

The question was, "Who were the Essenes, or Essenite's?" Nowhere in the Gideon, or any other Bible, are the Essenes mentioned. I knew who the Essenes were because I had read the book of Josephus, who dedicated a whole chapter of his book to them, I protested the question but was told to answer first. I did answer satisfactorily and chose to quit. I said that they were cheating. "Well," they said, "the Essenes are mentioned in the footnotes of the 1888 edition of the Oxford Concordance Bible, on Page 1,002." It then dawned upon me, after having answered thirteen questions, what a vast subject the Bible was. After they deducted taxes, I took away 27,500 pounds, which was a fortune.

I now lived in England, and worked in the coalmines of the English midlands, and my wife was a very well-paid photo and fashion model in London. On weekends, if she had no commitments, she would come north and visit me, and every second weekend I would ride my motorbike to London and be with her. It was a good life, and we enjoyed our honeymoon-like weekends. She was earning ten times more than I did, but that didn't bother me one bit.

One day, on my way to Brighton, a resort town on the English Channel, where my wife was working that weekend, I stopped in Stoke to see my old friend, Tom Simpson. We met at his club, and there was the fellow with the Jaguar, still selling the car for the same three hundred pounds. I gave him two hundred twenty which was all the money I had with me, and my motorbike. I drove the Jag to Brighton. I had been a few hours at the hotel where the fashion show was on, when an old, typically English gentleman approached and asked me to raise the bonnet of the Jag so he could see inside. He then asked me to start the motor. He listened to it in silence for about a minute and then he said, "1939?"

"Yes," I answered.

"Will you accept five hundred pounds for it?"

"Five hundred pounds!" I exclaimed.

"Oh, alright," he said, "six hundred-fifty pounds. My final offer. Take it or leave it." I took it. I could not resist a profit of one hundred twenty-five percent in fewer than eight hours.

One Saturday morning, while having breakfast with a Hellene serving at a NATO Air Force base there, and two Cypriots, we decided to drive to Manchester and watch a football game. We all got into a car belonging to one of the Cypriot's and took off. Since it was already late, we decided to go through country roads to shorten the distance. That got us into Derby, a town in England that had not been bombed during the war and looked exactly the same as it did three hundred years ago. We got lost into the maze of narrow streets. We could not communicate with the natives to ask for directions because they spoke a dialect incomprehensible to us. All of a sudden, I felt very familiar with my surroundings. I knew exactly where we were, and I gave precise direction to the one driving, that got us to the Manchester Road. Evidently in a previous life I have lived in Derby.

I worked at another colliery, and this time I went for production—the best paying work. That colliery had possibly the best coal of England, called Type R, which is very hard coal and very high in calories. However, the seams were less than three feet which means one must crawl on all fours. The battery of the lamp which is necessary to see, is on the waist, and always catching on the rocks. In that place called Tophart, there was a piece of German machinery called 'the plow.' Indeed, it was like a three-pronged plow that had to be hammered into the coal, and then a pulley would pull the plow to the other end of the seam. The plow would break the coal into pieces which would drop to the belt conveyor. It was very good production, however on occasion the chain that pulled the plow would break. The English would say, "It's typical. The jerries could not do a proper job and make a good chain."

Having studied in Austria and knowing that the jerries do not have their equal in engineering, I was wondering why the German chain would break. I found that the chain was breaking because the plow was meant for German coal, which is much softer than the coal of England. When the chain would break, we would order a new chain from the factory in Germany. Of course, the new chain, after a while, would also break. So, I took a link of the chain, studied it, measured it, and I wrote to the Germany company to find out the steel type that they used to make the chain. I thought that if I were to use the same dimensions of the chain with a better quality of steel to withstand the hardness of the English coal, the chain would never break.

I submitted my study to the management, and I said that, instead of wasting our money to buy a chain from Germany, we could order that chain at Stanley and Baldwin, a big steel works in Wales. At that time the steel industry was also nationalized in England. Instead of wasting our money abroad, we shall recirculate it in England and we shall have an English chain. The English chain cost much more than the German chain, but it was also much better. When, eventually, the English chain came, and it never broke, the workers were saying, "It's typical. It had to be made in England to withstand."

During my two years of coal mining in England, at Nottingham, Stoke-on-Trent, Swinton, and in Scotland, I also attended the Universities of Nottingham, St. Andrews, and Glasgow, where I obtained a Master of Arts degree in History.

CHAPTER **21**

Greek Army Boots and the CIA

IN ENGLAND, WHEN I won all that money on *Double or Quits*, I decided to take an extended vacation from the National Coal Board. I bought the poor man's Rolls Royce, which was a 3-liter Rover, an English car, which at the time was a very good car. They called it the poor man's Rolls Royce because it had many of the characteristics of the Rolls Royce, like the ice tray, the crystal glasses, and the decanter at the back. It was all beautiful leather upholstery, and wood. In it, my wife Linde and I undertook a vacation whereby we went to all the wine producing areas in France, Germany, Austria, Italy, Croatia, and Slovenia. We drove south through Italy, and by ferry boat, we crossed to Greece.

It was a very pleasant occasion. In Greece, we visited only my father, because my mother wouldn't speak to me since I had married against her wishes, a 'German' girl—she never discriminated between Austrian and German, to her they were all equally bad. Especially the Austrians, because, she said, Hitler was an Austrian, Kaltenbrunner was an Austrian, Miller was an Austrian, those heavy-duty criminals of the Nazi SS. She thought the Austrians were just as bad, if not worse, than the Germans.

On our way back to Great Britain, they stopped me at the border of Greece with Yugoslavia, and they declared that I had not served my military duty in Greece. When I served in the British army, Greece was not yet a member of NATO—and it now applies that if you have served in one NATO army it's accepted in every other. They said, "As far as Greece is concerned, you are AWOL, you have not served." They held me at the border, and they told me that I would go back—to the boot camp. Linde drove the car, on her own, back to England.

I was sent to the boot camp where they were sending illiterates, Turks—which is pretty much the same because all the Turks which I saw there were illiterate—; AWOLS like me, my category, the ones who had not shown up when their year was called; people of questionable, either mental or physical health, like effeminate boys—there were a few whose testicles had not properly developed, and they were not shaving, they didn't have beards; some who were obviously acting like insane, demented persons—but the army was not certain whether it was pretending or they were really demented; people who had ulcers; people who had not an advanced stage of tuberculosis. There were Yehova Witnesses, accused of being spies for the Soviet Union, who refused to take an oath of service to Greece's army. In other words, that camp was meant for the misfits, and it was considered a penal boot camp. The only regular people who were at that boot camp were the Corinthians because Corinth is the place where the regular boot camp is located, and the Corinthians were not sent to the boot camp in their hometown so they would not have an advantage over all the others by being next to home. So, they were actually the victims because they were there among the worst debris that Greece could produce.

The boot camp had old fashioned Turkish lavatories: that is a hole in the ground where you have to actually aim; if you aim too well, the water splatters up, and you don't want that either. When I first went to that group lavatory which was serving some six hundred people, the feces covered even the aisles, it was abominable, it was the worst of the worst you can imagine, the stench was insufferable. The Communists at the boot camp were the ones given the duty of cleaning the latrines.

Something very peculiar happened to me. For nine days I did not defecate, and even though I was eating every day my three squares, still I did not defecate, and it became a mystery to me: where was all that food going? Luckily, nine days after I started not defecating, I was told, that because I spoke foreign languages, I had to go to Corinth and take a test of aptitude. I asked, how do I go to Corinth? They said, you can go by military transport, or if you want to spend your own money, any way you please. So, I took a taxi. It was two hundred fifty kilometers from Missolonghi to Athens. I took a taxi and went home to Athens.

By that time, my wife had returned to Athens from Great Britain, from London, and to my very great surprise, she had been invited to stay at my mother's house. Apparently, my mother had realized that her favorite musicians, which were Mozart and Beethoven, had composed their music in Vienna. Austria was to a degree acceptable. So, I was surprised to find out that they were both there. I found that out because I asked the taxi driver when we entered Athens to stop at the public telephone, and I called my mother to tell her to make sure than when I came home that there would be a bath drawn for me, and that nobody was allowed to come anywhere near me until I had washed. She said, "Your wife is also here." I was elated.

I went home and took a bath. My mother thought that my socks were dead rats. Meanwhile, they boiled my clothes, my mother threw the boots away, and sent the maid to the war surplus stores to find new boots because the ones I was wearing were stinking to high heaven. And I defecated for the first time after nine days, and I told my mother, and she wouldn't believe it. It is still a mystery to me.

I had a voracious appetite in that Greek Army boot camp, and even though the fare in the Greek boot camps was not even suitable for beasts, for some reason I liked it. One dish in the Greek boot camp I liked was *'patates* blm', Because the composition of the people in the boot camp was dubious as to their mental condition, the potatoes were supposed to be peeled with spoons. But because it is very difficult to peel a potato with a spoon, the cooks, or the assistants to the cook, instead of peeling the potatoes, were dropping them into the cauldron of boiling water as the potatoes were, with the dirt around them and the peel, and this dish we used to call *patates* blm because of the 'blm' sound the potato makes when hitting the water.

Another fare of the Greek army was *prasorizo* krits-krits. *Prasorizo* is leeks with rice—krits-krits means nothing, that's the sound you hear when you chew food which contains sand, because the leeks were never cleaned, and they contain sand. They were throwing the leeks and the rice into the cauldron to boil, and of course in Greece everything contains huge amounts of olive oil, so they were all quite nutritious. But when you chewed the leeks and the rice you heard the sound krits-krits because you were chewing sand.

The other fare was cod, but this was salted cod. When you looked at it, it looked like a piece of triangular cardboard. And it had to go into water and stay there for at least forty-eight hours for the salt to dissolve. But they didn't let it remain forty-eight hours in the water for the salt to be removed, in fact they were cutting it into pieces—or breaking it into pieces since they didn't have knives to cut it with, and just boiling it, so it was the saltiest thing you can possibly eat. It was like eating salty cardboard. Only on Sundays, the fare was to a degree, edible because that would be macaroni with a lot of meat and again a lot of olive oil, but at least there was no sand or dirt. So that was the interesting part of the boot camp.

That boot camp was in Missolonghi, famous because it is the place where Lord Byron died in 1824 during the siege while fighting for Greece during the War of Independence of Greece from Turkey. After I was finished with the boot camp, that's when my father is supposed to have pulled a few strings and I ended up in military intelligence which was in

Athens. And not sent somewhere abroad. The boot camp took forty-two days. After having served in the British Army, the experience in the Greek boot camp was the epitome of the ridiculous.

The Greek military intelligence service was organized into four divisions: Espionage, Counterintelligence, Personnel and Special Operations. My job was to translate, and our translation department was in the espionage branch, which shared facilities with Special Operations. The head of the espionage division was Lt. Colonel George Papadopoulos. That's where I met the Colonel, I could hardly say I knew him. I was a private, and having come from the penal boot camp, was not considered even a full-fledged soldier. My acquaintance with Papadopoulos was a factor in my later work in Moscow, Bonn Bad-Godesberg, and New York City for the military regime he led to power in 1967.

Our work was mundane, routine, and generally inconsequential. I was translating from English, French and German into Greek, and from Greek into English, German, and French. Boxes full of photocopies arrived to the translation office, which included five civilians and two soldiers, of which I was one. Whenever these boxes arrived, the head of the translating office, who was a civilian and an evangelical Protestant pastor—something very rare in Greece—would find an excuse to send me out of the office, usually to go and burn documents in Galatsi, a suburb of Athens. The military intelligence had incinerators for burning documents, in facilities that also housed Special Operations. He had been ordered not to let me see anything that came from Cyprus because they knew that I had served in the British Army, and I was not fully trusted.

One day that civilian, the head of the interpreter's department, was frustrated because he had difficulty understanding one of the documents that he was trying to translate. He was searching in his dictionary, but he couldn't find it, and eventually he said, "Michael, I need your help here." He asked, "What is a go-cart?"

"A go-cart?"

"Yes," he said, "What's that?"

"It's a big toy," I said, "It's a sort of racing vehicle meant for children, or teenagers which has usually a 50-cc engine and it goes on imitation racetracks in amusement parks." I was wondering what kind of intelligence was it that had to do with go- carts, and then he started laughing.

"You know," he declared, "I was told not to involve you in any translation which had to do with the stuff we receive from Cyprus, but this is ludicrous." What came as top-quality intelligence from Cyprus was photographs of the bulletin board of the non-commissioned officers mess in the British barracks in Nicosia. They were paying, apparently, someone there to go with a Minox camera, one of those spy cameras, and he was sending boxes, huge boxes, full of alleged intelligence which was just photographs of the bulletin board of the non-commissioned officers' mess, like this one which read, "Tomorrow there will be a go-cart competition for children, participation, ten shillings." That was the intelligence we were receiving from Cyprus.

One exception to the mundane nature of our work was a document we received from the Israeli Mossad. They advised us to change the airplane flight routes for incoming planes to Athens Airport, because even one six-ounce flask of poison could contaminate the Lake of Marathon, the only water source for all Piraeus, Athens and environs. I thought it was good of the Israelis to share that because Greece had never been especially helpful to Israel.

In 1963, when George Papandreou (the father of Andreas Papandreou, and the grandfather of the leader of the opposition in Greece recently, also named George) won his landslide victory and removed the right-wing party from the government of Greece, he won with a majority of fifty-three percent. It was incredible in Greece to get fifty-three percent of the vote, but the fifty-three percent of the vote was interpreted into something like seventy-five percent of the seats in Parliament, so he had hardly any opposition. Papandreou then began replacing the right-wing officers in military intelligence with left wing officers, and since no career officer in Greece was left wing, he was replacing our good officers with officers who had served in the ranks of the Communists during the civil war. Of course, their ranks were not earned in either the military academy or the national army. They had been rebellious, bandits, and guerillas of the communists, but they were all given amnesty and they had been, by George Papandreou, incorporated into the national army of Greece.

The CIA obviously was a little perturbed that their people were gone, so they decided to send a panel of CIA operatives to find out what the hell is going on with Greek military intelligence.

My new boss, who had replaced Colonel Papadopoulos, and who had served as a battalion commander during the civil war on the side of the Communists, ordered me to come to his office. I was still wearing a soldier's uniform. He said, "I'm told that you are the best English-speaking person here, is that true?" I admitted that I was.

"Tomorrow some Americans are going to come, and they want to address the new officers of Greek military intelligence. They will need someone to simultaneously translate from English to Greek and translate the questions from Greek to English. I was told that you could do the job better than anybody else. Do you have any civilian clothes to wear?" When I said yes, he continued, "You will wear civilian clothes and if they ask you under what capacity you work in military intelligence, you will tell them that you are on loan from the Department of Defense. You won't tell them you are a soldier here." He thought it would be degrading or demeaning for him to offer an ordinary private to do this job with the American officials. Not that the Americans could care at all whether I was a soldier or not a soldier.

There were three Americans in the panel, headed by Mr. Le Fleur, 'the flower,' but he had Americanized it, and he pronounced it 'Lefleur,' who was a Sovietologist, and he was probably in his fifties. Another was an active-duty marine officer whose specialty was concealed weapons that don't look like weapons and could never be considered weapons, but they were lethal. The other one specialized in secret communications, in other words, how to write a communication that could not be immediately detected as such. The easiest, obvious thing is to use your urine to write a message. Or to take a couple of aspirins, turn them into powder and dissolve them in water and use that in lieu of ink. That is the most primitive way. At some future time, add heat to make it show up. Mr. Lefleur gave me a list which he had prepared of words, with which he said I should familiarize myself. All of them were known to me, so I told him I was familiar with them. He said it was some kind of trade vocabulary that I might not know, but since I was translating all the time during my service there, I knew them. But I had never done simultaneous translation and it is a terrible headache. Not so much translating English into Greek but translating the idiotic questions those Greeks were asking into English.

It went well, the Americans were satisfied. They could assess those officers they were addressing—that was their job, to find out what was the new composition of the Greek military intelligence after the victory of the left wing, and how reliable Greece would be as a member of NATO.

When it was over, I think it lasted about a week, Mr. Lefleur asked me, "Michael, what is your capacity here in military intelligence?"

"I am a civil servant of the Defense Department on loan."

He looked at me carefully, "Why are you lying to me?"

"Because I was ordered by my commanding officer, in case you asked me, to give you this answer."

"Michael, could you come at about 5 o'clock this afternoon to the American Embassy?"

I did. Apart from those three whom I had already met, I also met the venerable Mrs. Anderson—she was the one who later took me as a partner to cheat in the Mexican Nationals at bridge. And I met the head of the CIA in Athens, the man who was murdered in Red Square in Moscow, thanks to an article using stolen classified information by Jack Anderson, the syndicated columnist, revealing his identity. I think his name was Pierce, but that may not have been his real name.

They told me they wanted me to work for them. I asked, under what capacity?

"You'll still be in the ranks of the Greek Army," one said. "We shall make sure you are promoted to officer's rank, and we shall send you to our office in Kavala, in Macedonia in northern Greece, and we have an assignment for you."

I said, "I shall serve in the Greek army for another sixteen months, and I'll be through with it. I'm not interested. If you have a commission you have to serve longer, and besides, I don't want any entanglement with foreign intelligence services."

The CIA at that time was using a peculiar method in recruiting foreigners. One was money, like the carrot in front of the donkey's face, and the other one was they always wanted to have knowledge of your skeleton in your cupboard, something that they could use to blackmail you.

They thought that my skeleton was that I had been discharged under very unfavorable conditions from the British Army. Little did they know that my father was elated when that happened, and that it didn't bother me too much. When they told me that they knew that I had been kicked out of the British Army, I said, "So what?" They were very disappointed that it did not happen to be a skeleton in the closet. It was, as far as my mother was concerned because she didn't speak to me for a couple of years. They couldn't entice me with money because I had more than enough.

That was the difference between the KGB and the CIA. The CIA never managed to recruit top quality people for the simple reason that they thought they would either buy them or force them by knowing something derogatory or something they could use as leverage to force. The KGB, on the other hand, presented itself as the savior of the world, the protector of the masses. They used ideology. They got good quality people usually.

The CIA officers said that what they had in mind was of tantamount importance to my country. I wanted to know what. They said I had to commit myself before they could tell me. I said I wouldn't commit myself unless I knew. They insisted that I could be assured that it was to the interest of my country. I retorted that, if it is to the interest of my country, that they should address some high-ranking officer. "Plenty of high-ranking officers in Greece are cooperating with us," they told me.

"Then why are you here? You came because you don't trust anybody."

"We don't trust anybody." There was a lot of haggling. I wouldn't commit myself unless I knew what they wanted. They wouldn't tell me unless I committed myself.

Then Mrs. Anderson said, "Michael, you will be a lieutenant in the Greek Army, which means you will collect a salary as a lieutenant,"—which at that time was less than fifty-five dollars a month. "You shall have PX privileges, you shall have three hundred-fifty-five a month from us, and you shall have a Jeep." The Jeep, that was enticing.

I didn't know exactly what the PX was, but the PX was supposed to be better than the NAAFI—that was the British equivalent of the PX. She said, "They have much better merchandise and much cheaper. You can buy a carton of Camels for less than ten drachmas."

I said, "Really?"

"Really."

"Ok, fine, I'm your man." The tobacco got me, that, and the Jeep.

So, from the end of 1962 until 1965, I was engaged in military intelligence for the Greek Army.

CHAPTER **22**

The Family Enterprises

OUR FAMILY WAS connected to the gossip circuit as well as its political and business connections. I was acquainted with a courtier, a Lady-in-Waiting to Queen Frederica, Mrs. Maltsiniotis, a very attractive and very wealthy widow in her forties. When she would relate to me the queen's comments, I had every reason to believe her, and I can vouch for their authenticity.

In 1963, the First Lady of the United States, Jacqueline Kennedy, visited Greece. Jackie Kennedy was not popular in Greece. After having had a miscarriage, she apparently decided to take a vacation from America and American politics and do a tour of Europe. She spent some time in Italy and then she came to Greece as a guest of Stavros Niarchos, and she lived at Niarchos' private island, which he turned into a nature preserve. He had a cultured background and became a multi billionaire after building the first supertanker.

Only Niarchos and Onassis owned inhabited islands. And that was in contravention to the Greek Constitution which, as far back as 1843, abolished slavery. The Constitution would not allow any Greek to own an island, because if he owns an island, who owns the people on the island? But by plebiscite the inhabitants of Scorpios, Onassis' Island, and the inhabitants of Spetsopoula, Niarchos' island, said that they didn't mind if the islands were owned by those two tycoons, and they would be glad to be owned by them.

While Jackie was Niarchos' guest at that private island, while she was having a good time at Niarchos' island, the Athenian society went out of its way to throw big parties for the First Lady of the United States. Someone asked Queen Frederica, who was married to King Paul, why she was not inviting Jackie Kennedy, as opposed to others who were going out of their way to throw big and phantasmagoric parties for her. Queen Frederica said, in paraphrase, "That whore will never cross the threshold of my palace unless she is officially in Greece with her husband." And that is the queen's word.

And then Queen Frederica went on to explain. "I know that before coming to Greece she was running around in Italy with all kinds of Italians. Furthermore, I know that when her husband's father decided that his son should run for the nomination of the Democratic Party, she said she wanted a divorce, at which point Joseph Kennedy asked her, "How much?'" So, Jackie set a price. Nobody knew exactly how much, but Joe Kennedy agreed to pay the price provided that she was pregnant during the campaign, obviously she complied, and during the campaign she was carrying John-John. At that time, it was considered a total impossibility for a Catholic to win even the nomination, certainly not the presidency of the United States, and a divorced Catholic stood no chance whatsoever. The queen, outspoken and sometimes controversial, had a very low opinion of Jackie Kennedy and so did most of the Greek populace.

In the month of September 1963, she came to Greece as guest of Niarchos, and protocol demanded that she be received at the palace; in October she returned to America, and a month later her husband was assassinated.

Later, unlike the Americans who thought that their ex-First Lady marrying a Greek ship owner was a *misalliance,* the entire Greek population thought that Onassis could do much better, especially if he continued with Maria Callas. Perhaps the Greek populace disliked Jackie as a reaction to Onassis dumping Callas. After all, Callas was at the time considered the best Greek diva of the opera, and all Greeks were very proud that she was Greek. She was coming every year to Greece and singing at the Athens Festival, so the populace loved her. I did. She was desolate, disappointed, and from that time on, in decline.

The courtier, the very good-looking Mrs. Maltsiniotis, had a son who was sixteen years old, and he was going to Athens College. He was a colleague of my cousin Alexander.

When King Ibn Abdul Aziz Ibn Saud was expelled from the luxury Hotel Negresco in Nice, France, he then bought a palace in Semmering in Austria, but for some reason the royal Saudi family didn't like Semmering, so they came to a brand-new hotel in the vicinity of Athens where they rented the entire hotel. There were four top royal dignitaries: the Crown Prince and three more who were official wives. There were another fifteen women who were not official wives, but members of the harem. According to Islam one can marry four wives, but it doesn't preclude from having children from another hundred or so. The Greek press was making sort of fun that the Crown Prince had $4,000 a day as spending money from his father. The three sons of the official wives had five hundred dollars a day, and the rest, less, but everybody was getting paid every day from the royalties that Ibn Saud was collecting from Aramco.

The Crown Prince, who apparently didn't like living with the rest of the royal family, had rented the presidential suite of the Athens Hilton. He was staying at the Athens Hilton, and he was having an affair with Mrs. Maltsiniotis—to the detriment of her son who was getting hazed and jeered at school because his mother was having scandalous sex with an Arab. It was known all over Athens.

The Maltsiniotis' owned a big steel factory, so the young Maltsiniotis obtained an International Harvester four-wheel-drive car, similar to a Jeep, took it to the factory, had it beefed up with extra bumpers and reinforcement in the chassis to the point that the car was really a tank. He drove the car to where the driveway of the hotel enters to the main thoroughfare, a beautiful eight-lane avenue with eucalyptus trees in the divider in the middle—a beautiful street. He knew that the crown prince had to go every day to his father's hotel, to collect his money from his father. So, the young Maltsiniotis waited and when he saw the red Ferrari coming down the driveway of the hotel, hit it as fast as he could with his International Harvester.

He turned it into a total wreck—the way that you grab a piece of paper and crumple it in your hand, that's how the Ferrari looked. It ended up at one of the eucalyptuses in the middle of the street. Since all of Athens knew and disapproved of Mrs. Maltsiniotis illicit affair with the Crown Prince of Saudi Arabia, the boy was not even charged with murder. It took an hour to disassemble the car to extricate the body out of the car. It was considered a traffic accident, and the Arab was to blame because allegedly he didn't stop at the red light. The young Maltsiniotis was not hazed or jeered any more at school, in fact he was treated as a hero.

A few weeks after that incident, Ibn Saud lost his throne. His brother usurped the throne, so the crown prince would never have become king anyway. The place where the hotel stood, and the name of the hotel is Lagonissi.

By 1965, I was applying myself fully to the family enterprises in abrasives, refractories, and munitions as Technical Director. On the island of Skyros, the family had a marble quarry in which my uncle Alexander and I each had half interests in a limited liability company. The share of whoever died first would go the other party. He was born in 1901, so it was naturally assumed that he would die first, since I was thirty-three years younger. That happened, and in 1991, I inherited one hundred percent of our interests on the island.

For almost ten years that quarry had operated exclusively for the Sheik of Kuwait. He built his palace with it and almost everything else pertaining to the palace. Because the sheik was buying it, all the Kuwaitis wanted to have also a piece of that marble. When the palace was finished, the sheik invited my uncle Alexander and me to dinner there. We had insisted that the floors should not be made of that marble because it is not a hard marble, like the white marble of the Acropolis. It is a rather soft marble, and it is not impervious to the damage perpetrated by women with high heels. The sheik said, "I have no problem with that. Women in my palace walk barefoot."

At dinner, there were only men, sitting on pillows on the floor, and a number of wenches coming, barefoot, with the trays. One had to serve himself with his fingers, which I didn't particularly care for, but my uncle told me, we are guests here, we have to do as the Arabs. At one point a wench comes with a tray full of white things with a black stripe. I didn't know what those things were, so I questioned my uncle, in Greek, "What is that?"

He answered, "It's ewe's eyes." The eyes of sheep.

I asked, "How do you eat that?"

"Just pick one up, pop it in your mouth and swallow."

When the banquet was over, we were supposed to burp. No alcoholic beverages were served. I did not enjoy the Arab banquet.But we had sold over ten million dollars' worth of marble to the sheik. He selected our company because he loved the colors. Our marble may not be good quality, but it has a magnificent combination of strawberry and peach. It seemed that those were his favorite colors. Because it's not hard marble, only some items can be made with it, like lamp stands, windowsills, mantle pieces, and objects of art. It is certainly not meant for floors, or steps. Tables can't be made of it because, where the strawberry and the peach come together the binding is not very strong, and if it's a table, eventually it will collapse. It is poor quality, but beautiful marble, that's why it hasn't been touched since 1974. After the Iraqis devastated Kuwait, and the palace was destroyed, I hoped that perhaps the new sheik might want to build his father's palace the same way it was, with that marble. But the new sheik evidently wasn't interested.

We had a marble quarry in Naxos which was excellent quality. A famous opera by Richard Strauss, *Ariadne Auf Naxos* memorializes Naxos. It is a bigger island, much bigger. We had a beautiful quarry there where there was porous green marble, very hard, and all kinds of floors could be made with it. The quarry was sold. In the Pentele Mountains outside Athens, there is a marble called penteli, the white marble out of which the

Acropolis was made, but we had no quarries there. The General Motors building in New York is made of it. Walking out of the Plaza Hotel, the first thing one sees is the General Motors Building with the pentelic marble.

Our family had extensive emery mines, and before the First World War we had a virtual monopoly of the top-quality emery in the world. Whatever abrasives were used by the Italian industry were ours through the Pallavicini's, who established a trading post in Milan, which eventually over the years also became an auxiliary or secondary plant for the abrasives. Dimitrios Panayotopoulos had a Vatican title, a papal title, and 1868, a marriage to Princess Elvina Pallavicini.

The name of our company was Smiris, Limited. *Smiris* means marble. We had the monopoly of abrasives all over the world. We had sold to the United States from the quarry in Samos, which was of a lesser quality, but the last shipment to the United States from Samos was in 1912. After that the United States was covering its needs in abrasives from the Philippine Islands.

In 1965, my cousin, Micky, attempted to reopen the American market. We hadn't sold to America for over fifty years. The family in Greece at the time had given up mining activity except for the emery mines in Naxos and the marble quarry on the island of Skyros. We still owned a minority share in the munitions factory and maintained full ownership in the abrasives factory. We made most of our money from exports and imports—trading, rather than manufacturing. I personally had a very good client in Germany, WARTHA, to whom I was selling battery grade manganese.

One day, a 10,000-ton order came to us from America for low grade emery. We had never heard of the company placing the order: Intercontinental Mining and Abrasives Company, Ltd. I checked with Dun and Bradstreet and in this way found that Micky was behind the order. The problem was that he wanted the—to us—enormous quantity, on credit. It would be, including shipment, about $200,000, at the time a very substantial amount of money. We still didn't know who the end recipient would be, and if we should take the matter seriously. We convened a family council and my father, who had the decisive vote, said that if we had a chance to help Micky establish himself as a businessman in America, we should do it.

Micky was in America because, in 1963, after having committed a series of frauds, he fled Greece with a stolen English passport, chased by the police. He reached Mykonos in a stolen 'cigarette' power boat capable of one hundred km per hour speeds. Nobody had yet seen so fast a boat in Mykonos and that aroused everybody's curiosity. He managed to get himself invited by the Guinness's whose yacht was at the time in Mykonos.

The Lord and Lady Guinness invited him for tea on board. Another guest was James Galanos. He was the very 'in' fashion designer at the time, whose best client was Jacqueline Kennedy. Galanos offered Micky twenty thousand dollars to buy the boat, on the spot. Micky did not need persuasion and sold it the moment the Guinness's invited him to join them on their cruise to the Riviera. Galanos loaded some of his models on board the 'cigarette' and departed for Piraeus. When he docked, he was arrested for having stolen the boat. And Micky had the Galanos cash securely in his pocket.

By then, the Interpol was also after him, but the stolen English passport had not yet been reported so he was temporarily safe. He went to Paris and visited his mother. He forged her French passport by inserting his photo and changing 'Marguerite' to 'Michel' and the 'Princess' to 'Prince.' He now had a more or less valid French passport as 'Michel, Prince de Polignac.' Polignac is a French noble house important in European history since 1050, and from which is descended Prince Rainier of Monaco.

Somehow Micky met an old sweetheart from the time he had been a student in London, an English girl named Moira Charles. She was then a resident of New York and was employed as a buyer at Macy's Department Store. Micky instantly saw her as his ticket to America. They married within days. Micky bought an old and dilapidated, but big, motorsailer for the trip across the Atlantic. Moira's two brothers and her sister offered their services as crew, not knowing what a life-threatening adventure on which they were embarking.

Micky managed to bring the ship and his crew safely into the Long Island Sound and was instantly in the news: 'French Prince Sails into Long Island with Newly Wed Wife and In-laws.' The American affluent are fascinated with European aristocracy. The poor appearance of the yacht was attributed to the Atlantic. The invitations to parties and cocktails started raining on them. But Micky had only three hundred dollars left and he had to earn a living. Moira had to go to her efficiency apartment in Manhattan and resume work at Macy's. Micky sold the yacht for peanuts and got a job at New York Life attempting to sell insurance.

Micky was hardly making a living when he met an old school mate of mine, Basil Lilios, who had emigrated to American and had a job at American Broadcasting Company, ABC. Micky convinced Lilios to entrust Micky with his savings—roughly $2,000—and become his partner in a venture they called Intercontinental Mining and Abrasives Company, Ltd. They rented a cubicle at 100 Fifth Avenue and printed very impressive stationary. Micky wanted to work as an independent factotum of the family business in New York but had not taken the trouble of informing us of his intentions.

It was 1966, and since 1912 we had not sold a penny's worth of any merchandise to an American client. This low-grade emery was a product of the Island of Samos and the mines and quarries there had been idle since 1912. Once it was decided to fulfill Micky's order, I went to Samos with my wife to restart the operation. I walked so many miles in that mountainous terrain that I got my first attack of gout there. I was only thirty-two at the time. It took two months to set the production up and we shipped the ten thousand tons within the time limits specified.

We eventually found that the clients were Bethlehem Steel, and Pittsburgh Metallurgical. Micky actually paid almost all that he owed us for the shipment. Then, two more orders came, and the Samos quarries were in full swing.

Emery had the abrasives monopoly, but with the Second World War the Germans developed a synthetic abrasive called electro corundum, and the Americans developed an alternate abrasive called carborundum, and after the Second World War those two put us out of business. Emery is an abrasive, and it comes from a mine. It is a rock which is comprised of approximately sixty percent aluminum oxide—which is the abrasive part. Aluminum oxide appears in nature in many forms. If it's watery and very soft, it's called bauxite, and bauxite is the major mineral out of which aluminum is made. If it is hard, very hard, the hardest mineral next to diamond, it's called corundum, but corundum does not appear as such in nature. Good quality emery has at least sixty percent corundum, thirty percent iron oxide, and ten percent other minerals.

Corundum appears as sapphire if it happens to be from white to blue; it appears as ruby if it happens to be red. The only element that is fully aluminum oxide and found in nature is sapphire or ruby. It appears on the island of Naxos and on the island of Samos, in fairly large commercial quantities, and in some other parts of the world. If the percentage of corundum is below forty percent, it appears in many parts of the world and is called sillimanite. There is a lot of sillimanite in the Philippines, and in Africa, and some in South America.

Corundum is a fully crystallized aluminum oxide, the hardest substance next to diamonds. Corundum is an industrial product; it is not in nature. I wanted to redress the quality of our emery, which was about seventy percent corundum, the most powerful abrasive on earth.

In 1966 I obtained an international patent from the *Deutsches Patentenamt* in Munich, Germany for the enrichment of emery to 98.8 percent purity of corundum. What I wanted to produce was quite important, commercially speaking. It is better than the American silicon carbide, and much better than the German electro corundum. It could possibly be used as a refractory, to make bricks, to build blast furnaces, or steel ovens, and better than the ones that were used at the time.

The idea was that I could eliminate all impurities and produce at the factory level, at the plant level, better than at the laboratory, by implementing a counter-crushing device. Inside a large rotating cylinder, particles of the enriched product would hit each other, crushing. Because nothing is harder than corundum, it can only be crushed with itself, it can't be crushed with steel balls, it's harder than steel, so I thought of self-crushing. The idea existed and was used in wheat. Instead of having wheat pulverized by mills, by stones rotating at a difference, one counterclockwise, one clockwise, a kind of collision crushing is used in Holland and in other countries, for wheat. That produces a finer flour.

So, I thought, why not use it for corundum? We produced out of the plant about 99 percent purity. In the laboratory I had produced 99.8 percent pure corundum. I could not make it 100 percent because within the molecules of corundum, which are not regular shapes, there might be some impurity that it was impossible to get out, not really impossible, but extremely difficult. At the pilot plant I could only produce up to 98 percent purity. That's fine for abrasives, but not good enough for refractories, so the Bank of Greece, which was a state bank, would not give us the money to build the crushing device. My uncle got loans from banks abroad: Bering Bank with whom we had a relationship going back almost one hundred fifty years, Lloyd's Bank, and the Deutschbank of Germany, because after all it was a German patent. It cost us quite a bit. On the basis of the patent, my uncle Alexander and I got a loan from the Investment Bank of Greece, justified by where I had obtained the patent, and also the commercial amounts.

My family's munitions factories had been supplying all NATO Armies with the 81 mm mortar. When the plant was appropriated by the Socialist government of Andreas Papandreou, we had $200,000,000 worth of orders pending, and we had a total of 600 blue collar and white-collar workers at that plant. Within four years the Papandreou regime increased the payroll to about 2,500, discharging most of the old veterans who knew what they were doing. Even though they quadrupled the number of workers, they did not manage to fulfill even a fraction of the pending orders, so they lost the contracts.

My wife couldn't stand the living in Samos, and in our seventh year of marriage, we felt a strain. We agreed to separate for as long as it took either one of us to feel the need of the other. I put her on the train for Austria and decided to remain in Athens, because by then, I was also sated with Samos. The emery operation could proceed without my continuous presence. It was simple surface quarrying, no mining or tunnels involved. Once every two weeks was enough for me to go just to supervise and direct.

After Linde had been gone for seventy-two hours, I missed her terribly. I went out with friends, but even the idea of copulating with another woman was totally repellent to me. I would sit by the hour all alone in my house, watching the telephone and praying to the gods that it would ring, and that it would be Linde asking to return home. My Greek machismo would not allow me to be the first to yield and make the call. I wanted her to be the one to relent. A week passed, and all I received was a bland note telling me she was in good health and happy to be with her relatives. I was not happy with that. I was putting in sixteen hours of work every day to keep my mind away from Linde, but when I came home, exhausted, I would sit by the telephone waiting for a ring.

CHAPTER **23**

A Congo Mercenary

ONE NIGHT, LATE, the ring came. But it was not Linde. It was Mrs. Anderson, the CIA operative in the American Embassy in Athens, offering me a job in the Congo.

"Michael," she enthused, "you will have a good time. It will be like a safari with no season restrictions and no bag limits." She failed to say that the game was shooting back with Czech made assault rifles. "We need you," she confided, "to get yourself recruited by the French-speaking Commando and be our eyes and ears there."

"Why not the English-speaking Commando?" I asked. "I am more fluent in English than French."

"We own the English Commando," was her answer, "but we have nobody in the French."

The whole idea was absurd. I needed no money at the time. I was quite wealthy and my prospects, with the opening of the American market were very promising. Mrs. Anderson was enumerating the financial advantage. "You will be paid $2,500 by the Katanga government and another $1,250 by us, each month."

The problem was, how many months did one survive to collect? No doubt the money was good and quite tempting, but I did not need it. My only African experience had been the six months I spent in Kenya while serving in the British Army. I had no combat experience. My job there had been more of an executioner, shooting burning Kikuyu while the Royal Air Force was dropping napalms on their villages.

What prompted me to listen to Mrs. Anderson, rather than cut the conversation short, was the thought that, should I go to the Congo, I would have no access to a telephone and could not call my wife. I felt great relief at the idea.

In late 1966, I left Athens and joined the mercenaries in the Congo and served in Katanga. I was in the Congo for nine months before being captured and repatriated to Greece.

I joined the Francophone mercenaries, but I spoke German most of the time because I was assigned to the German platoon commanded by *Obersturmbanfuhrer* Richard Schmidt. He and all of his men were Waffen SS who had survived the Eastern campaign in Russia, the French Vietnam debacle in Dien Bien Phu with the Foreign Legion, and the struggle for independence in Algeria. The Germans whom I met in the mercenary commando were incredible survivors, and the best possible fighting machines. My admiration for their sterling qualities had no limit. They were brutal and could be cruel at times, but their discipline, organizational skill, dedication to duty, camaraderie, ability of improvisation, courage and fighting prowess left me often speechless.

When De Gaulle allowed Algeria to become an independent country, the French Foreign Legion—which was stationed in Algeria, Algeria being its home—was homeless. It was decided that the Legion would transfer its flag and its home to the island of Corsica. From its original corps strength, about 45,000 men, the French Foreign Legion shrank to the size of a brigade of about 5,000. And all who were over forty years of age were let go. That meant all the German World War II veterans.

The Congo had been a Belgian Colony, and the Belgians had been pressured by the United States and the United Nations to abandon their African colony. It looked as if the United States always was envious of the countries that had colonies—the Americans never admitted that either Puerto Rico or the Philippines were colonies. They seemed to have a sort of inferiority complex *vis a vis* the empires of Europe, and they wanted to see them lose their empires, and in this respect they succeeded.

Belgium was coerced to abandon the Congo in 1958. Unlike the British and the French, who at times did attempt to elevate the colonial people to some semblance of westernization and civilization, the Belgians had done nothing of the sort. When Belgium was forced to abandon Congo, there were only one hundred men in Congo who had the equivalent of a high school diploma. One hundred out of 40,000 attest that Belgium never attempted to do anything to elevate the colonials, as opposed to the French who took their *action civilisatrice* more seriously. The ex-French colonies are the least troublesome and the best governed.

The withdrawal of the Belgians from the Congo created chaos and brought forth old tribal disputes and petty quarrels that had been suppressed for the eighty-eight years of Belgian rule. In the chaos that ensued the Belgian withdrawal, the Soviet Union decided to take advantage. They managed to create, with Patrice Lumumba and Joseph Kasavubu, a

Communist influenced regime to govern Congo. There ensued a struggle for power between Lumumba as Prime Minister and Kasavubu as President, in which each attempted to dismiss the other. Lumumba was ousted by Kasavubu with the aid of Congolese Army leader, Colonel Joseph Mobutu, and in 1965, Mobutu deposed Kasavubu, who retired from politics. Mobuto eventually changed the place name to Zaire, and his own name to Mobuto Sese Seko.

The province called Katanga is probably the most precious piece of real estate on our planet. Katanga, roughly about the size of California, has every conceivable precious metal and important mineral in overabundance. It has uranium; it has platinum; it has elements of gold; it has copper; it has oil and about everything else. In copper, Katanga was only second in production to Chile. The interest in those precious metals and minerals were in the hands of a company called *Union Miniere de Belgique*. The main shareholder of *Union Miniere de Belgique* was the Belgian crown, but it had also British, French, and American shareholders. There had been excessive exploitation of this mineral wealth and there were vast investments and modern facilities for the production of the mineral assets of Katanga.

Rather than see Katanga revert to Soviet ownership it was decided that Katanga should secede from the Congo, become an independent country, and safeguard the interests of the company *Union Miniere de Belgique* which owned the mineral rights. The Belgians found one of the one hundred high school graduates of Katanga who was of Simba origin—Simba is the name of the tribe that inhabits Katanga. Simba means 'lion.' The man's name was Moise Tshombe. They appointed him Prime Minister of Katanga, then seceded from the Congo and continued the operation of the mines. The Belgians had armed about 20,000 Simba's with the most modern arms available to Belgium—and Belgium was the best manufacturer of infantry small arms.

The rest of the Congo, under the leadership of the two Communists, Kasavubu and Lumumba, and under the auspices of the Soviet Union, with East German, Hungarian, Czech, and Polish advisors, decided that secession of Katanga was obviously not in the interest of the rest of the Congo. With the support of the Soviet Union and her satellites, they decided to bring Katanga back. The Congolese, armed, trained and advised by Czechs, invaded Katanga. To everybody's surprise, the Simba's, the moment they were shot at, threw down their weapons and started running. The Simba's were among the smartest and best equipped soldiers Africa has ever seen. They wore excellent Belgian paratroopers' fatigues, excellent Belgian boots, and they were armed with the best Belgium could provide. The one thing the Belgians could not provide was bravery and defiance of the enemy. The Simba's name means 'lion.' In battle they were more like mice.

It was feared that the Communist-led Congolese would succeed in incorporating Katanga to their peoples' republic. Since the Simba's were so ineffective in the maintenance of Katanga's independence, it was decided to augment them with mercenary troops who would be paid by the mining company.

The demise of the French Foreign Legion after Charles de Gaulle granted independence to Algeria turned out to be opportune. Most of the legionnaires flocked to the Congo, to Katanga, to become the mercenaries who were supposed to strengthen the Simba's. The ex-legionnaires, initially a few thousand of them, were not plentiful enough to sufficiently reinforce the Simba's so it was decided to increase the mercenary troops and entice them with more money. At which point there were two mercenary units: one Anglophone and one Francophone. The Francophone was comprised primarily of ex-legionnaires, the Anglophone was composed primarily of British and Colonial people who had combat experience.

When I joined, the Francophone Commando numbered about 300, the Anglophone Commando numbered 3,000. The brunt of the battles to prevent the occupation of Katanga by the Communist-led Congolese was not anymore in the hands of the Simba's but was exclusively in the hands of the mercenaries. There were battles fought practically every day. The mercenaries were dramatically outnumbered, sometimes ten to one, and sometimes even worse.

In the Congo, it was a matter of day-to-day survival being extremely outnumbered. The mercenaries in the Francophone were comprised of about forty Germans: ex-legionnaires, ex-veterans of the Eastern Front, and about another two hundred sixty cutthroats from all over the world—about the worst conglomeration of criminal humans imaginable. Colonel Jean Schramme, the Belgian paratroop colonel, was nominally in command of the French speaking commando. The French speaking commando, however, was outnumbered by Germans, so the *sturmbanfuhrer,* the Nazi equivalent of lieutenant, was pretty much in charge. The French also called him *sturmbanfuhrer*. The *sturmbanfuhrer* had determined that we should attack only at night because Negroes are afraid of the night, and that we should use an excess of fireworks that somehow had found their way to the Congo from China. The ones that go up with a zoom and then burst were the ones which terrified the Negroes the most. Using foghorns and fireworks, we would attack at night, instill panic into the Negroes and then shoot them while they were fleeing. The enemy was the Congolese.

We avoided any confrontation during the day because we were so awfully undermanned.

I found that I was unexplainably affected by voodoo. The *juju* men were inserting small sticks in our foot tracks, not only mine, everybody's. They looked like sticks, ordinary sticks from trees, little twigs. It was a curse—to hurt our feet. The effect was successful. We couldn't walk. I was thinking, how can I be affected by voodoo when I don't believe in that? I had hired a Negro to wipe away my tracks so that the *juju* man could not find them and put his sticks in them. After that, the moment I would see a *juju* man I shot him, regardless of whether he had done anything or not. I must have shot at least five of them. It felt worse than gout. I had not the worst effect. Others could not wear their shoes because their feet were swelling.

The United Nations peace keeping groups in the Congo originally were a motley group from various nations: Poles, Yugoslavs, Columbians, Peruvians, but the mainstay of them was a Gurkha regiment from India. The Commander in Chief of the United Nations troops was the Gurkha colonel. One didn't want to mess with the Gurkhas because, first, they are professional soldiers; second, they are fearless; and third, they are lethal. So, we tried to stay out of their way.

We wanted to get rid of the Gurkhas because they are fierce fighters, and we were afraid of them. They were not fighting. They were there to maintain peace. They were there for the same reason that UN troops have been in practically every dangerous or unruly spot on earth since that ridiculous organization has been established, and never with any amount of success. In fact, the presence of UN troops all over the world has proved to be possibly the largest failure of the United Nations. They didn't prevent the genocide in Rwanda, they didn't prevent the genocide in Bosnia, and they didn't prevent the five wars that have been fought in the Middle East.

However, we needed to get rid of them, and we did. It happened because of the narrow size of the American World War II hand grenades. One day we saw the Indian Gurkha colonel and his driver, who had stopped to relieve themselves, walk away from their Jeep. While they were out of sight of it, I crept up with an American World War II hand grenade. It was a Jeep Willys whereby the fuel tank was under the driver seat, and the American hand grenade fit perfectly to go through the opening. I pulled the pin and attached the release mechanism with three rubber bands before the two Indians returned to their Jeep. They drove away, and within a few minutes the gasoline had eaten up the rubber bands; they had hardly driven more than a mile when we heard a detonation and we saw the flames. That took care of the colonel of the Gurkhas, and after that the

Gurkhas were withdrawn, so we were quite relieved.

Dag Hammarskjold, the General Secretary of the United Nations, had made four trips to the Congo, and took an active role in the peace keeping efforts in the Congo. He exchanged the various UN units that were stationed in the Congo exclusively with Scandinavians: Swedes, Danes, and Norwegians, so he could communicate with them. The Soviets denounced his decision to send a UN force to keep peace in the Congo and demanded his resignation. In September 1961, he was killed in a plane crash while enroute to negotiate a ceasefire between non-combatant UN troops and Katanga troops of Moise Tshombe.

When I was a younger man, it was accepted in Europe that the most civilized people in Europe were the Swedes. However, in the Congo, I realized that if you scratch a Swede—and you don't have to scratch too much—you will find the Viking underneath. Dag Hammarskjold had heard that Lumumba, the Communist leader of the Congo, had been to Katanga, and he was looking for him. Eventually Dag Hammarskjold who had now assumed the role of Scandinavian marshal in charge of his Scandinavian troops, went to a village where he had scant information that Lumumba had been at one time. He ordered his troops to gather the elders of the village, and in his poor French, he tried to interrogate them. The villager elders were unwilling to cooperate, so the Swedes began hitting them with the butts of their rifles and hitting them while they were lying on the ground. I thought it was very peculiar for the most civilized Europeans. Eventually Dag Hammarskjold said, *"Jela Lumumba, jela Lumumba?,"* which means, "Have you eaten Lumumba?" The one who had received the most punishment said, *"Seulemont le fois,"* which means, "Only the liver."

The only women we got were victims of rape. I was never interested in rape. Gang rape was common among the non-German mercenaries. The Germans—and I—maintained the strict discipline of the Waffen SS. Rape was not permitted in the *Wehrmacht*. I helped myself to a few pickaninnies—boys. It was common.

Following a battle, near a settlement, I was first on top of a nearby hill, where I was met by a Mother Superior. There were other nuns in a dwelling behind her. She extended her open palm and offered ten gold napoleon coins. "This is all I have." She implored me, "Please! Make sure my girls don't get raped! They are so frightened. And I told them the whites are civilized and they don't do things like that."

"Oh, Mother Superior," I said, "you should not lie to your girls." The next one to come on top the hill was a Sicilian, who saw that there were women. "Forget it," I said, "they are under my protection." He scoffed, "Why? You want all of them?"

"No," I told him, "I don't want any of them. But you don't get any either." Giovanni didn't like it.

Two Germans arrived, and I told the Germans that the Mother Superior had told her girls that whites don't do such things as rape, and we were here to prove that she was not a liar. The Germans told Giovanni, "Get the hell out of here unless you want to be shot."

More Germans came, and then the whole troop, until there were about sixty of us, and the nuns were safe. Of course, I kept the coins.

In early summer of 1967, everything collapsed: supplies, transportation, and our communications with the Katangan government. We had nominally taken orders from Tshombe and the Katangan government, but our real instructions came from representatives of the Belgian mining company.

When anarchy became total, the last Europeans prepared to leave. Our final orders were to defend the last departing train about twenty kilometers northwest of Stanleyville. The train was thought to be carrying in addition to the Europeans, precious metals and jewels, an exaggerated rumor, but it was attacked by the Congolese army, and in the pitched battle, the train was destroyed. I don't know whether, how, or how many of the Europeans escaped, but there were Red Cross, Belgian medical, and other emergency road transports evacuating everyone possible. We suffered our first significant casualties in that last battle, about thirty wounded, and three killed.

The next morning, the second-in-command of the Anglophone commandos, 'Titch'—meaning short, but he was a handsome six foot-seven—Williams arrived. He and his commandos had neither fought nor observed the battle to save the train and defend the departing Europeans, but he told us, "Well done, boys. You can go now." He did not say where we were supposed to go, or how we were supposed to get there.

He was accompanied by 3,000 Anglophone commandos who had set up threatening battle lines and artillery to persuade us to leave quietly, so we had no chance to loot for provisions. It had been some time since anyone had been paid by the Katangan government, the Belgian mining company, or anyone else.

What transportation existed was inadequate for the European civilians, and certainly not available to us. We realized that without transportation, making our way with our few vehicles which could accommodate perhaps sixty of us, we would never reach the Atlantic. Leaving behind our sick and wounded, about 250 of us turned around and walked east, not west, towards Lake Tanganyika, to reach either Kenya or Rwanda. We had four jeeps, two lorries, and a lot of gas. With no medical supplies, we would be vulnerable to all the infections and diseases of the African jungle, and we would have to forage for food on the way.

We lacked not only food but water. When we left Katanga and entered the western Congo, a drought made water an urgent issue. We made for a village about thirty miles southwest of the Congo River in search of water. Instead of water, we found a settlement of perhaps four to five thousand Lilionga people dying of thirst. Their fields were parched, most of their animals had died, and the people were more or less waiting for death. After the local waters had dried up, the women had for a time walked thirty kilometers to the Congo River and carried water back in jars on their heads, but by the time we arrived, they had become so dehydrated they lacked energy to make the trip.

In our search for water, we found crates containing a drilling rig. There was also a generator, and at least six twenty-gallon containers of diesel fuel. I was familiar with that kind of drilling rig, so the Germans and I read the French language manuals, assembled the rig and started drilling. I knew that since we were only thirty miles from the Congo River, we had to be within range of the underground water table. In about an hour we had an artesian well spouting enormous quantities of cool, fresh water out of a two-inch pipe.

When I asked the village elder, who spoke French, why they were about to die of thirst instead of studying the manual and putting the rig together, he said he didn't know about the manual. Furthermore, he blamed the Belgians for not setting up the rig themselves.

About a month out of Stanleyville, we were suddenly and unexpectedly strafed by an old American Mitchell Bomber, the kind that performed many of the bombing runs in World War II. The plane was painted entirely white to disguise any affiliation. We were confounded. We knew the Czechs or East Germans would not fly a Mitchell. Who, allied with the Americans, would attack us? The next day, in anticipation of another attack, we positioned our four Jeeps and 50-millimeter machine guns in a crossfire for their arrival.

Sure enough, the plane came again, and this time we caught it by surprise. We hit the right engine, and it crashed in the jungle close enough for us to make our way to it. The co-pilot was dead, having been seated on the same side as the engine we hit. The pilot was alive, and his right arm was injured, but he was trying to reach across his abdomen for a gun in his right holster. "Communistas!" he yelled.

Now we were doubly confused. Why would he think we were Communists, when we had been hired to defend the anti-Lumumba, anti-Communist side of the Katangan rebellion? None of us spoke Spanish, but we asked one of our Portuguese commandos to interpret as best he could. We deduced that the pilot was a Cuban stationed in Guatemala, which we knew had been the American base of operations for the Bay of Pigs and other anti-Castro insurgents funded and organized by the American CIA.

That is when we realized that the Americans must have switched sides. We did not know that the Americans and their allies had installed Mobutu as the Congolese strongman to replace Lumumba. Much later, when I was in Washington, DC, I learned from someone in a position to know that the Americans had indeed redeployed some of their Cuban commandos to fight in the Congo, in part to make the accusation that Castro and the Communists were active in Africa.

We were now only 175, our numbers having been depleted by disease and constant infections, as well as our first serious casualties at the last battle.

Our last battle in the Congo was in Bukavu, where there were 25,000 Europeans, mostly French and Belgian, and a few others. The town was occupied by the Congolese Army, so on our way out of Katanga we decided to go and liberate Bukavu.

The battle became a major story as it was very important to the Francophone world. It was considered an enormous victory for the liberation and evacuation of the Europeans trapped there. My photograph appeared on the cover of the August 26, 1967, French magazine, *Paris Match*, which had a circulation of twelve million. I didn't know when they took the picture and wrote the article, I had no idea. Many French journalists were in the Congo.

We were, according to the article, 117 men. We had the element of surprise because the defenders of Bukavu—or the occupiers of Bukavu—had no idea that so few would dare attack them. We took them by surprise; we captured their leader, in *flagrante delicto* in his bed with a white woman. We took him prisoner and the rest fled. We kicked them out of Bukavu. Then they woke up. They realized how few we were, and they started a series of frontal attacks.

We had four .50 caliber machine guns mounted on Jeeps, and the Congolese were attacking in the crossfire of those machine guns. They were mowed down like wheat, like corn, with a scythe. Thousands were killed with only four .50 caliber, about the biggest you could get, machine guns. At the lull of the battle, we went to collect their weapons and munitions because we were running very short. We realized that all the dead bodies had dilated pupils, which is indicative that they were drugged, because only a drugged idiot will attack in a machine gun crossfire.

Eventually we ran out of ammunition altogether and it was time to leave Bukavu. The town of Bukavu is on a lake called Lake Kiva, which connects to Rwanda, so we appropriated all the boats available there, crossed the lake and went to Rwanda on our way out of Africa.

However, we encountered the Tutsis, the nastiest of Negroes, kissing cousins of the pygmies, slightly bigger, and extremely primitive. The Tutsi, however, had knowledge of a lethal poison into which they were dipping the points of their blow darts. They were using bamboo to shoot blow darts, with air power, air pressure of their breath. Our orders from the *sturmbanfuhrer* were to not waste any ammunition since we had very little then. At one point, I was confronted by a Tutsi. I didn't provoke him in any way, I didn't say a thing, and he shot me with his blow dart. Their darts are like crochet needles, they have a hook, so his dart was hanging from my chest. I fired three 9 mm bullets into him, and he almost was cut in two. The *sturmbanfuhrer* heard the firing, so he approached and said, "Didn't I tell you not to shoot?"

I showed him the dart, still hanging from my chest. He asked, "What did you do to him?"

"Nothing," I declared.

"Do you mean to tell me he shot you without provocation? That's a different story." He gave orders, "Shoot all the Tutsis you can see." We must have killed about a hundred of them. To the great relief of their enemies.

We walked across Rwanda, and we walked across a small part of Tanganyika, which is now called Tanzania. We reached Lake Tanganyika, went to a little village there, commandeered the pirogues they had, and rowed ourselves to the north part of the lake, which can be either Uganda or Kenya. We were in Kenya. In expectation of us, the Kenyan army had deployed with tanks and artillery and when we were in hearing distance, with loudspeakers, they ordered us to surrender. Considering we had zero ammunition left, that was an order to which we could only comply.

All 110 of us were arrested by the Kenyan army. I don't know what procedure was followed with the rest of them, but when it came to me, I told them that I was Greek and requested to be taken to Nairobi to the Greek Embassy. They agreed. They took me to the Greek Embassy, and the Greek Embassy, upon establishing my *bonafides*, gave me a ticket back to Athens.

The rest of the men were scattered between Rhodesia and Angola. The Germans had no place else to go, other than to stay in Africa. I had no interest in remaining in Africa. I had enough of Africa to last me six lifetimes. I was there nine months. I had walked in Africa a distance equal to Key West from Montreal. I walked enough. Africa is extremely long. The maps don't truly show how long Africa is.

A story of Bukavu and a walk from Africa.

This photograph of me appeared on the cover of Paris Match, the French magazine, issue of August 26, 1967, when I was a Congo mercenary of the Fifth Commando, and a CIA operative in Katanga, as Belgium left their African colonies and the Soviet Union and Communism moved in.

Paris Match N° 959 Du 26/08/1967 La Terre a Tremble

CHAPTER **24**

The Colonels

ANDREAS PAPANDREOU HAD established himself as a Proconsul of the Centrist party of Greece. He started flirting with the Communist Party of Greece and became a vociferous critic of America and a great admirer of the Soviet Union. The honeymoon of Andreas Papandreou with the Communists, and the fact that a good proportion of the Centrist Party followed him, made it appear that if we had elections sometime in the foreseeable future it was possible, or probable, that the coalition of the Centrist Party and the Communists might win a majority. In order to prevent such a contingency, the Pentagon and NATO and the CIA called into play a program called the Prometheus Plan whereby units of the Greek Army should take over the governance of Greece to prevent such elections from happening. The Prometheus Plan was a NATO formulated plan that called for neutralizing a Communist uprising in case of an attack by a Soviet bloc country, whereby the government is overthrown, and martial law declared. It was not a Greek scheme. It was an American scheme, conceived by the CIA, and studied and promulgated by the computer in the Pentagon. However, a number of Greek officers were introduced to that scheme, and they were part of it.

In 1965, the young King Constantine II of Greece, who in 1964 had succeeded his father, King Paul, realized that there was a political crisis brewing in Greece with Andreas being a vociferous critic of the United States, and of the North Atlantic Treaty Organization. Andreas wanted to move Greece way further to the left than would be reasonable or healthy for Greece that was supposed to be. King Constantine II, possibly misguided, dismissed Andreas' father, George Papandreou, from the premiership and offered portfolios to various members of the Centrist Party. By doing so he actually split the Centrist party. This didn't sit well with the people. The people resented the fact that the king, possibly in contravention to his constitutional rights, had interfered in politics in a degree that the Constitution did not allow the monarchy to do.

Andreas Papandreou had attracted a number—about thirty percent—of members of Parliament that belonged to his father's party, and he was openly flirting with the Communist Party, so it was understood that a coalition between Andreas Papandreou, the left wing of his father's party, and the Communists, in view of the outcry of the majority of the people against the kings intervention, would win him the electionIndeed there was a political crisis in Greece. In 1963, there was a political assassination of a popular leftist member of the Greek Parliament, Grigorios Lambrakis, MD. The film Z was based on this. The assassination was blamed on the right wingers of Greece. In actual fact, it was the Communists who assassinated him and put the blame on the right wingers in order to augment and increase the extent of the crisis. Those were the prevailing conditions in Athens between 1963 and 1967. There was turmoil, there were strikes, there were demonstrations on the streets. There was an outcry against the king's intervention. In the summer of 1966, you could hardly walk in the streets of Athens because they were saturated with tear gas that the police were throwing to disperse the demonstrators. And there were battles with striking construction workers, the police throwing tear gas, the strikers throwing bricks and pieces of cement.

At that time, in 1966, my father died, He had cancer of the liver.

Under those conditions, in 1967, the Prometheus Plan was implemented by a cabal of middle-ranking army officers led by Colonel George Papadopoulos, Colonel Nicholas Makarezos and Brigadier Stylianos Pattakos. Those men were eventually to become my chiefs. The brigadier was not actually a member of the initial CIA-employed officers, but he was needed because he was in charge of a tank brigade. His tank brigade was instrumental in eliminating the possibility of the Royal Air Force taking an adverse position, since the Royal Air Force was, as the word says, royal. The tank brigade was also instrumental in neutralizing the Royal Navy of Greece, which was also royal, meaning loyal to the king.

One of my assignments while in the Greek Army had been to translate the Prometheus Plan, which was written by the American Pentagon. It provided specific plans for a military takeover in the event of an election victory by George Papandreou's son Andreus. Like the Americans, and like the colonels who executed the coup, I considered Andreus Papandreou an avowed Communist and was glad to help put in place this contingency. The military colonels who planned and staged regarded themselves loyal to the Greek Crown, with a duty to preserve national order and honor against an internal revolution.

King Constantine II was not a member of the Prometheus Plan. He had no idea about it. However, the officers who implemented the plan did it in the name of the king. Greek officers take their oath to the King, not to the Constitution like American officers. The king takes an oath to protect the Constitution, but the officers take the oath to the King. So, it is up to the king to use his officers to protect the Constitution, but the officers do not have an obligation to the Constitution. Their obligation is to the King, and it is his obligation to preserve the Constitution. Even though Colonel Papadopoulos, Colonel Makarezos and Brigadier Pattakos acted in the name of the king, the king had no idea, and he didn't like it.

The day was April 21, 1967. When the military took over there were only two drops of blood spilled, and they were from the finger of Andreas Papandreou. The orders of all the units that were implementing the coup were to go and arrest all the Communists in Greece, and to arrest all the politicians regardless what party they belonged to. When a young lieutenant and a few soldiers burst into Andreas Papandreou's bedroom, Andreas opened the drawer of a side table next to his bed, attempting to grab a pistol. The young lieutenant kicked the drawer and that was the only blood spilled.

The Communists were all corralled in the various football stadia of Greece. The politicians, on the other hand, were confined in the Athens Hilton. It was a lightning coup. Nobody was hurt. Nobody was really particularly disturbed.

I was not in Athens. At the time, I was serving with the mercenaries in Katanga in the Congo. My wife, who was there, related that she was listening to the American Forces Network, the AFN, which was operating out of a huge Air Force base the Americans had in the south of Athens, called Glyfada. She said it seemed that the Americans knew beforehand about the coup because they were telling the various personnel of the Air Force Base that, tomorrow, consider it an ordinary day and go about your business as if nothing has happened. The name of the Air Force Base, Glyfada, inspired a parody of a song then popular in the United States, and the Americans would sing, "Hello, Muda, hello Fada, now we are going to Glyfada."

Linde had returned to Athens months before my arrival from the Congo and was eagerly waiting for my return. She had no idea how often she had come very close to widowhood. She had developed a business, a line entirely her own, out of synthetic waxes of *Farbwerke Hoechst*, and was manufacturing and wholesaling floor polishing materials and shampoo.

I returned to Athens in September 1967. Two things of great significance to my future had happened in my absence. The first was that our abrasives plant had been appropriated by the Port Authority of Piraeus, so I had no job. Second, the Greek Army had established a military dictatorship in Greece. The compensation our family got for the emery plant was quite fair, and my uncle Alexander suggested we expand our marble quarries both in Naxos and Skyros, and that I manage them. Upon my father's death a few months before I went to Africa, I had become the major shareholder of the family business. I agreed to expand the marble quarries, but I did not want to engage myself full time with them.

I had met a few of the officers in charge of the dictatorship when I served with the Greek Army intelligence, and I was in full agreement with their policies and approved of their methods so far. I felt that it was time for me to fulfill my mother's wishes and become a civil servant.

I visited the officers and asked them if I could be of any use to them. They were astonished to see me because the Athenian elite were diagonally opposed to them. The rich in Greece, with very few exceptions, were opposed to them because they had acted behind the king's back and without his knowledge or consent. I never cared about the Greek monarchy or the persons in it. It was Danish-Russian-German, with not a drop of Greek blood.

The Colonels were delighted that I was offering my services and suggested I take the entry exam for the Foreign Service. They did not trust—with good reason—the career diplomats and wanted to infiltrate legally. That meant instead of appointing me, I had to take the test. A characteristic of dictatorships all over the world is that they deliberately discount their most egregious transgressions, like abolishing the Constitution, but pay too much attention to trivial detail. I took the test and scored top of 154 contestants. My German was as fluent as my English or Greek. For ten years my main language was German.

Greece, when the military took over on the twenty-first of April 1967, was considered by the United Nations as an underdeveloped country. The per capita annual income was $731. The Greek economy was in shambles, and worst of all we had a deficit in the balance of trade which was almost thirty percent of our gross national income. The only way that Greece could cover such an enormous gap was through the remittances of her sailors in the merchant navy—the money they were sending to their families—and tourism. But tourism had also suffered because of the disturbances and turmoil. Thanks to the military regime, seven years later, the per capita annual income of Greece was $1,850 dollars, and the balance of trade was less than two percent of the gross national income. The infrastructure that the military regime built in Greece made her eligible for full membership into the European Economic Community, the forerunner of the present European Union.

It improved so much in seven years—the dictatorship lasted seven years—because when you have a dictatorship, when you impose martial law, when you abolish the Constitution, you can rule and do whatever you please and whatever you think is in the interest of the country. You don't have an opposition to object to whatever you have in mind to do, you don't have a parliament to say yes or no as far as expenditures go. You can spend, if you have the money, for whatever purpose you wish to spend, and under a military dictatorship, at least in the beginning, you have no graft and no corruption. And under martial law you can overcome the worst enemy in every government, which is entrenched bureaucracy.

Under martial law there is no opposition, nobody dares present an opposition, and the press in Greece was genuinely in favor of the military dictatorship. The military dictatorship had automatically and finally put an end to all the turmoil, the tear gas, and the disturbance, and it was obvious that under all this tranquility imposed by the military Greece had a chance to revive.

It was autumn, 1967, and given the climate of Athens, winter hardly lasts more than a few weeks per year. Yet, my wife tells me that it is time for a new fur coat. "What's wrong with the one you have?" I asked.

"Everybody has seen it," she said. "It is not a fashionable coat anymore." I liked that coat. It was black and curly and very warm, the Persian Lamb coat I had bought her in England in 1958. I saw no need for a new one, especially in Athens where there is hardly a need for a coat, especially a fur. But she insisted.

I had a friend who was barely scraping a living selling live chinchillas. I had first thought of it as a joke, but now I began thinking about him. He had told me that he would sell the six-month-old males to furriers for twenty-five to thirty dollars each, and they make hats or stoles with them. There is always a market. He would keep the females, unless they are either too dark or too light, and create new families of five females and the best quality male. That goes on until there is the 1,500 needed for a coat. He had told me that it takes at least 1,500 pelts to select the 800 almost identical ones for a full-length coat. In the case of my wife, given that she was 5 feet, 10 inches, tall it would take more.

The chinchillas were sold in a rectangular cage, about five feet in length, with five compartments and a corridor. The females—which are larger than the males—live in the compartments. The male has the corridor and eats and drinks with the females. The females have no access to

THE PRIME MINISTERS

Venizelos, a Liberal, dominated between 1910-1936, to whom my father told the real story of the capture of Serres.

Ioannis Metaxas, a Monarchist, appointed by King Constantine, 1936-1941, promoted my father from exiled rebel to Military Attaché in Berlin.

Georgios Papadopoulos, a Military Dictator 1967-1973, under whom both Greece and I thrived as a diplomat in Moscow Bonn and New York.

THE KING   King Constantine I Loyalty to his royal relatives on Europe's thrones determined Greece's foreign policy and he was exiled, but politics brought him back.

THE COLONELS   Brigadier General Stylianos Pattakos, Colonel George Papadopoulos and Colonel Nikolaos Makarezos. Military Junta 1967-1974.

the corridor. When a female is pregnant, she becomes inimical to the male and aggressive, so her compartment is shut off so that the male cannot visit her and get injured. They give birth five times a year to one or two, rarely three, offspring. After seven months, the new females are ready to breed. They eat pellets made of wheat and alfalfa and some protein additive. Their only luxury is a bath in pink Bermuda sand. This special sand has no rough edges to injure the pelt and is necessary for keeping the pelt clean. One top quality male, the five medium quality females, the cage, three months' supply of food, and a hundred pounds of Bermuda sand cost me close to $500. When I came home that day loaded with the cage and its contents, my wife was perplexed. "What's that?" she asked.

"Your new fur coat," I replied. "Very few women in the world, and none to my knowledge in Greece, own a full-length chinchilla coat. It will take two to three years, but you will have something absolutely unique and terribly expensive."

I think her first impulse was to take the cage and throw it at my head, but when I told her it was $500 worth, she started thinking. "Well," she said, "I might never get a coat, but it will be fun to watch the gray rats grow."

By the middle of 1968, there was no room in our house to put more cages, and it had become a full-time job for my wife, so I decided to move my chinchilla farm to a house my family owned in a suburb of Athens called Kifissia. It was a four-room house, made of stone, with kitchen and bathroom. It was built in 1930 and was in poor shape. It was in the middle of a grapevine field, approximately ten acres, that produced the worse tasting wine imaginable. We called it 'Chateau Kif,' and bottled it and sent it to people we disliked. There was also a cottage for the servants and a building for the wine making. A retired gendarme, his three daughters and one goat lived in the cottage. I placed the chinchilla cages in the house and hired the gendarme and his daughters to take care of them. I had no usage for the goat, which was feeding on the grapes.

It was the fourth of July 1968, when the gendarme called me on the telephone and told me the chinchillas were dying like flies. The temperature that day reached 106 degrees. It was double indemnity because they could not be skinned, and I had a total loss of at least $1,600. I called the man who had sold them to me. He said that their native grounds are the peaks of the Andes Range in South America, and their thick fur was meant for that environment. He suggested I immediately buy air-conditioning units if I didn't want to lose them all. I proceeded to the dealership of Carrier and bought four units that stood on tripods, one for each room. They cost me a total of twelve hundred dollars. The heat wave continued for the rest of July, but I didn't lose any more rats. It was my birthday and Linde and I were sweating in our bed, suffering from the heat and I said, "Why should the rats have air-conditioning, and not us?"

I thought that if I could spend so much money for air-conditioning the chinchillas, why shouldn't I spend the same for myself? So, I bought a window unit that cost an arm and a leg because our house in Athens had stone walls three feet thick. It was an old house, and the best feature in it was the gas water heater in the bathroom that was made by Siemens in 1888. The huge blue and white porcelain bathtub on iron legs under the water heater must have been of the same vintage. I really hated air conditioners because of my aunt Dorette.

Aunt Dorette had married my uncle Alexander in 1943, and she loved American cars and Italian chauffeurs. One very hot day in the summer of 1964, I was walking along the *plage* of an Athenian suburb, the temperature must have been 104 degrees, when a Buick Riviera stopped next to me. It was my aunt offering me a lift. The car had 'climate control' and the temperature in the car was set at 68 degrees. I almost shivered sitting in it and by the time we reached my destination, from the very cold environment of the car back to the insufferable heat of the outside, I caught the worst cold of my life that tormented me for a month.

Because of the loss of so many chinchillas that July, the coat was postponed by two years, but in 1970 Linde came to Germany to visit me, wearing it. Because she was so tall and the coat so thick, she looked like a giant gray grizzly bear. It was a very long coat, reaching her ankles. She wore a matching chinchilla hat. It made quite an impression among the wives of the diplomatic corps of Bonn-Bad Godesberg. I thought it was grotesque, but I did not comment. I still preferred the black astrakhan even though it cost peanuts in comparison.

While I was in Katanga getting shot, Micky was by then an established supplier of emery to the American steel industry. He was on speaking terms with most of the CEOs and managing vice presidents of some of the biggest corporations.

He had arrived at this elevated position partly through his habit of reading, every morning, the two columns on the front page of the Wall Street Journal that have a short précis of all the news contained in the paper. One day in the last months of 1964 he read that INCO, the Canadian nickel company, the biggest in the world at the time, was going to have a strike. INCO was the major supplier of nickel to the US steel industry, and nickel is an absolute necessity for the production of top-quality steel. Millions read the Wall Street Journal every day, yet Micky is the only one

I know who made millions of dollars out of it. He instantly thought that if the strike were to last for a lengthy period of time, the price of nickel would skyrocket.

His sister, my cousin Helen, who lived in Paris, was married to the nephew of the richest man in Greece. Not the richest Greek—none of them lived in Greece at the time. This man had on his payroll close to 25,000 people in all kinds of enterprises. Among them was a small nickel refinery that had only started that same year. The nephew, Micky's brother-in-law, was in charge of all of his uncle's mining enterprises, including the nickel refinery called Larymna. Micky's idea was to sign a long-term contract with his brother-in-law at a price slightly higher than the market price on the day the strike started.

The brother-in-law, Alexander Athanassiadis, knew Micky was a felon and did not trust him, so he agreed only to a trial order of only thirty tons on a prepaid letter of credit. The current price per ton was $1,460. Micky agreed to pay $1,480. Micky actually lost six hundred dollars on the first shipment, but now Alex was pleased with himself for having—he thought—outsmarted Micky and was also pleased for having sold his merchandise in the American market. So, when Micky came up with a three-year contract for all the production of Larymna, approximately 3,000 tons per year, at $1,600 per ton, the brother-in-law was eager to sign. The tons referred to are European, or metric tons: 1,000 kilos, or close to 2,400 pounds; the American tons are 2,000 pounds. These differences were to have some significance.

Micky had, in essence, nothing to lose with his gamble. Should the INCO strike be short lived, he would obviously be in no position to fulfill his contractual obligation, but he owned nothing, and had no reputation to lose. Quite the contrary, he was a fugitive of justice, a known criminal, and it was only family ties that kept him alive and well. On the other hand, should the strike last long, the price of nickel would soar, and he stood to make a fortune.

The strike lasted for almost three years. After the third month of the strike the price went to $2,000 a short ton. The American economy, at that time of the Vietnam War, was in full gear, and demand for steel was at its highest. Micky was buying nickel from the brother-in-law at $1,600 per metric one. It was obvious to the brother-in-law that he had been had. His uncle was furious and demanded to be rid of the contract. One lawsuit followed another. Alex was trying to extricate his company from the contract and was also in breach of it for selling to other parties. Micky, with outstanding representation by the best lawyers in Athens, won the suits and even imposed inspectors to make sure that all the production of

Larymna came to him in the USA. The only concession he made was that if Larymna could produce and refine more than 3000 tons a year, the surplus could be sold on the open market. After a year into the INCO strike, the strategic reserves of the Pentagon were depleted, and the price soared to $5,500 a short ton. By the time it reached $7,500, Alex was able to convince the Greek government that it was Greece who was losing money by selling a national product at such low prices. Justice may be blind, but she is not deaf. She can hear the sound of coins dropping into her scale. The government passed a law that negated the contract on grounds of national interest.

By then Micky was a multi-millionaire. He bought a mansion in Sands Point, Long Island with five bedrooms, five bathrooms, six acres of manicured gardens and a half Olympic size pool. The furnishings were also extremely expensive, but not in good taste, given that Moira, his English wife, was of the people, and more prone to buy costly kitsch. He bought a luxurious house in Fort Lauderdale, Florida on a waterfront corner, where he could dock his 172-foot Burger yacht. He had at least eleven cars of exquisite marks like Facel Vega, Maserati, Jaguar, Aston Martin, and Ferrari. And there was $7,000,000 in cash collecting dust in the bank. My schoolmate, Basil Lilios, Micky's original partner, also became wealthy.

Micky's next endeavor, in partnership with our family's firm in Athens, was to engage in the 'triangular business' whereby one would buy Soviet products and find ways to bring them legally into the USA. The most sought after Soviet raw material was chrome. The demand had been created by both the British and American governments boycotting Rhodesia—today's Zimbabwe—for having declared her independence in defiance of Britain's demand that the Negro majority be the successor to colonial rule. Rhodesia was the biggest producer of chrome in Africa at the time. A disadvantage for Rhodesia is that it is a land-locked country, and her only access to the ocean is through Mozambique, then a Portuguese colony. The Soviets, East Germans, Czechs, and Chinese were openly trading with Rhodesia in spite of the United Nations sanctions. In the triangular business the Soviets would buy Rhodesian chrome at $29 a ton and sell theirs at $54. Soviet chrome is of superior quality, but not such as to justify the big price differential. After three or four Soviet chrome shipments reached the United States through Micky's triangles, the Soviets became more demanding and hiked the price to $60 a ton.

All this happened while I was in the Congo trying very hard each and every day to stay alive, but eventually, by the end of September 1967, I was back in Athens.

Micky had taken his pregnant wife, Moira, on a luxury cruise to

Morocco and the Cote d' Azure, and while they were in Rome, the Interpol knocked on their hotel room door and arrested him. She boarded the next plane to Athens and came to meet for the first time her husband's kin under those disagreeable conditions. Money talks, and Micky had tons of it. First, we had him extradited from Italy to Greece, and there he stood trial on eleven different counts of felony. All his accusers had been amply compensated, bribed or threatened, and he was acquitted. The whole thing took about two months.

While Micky was in jail in Athens in 1968, and I was waiting for my first appointment into the Greek Foreign Service, we planned how to buy ourselves Rhodesian chrome and sell it to the United States.

We bought a 20,000 BRT bulk carrier for $2.5 million dollars from the Eriksson's in Norway and sent it to the Sudan where another school mate of mine owned a chrome mine. All he could sell us was twenty tons, but for less than $5,000 in combined bribes, we got signed and stamped papers, bills of lading, and certificates of origin showing that we had actually bought 20,000 tons. Then the ship sailed to Lourenzo Marques in Mozambique and loaded the real 20,000 tons of Rhodesian chrome for $27 per ton. It was sold in the United States for $49 per ton as a product of Sudan. It was a pure profit: $400,000 in a single trip. We used the money and the ship as collateral to buy another bulk carrier. It was bigger, 40,000 BRT, but in bad shape, still it made two or three trips per month for almost a year.

The American customs authority had introduced phasmatoscopic analysis which proved that our chrome was Rhodesian and refused it from being unloaded at an American port. We merely sold it to a Canadian customer at a reduced price. After that we suspended the smuggling operation, and Micky entrusted the management of the two bulk carriers to Tidal Marine.

Pending his trials, while Micky was in jail in Athens, his wife Moira gave birth, in 1968, to an ugly baby girl. When she grew up, she was not ugly. She went to Colorado and published a horse magazine. Micky was free, very rich and without a care in the world. He returned to America with his family, but it was quite clear that he wanted to rid himself of Moira.

Most Greeks, especially the rich ones, believe that taxes are paid only by fools. They sometimes spend more money to avert the payment of the taxes that the tax amount would have been. Micky was no exception. He was playing the stock market in a big way and was very disturbed that each time he sold at a profit he had to share it with the IRS both as income and capital gains. To avert this, he moved his family to Bermuda and opened shop there with a white native Bermudian. He bought a beautiful house on an acre of land near the Southampton Princess Hotel. The stocks were then bought and sold from Bermuda and there were no taxes to be paid. Moira and her daughter were now banished in Bermuda, and Micky spent most of his time in New York living the life of a playboy.

CHAPTER 25

Moscow: Blue Jeans in the Diplomatic Bag

MY FIRST ASSIGNMENT in the Greek Diplomatic Service was as a courier in the Greek Embassy in Moscow. I didn't like anything about my job, or Moscow. But soon I learned there was a thriving black market in blue jeans, and I got very much involved smuggling blue jeans in the diplomatic bag and selling them for a hundred rubles each. The rubles I was earning by my smuggling the jeans could not be spent outside the Soviet Union because the ruble was totally worthless. It was even worthless in the satellites, and if you showed up with rubles in Prague, good luck to you. But you could spend them to buy antiques in Russia, so I was converting my rubles to antiques—also on the black market—and selling them to an antiquarian whom I knew in Athens. Some of the antiques were made the week before, but on occasion one would get one which was a genuine antique. Still, my margin of profit was one thousand percent, and I could easily sustain the eventual loss.

Sometimes I sold or bartered the jeans with the KGB guard who stood post at the entrance to the Greek Embassy. One day he asked me to meet him after his work at a designated spot in Gorky Park, where he would exchange something very valuable for two pairs of jeans. He gave me an object wrapped in old issues of *Pravda*, and I gave him the jeans. I thought he might expose my black-market trading if I did not comply, so I asked no questions. When I got back to the embassy, I took out from the newspapers an ugly black tempura on wood icon, depicting the Madonna and Child. I didn't particularly want it but felt I had to accept the exchange.

Back in Athens, I took it to the Armenian antiquarian. He examined it thoroughly with magnifying glasses and asked me where I found it. I told him that it cost me two pairs of jeans and had been given to me by a KGB soldier. He replied that was possible and told me it was a tenth century Madonna Nikopeoea from the Ukraine, and that there were only eleven known to exist. Later I found out there were only nine. When he offered me fifteen hundred American dollars for it, I immediately accepted. It had cost me twenty bucks.

I thought no more about it until years later in 1972 when I was posted to the Greek Consulate General in New York City. I was assigned the hopeless task of recovering a Greek vase recently acquired by the New York Metropolitan Museum of Art, a priceless object from Grecian Sicily that had been a major art story for months. It was painted by Apellis, the most famous vase painter of antiquity. It had been the cover picture and feature of the New York Times Sunday magazine.

When I went into the office of the curator, I spotted on the wall the icon I had bartered for blue jeans in Moscow. "How did you come by that?" I asked him

"We purchased it legally," he replied, somewhat defensively, anticipating our discussion of whose nation, and what museum, should have the Greek vase.

"And how much did you pay for it?"

"Twenty thousand dollars," he answered. "It was a steal." He had the receipt from the Armenian antiquary to show me. The icon was apparently one of only nine from tenth century Ukraine, from the period when they were just starting to produce icons. It was an Icon Nikopoea, showing the Madonna and Child in a stylized pose and setting. Its historical value must have trumped its artistic value, because it hadn't improved in the interval.

So, I had rubles. Diplomats of the Soviet Union were given a map of Moscow and they had a radius of twenty-five kilometers where they were allowed to go, with the center of the circle being the Red Square and the Kremlin. Within those twenty-five miles of radius there were marked areas where we were not allowed to go. And of course, we were not allowed to go anywhere outside Moscow. In order to see to what extent money could bribe a Soviet functionary I asked a 'favor' of my counterpart in the Soviet Foreign Ministry. He spoke Greek because, before becoming a member of the Communist party, he had gone to a seminary to become a priest. All Russians who go to seminaries learn Greek, thanks to Orthodoxy. His name was Vasily.

I ventured, "Vasily, I want to go to Leningrad."

"Well, it won't be easy, but I will get you permission to fly there." "No, Vasily," I protested, "you don't understand. I don't want to fly to Leningrad; I want to drive my car to Leningrad."

He objected, "That's impossible."

I produced a 100 ruble note which was about one third of Vasily's monthly salary, and I said, "Will that get me the license to drive to Leningrad?"

"Certainly not," he declared emphatically. So, I showed a second 100-ruble bill, and said, "How about that?"

"It's impossible. Even if I attempted to get you such a license, I would be putting my career on the line. If you want to go to Leningrad, I'll get you an airplane ticket."

"No, I want to drive," I repeated. Then I offered a third 100-ruble bill. That was his salary.

When eventually I produced 500 rubles, Vasily conceded, "It's difficult, it may cost my head, but alright, I'll get you the license." The reason I had so many rubles was that every week I was smuggling in the diplomatic bag ten Levi's jeans which I was buying in Athens in retail for ten dollars. I was selling each for a hundred rubles. At that time, 100 rubles in the official market were $110. One dollar was officially ninety kopeks, not even a ruble. But in the black market you could get not less than five rubles to a dollar. So, my jeans, which cost me ten dollars each, were selling for a hundred rubles, which under the worst of circumstances meant fifty dollars. The ten jeans would sell outside the Greek Embassy within an hour. People were waiting for them. The reason that the Soviets in Moscow were paying a hundred rubles for a pair of jeans was not that they were so desperate to have a pair of pants that cost them a third, or close to half, of what they earned a month. It was an act of defiance. Wearing the American jeans was protest that would not end in Siberia. But it had to be Levi's, they wouldn't touch any other brand.

I did drive outside Moscow to Leningrad, and I also obtained firsthand experience of how easy it was to bribe a Soviet official. That was a lesson to me because I found out that the whole farce of defense spending was meant to consolidate and establish the American government and the Soviet government. If the American government were to spend one tenth what they were spending on defense to bribe the Soviet hierarchy, they could accomplish more.

It is a little over 750 miles from Moscow to Leningrad. It took me about ten hours. When one leaves Moscow there is about fifty kilometers of a good, wide, but undivided, paved road, but after fifty kilometers, abruptly, without any sign, without any warning, the paved road stops. And it stops about four feet above the surface of the dirt road, so one has to know, and get off the paved road into the field in order to get onto the dirt road. If you don't know, you take a plunge. I didn't know, but I managed to put on the brakes and stop before hitting the precipice. Then you have the white *rollbahn* as the Germans used to call them, which are dirt roads, and fortunately, there was scarcely any circulation of vehicles. But if there was circulation it was convoys of military vehicles, which means that one has to wait until they all pass, because the dust they were creating would blind you. When I arrived in Leningrad my car was beige, but it started as black. My eyebrows were beige, my eyelashes were beige, and I was spitting beige spittle. The same thing also occurs when arriving in Leningrad. There were fifty kilometers of nice, wide paved road, about four feet above the surface. Again, one has to go to the field and enter the paved road from the side. But one can drive on the *rollbahn*, the dirt road, and drive as fast as you can go because there are hardly any encumbrances. There are no ditches, left or right, so even if you deviate from the road you get into a field. It was an experience driving in Russia.

In Leningrad, I went to the Winter Palace, the famous Hermitage Museum. I was in Leningrad less than forty-eight hours. I was not interested in prostitutes in the Soviet Union because all were KGB informers. So, yes, I drove outside Moscow to Leningrad. So, yes, I did go to the Hermitage by car. And a few weeks later I was expelled from the Soviet Union.

Due to my smuggling, life had become bearable in Moscow, and I even enjoyed it on occasions when I was invited to the pub at the British Embassy to play darts. My only recreation in Moscow had been to establish good relations with the English diplomats and to be invited to their pub. I could go and play darts, read the English newspapers, and listen to Kim Philby, the famous traitor. He now was a Colonel of the KGB. Still, he was going every day to the English pub at the British Embassy to play darts and read the English newspaper and play the pools. He was not wearing a uniform. Of course, the British knew, but they were not making him stay away. He wanted to win Littlewoods, that is, the English football pools. Some people became millionaires playing pools. I asked him once, "If you win the money, what are you going to do with it? You can hardly go back to England to spend it."

We had conversations. He was an avowed Communist. He was both an avowed Communist, and like his father, a great admirer of the Arabs. His father, Sir John Philby, was one of the most ardent supporters of pan-Arabism among the foreign office functionaries. Sir John Philby was not a Communist, but the son became one, thanks to the professors of Cambridge. He was interesting. He knew he was a traitor, but even though he was now a Soviet citizen and a KGB colonel he still maintained his anglicity. He had no regret, he was an affirmed Communist, and he felt he had done humanity a service because Communism, in his opinion, was the solution of all human problems and the way to make our planet paradise. I'm sure he didn't particularly enjoy his life. That is why he spent most of it in the pub. He may have been a loyal ideologue, but his Englishness was still very strong. In 1963 Philby had defected to the Soviet Union, and in his 1968 book *My Silent War* he claimed to have been a double agent for the KGB, the Soviet spy agency, for nearly two decades. He lived the rest of his life in Russia, a recipient of the Order of Lenin and an official Soviet hero.

I didn't like his personality. I saw him like a human rat, or, actually, a rat in human form. In fact, I despised him, more so than did his English compatriots. I didn't agree with him that Communism was the solution, and I thought betraying England was a major offense. He was very friendly. He yearned for British company and the British environment provided at the pub of the British Embassy. We both had the same favorite football team: Chelsea. He was in his late fifties at the time. He died in 1988.

The British saw in him 'Lord Haw Haw' in red drab, like the traitor who was broadcasting every day from Berlin to England during the Second World War. The one most often identified as 'Lord Haw Haw' was William Joyce, the chief broadcaster used for broadcasts to Britain. The hard news presentations were quite accurate and often scooped the BBC in announcing important wartime events. The propaganda commentary was wickedly clever and aimed at demoralizing the British Home Front, and very anti-Semitic. Joyce was actually an American born in New York of Irish immigrant parents, but the family settled in England where Joyce was involved in British Fascist movements. He fled to Berlin in 1939 and offered his services to Joseph Goebbels as a propaganda radio broadcaster. He became the mainstay commentator for the Nazi Propaganda Ministry's Overseas Radio Broadcast Service. Joyce was captured by the Allies, tried as a war criminal, found guilty and hung in 1946.

The damage that Kim Philby did was not so much the information, the intelligence, that he transferred to Russia; the damage was that he put a wedge in the relationship between the CIA and the MI-5 to the extent that the Americans after that never trusted the British. Philby, as head of the British MI-5, compromised the CIA. The intelligence is ephemeral, it doesn't have long legs. It may do damage at a specific time, but it's not irreparable. What was, however, irreparable, was that it was at least fifty years before the Americans began trusting the British again.

Cambridge did a big damage to Britain. If people have sons, they should not send them to Cambridge. Harold 'Kim' Philby was the privileged son of a British diplomat. As a student at Cambridge in the 1930s,

Philby was drawn to Marxist ideas and was an associate of what came to be known as 'The Cambridge Spies,' Guy Burgess, Donald MacLean, and Anthony Blunt. Burgess, MacLean and Philby were apparently recruited in the 1930s to be Soviet spies, possibly by Blunt. In the 1940s they began working for British intelligence, and Philby rose in the ranks to be a respected member of the intelligence community. In 1951, under suspicion of being double agents, Burgess and MacLean disappeared, surfacing in Russia in 1956 as defectors. Philby was questioned and accused of being 'the Third Man,' the one who warned Burgess and MacLean to flee as investigations closed in, but he was never officially charged.

Kim Philby was quite vociferous in his harangue against the Greek military dictatorship. He said, "How could you, in Greece, have a military dictatorship?"

I reacted, "How could we not?" We have had a military dictatorship pretty much ever since we have existed. What better military dictatorship than Sparta? It lasted 900 years. I think Sparta still holds the world record. I can't imagine any other country that had an uninterrupted history under the same regime; possibly Japan comes close. The Spartan regime started in the year 880 before Christ. Even though the Romans never conquered Sparta, not even attempted to conquer it, it gradually declined; it became Christian, and it became part of the Byzantine Empire sometime in the year 350 AD, so from 800 BC till 350 AD there is more than nine centuries.

At the beginning of August 1968, Czechoslovakia, under Dubcek and the moderates—the so-called 'spring thawing'—was deviating from the Kremlin's directives and following a liberal and independent policy with opening to the West. Everybody was wondering and pondering how the Soviets would react if Dubcek continued with his defiance. One Friday morning, I was waiting at the Foreign Ministry in Athens for my diplomatic bag to be ready so I could catch a flight to Moscow early that afternoon. My immediate superior saw me waiting there and urged, "Come with me. We have a highest level conference in two minutes, and I want you with me."

I was honored to be taken to a conference presided over by the chief dictator, Colonel Papadopoulos. On the other hand, I felt a little out of my element. I was a simple courier, the lowest rank in the diplomatic service, and the room was filled with generals, admirals, and top mandarins of the various ministries. My supervisor introduced me as "our man in Moscow." I was their man because I had started in the diplomatic service after the military had taken over in Greece; therefore, I was loyal to the military dictatorship whereas the career diplomats were ambivalent or outright disloyal.

The subject of discussion was what would happen in Czechoslovakia, and how should Greece prepare for any contingency. Almost everyone present offered an opinion, and most of them agreed that the Soviet Union would not use military force to topple the disloyal regime of Dubcek. Only Colonel Papadopoulos and I had not said anything. He looked at me and said, "How do you see things, Mr. Panayotopoulos, from the insider's perspective?"

I said that although I spent more time in Moscow, it made me no insider. People outside Moscow were usually much better informed, and I had no access to anybody who worked for the Presidium or the Party Secretariat, or the KGB. "However," I went on, "one does not need to be in the Kremlin having tea or vodka with Leonid Brezhnev to know and expect that within days, if not hours, the Soviet tanks will start rolling in the streets of Prague." That burst in the room like an explosion. Everyone disagreed with me. Everyone, that is, except the prime minister, who said nothing.

"This is not 1956," one of the generals said, "when the Soviets occupied Hungary and drowned the rebellion with blood."

"Yes," I agreed with him, "In 1956 the Soviet Union was much weaker than she is today. Now she has parity in nuclear arms with the United States, she has dozens of nuclear submarines armed with ballistic missiles that can reach any target in the world, she has the S-20 medium range nuclear missiles in Europe, to which we have no counter measure, and she has ten thousand tanks more than NATO in Germany, alone. Who is to stop her if she decides to invade Czechoslovakia tomorrow?" Not only did they disagree with me but were abusive and questioned my qualifications to be there in the first place. I told them, "If the Soviet Union were to allow her satellites to defy her, then the whole Soviet Empire would unravel."

They declared that I was an idiot. There was shouting and disorder, at which point the prime minister stood up and said, "Thank you, gentlemen. That will be all." He looked at me, smiled, and left.

"I should have known better than take you with me!" My supervisor was very mad at me. "Now you made a fool of me. How dare you disagree with generals and political analysts who have been in government for twenty years?" He dismissed me, and I thought I would be fired.

I had missed the flight to Moscow, so I decided to spend a quiet weekend with my wife and our roses and chinchillas. It was past midnight on Sunday when my phone rang. On the other end of the line was my supervisor at the ministry. "Have you heard the news?" he asked. "As we speak, the Soviet tanks have invaded Czechoslovakia from all her borders and are rolling into Prague with no resistance."

I had also predicted, during that conference, that unlike the East Germans in 1953, or the Hungarians in 1956, the Czechs would not fight. My supervisor was very humbled and apologetic. I could tell by his voice that he felt very ill at ease. "The Prime Minister telephoned me a few minutes ago," he said, "and ordered me to call you and offer you any post you want. He also ordered that you be promoted to first embassy secretary." That was quite a promotion. It compares from second lieutenant to colonel, three full ranks. And, from $550 a month to $1,000. "Where would you like to go?" My answer was London.

"I have a request that I would like you to consider," he ventured. "I need someone with your talent, intelligence, and knowledge to take over the Press and Information Department at our embassy in Bonn. I know it is *un post du combat*" —that is diplomatic jargon for a post that requires some work and is in trouble— "and it might turn dangerous. But I need to send my best man there. If you accept, I promise you that I shall assist you to the best of my ability. The center will be at your disposition. I will also send three of our top German-speaking attachés to serve under you."

I couldn't resist the aside, "How, from being an impertinent idiot forty-eight hours ago, have I become our best man? If you are so shallow in your judgments, don't you think you should resign for the good of the service?" He was more gracious than I. He said he was sorry, and he said that I wouldn't regret taking the post.

CHAPTER **26**

Bonn, *un post du combat*

THE *POST DU combat* that I had been asked to take in 1968 was the Press and Information Department at our embassy in Bonn. It was well known in the circles of the Foreign Affairs Ministry in Athens that the *Presseabteilung,* the press department of our embassy in Bonn was a career killer. Everyone had heard of Fraulein Fausten and how she ate the various press attaches for breakfast and spat their bones. The most recent fellow who had been the *Presserat* in our Embassy was a good acquaintance of mine and he was describing Fausten as a two-legged monster straight out of hell. I knew it would be a challenge.

There was not a single German newspaper, magazine or radio or television station that was not inimical to our form of government. Once the Germans learned 'democracy' they were determined to prove what good democrats they had become by demonizing the Greek military junta. In reality, we were anti-communist, but truly apolitical. We implemented programs and policies that were from the extreme left to the extreme right and everything in between. All workers in Greece were given a fifteen percent raise in wages and any increase in prices would be punished by imprisonment or worse. You cannot imagine how beautiful it is to govern under martial law and eliminate bureaucracy, graft, corruption, and incompetence.

I accepted the post in Bonn and knew that truth was on my side. It was up to the Germans to remove the *scheuklappen* of democracy and judge Greece and her Colonels by what they were accomplishing, not what they were falsely accused of being. The military dictatorship had certain plans that it wanted to implement. Even though we were accused of being Fascists, or of being extreme radical right wingers, in essence, and in actual fact, we had no ideology other than what to do to improve Greece's economy and the lot of the Greek people. One thing that Colonel

Papadopoulos and his immediate entourage had in mind was to electrify the whole of Greece. There were thousands of villages in Greece that didn't have electricity and the only source of water was the communal well. Sometimes in order to have water you need electricity to operate pumps. So, the first task was the electrification of the country.

Concomitant to the electrification of the country, Colonel Papadopoulos invited to a conference all the industrialists of Greece, in other words everybody who employed a hundred or more workers. I was among the ones who participated in that conference. I had not as yet joined the government. He told the industrialists, paraphrasing, "Gentlemen, a Damocles sword is suspended over your heads. I want a fifteen percent increase in pay for all workers of Greece, and I do not want to see any kind of increase in price." Yes, we were a police state, and yes, we could regulate price anyway we pleased.

The industrialists said, paraphrasing, "This is impossible, we can't do it." They suggested, "How about eight percent now and the other seven percent next year?" And Papadopoulos agreed to that. This was the first time in many years that workers obtained an increase in pay that was not eaten up by an automatic increase in prices. Until then, if the workers got, say a ten percent increase in pay, prices next day went up twelve per cent, which means they were poorer than before they got the raise. This time it worked, and Papadopoulos became the saint and savior of the masses of the Greek proletariat. That meant that the Communists were losing their base and Papadopoulos was gaining it.

The electrification of the country was implemented immediately and was accomplished within less than a year. By providing each and every village in Greece with running water, he became also the saint and savior of all the Greek farmers and all the Greek peasants. The next thing he did was to appropriate monastery and ecclesiastical lands, and he gave it to the landless peasants who were working them. The church didn't like that of course, but the peasants did.

We were definitely staunch anti-communists. All the Communists of Greece, that is, all the actual members, card-carrying members of the Communist party, about 12,000 of them, were confined in the worst islands of Greece which are not frequented by tourists. And the cadre of the Communist party was in jail, another, perhaps 8,000.

However, we did the best possible deal with the Soviet Union. At the time oil prices were fluctuating, and Greece had a terrible deficit in the balance of trade primarily caused by the importation of petroleum. Greece, under Colonel Papadopoulos made a deal with the Soviet Union whereby the Soviet Union would provide us with forty percent of our needs in petroleum in exchange for tobacco, lemons, and oranges. We exported to the Soviet Union the lemons and the oranges which had been rejected by Germany, and the third quality tobacco that not even Japan would buy. The remaining sixty percent of Greece's needs were covered by Colonel Moammar Khadafi, the dictator of Libya.

The Dictator of Libya, Colonel Khadafi, is a graduate of the Athens Military Academy. He served two years in the Greek army as a lieutenant, because that was his obligation for having studied for free in the Greek Academy. Khadafi never stopped being a friend of Greece. Our military regime made a deal with him, and he sold us oil at a fixed price and not for money, but for ware. Most of the ware that was going to Libya was plastic containers and plastic sheets, in other words, things that Greece could produce abundantly without high cost.

I met Colonel Khadafi while he was still a cadet. There is a spa in Greece called Kamena Vourla, which means 'the burnt bushes.' In that spa, which is about two hundred kilometers northwest of Athens, it is alleged that the water coming from a natural fountain there is radioactive. Whether it is or not, many people, thousands of people, believe that that water has healing qualities, and they flock to bathe or to drink the water. One who believed that was my father, and he used to go for at least fifteen days to spend in the water, drink the water, and swim in that water, in hope that it would reduce his suffering of arthritis. Another customer in that spa was Mohammad Idris al-Sanousi, King Idris I of Libya. He was the first leader of an independent Libya and headed a federal monarchy as chief of state. My father and King Idris became cronies and friends, and they used to play backgammon together.

One Sunday I was in Kamena Vourla visiting my father and watching him play backgammon with the king. The king was a typical Arab, wearing what looked like a caftan—a *jellabiya*—and a headscarf—a *keffiyeh*, the traditional Arab headdress of a square of cloth folded and wrapped—and he was a nice fellow. He spoke fluent Italian and some French, so he could communicate with my father. While they were playing backgammon, out in the open, we saw a cadet approaching, a cadet of the Military Academy of Athens. The uniform is dark blue with a lot of yellow trimming. And as the cadet was approaching, the face of King Idris had a subliminal look, and when the cadet came near, my father and I were also impressed because he had three stripes, meaning he was top of his class. King Idris stood up and embraced the man, and the man kissed his hand. King Idris told my father, in French, "This is the pride of my country. This boy is one of your best cadets." My father, of course, being a general, was quite impressed that an Arab was top of his class.

Moammar Khadafi obviously proved to be an ingrate. After he returned to Libya, three years later, he was automatically promoted to lieutenant colonel. Within weeks of his return to Libya, he and another group of officers deposed the king, who was his benefactor, and took over as dictator of Libya. King Idris lived in exile in Egypt till his death years later. Khadafi's first move was to eject the Americans from Wheelus Air Base in Tripoli and offer it to the Soviets.

In Greece, the deficit in the balance of trade was almost eliminated. The remittances of the merchant marine increased, and tourism took off like an avalanche, or a rocket. Which meant that Greece needed more beds. The military regime then made a policy that any citizen or any corporation, who had a waterfront property and wished to build a hotel on it, may do so with the money advanced by the Greek tourist organization at five percent interest. So, all of a sudden, Greece had thousands of Xenia hotels all over the place, and tourism, from 168,000 tourists, increased to a couple of million, and the economy thrived. In fact, we have a record during the three first years of the Papadopoulos military regime in Greece, which is only touched but not surpassed by South Korea. We had an eleven per cent annual increase for the years 1968, 1969 and 1970. No government, as yet, has come close to that. There were a number of works of infrastructure also implemented, among them, the road system of Greece, which was modernized and improved.

Greece had the largest merchant navy on earth, however, in 1967, even though Greeks owned 36,000,000 tons of shipping, only 7,500,000 tons of that shipping were flying the Greek flag. The rest, if they were tankers, flew the Liberian flag or other flags of convenience, like Panama, Honduras, Lebanon, or others, thus avoiding tax. The inventor of the 'flag of convenience' was Aristotle Onassis. He was the first one to fly the Panama flag, when Panama was neutral in World War II, in hope that the German submarines would not sink those ships.

Colonel Papadopoulos invited all the Greek ship owners to come to a conference in Piraeus. There they came, all of them, or almost all of them. I was present in that conference as an associate of Papadopoulos, not as a ship owner. At that time my family no longer owned ships, except two carriers which were serviced by Tidal Marine, a fraudulent company established in New York by my cousin Micky. Paraphrasing Colonel Papadopoulos, he began, "Gentlemen, what is it that I can do to entice you to change from Liberia, or Panama, or Honduras, or Lebanon, to the Greek flag?"

They answered, "We don't want to be subjected to the demands of the seaman's union."

"Fine, we can do that. What else?" he questioned.

They went on, "We want shipyards, which we don't have in Greece. We want credit, which we don't get in Greece. And we want telecommunications like the ones we have in London or in New York, which we don't have in Greece."

So, Papadopoulos said, "If I get you the shipyards, and if I get you the credit, and if I get you the telecommunications that you want, will you switch to the Greek flag?" And they acquiesced, "Yes." He finished, "It will be done. Is there anything else I can do that will entice you?"

And one of them insolently spoke up, "How about you dropping your pants and let me at you?" Papadopoulos responded, "I would do that, too, if you are going to bring all your ships to the Greek flag."

Even before I assumed the post at the Greek Embassy in Bonn in 1968, I knew that much of my success or failure would depend on how I got along with Vilna Fausten, the *Presseabteilung,* the chief secretary. Fraulein Fausten was a native of Koeningsberg and had a degree in *Germanistik* and mathematics from Göttingen. She had been in the same semester with our First Ambassador to West Germany, Alex Kyrou, who hired her the moment we opened our embassy in Bonn. She was in charge of all accounting in the embassy and was drafting most of the *'notes verbales'* to the *Auswertiges Amt*. She was the right hand of the ambassador and an indispensable member of his inner staff. When various directors of the *Presseabtellung* mismanaged or outright stole funds which were meant to use to 'influence' German journalists, the ambassador put her in charge of the day-to-day operation of the *Abteilung*.

She was a small, thin spinster that looked more like a schoolteacher than the *eminence grise* of the Greek Embassy. She did, however, have a very strong, forceful personality and could not tolerate incompetence or stupidity. She was apolitical and I never discovered how she voted. She was not a crypto-Nazi nor a left winger, but she was a real German who resented the partition of her country and hoped one day to walk under the Brandenburg Tor, the Brandenburg Gate, symbol of Berlin. Having lived most of her adult life in Bonn, she knew a lot of influential people. Frau Dr. Mildred Mendes, the wife of the third-party leader was her personal friend, as were many *abgeordenten*. She definitely was an asset to the embassy and to the ambassador. Almost all of my predecessors had tried to have her fired, but she was immovable like the Rock of Gibraltar.

Though I was quite charming and handsome that many years ago, and most women noticed me, I was told that Fraulein Fausten was not susceptible to such advances. The ones who had tried that lived to regret it. On the day I entered the *Presseabteilund* of our embassy to assume my post as the new director, I wore a blue blazer, gray flannels, and my regimental tie—the Argyll and Sutherland Highlanders. I think in all modesty, that I looked much better than Sean Connery or Cary Grant. Fraulein Fausten greeted me with reserved civility, and she was not the least impressed by my thick Austrian accent. Quite the contrary. In my attempt to break the ice, I asked her what was the meaning or significance of her name: Vilna. She said she was born the day that Vilna fell in World War I and her father was so enthused by the German victory over the Russians, that he named her after the city. *"Ober Sie schauen goar kein so alt gnaediges Fraulein,"* was my instant response.

"You know when Vilna fell?" was her astonished question. *"Gewiss. Es war der 17te September 1915, and und ich haete Sie niemals fuer 53 geshaetzt."* Vilna was a town in Russian Lithuania, known today as Vilnius, the capital of Lithuania. It was captured by German forces in September 1915 and occupied until the end of World War I when Bolshevik forces moved in to establish the Soviet Republic of Lithuania. Vilna was then seized by Poland in 1920 and was not returned to Soviet Lithuania until 1939.

After that, Fausten became a devoted and loyal member of my staff. She was also a snob and relished the fact that I was married to a *K & K Fuerstin,* a princess. She loved spending time with *Durchlaucht,* which is a title for royal personages. It is not true that history is useless. Or that titles mean nothing.

It was the first week of January 1969. In Berlin in the first week of January, they celebrated what was called the *Grunne Woche*, which is the Green Week. It is a one-week international agricultural fair where the various countries display their agricultural ware. I was freshly transferred from Moscow to Bonn and that was my first assignment away from the home base. Because the *Grunne Woche* seemed to be very important, most of the embassy personnel were there, including the ambassador. Many of the consul generals of Greece had assembled at the Greek Pavilion, where Greece was displaying early tomatoes, early potatoes, and grapes and the like. Our next-door neighbor at the fair, next to our pavilion, was the Iranian Pavilion. The Iranian Pavilion had a huge picture, like a poster, of the shah and his wife. Little did I know, because I hadn't kept current with what was happening in Persia, I didn't know that the Persian students hated their shah. The huge photograph became a target for many of the Greek tomatoes picked up on their way.

Our consul general in Berlin was a snobbish man, and he didn't know me. He had heard that I was the man of the military dictatorship, and that

I had just been transferred from Moscow. He threw a party for the Bonn visitors and failed deliberately to invite me. I was a little sad that I had not been invited, but, I thought, I will go and surprise my aunt whom I hadn't seen for at least twenty-five years. I knew she was in Berlin with her husband, Tofin, who was the French Minister. My aunt Raymmonde was another Princess de Polignac—one of the sisters who didn't marry a Panayotopoulos. I took a taxi and asked him to take me to the French Embassy in Berlin. To my surprise, it was a little palace on the outskirts of Berlin.

The French guard outside asked me what I wanted, and I told him I was a nephew of Madame Tofin, so he called. Madame Tofin was also having a dinner party, for the French journalists who were in Berlin to cover the Green Week, as France was also one of the exhibitors there. France was a major agricultural country and had the biggest pavilion. Permission was granted for me to enter, and my aunt Raymmonde was delighted to see me, especially since she hadn't seen me since the late 1940s, at least twenty-five years, when I was still a teenager.

"I see your family tradition is being propagated," she observed. "Your father was a military attaché serving a military dictatorship, and now you are a press attaché serving a dictatorship. Why are you not at the party of your consul? He invited us, but we do not go to functions of the dictatorship."

"I was not invited."

"Well! If he didn't invite you because he doesn't know who you are, we'll give him a good lesson!" When her party was over, and she made sure that her party would be over quickly, she took an official French Citroen of the embassy, with French flags flying, and with two French motorcyclists driving in front, she drove me to the Greek consulate in West Berlin. The Consul was alarmed when he heard that a car from the French Embassy had arrived, so he anxiously stepped out. My aunt told him, "I brought my nephew." That fellow did not snub me anymore.

CHAPTER **27**

Six Months Ago, She Was a Man

WHEN THE *GRUNNE Woche* was over, I met with my friend Michael Kakaras, who was our commercial attaché in Hamburg. He was a very old hand in Germany and had been in Germany for at least twelve years in the same position. He was a boyhood friend of mine and a perennial joker.

"Michael," I said, "I am not familiar with Berlin. Where can I go have some good time and enjoy a woman?"

He suggested a place, and assured me, "Michael, you will love it."

"Are you going?" I asked.

"No," he replied, "I have to go back to Hamburg."

So, I was on my own. I went to the suggested place, which was very crowded. If you dropped an apple, it wouldn't hit the floor. But, to my disappointment and surprise, everybody I saw there among the clientele were males. There was no room on the dancing floor, there was no room anywhere. So, I stood at the bar. The bartender was a buxomy, typical German woman, wearing a folkloric dirndl. I ordered a drink. Someone who was obviously homosexual and on drugs, was on the stage, entertaining and telling jokes. Berlin was possibly the only town in Germany where there is a semblance of humor, opposed to any other part of Germany which was totally humorless. He was telling Berliner political jokes which were quite funny. He, or she, was making particular fun of the then-Minister of Defense of Germany whose name was Strauss, and *'strauss'* means 'ostrich.' He, or she, was making a joke about the Defense Minister's guts, or courage, and comparing it to *'Strauss Eier'* which translates to 'ostrich eggs,' which an American could understand as 'balls.'

As I was standing there sipping my drink, I feel the presence behind me of someone quite acceptable. I turn around and there is a breathtakingly beautiful woman who was at least two inches taller than I. All my life I have been fantasizing or imagining about finding a very tall woman who wouldn't be gangly or ungraceful, and this one was definitely the epitome of my wildest fantasy. She saw me looking at her, almost mesmerized, and she said, "Is there anything wrong?"

"No," I said, "I just don't believe my eyes. I never suspected that you existed in reality."

She smiled, "I do exist, and I am one of the featured stars of the show. I sing here, and because I am so tall, they call me 'Eiffel Tower.' Do you want me to join you for a drink?"

"By all means, please." She stood next to me and ordered something.

After the drag queen had finished the jokes, the next number was a strip tease. There was a nubile blond, perfectly shaped, rather short, who did a strip tease and stripped everything. The 'Eiffel Tower' turned to me and said, "Who would believe that that was a boy only six months ago?"

I asked, "What do you mean?"

"Six months ago, she underwent the final operation." Then, because of my puzzlement, she said, "Apparently you don't know where you are."

"Well, where am I?"

"This is the nightclub of the transvestites," she said. "Everybody you see here used to be a man at one time or another."

Incredulously, I said, "Do you mean to tell me that you were a man?"

She smiled, "Actually, I am still technically a man."

"What about that buxomy bartender?" I pursued.

"She was also a man."

I don't know whether I was disappointed or not, but I thought to myself that I should find more out about transvestites. After the Eiffel Tower finished her song—she was singing in a very pleasant contralto voice—she joined me again. Meanwhile, some of the patrons had left so there was more room. We sat at a table, and first thing, she educated me about the operations performed only in Casablanca by one French surgeon, a gynecologist, Dr. Georges Burou. He had been removed from the medical profession in France because. his methods were considered illicit or illegal. She took a glove—after all it was January in Berlin—and she put her finger inside, and described, "That is, in essence, the operation that Dr. Burou performs. It eliminates the male sexual organ and turns it into a very small vagina. But I dread to take that operation because then I'll be rendered a total neutral. Dr. Burou, as yet, has not perfected his technique to create a clitoris, and without one you lose all sensational sex. So, I will not go and have the operation." She explained that, preceding the operation, there is hormone therapy which lasts between one to three years. There is of course, the castration, and the intake of a lot of female hormones whereby breasts start popping out and the fat concentration goes where it's supposed to go with females, so they all look perfect females.

After the establishment closed, she announced, "Now, if you want, you can come to our club. It is private, where only transvestites and their friends go." The one where we were was public. I thought, *I spent all my time with that Eiffel Tower, we'll see what the rest of the night has in store.*

I left with her, and we went, very near the Berlin Wall, into a building which was still a ruin. We descended some stone steps, and there was a big double oak door. We knocked on the door, and in the speakeasy way, a little window was opened, and we were admitted. We descended more steps, and there was a huge rectangular hall with tables. There was music which was extremely loud, and it played rock and roll. A few projectors were projecting various movies—one of which, strangely, was *Gone with the Wind*.

With the combination of so many movies being projected all at once and that horrible rock and roll, plus the constant change of light, I was not particularly happy being in that nightclub. The drinks were served even before I ordered one. I was thirsty, and I think the drink that I was served was a Gin Fizz. After I had a few gulps of my drink something very peculiar happened to me. Instead of seeing the movies projected, I would see green and yellow stripes on the wall, increasing and decreasing in height according to the volume of the music. But it was not the music that was being played, which was the unpleasant rock and roll, but the music that was in my head: Beethoven's *Fifth Symphony*. When in my head it went, 'dah, dah, dah, dun,' the yellows would go up and the greens would go down. Then when it would go 'da da da dun, da da da dun, da dun,' the greens would go up and the yellows down. It was a dancing of the green and yellow stripes according to the rhythm of Beethoven's Fifth. While still enjoying Beethoven's Fifth and looking at the display of green and yellow stripes, I could also consciously hear the rock and roll but not at the intense volume, and get some idea that films were still projected.

I suppose that the second stage of the 'trip' was seeing my life. It started with an excruciating pain that I felt on my neck, and that was the instrument that physicians use to pull you out: forceps. I felt the pain, I saw my birth. It went on, and things that I had forgotten or suppressed from my memory came to the fore, with the accompanying pain. I also saw the pleasant parts of my life, but it was mostly episodes or instances that I had either forgotten or deliberately suppressed from my memory.

When the influence of the LSD—because that's what was causing it—was starting to dissipate, I found myself on the steps banging on the door, but I have no conscious memory of ever having stood up from where I was sitting, or walking across that hall or climbing the steps to reach that door. While I was there banging on that door, I came to my full senses and again heard that ghastly cacophony of the rock and roll. The Eiffel Tower was next to me, and she said, "Well, did you enjoy your trip?"

"It took me unaware because I had no idea."

She responded, "That was the intention, because if you are aware of it, it might not work."

Looking at my whole life as if it were a kaleidoscope was not a bad experience, but I wouldn't want to have it again.

Next, we went to her apartment, and truly she was still a male. But we have a saying in Greece, actually a joke, that someone, instead of being served feta cheese was served a cake of soap that looked like feta, and when he put it in his mouth he started foaming. But he had paid for the feta cheese, and he said, "Foam or no foam, I paid my money, I am going to eat it." So, I thought, *male or not male, I spent all my time with that creature, and I am going to take full advantage of it*. That was two firsts in my life: having LSD and experiencing the 'trip,' which is a trip of your whole life, and sex with a transvestite. I was thirty-five years old, and I was married. That doesn't count as infidelity; it is a one-night stand, a fling, and not even a woman.

Years later, in America, I met a transvestite who had undergone the operation of Dr. Burou in Casablanca and had a clitoris.

Berlin had a French patina. It derived from its most famous king, the flute-playing Frederick the Great, who was a homosexual. When he became King of Prussia, Berlin was just a town in the little periphery called Brandenburg. When he died, Prussia was a major European power, thus the name 'Frederick the Great.' Frederick the Great befriended Voltaire—in fact two famous monarchs befriended Voltaire. One was Fredrick the Great, and the other one was his niece, Catherine, Empress of all Russias. Frederick would speak only French. He resented the German language. He thought it was vulgar and not meant for gentlemen to speak, so in all his life he spoke only French.

The few occasions when he spoke German are so small a number that they are easy to repeat. The first time that he used the German, at least to more than one person, was when 7,000 Prussians were bivouacked facing 70,000 Russians, and Frederick had given orders to the generals that next day they should attack. Before dawn the generals dared to go and confront their king. They said, in German of course, because most of the German generals couldn't speak French, "Majesty, we think it would not be opportune for us to attack, considering that we are outnumbered ten to one."

Frederick looked at them and he said, *"Meine herren..."* translated to, "Gentlemen, do not think. Leave the thinking to the horses which have a bigger head than you." Then he ordered that a pyramid of drums be made so that he could climb on it and address the troops. The troops assembled around their king who was also their field marshal, and he said, "Hunde ...., Dogs, do you want to live forever?" I suppose it can only take Prussians to be enthused with this admonition, so his troops attacked the Russians, and were victorious.

Another time it has been recorded that Frederick the Great spoke German, was after he was so successful in all the wars in which Prussia took part, usually with the English as her ally. Frederick, now in his sixties, decided to build an exemplary palace for himself in the suburb of Potsdam. He called it *Sans Souci* which means 'without worries.' He gave orders how he wanted it to be built. He wanted the gardens to be a facsimile of the gardens that King Charles II had built, for which George Frederic Handel wrote the *Water Music*. He wanted the gardens to be English gardens, and he wanted the palace to be more or less French rococo. He gave minute details how he wanted it to be landscaped. When it was built according to his demand, he took a tour of *Sans Souci*. That area is watered by the Spree River. The Spree River is quite winding and there was a little peninsula, a promontory, on the riverbank where Frederick saw a water mill to grind grain. It was an offense to his eyesight. It was absolutely against anything he had wanted for his country estate. He asked, in German, "What is that mill doing there?"

His factotum said, "We are sorry, Your Majesty, but the miller was not willing to sell."

Frederick commanded, "Bring that miller here,"

In front of him, all of them riding on horses while inspecting the grounds, they brought the miller. Frederick looked at the miller and said, "Erbbetielt.... He orders you—" because royalty doesn't use the first person— "He orders you to sell the mill and disappear from here."

The very typical Prussian miller looked at his king and said, *"Majestat...* Your Majesty, there are courts of law in Berlin."

Indeed, there were, and those courts of law dispensed justice in the name of the king, but Frederick was so taken aback by the audacity of his subject that he said, "Let it be." That mill stood there until 1961. In 1961, before they built the Wall in Berlin, they demolished the mill. When tourists were taken to Potsdam, in East Germany then, and the episode was explained—how a lowly miller defied his king and threatened to sue him—it just was inconsistent with Communist theory. Rather than tell the story, they chose to demolish the mill. The mill does not exist anymore.

Catherine the Great was worshiped in Greece. We were always hoping that the Russians would liberate us from the Turks. Catherine the Great did make quite an effort to destroy the Ottoman Empire. All the Turkish areas which today are independent little countries, became Soviet Republics, like Azerbaijan, Uzbekistan, Tajikistan, Turkmenistan., Kyrgyzstan, and Kazakhstan. All that was Turkish and part of the Ottoman Empire. Catherine the Great distanced Russia from the Ottoman Empire, and she wanted to demolish the Ottoman Empire. We Greeks hoped that she would give us our fair share. Among her multitude of lovers, Catherine the Great had John Paul Jones, the American hero. She made him also an Admiral of the Russian Navy.

But Great Britain had objections to the demolition of the Ottoman Empire because that would mean access for the Russians to the Mediterranean. The mainstay of British policy was to keep the Russians out of the 'warm seas,' a policy that Britain pursued without deviation for the better part of 200 years. Only when Britain was succeeded by her niece, the United States, did the Soviets have fleets all over the world. As long as Britain ruled the waves there were no Russian ships in the Indian Ocean, or in the Atlantic Ocean, or in the Pacific Ocean.

CHAPTER **28**

Phryne and the Playmate of the Month

EARLY IN 1970, there seemed to be an international monetary crisis and some currencies were being realigned against the dollar, and my 4,000 *deutschmarks*—my $1,000—monthly salary was down to 3,780 DM, making my budget more complicated than before. That was on my mind when the telephone rang, and the American on the other end of the line identified himself as the managing editor of *Stars and Stripes,* a publication that serves the American armed forces. His name was Tom. He volunteered that his paper was read by over a quarter million American servicemen in Germany and elsewhere in the world, and that it was printed in Frankfurt. That made it a German paper and therefore within the realm of my responsibility as the press attaché of the Greek Embassy in Bonn.

He then asked me if I read *Playboy* magazine. The regime I served had banned *Playboy* from Greece because of its alleged pornographic content, but I had transferred my subscription to my German address in Bad Godesberg and I continued to enjoy the entertaining magazine in spite of the official *verbot*. I told him I had been a subscriber since 1960 and that pleased him.

"Then you must know who Gloria Root is," he said. I did. She was the December 1969 Playmate of the Month, and I had amply salivated looking at her centerfold—my ten years of absolute fidelity to my wife were approaching their end. "Do you know where Gloria Root is right now?"

"How should I know?"

"She is rotting in a Greek jail in Athens," he complained. "What can you do about it?"

"What do you expect me to do? I am a Greek diplomat in Germany. Not a jailer or policeman in Athens. It has nothing to do with the Ministry of Foreign Affairs."

"A quarter million of our readers have voted her 'Playmate of the Year,' and they will be very disappointed if she remains incarcerated in Greece. You get too much bad press all over the world, do you want to add *Stars and Stripes* among your critics?" he cautioned.

"What can a press attaché do on a matter that belongs to the jurisdiction of the Justice Department?" I tried to explain to Tom. It was absurd, almost comic, but he was adamant in his insistence that I should do everything possible to free Gloria Root—she was called 'Babs,' maybe because of the boobs.

As a matter of routine, I made a report of my conversation with the Chief Editor of *Stars and Stripes* to my superiors in Athens and asked them to try to intervene with the appropriate authorities to see if there were any possibilities for the release of Gloria Root. The response I received was a total rebuke and mild reprimand, reminding me that we do not involve ourselves in other people's business. They didn't even tell me what the charges were. Meanwhile, Tom kept calling me every day and threatening me with anti-Greek editorials about the military dictatorship in Greece.

As a holdover of the negotiations with Germany for World War II reparations, we had a legal attaché at the Embassy—a true sinecure of the previous 'democratic' regimes—who had nothing, absolutely nothing, to do all day, but had been collecting a salary the same as mine for nearly twenty years. He was afraid that I might have him fired, because I was a true representative of the military dictatorship and not a diplomat of the old school. I had the advantage of his fear, and he was inviting me to bridge games at his house, and he and his wife were good bridge players, and knew everybody in Bonn.

I decided to put him to work for a change. When I went to his office to consult him about the Gloria Root matter, he was solving a crossword puzzle in one of the German magazines. He flushed with embarrassment and tried to conceal the magazine. "Relax," I told him, "My visit is for business. I want you to communicate with the Ministry of Justice in Athens and find out everything pertaining to the American, Gloria Root, and her incarceration. Next, I want you to research to determine if our jurisprudence acknowledged precedents, and how far back we can go."

Through him I learned that Gloria Root had been arrested at the Greek-Turkish border two months ago carrying fifty-six pounds, enough hashish and marijuana to be designated as commercial quantities: That means smuggling of drugs, which was a serious offense in Greece, especially under martial law. The penalty was at least sixteen years in prison, no parole, and no plea bargaining. Justice in Greece at the time was dispensed by court martial—military tribunals. Gloria Root's future looked very bleak.

As for precedent, Greece had only been an independent and sovereign nation since 1830, and we had cases going back to the 1860s that had been adjudicated accordingly. That helped. Only, the precedent I wanted to use went back to 358 B.C.

In that year, the *hetaera* Phryne was accused of being a spy of Philip, King of Macedonia and father of Alexander the Great. Athens and Macedonia were enemies, and the gold, silver, and lead mines that Athens had in her colonies in Macedonia were in peril. Because Phryne was a famous and most remarkable woman, her case of high treason was scheduled to be heard at the highest court of Athens, the Areios Pagos—this is the name of the court in which the Apostle Paul converted his first prominent gentile, the Areopagite Dionysus, who was eventually beheaded in Paris and became the patron saint of France: Saint Dennis. The evidence that Phryne had committed treason was irrefutable. The penalty was death. Her very able lawyer, Hypereides, knew that no argument could possibly save her. So, he decided to go outside the law and appeal to the love of beauty for which Athenians were famous all over Hellas. He brought Phryne to the center of the court and disrobed her. There she stood, completely nude, in front of the high judges of Athens. "Yes, men of Athens," Hypereides began his plea, "I freely admit that my client did commit treason, and I know that the rightful penalty is death. But can you, men of Athens, destroy such beauty standing in front of you? Is her ephemeral act of treason really worth the sacrilege of snuffing away such rare beauty? Will Athens be vindicated or mournful by killing her beauty?" The Athenians acquitted her.

In my final report, I took the risk to go over the heads of my superiors, a risk that might have me discharged, or worse, and I sent it directly to Colonel Papadopoulos. I made a plea that if we Athenians could forgive treason to save beauty, couldn't we show the same magnanimity to an American beauty who had only brought illegal drugs into the country and never had a chance sell or use them—nothing compared to treason—and prevent the waste of her beauty in a Greek jail? It worked. The colonel issued the necessary orders, and she was extradited from Greece, never allowed to return. He wrote me a personal note thanking me for bringing the matter to his attention, saying how pleased he was to be able to emulate the example of our ancestors.

Stars and Stripes threw a big party for her in Frankfurt, and I was, of course, the guest of honor. I was introduced to 'Babs' as her savior, but she was—unlike Phryne—a dumb, ignorant, banal, and uneducated American sometime-redhead with big breasts. She felt compelled to show her gratitude by going to bed with me. I was not really attracted to her, but the idea of copulating a Playboy centerfold enticed me. An inflatable doll would have been better—it was like sex with a piece of wood that could breathe.

Still, I consider my role in her release as one of my major accomplishments in my time as a diplomat.

A newspaper depicts 1969 December Playmate of the Month, Gloria Root, leaving a Greek jail for transporting 36 pounds of heroin. Manipulating a 358 BC Greek court precedent concerning Phryne, another famous nude, I got her out.

Playboy forbids seeing Gloria.

Phryne

Helmut Schmidt, German Chancellor, and Minister of Defense, to whom I owe my Order of Merit, Germany's highest honor bestowed upon a civilian, and the only Greek.

CHAPTER **29**

Emery, Whips and Education

I WAS ATTEMPTING, while at the embassy in Bonn-Bad Godesberg, to sell emery for the building of the new *autobahnen*. A very attractive woman, Christine von Schuetzenberg, was the final authority on the decision whether they would use emery or not. Not only was it a patriotic duty to promote a national product, I stood personally to make a commission since my family owned the emery quarries in Naxos.

Christine von Schuetzenberg was Hitler's dream of the ideal Germanic woman: blond, about 1 meter 70, with a wide pelvis and very *zaftig*. Almost Junoesque. She was at the time twenty-nine years old and had a doctoral degree from Darmstadt and held a position at the university. The only negative thing in her appearance were her cold gray eyes, and her lips were rather thin. Obviously, since the adoption of emery depended on her, I poured the charm by the gallon. She was interested in me, but not truly attracted. I was thirty-five at the time, in perfect health, with a good position and lots of money.

She would go out with me in Bonn, or in Koeln or in Darmstadt, and once we met in Osnabruck. But she would not let me kiss or touch her. Gradually, she told me that she felt only contempt for the entire masculine human race and that she had no sexual interest or desire for any man. She had been briefly married but did not discuss any details and I did not pry. After we had known each other for six months, and we were, on her suggestion, *per du*, I ventured to ask her if she were lesbian. She said, not really, but it did not disgust her if a woman kissed her. Later, I asked why she spent so much time in Stuttgart. Eventually, she told me that in order to keep her mother, the Frau Graeffin, in style, she needed more money than her salary would allow. In Stuttgart, she had a number of clients with perverted tastes that would supplement her income. This was, of course, a secret, and if known it would jeopardize her position at the university.

The more she rejected my advances, the more infatuated I was becoming, and very frustrated.

I had a lot of business in Stuttgart and Nuremberg where I was attempting to put Greek newsreels into movie houses frequented by Greeks, and Schickedanz, the owner of the Quelle and the Kaufhof, was our honorary general consul. One night, unknown to Christi, I followed her in Stuttgart, to her place of business. She was surprised, and very angry at my intrusion into her secret abode. It was a barren, windowless, cold room with a bathroom and a small closet. The only furniture was a bed with a nylon cover, no pillows or blankets or sheets, and a small coffee table with a metronome to tell how much time had passed. On the walls were all kinds of whips, shackles, and other instruments of torture. The floor was covered with a thick nylon sheet.

After she screamed at me for violating her privacy, and attempted to strike me, I was about to leave, and forget about the emery. But, as I opened the door, she called me back, then she put her hands around my neck, and kissed me on the mouth. She took off her clothes and, stark naked, went and lay on the bed without saying a word. She had very smooth, velvety skin and one of the best pair of breasts I had ever seen. Top Playboy material. Her body was firm, almost muscular. Had she been made of stone, it would not have made any difference. She lay there on the bed with a totally expressionless face and no movement or reaction or sound. It was like copulating with a corpse that still barely breathed. No matter how hard I tried, I could get no reaction out of her. I had never been so hopelessly thwarted and overwhelmed by a feeling of ineptitude. After an hour, soaking with sweat, I got off the bed, never having had an orgasm myself, my testicles hurting like hell, put on my clothes, said, "*Lebewohl,*" "Be well," and left.

After leaving her room of business, I doubted that I would ever again see or hear from her. Two weeks passed and I was familiarizing with the idea that it was over, and the millions I was reflecting to earn out of the emery deal were gone.

One cold Friday evening Christi telephoned me at the embassy, from Darmstadt, and asked if I would see her in a few hours, when she returned to Bonn. I had mixed feelings. My ego was gratified by her initiating the resumption of our affair but the thought of even attempting to make love to a cadaver repelled me. I encouraged her to come, however, because if there were any chance to put emery in the autobahn, no matter how remote, I did not want to miss it.

It was close to midnight by the time Christi arrived in her inelegant Volkswagen station wagon. The Dresden, my favorite hotel in Bad

Godesberg, was full. So were most of the hotels in Bonn. So, I called the Peterhof, and they had a suite. By that time, the ferry had stopped its runs, so I had to drive all the way to Bonn, get over the bridge, and drive to that most magnificent hotel. The room was a combination of black and gold that perfectly matched her complexion. She was behaving like a kitten, not her usual remote and cold self. She told me she was willing to give it a try, but that I would have to work very hard to awaken the woman in her. And hard and painful work it was.

I have done a lot of manual labor in my life, mostly as a coalminer or steelworker, but no amount of hard labor can compare with the awakening of that woman's sexuality. She wanted me to press as hard as possible, with our bodies locked, and not move, but to increase the pressure. The bone at the pubis started hurting, and my arms were trembling from the exertion, but she was urging me to press harder. I was about to faint, when suddenly, under me, a volcano started erupting. In all my years before or since, never have I experienced such an explosive orgasm. Vesuvius and Etna combined couldn't be more dramatic. At that moment, I was the happiest man alive.

From that moment on, Christi's attitude and behavior changed. She was now the devoted, obedient, and passionate girlfriend—the ideal lover. Getting her to orgasm became gradually less of a hard labor ordeal than the first one. There was, however, still something that bothered me: the secret life and business in Stuttgart. I wanted her to give it up and find another occupation to substitute her income. I even offered her a stipendium of DM 2,000 per month out of my pocket. That was $500 back then, a lot of money. She refused it and appeared to be hurt by my generosity. She maintained that it was not in her character to be a kept woman or depend on anybody. I could not comprehend such ardor in pride by someone who was a whore to perverted old fools. Frankly, I was jealous and did not want anyone near her. In matters with women, my Greek machismo and the Mediterranean blood always shoved the Scottish half away.

She assured me that there was nothing to be jealous about, that there was no sexual or other contact involved, and said that I should trust her. I asserted that if such was the case, why did she need a bed in the room? Our arguments on this subject were the only dark clouds on what was the perfect affair for me. Christi was the woman that ended my ten-year fidelity to my wife. I wanted to be her only master, the axle around which her life would rotate until death did us part. German women are known to be stubborn, and she was no exception. Eventually, short of breaking up because of my jealousy, we agreed that I would be allowed to hide in her closet while she was in session with a client and hear for myself that there was no sex involved, and no ground for me to be jealous.

At this time there were 400,000 young Greek men working and living in Germany as *Gastarbeiter*, and about 75,000 young Greek women. Some of the men were married and had brought their wives with them, and their children. We never had a precise figure of how many Greek children lived in Germany at the time, but an estimate was 16,000 of school-going years. Those figures may be small for Germany, but for Greece, it meant one-third of her active male population. Most of those Greeks were of peasant stock, good, healthy, and very religious. It was customary for young peasants to marry a girl from the same village or the closest neighboring villages, but—God forbid! —never outside the province. So, many a girl would put together their dowries, hire a taxi and have themselves driven to Germany, to Munich or Nuremberg or Stuttgart or Neuss, where they expected to find their future husband. So, Greece was actually suffering population drainage of her best stock, ancillary to large population figures of Greeks in Australia. The only compensation was that a good proportion of the earnings in Germany were transferred to Greece, to family and for the future. But with so many girls leaving home to find a husband in Germany and subsequently, with so many children born in Germany, these remittances became less and less.

Even though the matters and problems of the *Gastarbeiter* were not part of my duties, it was a subject that concerned all of us at the embassy. I was the only one who had extensive traveling expenses, and I was paid a per diem for nineteen days out of the month, so I had assumed an extra responsibility that involved entertainment—propaganda—and the schooling of the Greek children.

Germany, in her generosity, availed free schooling to all children regardless of ethnic origin. Education in the *Bundesrepublik* was determined and administered by the individual *Laender*, or states. There was no *Bundesministerium* in Bonn. Because of my traveling, it became my job to attend to the schooling of the Greek children to make sure they did not forget what they were. I was working mostly with Greek priests. The Greek teachers who had been hired by the various *Laender* to offer some hours of Greek lessons to the Greek children in the German elementary schools were very happy with their pay and their living conditions. The German schools, like everything in Germany at the time, were top quality and very efficient. Our problem began with high school. Germany, Switzerland, Austria, France, and Japan have the best and most demanding high schools in the world. A German high school diploma or a French baccalaureate are three times more education that the best college degree in America. The Greek children, with few exceptions were not up to the level of the German children and could not follow.

The various *Laender* that had hired Greek teachers for the elementary schools were not willing to hire teachers for high schools. Their position was understandable and logical: Germany was not a country of immigration. That policy was made amply clear. The *Gastarbeiter* were there to serve the needs of the ever-expanding German economy, the result of the combined efforts of two geniuses: Adenauer and Earhart, and only for so long as those needs persisted. They or their children could never become German citizens or obtain permanent status.

Giving children, by law, six years of schooling, was the limit the *Laender* would go. High school—gymnasium—was also free, but the hiring of extra teachers for children whose future was not necessarily in Germany, children who did not show either the adaptability or the capability to fully attend a German gymnasium, would be, in their opinion, a waste of money and effort. I rather agreed with them, but my government's position was to pressure the *Laender* to provide the money for Greek high school teachers, or better still, build or offer buildings that could be converted into Greek high schools, but paid and run by Germans.

It was a preposterous demand, but it had worked in Australia and my superiors in Athens thought we could also manipulate the Germans. They refused to see the difference between Australia and Germany. Australia begged for Greek immigrants because Greeks never become parasites on the government's dole. They open businesses and thrive. Thanks to the Greek immigrants, Australia became a major tobacco and wine producer and exporter. Germany, on the other hand, could rid herself of all the Greeks and replace them in one day with Yugoslavs, Turks, Spaniards, Italians, and more.

I had, however, one trump card. The biggest and most important land was Bavaria, and in Munich we had a Greek high school that was established in 1836 by the King of Bavaria, Ludwig—the mad one. The school had a mix of Greek and Bavarian teachers. It was a school with a proven record of 134 years of uninterrupted and successful function; a school inspired and paid for by the Bavarian land. It was the living example of what we wanted the other *Laender* to undertake. The doors in Cologne, Hanover, Bremen, and Hamburg were shut in my face with a resounding, "*Nein*." In Saarbrucken and in Frankfurt, they did not outright say no, but they didn't say yes, either. My best hope was in Mainz, and most importantly, because of the great number of Greeks there, Baden Württemberg.

It was again a very cold Friday, when the telephone rang at my office and Christine von Schuetzenberg, my Christi, posed, "Can you be in Stuttgart in five hours?" It was time for her to prove I had no reason to be jealous. My Mercedes, that I named 'Lazarus,' because he had been resurrected twice with burned up engines, could not do 240 kilometers per hour, so I hired a plane, which cost a small fortune, and I was in Stuttgart in time.

The arrangement was that I would be locked in the closet and listen to the proceeding, but I was to make no sound, and remain there until the closet was unlocked. I didn't like it, especially since there was no heat in that nasty place and there was no stool to sit in the closet, but I decided to rough it and satisfy my curiosity as to the asexual nature of sadomasochistic encounters. After she closed me in, she left to go pick up the client. I was in a pitch-dark closet with only standing room, and very uncomfortable. If I had any claustrophobic tendencies, I would easily have gone mad there. But I had to play by her rules. Before she left, she warned me of the stench that would assail my nostrils, of the pleas for mercy by the client, the screams of pain, "but don't you make a sound, or else."

It couldn't have been more than ten minutes that I was confined in the dark, dank, and smelly closet, but it felt like hours. I heard the door opening, and three people came in. The sound of their voices revealed another woman, and a man who sounded like he was in his late forties or early fifties. His German was refined and sounded more Heidelberg than Schwabenland. The preliminaries and the financial arrangements were conducted in a very polite, civilized tone. The metronome was started, and then, very abruptly, hell broke loose. The two women began screaming, insulting, and abusing the man who was begging for their mercy. I could hear the whiplashes on his body, and the sound of being walloped with a paddle or cricket bat. I could hear the thump of kicks, and by his screams and groans, I knew it was real. He was calling one *"meine Goettin,"* "my goddess" and the other *"meine Herscherin,"* "my ruler." I could not hear the metronome, but obviously, the moment it stopped, there was a pause until more money was paid, and then the torture resumed.

I was ordered not to make a sound, or smoke. That ordeal must have been going on for an hour, and I was stiff with cold, tired from standing motionless for so long, and yearning for a smoke. I was also disgusted and appalled by the punishment the man was enduring. At one point, there was silence, and I could only hear the man crying, and the two women breathing heavily after all the energy expended on the merciless abuse of 'Kunde.' I had enough. Disregarding my orders not to move, I smashed the door of the closet, lit a cigar, and got out.

The two women were lying on the bed, resting after all their labor.

The man, stark naked, bleeding from his nose and mouth and with dozens of ugly red welts all over his body, some also bleeding, was lying on the floor in a slime of urine, blood and sweat. The women were wearing imitation leather outfits, very tight, that covered their bodies from neck to thigh with only their breasts and genitals exposed. They wore high heeled boots of the same leather, that came up to their thighs. The boots had metallic points. Christi was wearing a mask. The other girl was smaller, a size six, I would guess, with raven black hair and very fine, gentle features. She certainly did not look like someone capable of such cruelty. She was astonished to see me there. Obviously, Christi had not warned her there would be an audience. Christi was very mad at me; I could tell in spite of the mask. The girls were tired, and perspiring. The man on the floor had a smile of relief on his battered face and evidently welcomed my abrupt and unexpected appearance. "I will pay you five hundred marks," he said to me, "if you f— those two and let me watch."

"I'll do it for free," I said. Christi hit me with her whip across the face. I had a welt that lasted for a week.

"Get your clothes off and come to the bed," she snarled, and she ordered him, "Put the five hundred marks on the table."

The five hundred marks were paid and I was dragged by the two women, unclothed, and before I knew what was going on, Christi was astride my face and the other one was riding me like a mule. Then, Christi switched with the other girl. That went on for quite a while. My mouth was full of pubic hair. When, after an hour had passed, and they thought the five hundred marks had been well received, they stopped. The man was trying to masturbate, but apparently, he failed. I was disgusted, I was unhappy, and my cheek was hurting me. With all that slime in my mouth, I spat in his face. The session was over. The girls pushed him out and threw his clothes after him. The other girl collected her share of the money and left.

Christi was now free to vent her rage. She screamed, "I told you to stay in! He was my best customer! Now I've lost him!" So, we parted, more or less unfriendly to each other.

I had been trying to convince the various *Laender* of Germany to extend the expenditure for educating the Greek children in Germany beyond elementary school and when I received a letter from the Education Ministerium of Baden Württemberg, of which Stuttgart is the capital, to go and discuss the possibility of a Greek high school in Stuttgart, I was elated.

I went to Stuttgart for an appointment with the Minister, and I was shown into his office. I recognized the Minister of Education of Baden Württemberg as the pervert that a few weeks before I had seen being tortured by those two females. As he began to identify me, he reddened, and he said accusingly, "You did not have to go to all that in order to get my approval. I was determined to approve the request of Greece to build a Greek high school without you compromising me the way you did."

"Sir," I said, "first of all, please accept my apology for having spat in your face," probably unnecessarily adding to his embarrassment. "Secondly, I am neither that clever nor that diabolical to entrap you in that manner. It was pure coincidence."

Greece got the high school in Baden Württemberg at the German expense, with the Greek teachers being paid by the German *Laender*, and I began to realize that the perversion of the German male goes even beyond my wildest imagination.

CHAPTER **30**

Commercial Women

ONE DAY I received a telephone call from my close, boyhood friend, Michael Kakaras, in Hamburg, where he was the commercial attaché. It was Michael, who, when I last saw him in Berlin, steered me to the club of the transvestites. The post of commercial attaché in Hamburg was very important because Hamburg, being the third largest seaport in Europe and the largest one in Germany, gets an inordinate number of Greek ships docking there and many thousands of Greek sailors. So, the commercial attaché in Hamburg had extended duties beyond just commerce. Michael had been there for twelve years; he knew a lot of people and he was quite popular. He said, into the telephone, "Michael, there is going to be a wife swapping party at the house of the harbor master." Of course, the harbor master in Hamburg is a very important position, a very important function.

"So, what do I care?"

He rejoined, "We have been invited."

"You don't think that I will bring my wife from Greece to go to a wife swapping party, do you?"

"No," he retorted, "They don't know who our wives are. I know two German whores who specialize with Greek crews. Whenever a Greek ship is in the harbor those two girls go on board the ship and entertain the crew, so they speak Greek, they can dance Greek dances, and they can curse like stevedores. They will take the role as being our wives."

I didn't think that it would work, but I had nothing to lose, so I went to Hamburg, and I was introduced to those two. They were very Germanic in appearance. They were both Junoesque—meaning overweight—they were both blond, one had gray eyes, one had blue eyes, and they didn't even remotely look like Greek women. But they certainly spoke Greek, the worst Greek possible, the Piraeus *argot* of the Greek merchantmen.

We went to the wife swapping party. A rule of the wife swapping party was that the host, or the hostess, is not allowed to use their conjugal bed, other than that it is a free for all. Apparently, the wife of the harbor master was very interested in Michael Kakaras and probably arranged the whole thing because she wanted to have him. When we entered, the moment she saw him, she disengaged herself from whomever was copulating with her. She came to Michael, seized him, and in breach of the rules, she took him to her bedroom.

After the wife swapping party was over, we left, and my alleged wife announced, "You owe me eleven hundred marks."

I said, with some surprise, "What do you mean?"

She responded, "I charge one hundred marks per trick. I had eleven tricks; therefore, you owe me eleven hundred marks."

"Listen," I said, "there were a total of eleven pair there, and I know I certainly didn't screw you, and neither did Michael. That leaves nine."

"So," she came back, "some of them did me twice."

I have that also as a mark of German perversion. Perhaps wife swapping parties do happen elsewhere, but I never partook in one.

A diplomat is often afforded close encounters, which may be rebuffed or consummated, with beautiful, famous women.

There was a famous singer and actress—she lives, so I will not mention her name—at a Greek diplomatic reception honoring her. Our conversation was interesting, and when I learned she was leaving that night for her home in London, I got her a first-class ticket on Olympic Airways and went with her. We became better acquainted under a blanket on the plane and intended to effectuate it at her apartment. When we arrived, she excused herself, saying she would be back, while I waited in bed. But, alas, when she returned, she announced that her husband—she was married to a well-known producer—had called and is coming over, "So, pop off, Michael, can you?"

Also in London around the same time was Twiggy. On the occasion, she said to me, "Why aren't you paying attention to me?" To which I replied, "If you and I were the last two humans on this earth, the species would go extinct."

The original Bond girl from *Goldfinger*, Honor Blackman, I dated when she was with *The Avengers* television show. After several dates I proposed we go to bed, but I was rebuffed.

Micky was planning a trip to Europe and wrote me a letter announcing his forthcoming visit. Things were going well. It was now approaching the end of 1970. Micky was engaged to Kemper Penney and lived in New

York. Linde was expanding her business, ran the family company on behalf of Micky and was also chartering our yacht during the summer. Moira was happy in Athens and became very attached to Linde.

I was in Germany dedicated to my duties there, and even though overworked, I loved every moment. Since Linde chose to remain in Greece and only came once or twice a month to visit me, I had compromised with my loyalty principles and allowed myself sex with whores. In this respect Germany was paradise. Prostitution was legal except in Bavaria. My reasoning was that since there is no emotional attachment, it is not adultery or being unfaithful. When I was in Munich for the *Bayerische Rundfunk*, I kept company with my half-sister in Dahau, or her mother in Berchtesgaden, so I stayed away from whores. In Frankfurt, where I had established a very good relationship with both the publisher and editor of the *Fr. Algemeine*, I was a good client of those incredibly elegant and beautiful *Kirchnergasse* girls, diagonally across the Frankfurter Hof. They used to wait in their sports cars, Ferraris and Maseratis, Iso Griffos, and Iso Revoltas, Jaguars and Aston Martins. The Porsches and Mercedes looked like poor relatives there. In Hamburg, it was even better. A magnificent and very chic café with waiters in *frac*, long white tails, a live string quarter playing classical music, and the girls dressed in exquisite French gowns. It was too good to be true. Finally, in Duesseldorf, there was the municipal brothel where I had met the most esthetically perfect woman I had ever seen.

By that time, I had established a cordial relationship with Helmut Schmidt and felt almost at home in Hamburg. My residence when there, was No. 2 *Jungfrauenplatz*. That was the house of Michael Kakaras,.

In Micky's letter to me, he warned that he wanted to have girls waiting for him. I had no girls. The only thing I could offer him when he arrived at Bonn-Wahn was my car waiting on the tarmac next to the plane—a special privilege because of my diplomatic plates. I was driving, at the time, a Cadillac Fleetwood to shock the bourgeois who expected everybody in Germany to drive a Mercedes. My Mercedes, 'Lazarus,' was in the garage suffering of ball bearings. Micky was impressed, but also disappointed when he didn't see women in the car. "Where are the girls? he asked. "Didn't you read my letter?" I said I had no girls.

"Well, what do you do, with Linde in Athens?" "I go to prostitutes," was my answer.

"I have never paid for it in my life," he retorted, his voice full of contempt. I tried to explain my theory, but he wouldn't accept it. "If this is the case, and you don't have any girlfriends, then I leave tomorrow."

I said that tomorrow I was scheduled to go to Hamburg and was hoping he would come with me. He reluctantly agreed to come along. I had an appointment with *Augsteinof Der Spiegel,* the chief editor and did not want to miss it. I explained to him that he could enjoy the company of my friend, Michael Kakaras, the *der Handel* attaché, while I made my tour of *Augstein* and von *Brauchitz of Die Welt*. This was Micky's first time on the *autobahn* and he was petrified by the speed. 'Kadillo,' the Cadillac, was too slow. She could hardly do over 120 miles per hour. All the Porsches, most of the BMWs and the Ros' would pass us. It was a toss-up with Mercedes. All that horsepower for nothing.

Micky was pleased to meet Kakaras, who was a congenial host and companion, and that evening I suggested to my cousin to accompany me to my favorite spot in Hamburg. Even a sophisticated *homme du monde* like Micky was impressed. He was pointing at the girls and asking me if they were indeed prostitutes. "Behave yourself!" was my answer. "Don't point with your finger, it is rude. This is a high-class meeting locale, and everybody is expected to act accordingly."

"Neither in Paris, nor in London, nor in New York, have I seen so elegant and beautiful whores," he said. "I cannot believe my eyes." Indeed, it was beyond belief how vivacious, graceful, and dazzlingly attractive those girls were. The etiquette of the establishment was that one would ask the waiter to convey one's interest to a specific girl and it was up to her whether she would respond or ignore the invitation. They always ignored the Japanese because, as they explained to me, their penis was too small for the German condom, and no self-respecting German whore would have sex without a condom.

I was a steady customer, so I didn't need to ask the waiter. Two girls that I had known from previous occasions approached our table and were invited to sit. I introduced my cousin and told them that he was new in Germany and could not speak the language. The girls could understand English.

Micky, who had 'never paid for it,' was now anxious to leave with them. We went to their working apartment, with very plush carpet, mirrored walls, and ceiling and with two beds, and hardly any other furniture. German whores are too professional and never fake an orgasm. They consider it cheating. They are there to please their client, not themselves, so while I and my mate were on one bed, we heard the girl with Micky screaming. We saw that Micky was between her legs, and she was experiencing his 'iron tongue' while she writhed in delight. 'My' girl asked me if he would do that for her, also. I assured her that she would have her turn. Hardly do any johns do that for whores. But Micky treated then as girlfriends, and they were very appreciative.

After the 'commercial' part of our session was over, Micky asked them if they knew where we could buy marijuana. They did, so we went and bought one hundred dollars' worth, then Micky asked them where the best hotel in Hamburg was. They both suggested the Hotel Atlantic. We went there and rented their best suite. We ordered from room service, beluga malossol and Taittinger Blanc de Blanc; they didn't have Roederer Kristal. We smoked the joints and copulated till the wee hours of the morning. The girls said they had never had a better time in their lives. Even though the tryst at the hotel was meant as *privat* and not part of a commercial transaction, Micky gave each of them two hundred dollars. They were the happiest girls in Hamburg that day.

A month later I was in Athens telling the story to Moira and Linde. "'Never paid for it?'" Moira scoffed. "When you see him again, ask him about the $54,000 he paid to have Dianne Durham."

When I saw him again in New York, I did ask him. He had an entirely different theory about that. "I bought the lighters on my Bermuda account. The Bermuda company sold them to the New York company for $75,000. The New York company incurred a total loss, so I gained at least $13,000 in taxes. Dianne attracted me, but I bought her lighters so that she would stop sniveling and disturbing the harmony of my flight."

CHAPTER 31

The Spy

WILLY BRANDT ABSCONDED from Germany in 1938, primarily to avoid the draft, but also because evidently, he was opposed to the Nazi regime. He surfaced in Norway and married a Norwegian woman and became a subject of the King of Norway. In 1945 he came back to his native Berlin wearing the uniform of a Norwegian officer. He managed to get himself elected *Burgermeister* of Berlin. He made a name for himself as the hero of Berlin during the blockade when the Soviets had disallowed access to West Berlin, and the British and the Americans decided to supply and feed the population of West Berlin through an airlift. The airlift was considered a heroic task on the part of the Anglo Americans because they had to transport everything by air. Everything, from coal to use for heating, to food stuffs, to water. Through the efforts of the Anglo Americans and the tremendous bravery of the pilots, Berlin was supplied for a number of months until the Soviets realized the futility of the blockage and decided to lift it.

During this period of time, Willy Brandt, who was very visible, became extremely popular. He took advantage of this popularity and went to West Germany, and in a few years, he assumed the leadership of the Social Democratic Party of Germany. From a period starting in the mid-1950s till the late 1960s, he at times had been the Prime Minister, in Germany called the *Bundeschancellor,* or he had been the Minister of the Foreign Affairs of Germany. And of course, he was the leader of the Social Democratic Party.

The Social Democratic Party of Germany, not unlike the Democratic Party of America, some fifty years ago, had a very wide range. The extreme left, called the Social Democrats, touched the Communists, but the extreme right of the Social Democrats in some respects exceeded the right of the Christian Democrats. I compare it to the Democratic Party in America because during, say, Roosevelt's time, the left wing of the Democratic Party, which was restricted to the north, was extremely left. It was even granting monopoly status to the trade unions in contravention to both the law and the Constitution of the United States. On the other hand, the right-wing branch of the Democratic Party, as represented, by, say, Governor and Senator Talmadge of Georgia went way beyond the right of the Republican Party of the time.

Helmut Schmidt, in 1970, at the time I served in Germany as press attaché of our embassy in Bonn, was the Minister of Defense in a coalition government of the Social Democrats and the Liberals. The Christian Democrats at the time were the opposition. Willy Brandt was the *Bundeschancellor*, and at one time he held the portfolio of Minister of Foreign Affairs. Willy Brandt and Helmut Schmidt were almost diametrically opposed in both ideology and character.

My job, apart from reading the German press, watching German television, and attempting to promote a more balanced and objective reporting on Greece, also was to keep an eye on the Greeks in Germany and present Greek information to them. At that time, we had 400,000 guest workers in Germany. For Greece, it represented close to one-third of her active population. Their savings in the German banks were estimated at fifteen billion marks and we also wanted them to reinvest their German savings back in Greece. To us those men were extremely important.

It came to my attention from some of our guest workers at the Porsche plant in Stuttgart that an agitator, perhaps working for Yugoslavia's Tito or some other Communists, was trying to persuade the Greek workers—most of whom came from the Greek province of Macedonia—to unite with Yugoslavia.

The Greek Macedonia, the home of Alexander the Great, is an ancient Greek province adjacent to the present Yugoslavia. The Yugoslavian dictator Tito had created an artificial province with the same name, Macedonia, next to it in Yugoslavia, with obvious intentions to annex the ancient Macedonia, the province of Greece. The people of Tito's 'Macedonia' included a few Greeks. Like Tito's 'Macedonia', Yugoslavia itself was an artificial creation. In the boundary settlements after World War I, a Balkan territory of the former Austro-Hungarian Empire was established and named 'Kingdom of the Serbs, Croats, and Slovenes.' After World War II, Tito created the Federal Republic of Yugoslavia, meaning 'south Slavia.'

I obtained the permission of the Porsche management to go into the factory to address the workers and counteract the agitator's propaganda. Suspecting that he must work for Tito or some other Communists, I decided to track him, and discovered to my astonishment that he went regularly to East Berlin. At Checkpoint Charlie, he was admitted without hesitation. That certainly intrigued me. What business does an ordinary Greek worker have in East Berlin? And why would he go there? Getting back and forth between East and West Berlin was not that easy. It confirmed my suspicions he was working for the Communists.

I approached the military attaché who was the actual person in charge of the embassy. After all, we had a military regime, and the military attaché was the true superior. I reported to him that I have seen that a Greek goes frequently to Berlin and then he moves to East Berlin. I said I would like to see if I can find out what he is doing there. We had no diplomatic relations with East Germany, and it would be very dangerous for me to go there. The military attaché said, "You know East Berlin is out of bounds for us."

There is a suburb of Hamburg, on the Elbe River, called Wedel, and in Wedel there is an open house café very well situated on the top of a hill, and on the summit of the hill is an observation post, and in that observation post there are people who greet each and every ship entering the harbor of Hamburg. They say, for instance, "Welcome, Captain John Oulanbis to Hamburg, and thank you for bringing us—whatever." They know what the cargo is on that specific ship. When a ship leaves, they usually play the national anthem of the flag of that ship, and they say again, "Farewell, and have a good journey, Captain Oulanbis, and we hope to see you again." It was an act of courtesy on the part of Hamburg Harbor, and I loved that because I could hear the national anthem of Greece at least fifty times while I was sitting drinking coffee there. Wedel is the constituency of Helmut Schmidt. At one party to which I was invited, I was introduced to Helmut Schmidt. When I found that his constituency was Wedel, I told him how much I enjoyed his constituency. He replied, "One day we have to be there together." That was how I established a sort of acquaintance with him. Since he was the Defense Minister of Germany, I thought it would be incumbent to my duty as a member of NATO to tell him about that peculiar Greek who was going to East Berlin. And I did.

Helmut Schmidt was interested. He said, "Only an Austrian or a Bavarian might detect that you are not a native of Austria. So," he continued, "I have a suggestion. I shall arrange for you to obtain a genuine Austrian passport; I will even get you an Austrian-made car with Austrian plates." He finished, "And, I will get you a cover story of being an industrial representative. In this way you can go to East Berlin and follow that Greek wherever he goes."

I didn't much like the idea because I had never done any spying in my life and going to East Berlin was not my cup of tea, however I saw the advantages. Since Helmut Schmidt said this would be strictly between the two of us, I didn't tell anybody at the embassy. I had nineteen days out of twenty-five working days away from Bonn because, in my capacity as press attaché, the newspapers that were my target were all over Germany, except Bonn. Bonn was a small provincial town which during the weekend when the civil servants went home, was totally abandoned. The reason that Bonn had become the federal capital is that, because of its insignificance, it had not been bombed during the Second World War, so it was the only German town which had enough buildings standing to become the federal capital. There was an area north of Bonn which was also intact, and that was where all the embassies were gathered.

I reluctantly agreed with Helmut Schmidt. Indeed, within less than two weeks I had a genuine Austrian passport, I had an Austrian-made Fiat, and I had a story. According to the story, I was an industrial representative—in other words a high-level salesman. I went to Berlin, and I waited to see that Greek cross Checkpoint Charlie. When he did, I crossed also, he on foot and I in my newly-obtained Fiat. He went to the public library of East Berlin. Parking was not a problem back then in East Berlin—there were very few cars—so I followed him there. The public library was one of only a few places in East Berlin where one could go without need of any credentials or any specific documents. Furthermore, it was one of the very few places where one could use foreign currency without having to exchange it for the local currency. I saw him go to a specific aisle of the library, pick up a book, and pull out of the book an envelope. He put it in his pocket, and then he went to a movie. At that point, I lost him. I drove back to West Germany, and I reported to Helmut Schmidt. He said, "Well done, Michael. But we have to find out what is in that envelope and where does the envelope go."

It took me about three months to reestablish contact and again have the opportunity to follow him to East Berlin. This time I went to the movie also. I'm glad I did go to the movie. They showed a one-hour documentary made by a Soviet television team, but it was, of course, dubbed in German. The subject of the documentary was *Misery in America*. It showed the winos at the Battery in Manhattan; it showed the homeless sleeping on the benches of Central Park in New York, covered with newspapers, and the winos and the homeless in Washington, DC who slept over the grates.

Among other examples of poverty and misery in America, it showed Negro tenements in Georgia, tenements made of cardboard and tin, and the squalor under which those Negroes lived. I, being unfamiliar with reality in America, had formed my opinion from the magnificent movies we had seen, shot in Manhattan. I had read everything that I knew about America in *Readers Digest*, in *Time* magazine and in *Life* magazine. I thought that whoever made that documentary must have been a genius of a cinematographer, because I didn't believe that that was reality in America. I was just wondering where they found sights in Moscow that resembled so much in New York. The movie was about the Russian hero, Onege. I didn't particularly enjoy it.

I followed the Greek after the movie was over. Apparently in the theatre, he made another contact, but that I failed to fully document or see exactly what was going on. But I followed him, and he returned to West Germany. He then went by train to Darmstadt, and I followed him in the train. In Darmstadt he went to the University of Darmstadt, and at the Office of Weights and Measurements—it was an official federal office—he met with a professor. I assumed he was a professor—I didn't know who exactly he was. The Greek gave him the envelope and collected money.

I duly reported all that to Helmut Schmidt. The professor whom I described to Helmut Schmidt was arrested, and after his arrest, others, then four German generals committed suicide. They were Generals of the new German—the West German—Army, the *Bundeswehr*. It became known that whole missile rockets had been shipped in the open, aboard open railroad cars, from West Germany to East Germany as cargo. Those were actual NATO rockets, possibly with nuclear warheads. The generals apparently were spying against NATO and West Germany, but it happened that 'suicides' often occurred during interrogation.

Within a few weeks I was unexpectedly, and unhappily for me, because I enjoyed being in Germany, transferred from Germany to Greece, and thence to New York.

Apparently, I unknowingly became a part of governmental deception as it unfolded in Germany during the Cold War era. Both the leftist German Democratic Republic and the more leftist Federal Republic of Germany governments were infiltrated by ominous eavesdropping Communists during the Cold War era. An East German Stasi spy—the feared East German secret police—Gunter Guillaume, was successfully embedded in the office of Chancellor Willy Brandt during 1969 to 1974.

There were political complexities and the conflicts of a new multi-party Germany, and conflicting personalities and ambition. Brandt was the progressive leader who led the nation out of the Nazi-polluted era. His private secretary since 1955, Gunter Guillaume, whose job it was to keep his boss and the government office informed about public opinion, regularly diverted reports of meetings, and copies of documents back to his Eastern Bloc operative. Guillaume's Communist contact was Arno Kretschmann. Herbert Wehner was the agitating Bundestag Party leader, and Helmut Schmidt was the chancellor-in-the-wings. After the discovery that his secretary was an East German spy and the arrest in 1974, Willy Brandt resigned, and Helmut Schmidt then became the undisputable head of the Social Democratic Party and the next *Bundeschancellor*.

CHAPTER **32**

Living the Good Life

MICKY HAD PRECEDED me to America, first arriving in 1963. After leaving Greece in 1968, he ensconced Moira in Bermuda and worked at being a playboy. Being a restless and adventurous type, he did a lot of traveling all over the USA looking for his next money-making opportunity. One morning, he was in the first-class compartment of an airplane that had stopped in Dallas, Texas, on the way to Florida from Los Angeles. A stunning beauty boarded the plane in Dallas and was seated next to him. As the plane took off, she began sighing and crying, and making Micky very uncomfortable. He asked what the matter was. With an effort, she told him that she had invested most of her money in a large quantity of disposable BIC lighters, and she was now stuck with them and could not sell them. Micky asked how much money she had paid for the lighters, and her answer was, $54,000. He pulled his Bermuda bank check book out of his pocket, wrote a check for $54,000 and asked for her name. She told him that it was a joke in bad taste, to make fun of her. "It is no joke," Micky assured her. "I am buying your damned lighters so I shall have peace and quiet the rest of the flight." Her name was Dianne Durham. Mickey gave her the check and his office address in New York. She was very doubtful that the check was valid, but Micky told her to first cash it, and then deliver the lighters. She was an outspoken Texan and told Micky that if he thought that this phony gesture would get him sex with her, he was mistaken. "I wouldn't mind," Micky told her, "but my purchase of the lighters is purely for the sake of my tranquility." They had a pleasant conversation the rest of the flight, but Dianne was convinced than the check was not genuine. She refused to give him either her address or telephone number, but Micky had no difficulty tracing her to Neiman Marcus in Dallas. She had a well-paid position as a model, buyer, and public relations spokeswoman.

The episode was almost forgotten, when three weeks later, an

18-wheeler truck stopped in front of the building at 100 Forty Sixth Street where Micky's office was located in Manhattan, wanting to deliver 5,000 gross of BIC disposable lighters—almost 700,000 lighters. There was no room for so many boxes in Micky's office, so the truck was directed to his warehouse in Brooklyn. A few hours after the truck, Dianne showed up, dressed in the best Neiman Marcus had to offer. According to Micky's description, she was breathtaking. She was full of apology for having doubted Micky's veracity and wanted to show her gratitude. That she did for a week at the New York Plaza Hotel where they made their love nest. After that, Micky was hooked. He practically moved to Dallas, and Dianne became the axis of his life.

Moira found out and came to New York to confront the situation. She and Micky had a brawl during which Moira stabbed him with a kitchen knife. The wound was superficial, except it bled too much. To avoid criminal recriminations, Moira agreed to a divorce. She was to be exiled in Athens in a luxurious condominium across from the ancient Amphitheatre at the foot of the Acropolis, purchased in her name; she was to receive for life, or until she remarried, $2,500 per month; child support was set at $24,000 per year, increasing by $600 every year until Samantha—she was conceived while they were watching *Bewitched*, the television show—reached her eighteenth birthday, at which time she would draw on her trust fund. Finally, Moira could still order her groceries and other incidentals to be shipped to her from America.

Probably Micky was setting his sights on a marriage with Dianne Durham, who was glamorous and spectacular, but the lighters changed all that. The lighters of which Mickey was in possession of almost a million, were the first ever made disposable lighters. They did not have a controlling screw or lever accessible to the user to increase or lower the flame. All were defective in that they produced either a very high flame that would singe eyebrows, or no flame at all. They did have an adjustment screw, but it was inside the body of the lighter and could only be moved by means of a tiny wrench. Micky hired dozens of teenagers to adjust the flame of the lighters, but most would give up after a few hours or days. He had a secretary who recommended her roommate to come and work on the lighters. She was, as they say in America, between jobs, having recently been released by the Ford Modeling Agency.

Her name was Kemper Willa Penney. She was a good looking blonde with a perfect figure, but very tight skin. Medium height, medium weight, medium everything else. Micky hired her at $2.50 an hour, the minimum wage in 1968. She turned out to have the patience, and the eyesight, and the skill to turn the tiny screw and make the lighters function. She could work on two hundred lighters per eight-hour day, and never complained or asked for anything. Micky advertised the lighters in the newspaper, three for two dollars, or five for three dollars, and started selling them fast. He sent a few dozen to Athens, but we couldn't even give them away. The disposable mentality had not yet reached Greece.

Dianne Durham, meanwhile, was promoted and sent to the Nieman Marcus store in San Francisco. Micky had to fly there to see her, and it was becoming a burden. One day he received an invitation for a black-tie dinner at the house of the executive vice president of Air Reduction Corporation. Moira was at the time exiled in Greece. Dianne was in San Francisco, and he had no date to take to the dinner.

In desperation, Micky approached Kemper and asked her if she was free that evening. Kemper had been waiting three months for him to acknowledge her presence and was delighted. Micky told her it was a black-tie affair, and suggested they go to Bloomingdale's to buy her the appropriate dress and accessories. Kemper told him, no, thank you, that she had everything needed. Micky was dubious that she understood it was a very posh dinner party. But she assured him that her wardrobe was quite adequate for the occasion. Micky said, let's go to Tiffany's and I will buy you some good jewelry, but again Kemper declined, saying she had all she could possibly need. Micky was perplexed. First, how could a girl that works for $2.50 an hour afford anything luxurious, and secondly, what kind of woman rejects such offers. He was afraid his 'date' was either stupid or too good to be true.

With ill forebodings about the fiasco he might be heading for, he drove the Facel Vega to the basement apartment on Seventy-Third Street that Kemper was sharing with Micky's secretary. He was astonished. His date was one of the most elegant, attractive, glamorous girls he had ever seen. There was a diamond tiara across the beautiful long blond hair, matching diamond earrings, ring, and bracelet. She wore a platinum cross around her neck with a large diamond in the middle. Micky assumed that all those diamonds might be fake, but the gown she had on was very much Paris. It was Givenchy. Micky told her she looked like a million dollars. Not quite, she said, but almost. To his even greater surprise, she knew how to behave among the plutocrat, and spoke French to the Ambassador of France. And it was very good French for an American. Micky was astounded. Who the hell was Kemper? How could the girl working for him for minimum wage afford all these luxuries and comport herself like a princess?

Eventually they were seated at the tables, and Kemper was placed to the right of the host. Micky was the guest of honor. They had hardly begun which the host stood up and addressed Micky. "Michael, to us Americans, our heiresses are what to you Europeans are your royalty. Thank you for honoring my house with Kemper's company."

Micky was totally bewildered. He had no idea what his host, Theodore Dunn, was talking about. Eventually he came to realize that Kemper was J.C. Penney's only granddaughter. To a Greek, it was inconceivable that a girl from so rich a family would work. Especially at such a demanding, boring job for pennies a day. After the dinner party, a dazed and mystified Micky was invited to the apartment for a night cap. Next morning Kemper was fired. Said Micky, "I cannot have my future wife working at such a menial job."

Kemper at first did not accept the marriage proposal. She was infatuated with Micky and after having experienced his *langue de fer*, iron tongue—Micky could do sit ups with his tongue—she was even more attached to him. But she was engaged to marry a Dupont de Nemours; if she broke the engagement, it would displease her grandfather. The American well-to-do have the tendency to intermarry so the money stays intact in the right hands. They are a tribe all their own and live on their own planet. Micky kept dating her and pressing his suit, but to no avail. Marrying Micky would mean loss of inheritance, and his tongue, exceptional as it might be, was not worth $60,000.000. Then, the fellow with whom she was engaged, whom she had known for most of her life, and who was homosexual, broke the engagement himself to help her in clearing the way for Micky.

Still the Penney's were reluctant to give their blessings. Micky had millions, but they had many more. Huntington Hartford was their next choice for Kemper, the heir of the A&P Empire. The company, no longer in existence, was one of the oldest on the American continent. The full name was, the Honorable Atlantic and Pacific Tea Company, and it was established in 1716. Huntington was a notorious playboy and spendthrift, and he squandered the money. Had he married Kemper, A&P might still exist.

Micky's chance came when the best friend and schoolmate of Kemper's decided to elope and was getting married in Seattle. She had invited Kemper to be her maid of honor, and to be the only guest at the wedding. But the elopement came very abruptly, and Kemper couldn't get an airline flight that would get her to Seattle in time. She was crying her eyes out.

Micky went to Standard Oil where he knew they had their executive plane for sale and bought it. Just to fly Kemper to Seattle on time. Micky bought, right there on the spot, the biggest private plane that Standard Oil, now EXXON, had for sale, and also hired the pilots. It was a converted B-26 Mitchell bomber turned into a luxury means of transportation for one of the Rockefellers. In that plane, they made it in time. Kemper was so happy, she at last accepted Micky's proposal and planned for their wedding soon after.

Micky was not in love with Kemper. He liked her, but he still loved Dianne Durham. He wanted to marry Kemper because he saw her as his ticket to the top. She would pave his entry into the realm of American plutocracy. At this stage, the sky would be the limit of his ambitions. Six months prior to their wedding, but with her parents' acquiescence, Kemper moved into Micky's mansion in Sands Point, Long Island and started converting it from Moira's middle-class kitsch into American not quite *nouveau riche*. Paintings costing into the hundreds of thousands were purchased at Christie's and Sotheby's. Marble, teak, and ebony replaced the wall papers and imitation parquet floors, and the furniture was imported from Greece, Italy, and France. Even the bottom of the swimming pool was painted by an artist. To Micky's chagrin, Kemper had studied 'history of art' at the Sorbonne for four years. She had also spent all her European summers in Italy, Germany, Spain, and Greece, and she knew where the really good and expensive objects were to be found.

The only thing she kept from Moira's household was Claudella. She was a very nice and competent Negress from Montserrat in the Leeward Islands that Micky had smuggled into the United States and was now a very well treated slave. She had no papers at all, but she liked her circumstances, and was paid two hundred dollars a week besides all her clothes and whatever else she needed.

There was one thing that Kemper had that Micky—and later, I—could not stand: her Afghan Hound, a most obnoxious and foul tempered dog that Kemper loved with a passion.

The marriage of Aristotle Onassis to Jacqueline Kennedy had the effect of hydrogen bomb explosions in America. They were shocked. The woman Americans most respected, admired, emulated, adored, fawned over, and who many saw as a queen—while in reality she was nothing but a very expensive whore—had married someone they had hardly ever heard of. He was not British aristocracy or European royalty; he was a Greek ship owner. They were appalled. What was a Greek ship owner? Gradually, the tabloids and the rest of the print press serving the unquenchable curiosity of the public were full of stories about Onassis and the rest of the Greek shipping magnates, and the fabulous fortunes they had amassed with their super tankers.

It was at this moment that two Greeks, one a clerk at a shipping chandler's office in New York, Stelios Amanatides, and the other, John Livas, of London, who had a quarter ownership in an old freighter, conceived of a

THE NEW YORK TIMES, SUNDAY, APRIL 25, 1971

Kemper Penney Becomes Bride Of Mining Man

Special to The New York Times

Miss Willa Kemper Penney, a granddaughter of the late James Cash Penney, founder of the department store chain, was married here yesterday afternoon to Michael Alexander Panayotopulos of Sands Point, L. I., and Athens.

The Rev. Kenneth O. Jones performed the ceremony in the chapel of the Fifth Avenue Presbyterian Church, and

Mrs. Panayotopulos, the former Kemper Penney.

> *Cousin Mickey saw the J.C. Penney heiress as his ticket to the top.*
>
> *I liked Kemper, but her Afghan Hound was obnoxious.*

From The New York Times. © 1971 The New York Times Company. All rights reserved. Used under license
https://www.nytimes.com
Portraits by Bachrach Photography

Michael Panayotopulos To Wed Kemper Penney

Special to The New York Times

ORMOND BEACH, Fla., Feb. 20—Miss Willa Kemper Penney of New York and Michael Alexander Panayotopulos of Sands Point, L.I., Hinson's Island, Bermuda and Athens plan to be married in New York on April 24. The ceremony in the Fifth Avenue Presbyterian Church will be followed by a reception at the River Club.

The future bride, known as Kemper, is the daughter of Mr. and Mrs. Roswell Kemper Penney of Ormond Beach and Waynesville, N.C., and granddaughter of the late James Cash Penney, founder of the J. C. Penney Company, the retail chain. Her father is president of Roswell K. Penney, Inc., a real estate concern in Daytona Beach.

Mr. Panayotopulos is the son of Alexander Panayotopulos of Athens and the late Mrs. Panayotopulos. His father is president of Smyrls, S.A., a mining company.

Miss Penney was graduated from the Foxcroft School in Middleburg, Va., and from Briarcliff College. Her fiancé, an alumnus of the London School of Economics, is president of Intercontinental Mining and Abrasives, Inc., of New York and Athens.

known ughter oswell mond sville, presiiney, Fla,

son llos yrny n-

Miss Kemper Penney

Miss Cynthia Guyer.

William N. Lillios was best man.

The bride is a graduate of the Foxcroft School in Middleburg, Va., and Briarcliff College. Her husband, an alumnus of the London School of Economics, is president of Intercontinental Mining and Abrasives, Inc., of New York and Athens, a mining company. His previous marriage ended in divorce.

> *Mickey's moment came when Kemper was unable to get a flight to Seattle for the elopement of a best friend, so Mickey bought the Rockefeller private plane he knew was for sale by Standard Oil, hired the crew and flew her to Seattle. Impressed, she finally agreed to his marriage proposal.*

bright, and genius idea. The American public was lapping up every word written about Onassis, and the other Greek tycoons, but none of them had a company or corporation traded on any stock exchange. They could create a *public* Greek shipping company and offer the stock through the New York and London exchanges to the public: 'Participate and be a partner in the fabulous business that made so many Greeks multimillionaires.'

They chose the name Tidal Marine International and incorporated it in Delaware and the British Channel Islands. They needed, however, much more to qualify for acceptance in any stock exchange. Two more Greeks were brought in to enable the Tidal Marine idea to become reality. One was Steve Felouris, who had a high position in the second largest brokerage house in the world: Shearson, Hammill & Co. The other was Gregory Spartalis, executive vice present of the National Bank of North America. Tidal Marine got a sweetheart loan to buy full ownership of the Livas' freighter. Then using the freighter as collateral, they obtained a new loan to buy a small tanker.

Tidal Marine now had enough substance to barely qualify for entry into the NASDAQ, or over the counter exchange. Steve Felouris made sure of that, and started peddling the stock, using the prestige of his firm. From eight cents per share of stock in June 1969, it catapulted to $6.50 in three months, and over 18,000,000 shares were sold. At this point the shares were also introduced in London and a similar buying frenzy occurred there, too. With all the cheap money flowing into the coffers of Livas and Amanatides, they were buying ships as fast as they could, and used them as collateral to buy even more. All the major newspapers and magazines in American and Britain, the only exception being the *London Financial Times*, were carrying articles full of praise about the two fabulous Greek magnates. *Barron's*, which belonged to the *Wall Street Journal*, had an eleven-page account of the incredible genius of John Livas and Stelios Amanatides.

Mickey was fascinated, and a little envious of Livas and Amanatides who had made more millions, and faster than he had. He decided to approach them, and also emulate their method of turning the stock exchange into a money printing machine.

Mickey's office in Manhattan, for the Intercontinental Mining and Abrasives Company, occupied half the fourth floor of the 100 East Forty Seventh Street and Second Avenue corner building, two blocks from the United Nations. It was impressively furnished and equipped with a Xerox copier, IBM typewriters, and a fax machine. I had never seen one before—they were state-of-the-art in 1971. There were rows of file cabinets. If, however, one were to pull a dossier from the cabinets, it was empty or filled with newspaper clippings. Micky's office was a study in ostentation. It had a heavy oak desk, a sofa and armchair. On the wall behind was a map of the world with illuminated spots where the major minerals were to be found, with samples of those minerals positioned under the spotlights. His employees were a secretary who did very little—she was Kemper's ex-roommate—and an alcoholic geologist who was running errands, and an elderly woman who made the coffee and fetched lunch. Under the pompous title, Intercontinental Mining and Abrasives Company, Ltd., there was no substance of any kind. There were pictures on the walls of plants and mining sites, but none had anything to do with the present reality.

Our only source of income in New York came from the two bulk carriers which were managed by Tidal Marine. Micky could not be bothered with the details of running two ships, and the responsibilities of feeding York and paying a crew, plus chasing cargoes. Tidal Marine, by then, had offices in New, London, Piraeus, Hamburg, Hong Kong and Cape Town, and employed over fifteen hundred people. They owned or managed forty-two ships, mostly tankers. All flew the Greek flag, so Livas and Amanatides were treated in Greece like demigods. Micky was heavily speculating in the stock market with millions, but whatever gains he realized, if any, were in Bermuda.

J. C. Penney died on February 12, 1971, within days of my arrival in New York. The death of J.C. Penney was inconvenient for Micky because it postponed his wedding and the plans he had for exploiting the publicity the wedding would bring. His funeral was attended by six senators, dozens of Congressmen, four Governors, the Mayor of New York, and many other magnates. It gave me an insight to the rich and powerful in America. The whole family, with the exception of Kemper's father who was being treated for cancer of the esophagus at the Johns Hopkins Clinic in Baltimore, was there. I made good contacts and acquaintances that day. I wondered why the body in the coffin was wearing shoes with a hole in the sole. Why, if they own sixteen hundred stores that all sell shoes, couldn't they have a decent pair of shoes for the corpse to wear? I thought it was the extreme of tightness. I didn't know that it was his wish. It made a statement, for those who thought about it.

The widow took a liking to me, and when I told her I enjoyed playing bridge, she invited me to her club, the River Club, to come and play. There were only two clubs in New York as exclusive as hers: the Jockey Club and the Yachting Club. I went on the designated date, but the Negro majordomo wouldn't allow me entry. "This is a segregated club," he advised.

"What do you mean?" I queried.

"We do not allow Catholics or Jews," was his answer. I had given him my card from Germany—I had not yet printed cards in English—but the name was the same regardless of language.

"How did you guess I am Catholic? I asked him, more jokingly than seriously, "The name is typically Greek, and we Greeks are Orthodox, not Catholic."

"It makes no difference," he insisted. "We are segregated." It was apparent that Mrs. Penney had forgotten to submit my name to the guest list. While I was having my fun with that superior Negro, his telephone rang. It was Mrs. Penney, asking if her guest for bridge had arrived. The Negro almost turned white. He was shaking, and stuttered that, yes, he was at the entrance door. He looked at me beseechingly and started apologizing for the misunderstanding. I was more amused than offended and had my first lesson in the incredible levels of hypocrisy with which the American elite are endowed. I found out that something similar had happened to Aristotle Onassis the first time he went as a guest to the New York Yachting Club. He was very offended, however, so he bought the building and evicted the club.

Micky had to wait two months for his wedding. Meanwhile, he had discovered a defunct and almost bankrupt company in the state of Rhode Island called IMAC Foodstuffs, Inc., that was still listed on the NASDAQ over the counter exchange. His New York Corporation was Intercontinental Mining & Abrasives Company, Inc, and that could spell the acronym IMAC.

The IMAC Company had about forty fast food stores in Rhode Island and Massachusetts that had closed due to the competition of McDonald's, White Castle, Crystal, and Burger King. The IMAC stock had not been traded for over a year and was idling at forty-five cents per share. The value of the real estate owned by IMAC was estimated at less than a million dollars. There were 1,600,000 shares outstanding and another 900,000 shares in the hands of the management. Micky offered them $350,000 for their shares and they were delighted to sell them. He also, over a period of six months, started buying and selling the IMAC stock through brokers all over the country until it fell to seventeen cents per share. This is called stock manipulation and is highly illegal. When it reached that low price, he bought everything that was available.

A few weeks before his marriage he owned close to two million shares and the price was thirty-five cents. At this point he told me and all his relatives, friends, and acquaintances to buy IMAC stock. I bought 22,000 at thirty-five cents and another 10,000 at forty cents, and 3,000 at forty-five cents. I invested a total of $15,000. I was slightly annoyed when I found that Micky was the sole seller and was making one hundred percent profit out of his own relatives. Moira, his ex-wife, also bought about the same amount, and the Penney's bought close to a million shares. While he still owned the controlling share, he had legal papers drawn whereby IMAC Foodstuffs, Inc. bought the New York corporation, Intercontinental Mining & Abrasives Company, Inc. Then the 'Foodstuffs' was dropped from IMAC Foodstuffs, Inc. In this way his company entered the NASDAQ exchange, as IMAC, Inc., so he had the acronym of the name without meeting any of the requirements.

Next, he sold all the hamburger places for about seven hundred thousand dollars and used the money to aggressively buy IMAC stock, pushing it to $3.50. On paper he had made close to six million dollars in a few months without risking anything. He wanted to use the publicity of the marriage to push the stock even higher.

The publicity about Micky's wedding to the Penney heiress was extremely positive. It surpassed even our best dreams. Micky now reduced the personnel down to what it was before, and the daily dinner parties came to an end. His whole concentration and efforts were now dedicated to increasing the price of his stock.

He defied the laws and regulations of the Securities and Exchange Commission, and even hired people to peddle his stock. He had me advertise the stock to all the Greeks at the consulate. He spent $11,000 to bring, via satellite, the European Club championship in football between Ajax of Holland and Panathinaikos of Greece, and another $60,000 to buy the one hundred five minutes and have it televised live on *Channel 11,* a local New York television station. The only advertisements were dedicated to the sponsor, Michael A. Panayotopoulos and his *public* company, IMAC. The Greeks responded and started buying like crazy. From $3.50, which had been the price of the stock before the wedding, it now soared, within three months, to $12.00. Micky was now—on paper—worth $35,000.000. Public companies have to issue quarterly reports, have to abide and respond to Security Exchange Commission inquiries and have to hold an annual stockholder's meeting. Micky had nothing to report since there was no business of any kind behind IMAC. So, he dispatched his alcoholic geologist to Greece to establish some sort of nickel mining— or the semblance of it—and have something to report.

On various occasions the two Tidal Marine founders, Livas and Amanatides, would come to our house in Sands Points and have very secretive talks with Micky. Nobody knew what they were talking about, but it was not so peculiar since Tidal Marine was managing our two bulk carriers.

After the wedding was over, at the end of April 1971, we went to attend Bill Lilios' nuptials in Cleveland, Tennessee, where Micky was to be the best man. A few days earlier, when Micky had married Kemper Penney in New York, his best man was Bill Lilios, my childhood friend and schoolmate at the Athens College, the fellow whose meager savings Mickey used to create his American business and the millions that ensued out of that business. Since Bill Lilios was the best man at Micky's wedding, my cousin would be the best man at his wedding.

The Panayotopoulos clan, with the exception of my mother, who chose not to come to America—or the colonies—as she called the USA, boarded Micky's plane in New York. It was the converted B-26 Mitchell bomber that he had purchased from Standard Oil, which had been converted as the private airplane, with no luxury spared, for the comfort of the previous owner, David Rockefeller, Jr. All seven of us, plus Mickey's secretary, who was Kemper's ex roommate, and Claudella, the Negro maid, sat most comfortably in that plane.

Even though it was a sunny spring day, the plane was tossing and dropping as if it were flying into a storm. My flying phobia made me the joke of all the passengers. They were telling me that each motor was 1,500 HP and that it was a solid piece of machinery meant for war, but I was petrified and wanted to jump out. Eventually after ninety minutes of torture, we landed in Chattanooga, Tennessee. The municipal airport of Cleveland was not big enough to accommodate the B-26. Cars and limousines were waiting for us and took us to a motel in Cleveland.

We all went to a self-serve restaurant where the trays were placed on a rotating circular buffet, and one would reach to fill one's plate. It was $1.75, no matter how much you ate. We then went to a Baskin-Robbins for ice cream, where I experienced my first encounter with apartheid in America. With us was Claudella, the Negress that Micky and his first wife—his English wife, Moira—had stolen from Montserrat in the Leeward Islands and turned her into their servant. She had been illegally imported into the United States, but Claudella had been very happy to be in the service of Micky and Moira. And then she was even more delighted to be in the service of Kemper because Kemper was treating her almost like an equal, unlike her previous mistress, the English woman, who was of the people, and treated Claudella as a servant. Claudella was now elevated to almost being a member of the family.

When we were in Baskin-Robbins, about eleven of us and Claudella, we sat at the most convenient table, and nobody came to serve us. Eventually we started out for the waitress. The waitress came and said, "You have sat at the wrong side of the parlor. This side where you sit is for colored, only."

So, we all moved to the other side of the parlor. And again, the waitress wouldn't come. We said, "What's wrong now?"

She told us, "You brought with you the colored woman. We don't serve colored in the white section." We understood, then, we should sit in the one side of the store, and Claudella should sit by herself on the other side.

My uncle Alexander stood up and announced, "We are Greeks. We don't acknowledge your color codes, and we will go someplace else." Bill Lilios was engaged to be married to a typical southern belle, whose name was Amy Card, and she lived in Cleveland, Tennessee. Her mother was the great-granddaughter of Jefferson Davis, so they had tremendous Confederate credentials. The bride's father was one-third owner of Magic Chef, a company located there that manufactured kitchen appliances. He was also the owner of the Bank of Cleveland, and he owned the Ford dealership in Cleveland. Furthermore, he was the leading Republican in that part of Tennessee. In the early 1970s, it was probably pretty difficult to find a Republican anywhere in the deep south.

The wedding was a Dixie event. During the wedding, which was a typical Baptist wedding, no alcohol was served at the big banquet. After the wedding, at the reception at the bride's house, the only thing that flowed was California champagne, and of course, we, the Panayotopuli, were extremely displeased. We thought that they could at least buy some *Moet et Chandon,* if not *Veuve Clicquot* or *Dom Perignon* champagne. Of course, we did not expect Roederer Kristal in the boondocks of Tennessee.

One of the foremost guests at that wedding was Senator Talmadge. Senator Talmadge sounded—in whatever little I understood of his saying, because he spoke with such an accent—as if he was a Republican and an extreme Republican, at that. But he told me, "Hell no, I am a Democratic Senator."

An after-wedding brunch was held at Senator Talmadge's estate in Athens, Georgia. All the guests went to Athens, Georgia in a caravan of cars. As we were approaching the Talmadge estate, I saw tenements. I had a moment of *déjà vu.* It was the same scene that was shown in the Soviet documentary that I had seen in the theatre in Berlin when I was following the Greek spy. I saw the tenements made of cardboard and tin, and the squalor. At the earliest opportunity, I asked the senator, "Senator, do you remember at one time, a cinematographic crew coming here and taking pictures of your tenements?" He recollected there had been one from Germany.

"No, they were Russian," I informed him, "and they used your estate to make propaganda against the United States. Why is Georgia in such a bad shape? Why don't you have any decent roads in Georgia?"

"The Yankees are to blame."

That was 1971, and it perplexed me, and I asked, "What do you mean, 'the Yankees are to blame'?"

"Don't you know they devastated Georgia?" he countered. But, when? "In 1865." Then I realized that, to Dixiecrats, for everything that is wrong in the south, the Yankees are to blame.

Since the bride's father owned the Ford dealership, right after the wedding was over, I urged the bride's brother to open the dealership and sell me a car. I was determined not to fly back to New York and subject myself to the same ordeal. For seven hundred dollars, I bought a very nice, though seven years old, 1964 Thunderbird. We now had thirteen cars in the garage of Sands Point.

In September 1971, the IMAC stock reached its highest at $12.50, but stabilized between $10.50 and $11.50. The Tidal Marine stock was above $17.00 at approximately the same time. What Livas and Amanatides had been discussing, in their secretive way at our house in Sands Point, was swapping their Tidal Marine stock for our IMAC stock on a three to two basis. The reason was that you cannot obtain a loan from a bank with your own stock as collateral, but you can do so with somebody else's stock. Micky was at first reluctant to do the swap, mainly because he had no need for cash or loans. Eventually he got them to offer one for one, and he did exchange about 200,000 shares of stock.

At that same time, Steve Felouris, the high positioned Greek with Shearson, Hammill & Co the investment bankers of Tidal Marine, called me one day at nearly noon at my office and asked if I could be at the Périgord, a fine French restaurant in mid-Manhattan, in fifteen minutes. I said, "Sure," and took off.

Steve was there with a company of people I didn't know, but two looked familiar. We were introduced, and they were the Executive Vice President of Twentieth Century Fox; his assistant; the famous director Elia Kazan; the financial top executive of Twentieth Century Fox and his assistant; and Kimon Friar, an English scholar and translator of many ancient Greek texts and tragedies into English. I had met him when I was a pupil in the Athens College in 1952.

They told me that Twentieth Century Fox had obtained the rights to make a movie out of Mary Renault's book, *The King Must Die*. She was a famous and very well published author of books inspired out of Hellenic mythology and history. She had lived most of her life in Greece and when she died, in her will, she specified that no book of hers would ever turn into a Hollywood movie. I questioned how they could defy the last testament of Mary Renault, and it was explained to me in American legalese that I could hardly understand, that it had been done. Friar was already finished with the script. They had a budget of $15,000,000. Felouris told me that his firm would finance most of it as executive producers. The budget was based on Hollywood costs.

"How much can you save us if we shoot it in Greece?" was their question

I studied the budget for a few minutes. "At first glance," I said, "I could save you at least $2,500,000. If I study it for a day or so, I might come up with more savings." At that time, an extra that spoke not a single word of dialog got eighty-five dollars per day. In Greece, they could have all the extras they needed, and more, for nothing. "And," I pointed out, "given the Hellenic theme of the book, I might even get the Greek government to co-finance the movie for a percentage."

Felouris was ecstatic. "Michael, if you can save us that much and even get your government on board, I will personally pay you a $250,000 finder's fee and give you also half a percent of the net."

I declined the offer. Felouris looked as me as if I were sick. "You are either too stupid or too good. I don't know which, but here in American a finder's fee is legal and part of any big deal." He pondered, "But if you cannot accept it, I will give you a piece of advice that is worth more than a quarter million dollars. Tell your cousin to stay away from Amanatides and Livas. They are crooks."

Think of it. Felouris had worked from the initial stage with Amanatides and Livas to make their company public, and his firm, Shearson, Hammill, was the major financier and promoter of the Tidal Marine stock. He was putting his head in the scaffold with this advice given in front of people, in a public place. I appreciated candor, and that, like a typical Greek, he wanted to outdo me in amount of honesty. I threw away a quarter million dollars. He was putting his job and the reputation of his company in jeopardy. How much is that worth?

That evening, at dinner, I gave Micky my quarter million dollars' worth of advice for him. I repeated the conversation, and Micky looked at me as if I were dim-witted. He said, "Do you really think I needed Felouris to tell me they are crooks? I have known that all along. Your advice is worth nothing. You are a fool for rejecting the finder's fee."

Micky and the Tidal Marine principals kept swapping stock until Micky had no more left. He had by now over a million Tidal Marine stock worth close to $19,000,000 in market value. Our IMAC stock was trading at $10 while Tidal Marine was $18.75. Still the Amanatides-Livas duo needed more of our stock. Micky suggested to me, and to Moira, who was now back in New York, and to his wife Kemper, to trade their stock with Tidal Marine on an even one-for-one basis. I had 35,000 shares, Moira had an equal number, and Kemper had 200,000 shares. We did the trades and drank a toast to Amanatides for giving us such a great deal. We automatically made nine dollars per share.

A month after I made the swap, Linde came to New York, and I sold a thousand shares for twenty dollars per share—due to scarcity of Tidal Marine stock in circulation, the stock was going up—to pay for her shopping. According to appearances, the Shearson Hammill brochures, and the press, Tidal Marine was doing extraordinarily well. They had a fleet of fifty-seven tankers, twelve bulk carriers and eighteen general cargo ships, and in tonnage they were the third largest Greek shipping company. Only Livanos and Onassis were bigger, because of their supertankers. Nobody had as many ships. In fact, Germany or France did not have as large a merchant navy as Tidal Marine. These facts created a frenzy of demand for the Tidal Marine stock. The reality, however, was quite different.

By the time we had swapped all our IMAC stock with the Tidal Marine principles Livas and Amanatides, our IMAC stock was down to $9.50, while the Tidal Marine stock had reached $18. Between himself and Kemper, Micky had now accumulated a little over 1,500,000 Tidal Marine shares. Since he was no longer manipulating the IMAC stock, it was expected that it would gradually drop. Especially given that there was no substance of any kind behind the company. There were only misleading and outright fraudulent reports and accounts. IMAC had less than $60,000 worth of real assets, yet the equity represented in the stock was close to $16,000,000. About eighty-five percent of the IMAC stock was with four banks, where it was being used as collateral for Tidal Marine loans. The banks: Bank of America, the first largest bank in the United States; First National City Bank, which was second; First National Bank of North America, forty-first in size; and Westminster Bank of England, the second largest in England, may have been jittery with the IMAC stock going steadily down, but they were not willing to trade it at a loss.

It was at this juncture, April 1972, that Livas and Amanatides came to Micky with a new proposal. They offered to sell him five tankers, all with at least three-year time charters, for $18,300,000. They said that they wanted at least $3,300,000 cash and they would arrange, with their banks, the loans needed for Micky to cover the remaining $15,000,000. They also offered to service the loans, manage the ships, and pay Micky $50,000 per month. The loans would be for five years, after which time the ships would belong to Micky, free of all debts and encumbrances. It was a deal too good to be true. I was suspicious from the start, but there was nothing concrete I could criticize or object to. Why would anyone give five ships that made tons of money, for practically nothing, and pay you on top if it?

Micky was also skeptical, but he was fascinated by the idea. So, he sold about 200,000 shares of Tidal Marine and paid the cash. The National Bank of North America—one of this bank's five directors, Gregory Spartalis, had been among the first to contribute in the creation of Tidal Marine—lent Micky $8,000,000 for three of the ships. All three had four-year time charters with either BP or a German refinery in Hamburg. The time charters were the main collateral. A time charter for a ship is the equivalent of a rental lease for a house. The remaining $7,000,000 was lent by the Bank of America for the other two tankers. It was the same arrangement: three and four-year time charters, which by themselves covered the whole amount of the loan. Micky then became not only a substantial ship owner with five medium size tankers and two bulk carriers, but he was also one of the major shareholders of Tidal Marine. He explained to me that Amanatides had a temporary cash flow problem, and that prompted the sale of those tankers. Amanatides said he needed the $18,000,000 to plug some holes.

At the same time, the two principals of Tidal Marine were treated like gods in Greece. The military dictatorship held them in much higher esteem than Onassis whom they did not trust, or Niarchos whom they loathed. Amanatidis' mother, an elderly, half-illiterate peasant widow, lived alone on the island of Skiathos in the northwest Aegean Sea. The only means of transportation on the island was by horse, mule, donkey, or bicycle. She was complaining that she was too old to walk to church every Sunday—a distance of less than a kilometer—so her son sent her a golden Rolls Royce with an English chauffeur and the chauffeur's wife as her servants. The car arrived at the harbor of the island, but there was nowhere to go since there were no roads meant for automobiles. The dictatorship in Greece immediately ordered the army to go and build a road from the house of Mrs. Amanatides to the church. The road was built within seventy-two hours. That is the kind of treatment these two were receiving in Greece. In 1972, the Tidal Marine stock was also traded in the Athens stock exchange, but there were never enough shares available to satisfy the demand.

I was planning my annual vacation for the fourth of July in 1972. I had a full month and wanted to take advantage of the extra day due to the American national holiday. On the first of July, Micky called me on the phone, very early in the morning, and told that he planned to dump all his shares of Tidal Marine, starting at 10:30 that morning. He said, "I give you fair warning: sell your shares now, because when I start selling, stock will crumble and lose most of its value."

I had 33,000 shares left, at $19.50 per share. That was over $640,000. There was nothing I needed or wanted to buy of such value. It was 8:45 a.m. and the market in New York opened at 9:30 a.m. The idea of having so much money in cash made me nervous. So, I called Steve Felouris at Shearson, Hammill and asked his advice. He said that if Micky dumped all 1,500,000 of his Tidal Marine shares at once, it might draw the stock down to $17 or slightly less in the first hour, but since there was such a scarcity of stock in recent months, by the end of the day it would stabilize at present levels or even increase in value. He told me it was a blessing in disguise, and if I didn't need the money, I should hold on to them and I would not regret.

I followed his advice. Indeed, Micky started selling, after having also warned his ex-wife Moira. She sold most of her stock and bought a big house on Long Island. As Felouris had predicted, the stock fell to $15.50 in the first hour, but then it started gaining, and by the end of the session at four o' clock in the afternoon, it closed at $20.

The fourth of July was a Monday. When I boarded the plane for my vacation, I felt very secure and pleased with my financial situation. The plane arrived in Athens early in the morning of July fifth, and I asked Linde to drive to a central place in downtown Athens where there was a running light display of the Tidal Marine stock. It was $22. I felt on top of the world and told Linde we would have the most luxurious and extravagant vacation possible.

She told me that the Australian immigration minister was officially in Greece and that she had invited him and his wife, and the Australian ambassador—who was a bachelor—for a cruise on board our yacht. I felt a little annoyed at Linde for having planned the whole itinerary without consulting me, but I was very content for holding close to a million dollars' worth of shares that might go even higher.

I knew that Linde had developed a friendship with the Aussie, but like all husbands, I was the last to suspect that my wife was having an affair. Our yacht was a 42-foot ketch with a relatively small 85 horsepower Perkins diesel motor. It was a true sailing boat and could only sleep four with some modicum of comfort. There was definitely no room for five, plus the crew of two. "No," she said, "We will go and visit all the new Xenia hotels, built recently on the shores of the Aegean and sleep there." Only the crew would sleep on board. The only reason I needed the crew was because I wanted to relax and enjoy without having to use my energy pulling ropes or tinkering with the smelly engine.

Every detail had been taken good care of, and I liked the company of the Australian minister. The Xenia hotels we frequented were all clean and well-organized, and the food was superb. My cousin Helen, Micky's sister, and her multi-millionaire husband were also accompanying us in their yacht, an 85-foot motor sailer, and we competed in sailsmanship. I enjoyed myself, and I ignored the Australian ambassador who was obviously flirting with my wife. I was so happy that even the idea of shooting him did not cross my mind. Later, I learned that my cousin Helen, a notorious adulteress, knew all along about Linde's affair and evidently approved. I never could understand why women married to good, generous, and strong men are adulterous with others who are not up to their husband's standard. Helen was married to a demigod. Not only was her husband rich beyond measure, but he was also breathtakingly handsome, athletic, devoted and loyal. He was any woman's dream. And, without any false humility, I was also made of the same material.

CHAPTER **33**

The Highest Decoration

IN ATHENS, AT the end of 1970, I was studying the archives and preparing myself for my new assignment to the Greek Consulate General in New York, and to the United Nations.

Micky was delighted with my forthcoming arrival in New York. Meanwhile, Micky's mother died in Paris. Since the government would pay for the shipping of my household plus one car from Germany or Greece to New York, Micky suggested I go to Paris and pick up his mother's Rolls Royce and have it shipped to New York as my car.

Apart from the car, I had nothing else to ship because Linde was not ready to leave Athens. She said she needed at least three months to liquidate her business without incurring a loss. Her floor polishing products were selling at a one hundred percent profit to practically all hotels of Greece. She was advertising her shampoo on television, with herself as the model, and also making a killing. I knew she had no intention to leave Greece. Financial security, freedom and a 42-foot yacht, that she could now sail to perfection, were strong incentives to remain where she was, and ignore a life in New York. Before I left, however, she promised to come for a few days to attend Basil—we now called him Bill—Lilios' wedding. He had been my school mate and Micky's partner when Micky started his business with Bill's savings.

I had to spend three months at the Greek Foreign Ministry in Athens and study the entire contents of the archives dealing with Greco-American relations. Those archives start at the year 1818, about eleven years before Greece even existed as an independent country. They comprised of correspondence between a Liberation Committee of Greeks based in Paris and ex-President Thomas Jefferson whom those Greeks had met when he was American ambassador in Paris.

The Greeks were beseeching Thomas Jefferson to use his influence with the American administration and provide this Greek committee with weapons and munitions that America did not need any more since she had gained her independence. The correspondence was conducted in calligraphic French. On the other hand, Jefferson was advising and admonishing the Greek Liberation Committee that once Greece was liberated from Turkish rule, they should establish a pure and true democracy in Greece. He was giving them advice how to proceed in creating a Greek democracy. The response was, "Respectfully we acknowledge and appreciate your advice, Mr. President. At this point we are most concerned that, in order to obtain independence and create a Greek democracy, we need rifles, we need gunpowder, we need ammunition, and we need warships. We hope that you Americans who are friends of Greece might provide for Greece, since you don't need them yourselves." Again, the response from Jefferson was the same: once Greece is liberated from Turkish rule, make sure not to deviate from democratic rule.

After I studied, and learned by heart, the entire contents of the Greco-American relations archives of the Greek Foreign Ministry, I was sent to New York for what would be a three-year career.

I set foot for the first time on the American continent in February 1971 in Kennedy Airport. Micky and Kemper were waiting for me in her father's Mercedes. I had plenty of luggage and they explained to me that they didn't have a car big enough to hold so much. We drove Sands Point, Long Island into a gated and fenced area where each house had to have at least six acres of ground. It was called Harbor Acres and was one of the snobbiest and most expensive places in the world. There were fewer than one hundred houses within the fence, but they had their private police, and nobody could enter unless expected. I was very impressed with the house and the huge trampoline covering the enormous swimming pool. The garage contained eleven cars. One, a Mercedes 350 sport model, was Kemper's. All the others were Micky's. He always did like lots of toys, to the point of stealing them from Peter, when he was still a child.

He said, "You can pick any one you like to go to work, except the big Facel, or the Ferrari." All had diplomatic plates, not the real thing, issued by the United Nations. Micky said the moment I had presented myself and been admitted, I would be issued the real plates, and I would have diplomatic identification which he planned to use also for himself.

Sands Point was seven miles away from the Long Island Expressway, and another seventeen miles to New York City. I had to be at the Consulate General of Greece not later than 9:00 a.m. but Micky woke me at 6:00 a.m. I said we could do twenty-four miles in a quarter of an hour, why so early? I was thinking of my beloved autobahns and the one hundred miles per hour speeds. Little did I know that the Long Island Expressway was a moving parking lot. The average speed was ten miles per hour and sometimes less. Micky drove me to the consulate which was on Seventy-Ninth Street between Madison and Fifth Avenue, one block away from the Metropolitan Museum. He said he would come and pick me up in the evening and show me Manhattan.

Even before I arrived in New York, the German consul general had sent a letter requesting me to contact his office upon my arrival. I did so, and he told me that he had been ordered by *Bundespresident* Heinemann to bestow upon me on his behalf the *Bundesverdianstkreuz erste, zweite and dritte Classe um die an der Bundesrepublik Deutschland erworbenen Besondere Verdienste.*

The *Bundesverdienstkreuz*, the Order of Merit, is the highest decoration that a civilian can obtain from the German Republic. I was asked how many people I intended to invite to the ceremony, so the German consulate could prepare the banquet. When I asked why they didn't give me the decorations in Germany, I was told that there was no time. I invited all the personnel of the Greek consulate, the press office, and the Greek United Nations delegation, as well as the dozen people that Micky suggested. To my surprise, and disappointment, none of the consulate nor the UN delegation attended.

The German consul general revealed that my abrupt transfer from Germany had been requested by the German government for my own protection. My role in the uncovering of the spy activity might have consequences and I was better off away from Germany. He also conveyed the personal greetings and congratulation of Helmut Schmidt. I am still the only Greek to ever get the highest German decoration. It made me proud. Greece did not reward me, despite it was something that benefited the whole of NATO. I am still grateful to Germany. The Greek diplomats were green with envy. My black, red, and gold chest band with the eagle dangling at the end was my most valued possession.

At the consulate, there was no room for me in the Press and Information Office. In the beginning, I had to share the entry hall with another employee. The United Nations Delegation was the second floor of the building. No room for me there either. It came that I shared an office with two others. The third floor was the consulate, and the top floors were the residences of the United Nations ambassador and the consul general.

The ambassador was indifferent, so the consul general, even though junior in rank, ran the place as it were his own fiefdom. My immediate superior, the director of the press office, was an active-duty naval officer of questionable intelligence, poor command of English, and very narrow capabilities. He had clashed with the consul general. They were not on speaking terms, and they were both sending reports to Athens accusing each other of all kinds of offenses, from treason to utter stupidity.

The naval officer, a commander, was the only one of his kind to espouse the military dictatorship. All other naval officers were loyal to the king, and indifferent, or outright inimical, to the colonels who had taken over Greece. The military dictatorship led by Colonel Papadopoulos comprised exclusively of army brigadiers and colonels. The naval officer was loyal to the military dictators, but he was a troublemaker, so they exiled him to New York and made him Director of Press and Information Office. They sent me there to build up his office and his function. The consul general had proven his loyalty to the regime, and he was a protégé of my aunt Dorette, the very rich one with the Italian chauffeurs. I was very much in the middle, but I soon chose to support the naval officer because I couldn't stand the overbearing and arrogant attitude of the consul.

After a few weeks in New York, I had mixed feelings. I didn't like the environment nor the people I had to work with at the consulate. My salary was only fifty dollars more than what it had been in Bonn, in Germany. I had an hour and half drive each day to go to work. In the evening I would go to Micky's office, and we would wait until it was seven o' clock, having a beer and contemplating the future, so the drive back after the rush hour, was only an hour.

The positive aspects were, I was living rent free in a luxurious mansion in one of the best suburbs of New York. At the Greek consulate, I had very little to do, and there was hardly anything expected of me, other than wasting time at the General Assembly of the United Nations, which was at best, a charade. I had a millionaire cousin who was intending to increase his fortune. I had all the advantages of a millionaire's life without the problems or anxieties of losing the money. Our weekends were spent either on Long Island, or sailing—Micky had a 32-foot sloop at Sands Point, and a 72-foot Burger in Fort Lauderdale—playing with expensive toys or hunting in Tennessee. It was a very pleasant life. But it was not rewarding for me after my experience in Germany. I wanted some action.

The only thing that really bothered me was the Afghan Hound of Kemper's. He was a perfect exemplar of his breed, show material, really, but he was vicious and sneaky. Kemper adored him and she had stated very plainly that if we were to harm her dog or try to chase him away, she would also go. One reason Micky hated the dog was because, since Micky liked his steaks very rare and the dog was tall enough to reach the top of our dining table with his head, he would grab Micky's steak off his plate. Kemper would not allow us to put the dog out while we were having dinner. Kemper, and marriage to her, was an integral part of Micky's future plans, so we had to endure the dog. Although I did have a failed attempt to dispose of him.

In the consulate of New York, I had the title of Consul as far as the consulate was concerned, but I was in essence the Deputy Director of the Press and Information Service of Greece in New York. I was also a member of the Greek delegation to the United Nations. There my rank was First Embassy Secretary. Poor countries like Greece cannot afford to have a full membership representation at the United Nations. Greece had a skeleton of about five. In contrast, Cuba had about 130 personnel with her U.N. delegation, even though Cuba did not have diplomatic relations with the United States. Russia had about 300 members in her delegation. The Ukraine had about forty, and Byelorussia had another forty. The international theatre called the United Nations would draw the curtains every September, and all the heads of state and the ministers of foreign affairs assemble in New York. Greece, in order to man all the various commissions and committees in which she participated, would bring in the consuls from all over the United States, and Canada to reinforce her U.N. delegation.

I was sent to the Anti-Colonial Committee at one point. On the occasion, we were discussing Angola and Mozambique. Our NATO ally, Portugal, was also a dictatorship, so I felt a certain degree of affinity toward Mr. Salazar who had been dictator in Portugal for about forty-five years. I thought that the Portuguese policy that Angola and Mozambique were overseas provinces of Portugal was good enough policy for me. However, the anti-colonial powers wanted Portugal to lose her African colonies. It seems that the United States had its eye on Angola because there was at the time alleged that Angola has oil that had not been exploited as yet.

The matter came to a vote, which is conducted by colored bulbs. There are only three bulbs: a blue one which means yes, a white one which means abstention, and a red one which means no. If you vote either yes or no, you can't change that vote, but if you vote abstention, you have the right to revise and change that vote to either yes or no. An abstention is not necessarily an abstention, it is 'pause,' like 'passing.' The vote in the General Assembly at the United Nations is alphabetical: Afghanistan, Albania, and so forth. *F* is before *G* and when France's turn came, for reasons of her own, she voted against Portugal. When *G* came up, Greece, —represented by the Consul General of Chicago who was chief in the Greek delegation in that committee—without any hesitation voted against Portugal. I asked him if he had any specific instructions to vote against Portugal. He said that nobody had given him any instructions.

"Why did you vote against Portugal? I queried.

"Well!" he rejoined, "Didn't you see France voting against her?"

"So? Perhaps the French have their own reasons. After all, they are also a colonial power in Africa. Why would we vote against a fellow member of NATO and a fellow dictatorship?"

He shrugged, "If the French voted against it, that's good enough reason for me." With that, I had a very depleted opinion of how Greek foreign policy was conducted.

We both sat in the two seats which were reserved in the General Assembly for Greece, and when the vote was over, the Portuguese Foreign Minister approached us with a quizzical expression on his face, and he said, "Why?"

And of course, we had nothing to say. I could not speak, to tell him, "Because France voted against you," since the Consul General of Chicago was a superior to me, hierarchically speaking, in the Greek diplomatic service.

The Soviet Union had three seats in the UN; the Ukraine, White Russia, or Belarus as they call it now, and Russia, all three had representatives at the UN, and three different votes. If the United States were not a spineless oyster, she would have demanded forty-eight on the same grounds.

I would pontificate in the cafeteria at the United Nations, giving my opinion on everything, for example, after I returned from my one and only visit to the state of Washington. The first city in America I saw, after New York, was Seattle. In a rented car I went to admire Olympic National Park on the border between Washington state and British Columbia. That was my first pontification at the cafeteria of the UN. After returning from that beautiful place, I said to whomever wanted to listen in the cafeteria, that until recently I thought that the prettiest spot on earth was Delphi, but I was wrong. The prettiest spot on earth is Olympic National Park in the state of Washington.

Hearing that, a Ukrainian delegate, one of the Soviet Union's votes, spoke out. The Ukrainian said, "Have you ever been to Lake Baikal?" I had never heard of Lake Baikal, and I certainly had not been there. "No, where is Lake Baikal?"

"It's in Siberia."

I retorted, "How would you expect me to go to Siberia? I have been only a diplomat in your country, not a political detainee."

He urged, "The prettiest spot on earth is Lake Baikal."

"If one were to spend time in Siberia," I responded, "I doubt that the alleged beauty of Lake Baikal would be attractive enough." Apparently, Lake Baikal *was* one of the prettiest spots on earth, but they polluted it so much as to make it a dead sea. It is a great long lake in southwestern Siberia, near the Mongolian border. It is the largest freshwater lake in Eurasia, and at almost a mile in depth, it is the deepest freshwater lake in the world. Lake Baikal holds as much fresh water as the shallower lakes Superior, Huron, Ontario, Michigan, and Erie combined.

When I first came to New York I was fortunate, because what was supposed to be the most authoritative newspaper in New York was not against my regime. The *New York Times* was friendly because of Cyrus Shultzberger, a reporter who was married to Roxanne, a Greek woman from Rhodes. Cyrus Shultzberger had lived half his life in Greece. He was in Greece when the military took over, so he gave a true report, and he kept on reporting truthfully. So, the *New York Times* was friendly. I had established some good contacts with the newspaper, and I was on friendly terms with a man named Grousseu who eventually became the chief editor. We were discussing my admiration for Notre Dame University, and he told me jokingly, "More than half of our reporters are graduates of Notre Dame. It would be fair to say that the *New York Times* is a newspaper written by Catholics, read by Protestants, and owned by Jews."

I had added one new assignment to my duties as press attaché of Greece in New York. I was encouraging film producers to go to Greece to shoot their movies, where the military government was most accommodating in providing them with the free usage and services of the Greek armed forces. They could have any number of disciplined extras—whole battalions if need be—warships, airplanes, helicopters, tanks—all free. The reason was that movies made in Greece were portraying the country under a favorable perspective, thus negating the bad press, and it increased tourism which was the second most important source of revenue for Greece. The first most important source was the merchant marine, which was the biggest in the world.

I became a member of the Players Club in Manhattan and concentrated my efforts on meeting and befriending producers, directors, and actors. I had two vociferous and fanatic enemies: Melina Mercouri and Irene Pappas. Unfortunately, they were both exceptionally good actresses and well known in America. Their efforts at sabotaging my attempts to sway producers toward Greece were sometimes successful.

Irene Pappas was not as vociferous or as visible as Melina in her denunciations of the military regime of Greece, primarily because she was not in New York most of the time. She was more respected than Melina and much more representative of a typical Hellenic beauty. She played the part of the widow in the movie, *Zorba the Greek*.

A script came my way for a film with Greek characters. It was about how a Greek peasant mother reacts when she finds that her teenage son is homosexual. Irene refused the role if the film was to be shot in Greece, as she was averse to the military government. She had been offered $100,000 for six weeks of shooting. I approached an equally good actress, a little older than Irene, and with no resemblance to a Greek whatsoever. I asked her to accept the role, and she did, for half the money. It was Susan Hayward, an Oscar winner, and a very good person.

CHAPTER **34**

Archbishop of the Americas

WHEN I ARRIVED in New York, the consul general and the director of press and information services were not on speaking terms, and they were both sending reports to Athens accusing each other of all kinds of offenses. The main reason of their clash—other than their diametrically different characters—was the Greek Orthodox Archbishop of the Americas. My first secret order from Athens, before I left Greece, was to study the situation and send an objective report. Since I was Roman Catholic, they expected true objectivity from me.

In New York, I didn't tell anybody that I had this assignment. I just listened. I listened to my superior, the director of the press and information. I discussed the matter with the consul general, who was a graduate of the same school I attended in Athens, and I thought I would have some kind of affinity with him. Both were fanatic in their stands: the consul general supported the archbishop, and was a personal friend; my superior, the naval officer, took the side of the Greeks who opposed the archbishop.

Since the Patriarchate is in Constantinople, and the Turks determine who occupies that throne, they had made it absolutely plain and clear that Archbishop Iakovos stood no chance of ever becoming Ecumenical Patriarch. So, Archbishop Iakovos, a man of insatiable ambition, set his sights on becoming the first ever Patriarch of 'The American Orthodox Church' which he was planning to create by uniting all the orthodoxies in America under his scepter.

His first step was to introduce English in the orthodox liturgy. He did not translate the whole liturgy into English, less than a third, but that was enough to arouse the older Greek immigrants against him. They saw it as a sacrilege to adulterate the original language of the Gospels with the language of the heathen barbarians. Another step of the archbishop that made him more enemies in Chicago—there were over 4,000 Greeks there—was selling a Greek Church for $2,500,000 to the Black Muslims. All Greek churches in America are automatically property of the Archdiocese regardless of who built them. Many Greeks in Chicago accused him of stealing the money.

I decided to take my assignment concerning the archbishop seriously, so I flew to Chicago to find out about the harangue against him by the Chicagoan Greeks. I found that indeed the archbishop had sold the church to the Black Muslims, and indeed he had trousered $2,500,000. The Greeks there demanded, "How does he dare sell our church? After all, it is we who built the church." However, for a church to be accepted and consecrated by the archdiocese, if one reads the fine print, it says that the moment the church is consecrated and accepted, it becomes property of the archdiocese, not any more the property of the people who built it.

That church was in a neighborhood that had been taken over by the Negroes and the Greeks had fled to the suburbs. Hardly any of them ventured back on Sundays to attend the liturgy service. In the Catholic Church it is called a mass, and it is identical in both churches. Except for one part of the Apostle's Creed: the *Filioque*. They had built a new church in their present suburban location.

I asked, "Did you go to that church before the archbishop sold it?" "No", they asserted, "we couldn't. The whole area there is inhabited by Negroes."

"Well," I returned, "in that case, the church was not functioning."

"No," they acknowledged, "the priest also fled, and we built a new church in the suburb where we live now."

"So," I said, "the church was totally idle."

"Yes," they retorted, "but that doesn't mean that the bishop should sell it. To the Black Muslims!"

It was opportune for the Muslims, because all Greek churches face east, the same as the mosques. I thought two and a half million dollars was not a bad price. And I thought the archbishop has done pretty damn well. The sale was legitimate and justifiable.

In New York City, the most vociferous critics of the archbishop were George Kassavetes and Elia Kazan. George Kassavetes was the father of John Kassavetes, the Hollywood actor. He said that it is an outrage that the language of the Gospels is now being adulterated by English. He maintained that we Greeks have the unique privilege and advantage that our language is the one that was used to spread Christianity. Our language is the one in which the gospels were written. Our language is the one that the Jews translated their Torah. "And now," he accused, "we have this archbishop allowing English to adulterate our liturgy. It's sacrilege and it's an outrage."

"Mr. Kassavetes," I reasoned, "I see your point, and I agree with you that Greek is definitely, as far as Christianity goes, *the* language. But," I continued, "does your son speak a word of Greek?"

He admitted, "No."

Next, I went to meet Elia Kazan, who was a well-known screen writer and director. He was married to a Jewess, and his daughters spoke not a word of Greek. Elia Kazan told me that upon arriving in America—his autobiographical story is told in the film, *America, America*—he shed everything Greek about him. He changed his name from Kazantzoglou to Kazan. He married an American woman, and he made sure that his children would be raised like Protestant Americans. When he became a success in Hollywood, he began to realize that people from Mexico, from Poland, from Puerto Rico, and from other places, were proud of their origins. They were proud of their heritage; they were proud of being something other than born Americans. Elia Kazan thought, *if those people can be proud of their heritage, what about me? I have the most glorious heritage of any people on earth. Why should I differentiate from my Greek origins and from my Greek traditions?* He came to New York, and he became a super Greek. So, his arguments against the archbishop were not particularly convincing.

I asked how they could criticize the archbishop about introducing English into the liturgy when they had failed to teach Greek in their own families. Personally—even though I could see the archbishop's future plan—I thought that the introduction of English into the liturgy of the Greek Orthodox churches in America was a positive step to keep the younger generations interested into the Greek church. When they went there, they would hear something that they would understand.

We Greeks share a unique situation with the Jews. Our religion is also our ethnicity. All Greeks, with very few exceptions, are Greek Orthodox. The church is the invisible chain that keeps us together and reminds who we are. The longer this bond holds, the better for mother Greece. Our policy is to prevent assimilation of the Greeks in their new homes in the Americas and Australia.

All that, in minutest detail, was written in a memorandum which I typed myself because I didn't trust anybody in the consulate, especially since my superior was against the archbishop and the consul was pro-archbishop. I typed it myself, and I put it myself into the diplomatic bag on Wednesday morning, and I took the diplomatic bag myself to the airport and gave it to the hands of the pilot of Olympic Airlines plane that left for Athens on Wednesday.

On Friday, around 10:30 in the morning, I received a telephone call from Bishop Seles, who was the adjutant of the Archbishop Iakovos. Bishop Selas inquired, "Mr. Panayotopoulos, are you free for lunch?" Wondering, I said, "Yes."

"The archbishop would like you to be his guest for lunch here at the Archdiocese," he invited.

It was very unexpected. I didn't know if the archbishop knew that I am Catholic or not. I had only been in New York for a little over four weeks at that time. But I said, "I'll be more than happy to accept the archbishop's invitation. What time shall I arrive?"

The Archdiocese was diametrically across the street from the consulate, on Seventy-Ninth Street., only about a hundred paces. I went, full of curiosity. Why would the cleric want to have lunch with me? We hardly knew each other, and by now it was known that I was Catholic.

The archbishop was extremely cordial, as if we were long lost brothers. He served dishes that were my favorites, and also the wines I preferred. Even the cigar he offered me was an Upmann. It was uncanny. Instead of coffee after lunch, he served tea with scones and malted whiskey. He commented, "I could not find your grandfather's distillate on such short notice, but I hope Glenlivet will please you."

"How do you know my grandfather distills his own whisky?" I asked in astonishment.

"I know about your grandfather's still, and that he has a flock of geese guarding his vats. I know everything there is to know about you." I thought since he served Graves Superior and Riesling and *Châteauneuf Du Pape*, and my favorite cigar, he obviously did know a lot about me. "For what do I merit the attention of your Eminence?" I said, taken aback.

"I read your report, and I wanted to express my gratitude for your objectivity and truthfulness," he declared.

I was stunned. How could he have read my report? There were no copies, and I had made sure that nobody could have read it before I personally placed in into the diplomatic bag. The only possible explanation was that someone in the Foreign Ministry in Athens had read, or faxed, it to him. He saw my astonishment in my face and smiled, as if to answer, and said, "Never underestimate the reach or the capabilities of the Church. You and I shall be good friends." He paused, and continued, "I am appreciative, but I have one thing to ask. My request to you is, even though you are Catholic, I want you every Sunday at my church."

It was pain to drive all the way from Sands Point, but at least on Sunday morning, it only took me forty minutes to drive to Manhattan. When Archbishop Iakovos died from a pulmonary ailment at the age of ninety-three, in 2005, his obituary confirmed what my experience with him had been, and that he had not changed. He was known for reaching out to other religious groups and for his great efforts in ecumenism. His goals had obviously not changed, and he was driven out of his leadership in 1996 apparently because he supported the idea of uniting various Eastern Orthodox branches into a single American church. He was the first Greek Orthodox archbishop to meet with a Roman Catholic prelate and always sought to bring together and unite all people of faith.

He was born in Turkey and led the Greek Orthodox Archdiocese of North and South America, which has approximately 2,000,000 followers, for thirty-seven years from 1959 until 1996. The titular head of World Orthodoxy, Patriarch Bartholomew, came into direct conflict with Iakovos in 1994. It is widely believed that Bartholomew forced Iakovos to resign. Iakovos held a meeting with twenty-nine bishops from the ten North American branches of Eastern Orthodoxy and he recommended placing all the churches under a single administrative system while allowing their ties to remain with the separate 'mother churches' in Greece and Russia.

CHAPTER **35**

Apollo, the Jewish Baby

WHEN I HAD been in New York for only a short time, I arrived quite early one morning, before opening hours for the consulate. Usually, the department chiefs went there before the other employees to prepare work for them, so it must have been about 7:30 or eight o'clock in the morning. I was sitting at my desk reading the report of the 1970 census of Greece which I had to submit to the United Nations. To my great sorrow, I was reading that Greece was a dying nation, and that according to the census of 1970 deaths superseded births in Greece. I was thinking, what Romans, Turks and all other barbarians had not managed to succeed, we were doing to ourselves. Through emigration and poverty, we were having more deaths than births in Greece. The population was down to 7,800.000.

At that point, the telephone rang, and since there were no employees yet at the consulate, I answered the phone. It was a young woman on the other end of the line, and she said, "I am interested in adopting a Greek child."

The moment was not opportune for me to speak of Greek children. I was realizing that that was the problem of Greece, we didn't have enough children, so unfortunately my real self took over and I was extremely rude, which comes, unfortunately, naturally with me, and I barked, "Why, Madame, do you want to adopt a Greek child? Don't you think there are enough Negro children in America to be adopted?"

She divulged, "My neighbor adopted a Greek child, and it turned out to be very good."

I alleged, "Children are not like watermelons. Just because you went to a greengrocer and the watermelons happen to be good and sweet, does not mean that all of them should be the same. Children have different characters. Greek children included."

She responded, "I don't understand why you are so rude with me."

Then I became aware that I was indeed very rude to her, and I said, "I'm sorry for being rude to you, but you caught me on the wrong moment."

She told me her name was Mrs. Appelbaum, and that she was twenty-eight years old. When I asked why she didn't have a child of her own, she sighed, "For nine years, my husband and I have tried to have a child and we have failed."

"There must be some physiological reason why you can't conceive," I suggested. "Or perhaps either you or your husband has a defect."

"No," she protested, "We have been examined and reexamined by doctors. Neither my husband nor I have any kind of physiological or physical defect. It just happens that we can't conceive"

"How old is your husband? I pursued.

"He's twenty-eight, also."

"Where do you work? I continued my interrogation. and was told, at the First National City Bank, in different branches, and they lived in Flatbush. I asked her how much money they intended to spend for the adoption, and she told me they had saved two thousand dollars, which, in 1971, is much more than it is today.

I mused, "I tell you what. If there are no physiological or physical reasons for you and your husband not to have a baby of your own, I will give you a recipe, that you have to follow religiously, and you will have a baby of your own. If, after following what I'm going to tell you, you fail to become pregnant, then I will do my utmost to get you a Greek child from the orphanage of the Archdiocese in Brookline, Massachusetts. Can you and your husband take a vacation starting say, on the second of May?"

"Yes," she said, "We can arrange that."

"What I am going to tell you," I cautioned, "you must follow faithfully. Do not deviate one iota. And it will cost you probably less that the two thousand dollars you have set aside for having a baby. You and your husband," I instructed, "on or around the second of May, should book passage with Olympic Airlines to Athens. Upon arrival at the airport of Athens, don't bother about going to Athens and seeing the Acropolis. The Acropolis has stood for two and a half thousand years. She will be there when you return."

I went on, "Once you get out of the airport, you will see a lot of buses, tourist buses, Pullman buses. Read where those buses go, and once you see the bus which says Delphi, D-E-L-P-H-I, board that bus. It will take you about three hours of traveling on the bus, and you will reach Delphi, which my glorious ancestors believed to be the umbilical cord of the world. They thought it was the most beautiful spot on earth. When you arrive at Delphi, ask someone where is the Vouzas Hotel, V-O-U-Z-A-S.

Go into that hotel and book a room. Since it will be early May, chances stand that the tourist avalanche will not have booked all the rooms of the hotel. But whichever room you take, they are all the same."

"The Vouzas Hotel is built on the hanging rock of the mountain," I told her. "The top floor is actually the ground floor. It is amphitheatric, and all the rooms have the same view of that magnificent valley. Go into your room, descending on the elevator, and draw back the curtains and enjoy the view. Now the regimen starts for you to have your own baby. Tell the receptionist to wake you up at quarter-to-six. At quarter-to-six you and your husband walk to the Castalia Fountain. It's the fountain where the oracle used to drink water."

I advised her, "That water has peculiar qualities, one of which is fertility. The walking will take you about not more than ten minutes. Sit there, drink water and wait for the sun to rise. Enjoy the view, drink as much water as you can, and now walk back to your hotel. Go to your room and copulate in what we Christians call the missionary position, in other words, your husband on top of you, and in order to assure total penetration, take the pillows and put them under your bottom. You do that for fifteen days, each and every day, and if your period happens to come in between, ignore it. I know that you Jews avoid copulating during your menses, but in this case, it is part of the regimen. Ignore it and continue copulating with your husband every morning, first thing in the morning after you return from the Castalia fountain."

"Then," I concluded, "take the plane, come back to New York, and if you are not pregnant, call me."

About a year later—of course, I had forgotten the episode—my secretary said, "A Mrs. Appelbaum is on the phone for you." The name didn't ring any bells. I took the call, and a voice said, "Thanks to you, I have a baby boy!"

"Madame, there must be a mistake. I don't know you."

"No," she clarified, "don't you remember? I'm the woman that you sent to Delphi."

"Oh! So, it did work!"

"Yes! I got pregnant and now I have a baby boy. And because we owe it to you, we decided to baptize in the Greek Orthodox Church in Flatbush." I wanted to tell her that since her baby was conceived it Delphi, the Greek Orthodox Church had nothing to do with it. If she wanted to thank someone, it should be Apollo because Delphi was dedicated to the god Apollo, but I didn't go into that detail.

I said, "Are you sure you want to *baptize* it?"

"Yes, she affirmed, "we are going to baptize him in the Flatbush Greek

Orthodox Church. We have already spoken to the priest and the priest told the archbishop, and the archbishop decided to officiate the baptismal himself."

Then she announced, "We want you to be the godfather." I agreed. Since I would be the godfather, I decided to name the boy Apollo. It was a big occasion, the archbishop was both delighted and mystified because in the annals of the Greek Orthodox Archdiocese of all Americas, it had never happened that a firstborn Jewish boy was baptized a Christian. Very reluctantly, the family of the parents came to the Greek church and to my even greater surprise, the father's parents were Hassidic Jews, those Jews with the black coats and the black hats and the curls hanging down their cheeks.

The baptismal began, the archbishop was indeed officiating. In the Greek baptism the naked baby is placed into the water—which is the meaning of the word baptism anyway. The godfather, in order to prove that he is eligible to be a godfather of a new Christian soul, has to recite, during the baptismal, the Creed of Christianity—that little poem which was written during the Nicene Ecumenical Synod in the year 325 whereby the Christians at that time agreed on what they believed in. And it starts, *"I believe in one God, the Father Almighty, creator of heaven and earth..."* The only dogmatic and fundamental difference between Orthodoxy and Catholicism is within that little poem. In the filioque.

The archbishop knew that I was Roman Catholic, and he was a little apprehensive whether I would recite the Credo the Orthodox way or the Catholic way. The difference is in the Holy Spirit. According to Orthodoxy, the Holy Spirit derives from Father only: "But when the Comforter is come, whom *I will send unto you from the Father*, even the Spirit of truth, *which proceeds from the Father*, He shall testify of me," said Jesus. (John 15:26) It had been established in the Nicene Ecumenical Synod, as a symbol of faith, that there is one head: the Father, and both the Son and the Holy Spirit are subordinate to the Father, and Orthodoxy has adhered to that credo... "and in the Holy Spirit, the Lord, the Giver of life, Who proceeds *from the Father*, Who together with the Father and the Son is worshipped and glorified, and Who spoke through the prophets."

According to Catholicism, the Holy Spirit derives from Father *and* Son, because in the year 948, Pope Innocent VI, added a word, a Latin word, *filioque*, meaning "the son also," to say, ".... Who proceeds *from the Father and of the Son....*" That pope, by inserting *filioque,* made an invisible trinity, whereby Father *equals* Son *equals* Holy Spirit. That, of course, eventually led to the schism, the splitting of the church, in 1054.

When we came to that spot in my recital of the Credo of Christianity, the Archbishop looked at me, I looked at him, and I said, "the Holy Spirit, ... who proceeds *from the Father and the Son*," and the archbishop was really mad at me. In Orthodoxy, those who add "and from the Son," the filioque, sin against the words of Christ Himself. Then, I had to name the baby. The archbishop said, "And what will be the name of this servant of the Lord?" and I said, "Apollo."

The archbishop lowered his hands, and addressing me only, he said, "In my Archdiocese, I do not accept heathen names in a baptismal in which I officiate."

I turned around and looked at the father of the baby, and inquired, "What is your father's name?"

He answered, "It's Abraham."

I turned to the archbishop and said, "Your Eminence, will you accept Abraham as a first name?" He said yes. I pronounced, "The name of this servant of the Lord will be Abraham Apollo."

The boy was triple A: Abraham Apollo Appelbaum. That was a *faux pas* on my part because I didn't know that among the Hassidic Jews it is not allowed to name a firstborn after the grandfather. So, the Hassidim in the church were even further disturbed.

There was a Greek catering house very near the church in Flatbush and that's where the big baptismal party was to be held. After the baptismal we all went there. The archbishop, who was still very offended by me, approached me and said, "I want to know all the details. How did you convince those people to baptize their child in one of my churches?"

"Your Eminence," I recounted, "I used our mythology to convince the woman that the water of the Castalia Fountain in Delphi, has, among many other qualities, also fertility elements. And she believed it."

The archbishop insisted, "I want to know *all* the details."

"Your Eminence," I protested, "you are sworn to celibacy. I can't tell you the details because the details have to do with the sexual act." Nevertheless, he persisted, so I told him the whole story. He didn't believe me.

Archbishop Iakovos became a friend. He was astounded to be asked to baptize and name a Jewish baby Apollo, who came to be because I directed his previously unable-to-conceive parents to the Vouzas Hotel and the mythical waters of the Castalian Fountain in Delphi.

Greeks in general had a low opinion of Jackie and during the First Lady's September 1963 trip to Greece as a guest of shipping tycoon Stavros Niarchos, only royal protocol induced Queen Frederica, shown on the left, to receive her at the palace. In October she returned to America, and a month later her husband was assassinated. Later, unlike the Americans who thought that their ex-First Lady marrying a Greek ship owner was a misalliance, the Greek population thought that Onassis could do much better.

CHAPTER **36**

The Cultured and the Culture Minister

ONE DAY, I was listening to William Buckley on television. He used two Greek words that I thought he had invented himself. One word was *epiphenomena,* and the other word was *epistomonology*. William Buckley was one of the most caustic intellectuals in America and also a man of wit. I wrote him a letter thanking him for enhancing the Greek language with words sounding Greek, of his invention, since we Greeks for the last 2000 years have not managed to add a single word to our vocabulary. I, of course pointed out that neither *epiphenomena* nor *epistomonology* mean anything in Greek.

He wrote to me, "Indeed for the last two thousand years you Greeks have not done anything, including enhancing your language." He gave the definition of *epiphenomena* and *epistomonology* according to the Oxford Dictionary. From the Greek point of view *epistomonology* would translate '*the science of science*,' and *epiphenomena* is a pluralism. A phenomenon is already something unique, so you don't need the preposition *epi* to make it a more phenomenal phenomenon. A phenomenon is obviously not an everyday occurrence, so it doesn't need to be emphasized with the extra preposition. William Buckley, like most highbrow intellectuals, used Greek often in their sentence structures in order to show off their knowledge of the classics and their grasp of classic education.

I suppose William Buckley is the foremost among the highbrows of America. I had a good go myself at his primary debate adversary, the Canadian-born traitor called Kenneth Galbraith, or Professor, or Ambassador to India Kenneth Galbraith. I had a confrontation with him and Melina Mercouri, the two of them against me during the David Frost show in *Metromedia* in New York in 1972.

I found I was confronted by two instead of one when I had asked for equal time to rebuke what Melina Mercouri had already said to David Frost on a previous occasion. As if that were not enough, during that exchange of epithets and accusations, David Frost had assumed a comatose stance as if he were not even there, and I was very mad. At one point Galbraith said the dictatorship in Greece is far worse than anything in China. At which point David Frost seemed to be revived. He came out of the coma, and he said, "Professor Galbraith, have you been to China?"

Galbraith admitted he had not. "Well, I was there last year," said Frost. "Have you been to Greece recently?" Galbraith again answered no. Frost said, "I just returned from Greece a week ago and I can assure you, you are dead wrong."

So now I had an ally, and I felt invigorated, and I attacked them with all vehemence. Then I found out the truth. David Frost, because of his English accent primarily, was the darling of the American plutocracy, those rich nomads who trek from Southampton, Long Island to Palm Beach, Florida and back. He was invited to all their parties, to all their functions, and American wealthy succumb to an English accent. David Frost married a Negress called Diahann Carroll. The moment he did that the doors of Southampton were hermetically closed in his face. At which point the most inverted snob of America, Jackie Kennedy, decided to do something to upset the establishment of Southampton. She invited David Frost and Diahann Carroll to be guests of Onassis for a month on board the *Christina* and on the private island. So, under the conditions and circumstances that David Frost saw Greece, on board *Cristina*, obviously it was the best place on earth.

I had known Melina since I was a child in Athens. She was a tomboy and had a German governess, as did all the children of affluent Athenian Royalist families. We, the Republican liberals, on the other hand, had either British or French governesses. Melina had organized the German speaking youngsters, and was attacking and harassing us, the Franco-Anglophones. She was twelve years old when I was four, and I could not forget the ferocious kicks she had administered to my aching bottom when I was running away from her.

Her family was pro-Hitler and welcomed the German occupation of Greece. It was rumored that her first lover was a German officer. When by 1943, it was obvious that Germany would lose the war, she managed to reach Alexandria in Egypt and become an entertainer of the Greek troops that were stationed there. And there she married a very old and very rich Greek. He was at least seventy when she was eighteen. At the same time, she had an affair with a dashing and flamboyant Greek naval officer whom she married after her husband, leaving her a fortune, died.

They returned to Greece and her new husband became the Commandant of the Greek Naval Academy. The cadets of the era remember her shrieks at the numerous beatings she received from her husband for her many sexual indiscretions. By the time she was twenty-two, she was both a widow and a divorcee. At this point she went to the National School for Dramatic Art in Athens—the only school she ever attended—and after four years, graduated first in her class. She was automatically hired by the National Theatre of Greece and her brilliant acting career took off.

My father told me that during the New Year's celebration in 1948, he and a few of his cronies took Melina to a suite at the best Athens hotel, filled the bathtub with whipped cream, which she entered, and they licked her dry; then they bathed her in champagne and copulated with her for hours. It seems that her sexual lust was superlative and limitless.

Her father, the ex-royalist Germanophile, lost an election with the right-wing party in 1950, and in order to be reelected, he joined the Communists. She met and eventually married the film director, Jules Dassin, who had been blackballed in Hollywood as a Communist. One of his famous movies was *Rififi*. She brought him to Greece and had him direct her in a movie that she financed entirely. It was called, *Never on Sunday*. It was an international smashing success, and the music alone of the film, for which she had paid the composer five hundred dollars, made her millions. His compensation was Academy Awards he won for the music. In 1967, when the military coup occurred in Greece, she was in New York, on the eighth month of her Broadway show, *Ilya Darling* which was the musical rendition of the movie and made more millions. At least, the composer, Manos Hadjidakis, also made some serious money with that.

With this background, she was audacious enough to transform herself into an extremist of the left and a bitter adversary of my military government.

I had a *ZDF*, the German Television Network, confrontation with her in Cologne, while I was assigned in Germany, where she pretended she didn't speak German, and that she didn't know me. I reminded her that the first language she ever spoke was German and that the first man she ever copulated was a German occupation officer. She was infuriated—proving that she very well understood German—and attempted to scratch my eyes with her talons, but I was faster and punched her hard in the stomach. She fainted, but I am not sure it was not a fake. That made a good show on German television, but that round went to her because of my brutality. I had a second and third confrontation with her in New York.

With the next government, she did well; they made her the Hellenic Minister of Culture and called her a 'brave fighter of the resistance movement against the military regime of 1967-1974.'

There was a bookstore in Manhattan, the Rizzoli, that I entered one day, and to my surprise, I recognized that the music playing was music by Mikis Theodorakis, the Communist Greek composer. I was absorbed in listening when the manager approached and asked, "Do you also like this music?"

"I'm sorry," I said, "I cannot answer that, because I am Greek, I am a member of the Greek government, and the Greek government has banned the music."

She was a great admirer of Theodorakis, who had also been the recipient of the Lenin Order for his political activity as a leader of the Greek Communist Youth. He was a Communist type of Baldur von Schirach, the leader of the Hitler *jugend*. The woman and I became friends. She was German born and had a typical German syndrome. Her father had been a Nazi functionary and she needed to atone for that. She had volunteered her services and worked in a kibbutz in Israel to make up for the German stigma. She was an extreme liberal, and she took it upon herself to educate me in becoming a liberal. I allowed her to minister to all my needs and demands, and at her house I found that she had all the books of Nikos Kazantzakis both in German and in English translation.

Kazantzakis was accused of having leftwing tendencies, and he had been excommunicated from the Church, which biased me against him. I had attempted to read a book by him when I was a teenager, but I put it away with disgust. He used vulgar Cretan idiom to write his books and it alienated me even further. I opened the English version, and that's when that treasure of literature was opened to me. I enjoyed his books immensely because one can't translate the crude Cretan dialect. One has to translate it into English. It is a vulgar dialect. The word for 'lamb,' a small mutton, in the Cretan dialect is the same word as 'big shit' in the rest of Greece. If you are invited to go to their house and eat big shit, you don't like it. The word is *kouradi*. Kazantzakis was another whom I now consider a national treasure, though originally, I did not, because of his Cretan dialect, and his polemic against the Orthodox Church, and against the so-called 'protective powers,' which always somehow managed to harm Greece.

Konstantin Kavafi was an Alexandrian Greek who lived during the turn of the last century, 1863-1933. But he 'lived' in spirit during the Hellenistic period in Alexandria in the year 200 Before Christ. He felt and thought in the Hellenistic period 300 BC - 40 BC when the capital of the Hellenistic world was Alexandria, in Ptolemaic Egypt. The period ended with the defeat of Kleopatra and Marc Antony at Acton.

Kavafi has been translated in many languages including English. He was a homosexual who resented his affliction and in 1925 went to Athens and had an operation whereby his rectum was stitched together, and an opening was made at his lower belly. They call it *para physim edra*. In that way, with that terrible, and very painful, sacrifice, he stopped his homosexual activity. He died of cancer caused by this unnatural procedure.

Even though a homosexual, he is my favorite poet just as Tchaikovsky is my favorite composer. I hold Hannibal to the highest respect, in spite of his homosexuality, and I believe Frederick the Great was the best monarch Prussia ever had. One homosexual whom I don't hold in high esteem is Alexander the Great.

CHAPTER **37**

The Sabra, and Sophocles

I WAS AN exemplar of a husband, and for ten years, I was fully and totally faithful to my wife. Infidelity never entered my mind. In fact, in those ten years of being the most faithful husband, there had been many a wife who made a pass at me, and it was my pride and joy to reject them, and I bragged at how many I had rejected. The chapter 'Woman' had been hermetically closed, and instead of the words 'The End' was the word 'Linde.' She was all the woman I ever needed.

Our relationship had continued to erode when I was assigned in Germany, and it was her choice not to join me when I was transferred to New York, and she deceived me twice by saying, "Yes, I'll come and stay," and never did. She enjoyed thoroughly coming to New York. She would come with a tote bag, and leave with about six pieces of luggage, leaving behind unpaid bills that I had to cover, since I had provided her with the charge cards of Sachs Fifth Avenue, Lord and Taylor, Peck and Peck, Bloomingdale's, and more. I didn't mind. I had the money and could afford the extravagance, but it eventually dawned upon me that the marriage was really over

She agreed that she would come and stay permanently in the United States sometime in the summer of 1971. I went to Hertz and rented the largest station wagon they had, expecting that since my wife was coming to stay permanently, she would have a lot of luggage. I met her at the airport, and I began walking toward the baggage carousels.

"Where are you going?" she corrected.

"Don't you have luggage?"

"Oh, no," she said, "this is all." The tote bag she was hanging from her shoulder was all she had with her.

"Didn't you say you were coming to stay permanently?"

"I changed my mind. I still have business to attend to in Greece." That day I knew that it was the beginning of the end of our marriage. She, after I left Greece to join the Greek diplomatic service, developed a business of her own. She wanted to be financially independent, without the family's revenue or assets. Her business comprised of the manufacturing of a floor polishing material and a shampoo. Both the floor polishing material and the shampoo were based on the synthetic waxes produced by Farb Werke Hoechst in Germany. Once the military regime took it upon themselves to build as many hotels as possible in Greece her business thrived. The more hotels, the more floor polishing materials she was selling.

I can understand, to a degree. She was independent, she was wealthy, she had a yacht, and all the time to herself. Evidently Greece attracted her much more than either Germany or the United States. She came frequently to the United States, she enjoyed New York, she enjoyed Florida, she enjoyed California, where I never went with her. But to stay permanently, and be my wife, was apparently not in her schedule. After my renting the biggest station wagon, and her coming with a tote bag, that was pretty much the end.

So, I allowed myself to get emotionally involved. I had had sex with prostitutes, which I didn't think constituted infidelity or disloyalty, since there was no emotional involvement. I became very much infatuated with Ruth. When I met her in 1971, she was singing at a night club in Manhattan. She had been a beauty contest winner in Israel, where she was a sergeant of the Israeli Air Force. When she came to America, she became the *chanteuse* of a Greco-Jewish nightclub called Sirocco on Twenty-Ninth Street, between Madison and Fifth Avenue.

My friend Stathos, who used to be the chief editor of *Stars and Stripes*—that was how I had met him, in Germany—now three years later, was an employee of the *New York Daily News*. He was proud to point out to me that the *Daily News* was the newspaper with the number one circulation in New York, and the number two circulation in the United States, behind only the *Wall Street Journal*. The WSJ was printed simultaneously in three different cities, and that's why it had more circulation than the *Daily News*, he said. He had a byline in the *Daily News* which was called 'The Night Owl' and his job was to write gossip and to critique new restaurants, new night clubs, and report who was seen with whom where.

When Sirocco opened, he effused, "Michael, this is an absolutely unique night club, because it is owned by a Brooklyn Jew and a Greek Jew, and it tries to cater to both Jews and Greeks. Since Jews and Greeks don't mix, it will be interesting to see how the nightclub will fare. I'm going to write about that nightclub, and I want you to come along with me, because I think you will enjoy it." For some reason, I was quite tired and sleepy that night. Nonetheless, I accompanied him to Sirocco.

I was introduced to the Jew, the Brooklynese co-owner, and then I was introduced to Aris San. Aris San was a peculiar Greek Jew. He was born in a southern town of the Peloponnese to Jewish parents, but he was born in the year 1943. That was the year the Germans exterminated the Jews of Greece. His mother, in order to save her baby, baptized him into the Greek Church so that the identification card would say Greek Orthodox, and did not have him circumcised. Aris San grew up as a normal Greek, but of course he knew that his heritage and his parentage were Jewish. His father was killed by the Germans, but his mother somehow managed to escape. He had served in the Greek Army, and then he went to Israel. The policy of Israel was that anyone who claimed to be a Jew was accepted as such. Aris San joined the Israeli Army and participated in campaigns with the Israeli Army. Nobody would dispute that he was indeed an Israeli. I don't know if at a later date he had himself circumcised—I've never been to the urinals with him so I wouldn't be able to attest to the matter.

He was a very nice Greek and a very nice Jew—or Israeli. The nightclub, when Stathos and I arrived, was very crowded. You couldn't drop an apple and hit the floor. Aris San became the most prominent songwriter and composer of modern music in Israel. He wrote songs and composed the music for both Greek and Hebrew songs. Sirocco catered for a Jewish clientele from 6:30 to 11:00 in the evening, and for a Greek clientele until the wee hours.

That night the majority of the clientele was Jewish. There were hardly any Greeks. But the waiters were Greeks. The orchestra was Greek, with the only exception of Aris San, who was the bandleader, so to speak. Ruth came to sing her songs, and I, not intentionally, fell asleep. She complained to Stathos about his guest sleeping while she was doing her numbers. Stathos told me, in Greek, that I had disgraced him by sleeping while the star of the show was singing. I told him to say that I was very sorry, but that I shall come another time when I shall be in better mood, and I shall enjoy her singing. And that was it.

A few weeks later, I decided to go to Sirocco and apologize myself to Ruth. I went at about ten o'clock and to my surprise, the clientele was now exclusively Greek. Hardly any Jews, and when the orchestra played a song to my liking, in typical Greek fashion I broke my plates on the floor, at which the other Greeks took the cue and started breaking their plates also. The Brooklynese Jew rushed to the telephone to call the police. But Aris San exclaimed, "Wait! It's a Greek custom, don't touch the phone. Those plates are going to be judged as though they were made of gold. Let them break to their heart's delight."

Ruth came to sing and when she was finished, I asked the waiter to invite her to my table, and she came. She recognized me and remembered. "You should be ashamed, sleeping while I am singing." "That's why I came," I conceded, "I came to ask for your forgiveness. I was very tired, I had not planned to go out, and Stathos dragged me. But I'm very glad I came today, and I enjoyed your show. And you are definitely the most strikingly beautiful Israeli girl I have ever seen."

A sabra is a Jewish native of Israel. *Sabra* is the Hebrew name of the fruit of the cactus that grows in the Middle East. It is thorny outside and sweet inside, and that's how the Israelis think of themselves. What I saw in Ruth was not just a beautiful redhead with very white skin and green eyes, that looked more Dutch than anything else. It was in her that I saw both the antiquity of Israel and the vigor of the country that was established in 1948. I was vastly impressed by her. The impression turned into an immeasurable infatuation.

Le coup de foudre is that overwhelming feeling you experience when you see someone to whom you are extremely attracted. It hits you like a thunderbolt. It happens seldom in life. It is very intense but usually short lived—like a power surge that extinguishes all your lights and appliances. I had that with Ruth. She told me that even though she toyed with Gentiles, that she would only marry a Jew. So, I contacted a rabbi I knew and urged him to convert me to Judaism. I studied the Talmud and went to the synagogue every Friday night. I even studied Hebrew. Where the conversion stopped short was the matter of circumcision. My Hellenic subconscious would not permit the mutilation of my body for something religious.

One evening, it was late, I received a telephone call from a woman I didn't know, but it was the wife of Anthony Quinn, the actor. She demanded that I come get the woman who was waiting for her husband outside their apartment. It was Ruth, who had met Quinn at the club. I found her there, and furiously, jealously demanded an explanation. She said she was pursuing him because she wanted to become an actress. I explained how futile that was.

Ruth became my constant companion and eventually also my paramour. I would go to every function with her. I would go to family affairs with her, to the point that this gossip reached Athens. I was aware that my mother had two very strong hatreds: she hated Germans and she hated Jews. Her hatred for Germans had now dissipated because she realized from acquaintance, and eventually friendship, with her daughter-in-law that there is a lot to be admired with the Germans. But as far as the Jews were concerned, the hatred was still unadulterated. Upon my mother hearing that her son was consorting with a Jewess, she decided to do something about it.

She came to what she called 'the colonies' for the first time in her life. She came to New York, and I was there at the airport, with Ruth, waiting for her. This daughter of British aristocracy went out of her way to be rude and quite unaristocratic. The main characteristic of an aristocrat is *noblesse oblige,* but my mother utterly forgot that. When I introduced her to Ruth, she refused even to give her hand, and she turned her back. We went to my apartment in New York, not the mansion in Sand Point. There my mother challenged, "Michael, are you really serious about marrying a Jewish woman?"

The Jewish woman was standing there. "Mother," I objected, "she's a *sabra*, she's a native of Israel. She is not a Jew from the Diaspora. She is not the kind that you hate."

"Can you really condemn me to have Jewish grandchildren?" "Mother, they are going to be half Israeli, a quarter Greek, and a quarter Scottish. Perfect for being born in America."

My mother's rudeness certainly affected Ruth, and our idylium got cold. When my mother thought she had done her job by putting the spanners in the works, she announced, "Well, Michael, now I'll go and find our cousins in North Carolina."

I said, "I didn't know we had cousins in North Carolina."

"Oh," she alleged, "we have a whole regiment of relatives in North Carolina. Don't you know that when that unspeakable General Cornwallis surrendered his command, among his troops were the Gordon Highlanders?" Yes, I knew. "Well," she said, "the Gordon Highlanders refused to return to Britain because they had never surrendered either their colors or their arms. After the surrender they begged George Washington to be allowed to remain in America, and George Washington was more than pleased to have a whole Highland Regiment staying with him. And lasses from Scotland were shipped to America for them to marry. So, I know there is a huge Scottish colony in North Carolina and I'm going to see them."

My mother considered that she had next of kin two hundred years removed. She did not want me to buy her an airplane ticket. She asserted, "I want to go by bus and see the colonies." So, she boarded a Greyhound bus, and a week later she called me. "Michael, I searched all over North Carolina and they are not there. There are some Scots, but not related to us. The ones who are related to us are in Danville, Virginia. Come and join me in Danville and I'll introduce you to our cousins."

I found that there is a large community of Highlanders in that part of the world, and every year, they even have Highland Games. After I met the cousins in Danville, my mother and I both boarded a bus. I had gone by plane to Richmond, and by bus to Danville. Now my mother decided that we return by bus because she wanted to see the view from the other side of the bus.

My mother was quite happy with herself for having squelched the romance with Ruth. Indeed, the romance had cooled, but it was not over. Upon returning to Greece, my mother told my wife. My wife never thought that my affair with Ruth was really serious or that it would jeopardize her marriage, because she took me always for granted. But my mother coached, "I did my part, now you go and consolidate your marriage."

My wife telephoned me to say she was coming to New York. I picked her up at the airport. Usually she had the tote bag, but this time she had a piece of luggage. "Oh," I remarked, "how unusual."

We went to the apartment in New York rather than to the Sand Point manor. "Michael," she said, "I want to meet that paragon of woman who jeopardized my marriage, even though I never believed that you seriously considered divorcing me."

"Well," I demurred, "don't you think it's awkward?"

"Awkward or not, I want to meet her." Reluctantly, I agreed. I knew that Ruth wanted to get a job—a better job and more prestigious—at a nightclub that had opened in mid-Manhattan, as opposed to Sirocco, which was in lower Manhattan. The new club was in the Fifties, between Second and Third Avenues. It was called Le Cassino Russe. It pretended to be a Russian nightclub with balalaikas, and it catered to Russian Jews or Jews of Russian origin in New York, most of whom are fairly well-to-do. But Le Cassino Russe was owned by Greeks, they had only chosen to have a Russian theme. They had a female singer who was also a sabra, and they were paying her $1,000 per week. Ruth was getting only four hundred dollars at Sirocco. I knew that Ruth wanted to go to Le Cassino Russe, and she believed that she was a better singer than the other one. I had spoken to the owners, and they agreed to consider it. I thought that it was opportune to invite them to go with me and my wife to hear Ruth sing, so it wouldn't appear too blatant that I was there only with my wife.

Ruth knew, from sight, those two Greeks who owned Le Cassino Russe. They were both architects, and well-to-do like most Greeks in New York, or in the rest of the United States. After she finished her song, she was invited to come to our table. My wife, that night, looked like something out of *Vogue*. She was wearing a magnificent gown—that's why she had a suitcase—with her best colors which were black and white. One shoulder was exposed, and she had put all her expertise as an ex-photo model and ex-fashion model to appear like a million dollars. I would say she must have appeared like a million gold sovereigns that night. When Ruth came to our table, she complimented, "Michael, I knew your wife is beautiful, but I didn't realize she was so exquisitely beautiful."

My wife responded, "Tell her she's a lovely girl herself."

Ruth sat down, and we started negotiating her possible employment at Le Cassino Russe. However, if she or my wife wanted to say something to each other, they always addressed me, to be the interpreter. It was an awkward situation and I started cursing myself for having put myself in that condition. Ruth got the job, but only for six hundred dollars a week. When we were ready to leave, my wife declared, "Goodnight, Miss Ruth, and thank you for taking care of my husband when I was otherwise disposed, but from now on your services will be superfluous."

Ruth understood. Her eyes glistened. I knew that phrase was rehearsed because it sounded so much like my mother. When we went home, I asked Linde, "Did you come up with that phrase?"

"No," she admitted, "your mother taught it to me."

That definitely was the end of it. After that, Ruth pretended I did not even exist. I would go to Le Cassino Russe frequently, and she would totally ignore me. She never spoke to me a word again, and if I were made of air, it wouldn't make any difference. She was quite a pretty girl, not spectacularly beautiful like my wife, because my wife was taller, and as a professional, better versed in taking advantage of her femininity. Ruth went her way and I remained married to *Durchlaucht Fuerstin von Duerenstein*.

I did love Linde deeply, but it was not the *coup de foudre* which I experienced only once in my life with the sabra. What I felt for Linde was growing each year and the lust was giving way to more friendship and true companionship. She was to me more of a partner than lover. The feelings were not mutual. She chose to remain in Greece and pursue a business career. A marriage loses its substance when the spouses meet only three or four times a year for a few weeks each time.

That is when I decided to take revenge for the ten years of total and absolute fidelity on my part. I plunged into a life of reckless womanizing and turned myself into a playboy. I had a glorious time in New York. I had plenty of money, a prestigious title, youth, vigor, elegance, and good looks and most of all, diplomatic immunity—which meant I could park my Rolls Royce anywhere I pleased. Yet the fading away of my marriage left me with a constant bitter taste.

I used to rent a banquet hall in the Ansonia, the artists and actors hotel, on 173rd Street, almost Harlem, and do auditions. It is the easiest way to get women in New York. Simply put an ad in *Variety* that you are going to run a play at off, off, off Broadway and hundreds flock with their resume and their portfolios and their photos, and you can pick whomever you want—male, female, and everything in between. And you could rent that room in the Ansonia for a hundred dollars.

You have to be Greek and imaginative. It's very plausible because Greeks stage Greek tragedies. Everybody in acting has heard of Greek tragedies. Everybody has heard of Euripides, and Sophocles. That's what I was using, and it was very successful.

CHAPTER 38

Kissinger's Doctrine: Greece is Dispensable

IN 1974, WITH Henry Kissinger as the U.S. Secretary of State, an unfortunate episode occurred for Greece. In Washington the US administration was going through the worst stage of the Watergate scandal and the Nixon administration was on the verge of collapse. The foreign policy was totally in the hands of Henry Kissinger.

The Turks invaded Cyprus at the time when Cyprus was allegedly, or in theory, an independent sovereign country. But, it had, by treaty, the presence of a Greek and a Turkish contingent of armed forces. Both could not exceed 5,000 in strength. At the time both Greece and Turkey were NATO members. Brigadier Ioannidis, who in November 1973, had replaced Colonel Papadopoulos as the power force in Greece, wanted rapid action on Cyprus. He decided on a coup in which the Cyprus leader, Archbishop Makarios, would be assassinated. Ioannidis had made his plans clear to his CIA contacts, but for his own purposes Henry Kissinger wanted nothing done to prevent it. Makarios escaped, but it gave the Turks the pretext to invade and appropriate the northern third of the island, that Kissinger had been looking for.

On July 20, 1974, the Turks invaded Cyprus claiming that the Turkish Cypriot population was being 'threatened' and that Turkey had the right to intervene in order to 'restore constitutional order' under the rights granted by the Treaty of Guarantee of 1960. By July 24, 1974, Brigadier Ioannidis and the military regime in Athens had been replaced by a civilian government of Constantine Karamanlis. Over the next few days, a fragile ceasefire had been agreed on Cyprus following U.S. pressure. In late July, Turkey held about twenty percent of Cypriot territory and negotiations were taking place in Switzerland. On the fourteenth of August the Turks resumed their offensive and occupied thirty-seven percent of the island.

With the connivance of the United States and a spot of Kissinger's détente with the Soviet Union, it was agreed that Greece would be primed to fall into a trap whereby Turkey would invade Cyprus and take the island. It was expected that Greece would mobilize to attack Turkey. At the same time Bulgaria would mobilize and attack Greece while the Greek troops were engaged in fighting the Turks. Bulgaria would seize a piece of the Greek province of Thrace and thus indirectly enable the Soviet Union to have access to the Mediterranean.

Kissinger's engineering was thwarted by the vigilance of a Greek colonel, who before attacking into Turkey, checked to see the spare ammunition that he had. He found that the crates that were supposed to hold the ammunition were full of stones. He called the other unit commanders on the telephone, and asked if they had checked their ammunition, so they did. Stones. And then we realized that the Bulgarians had also mobilized, even though our move had nothing to do with Bulgaria. So, we didn't invade Turkey.

I don't know who put the stones in the crates. The rumor that circulated was that when Kissinger, during the Yom Kippur War, applied pressure to Israel to stop the advance to Cairo, in order to force the Israelis not to continue their advance, America stopped all military shipments to Israel. Since Israel and Greece have about the same type of munitions, it was rumored that my government had sold their munitions so that the Israelis could continue their advance. It's a tale that was not verified. I personally doubt that Colonel Papadopoulos would have done it.

The machination was the result of an understanding when Kissinger and Nixon went to the Soviet Union to meet with Brezhnev and the Soviet autocracy of the Politburo. Kissinger had implemented, perhaps for the first time since Monroe, a concrete American foreign policy. It was called *détente*, in other words, a lessening of the Cold War. Kissinger's trump card was China. that was now on the American side, which could be used as leverage for the Soviets to agree. The Soviets agreed with the proposals of Kissinger but demanded a balance. The American demand was the building of the petroleum pipeline from the Soviet Union to Europe, with the investment of billions of dollars in Siberia. Siberia is the same as Alaska, only it's five times the size of Alaska. There are tremendous riches in Siberia if one has the knowledge and the money to invest in it. That's what Kissinger, under détente, wanted to do. The Soviets responded, in essence, "Ok, anything you Americans say is fine with us—only we want two things: first, we want the Suez Canal to be repaired and ready for operation within eight months; and second, we want access to the Mediterranean."

In order to give the Soviets access to the Mediterranean, one of two countries had to be sacrificed: either Turkey or Greece. Kissinger thought that Greece doesn't weigh as much in the balance as Turkey, and he decided that Greece should be sacrificed. In order to engineer the whole thing, the Turks were given the green light to invade Cyprus, expecting that the Greeks in retaliation would try to take Constantinople. Once the Greek army was engaged in Thrace, at the outskirts of Constantinople, the Bulgarians would invade with practically with no resistance, and capture access to the Mediterranean on behalf of their Russian masters.

The Turkish invasion of Cyprus spelled the end for the junta in Athens. Three days after the invasion, Brigadier Ioannides allowed himself to be sidelined. President Gizikis and senior officers of all three branches of the armed forces invited Constantine Karamanlis to return from exile in France to restore democracy. The French President, Giscard d'Estaing, placed a plane at his disposal, and he flew into Athens, landing at Athens Airport on July 24. A large part of the population of Athens had turned out to greet him. He had changed from the man who left Greece years beforehand, friendly to the United States. He withdrew Greece from the NATO military command, legalized the Communist Party, distanced himself from the Americans and secured Greece's entry into the European Economic Community.

As a Greek, of course I despise Kissinger, but as an American, with the piece of paper that makes me an American citizen—which does not necessarily make me an American—I would consider Kissinger as an asset to the United States and not a liability. I don't like detente. I don't think it would have worked. I think Reagan had the right idea to force the Soviet Union into submission by increasing the defense spending exponentially.

But at least I can acknowledge that Kissinger was the first American since President James Monroe to create foreign policy in this country. Ever since Monroe the only foreign policy we had can be stated, "Europeans, stay out of our sphere of influence in America and we shall not interfere with your affairs in Europe." Monroe, by implementing his doctrine, followed the advice of George Washington, when upon leaving office after eight years, advised, "Be friends with everybody, be allies to nobody." George Washington was against America forming any kind of alliance.

The Monroe Doctrine was violated by President Woodrow Wilson when he declared war for no reason, because Germany was no threat to the United States. After that America did not have a policy. America could be compared, as far as foreign policy goes, to a giant amoeba which had reacted to stimuli. From one day to the other, no American, whether an ordinary citizen on the street, or whoever happened to be secretary of state, knew what the policy was.

After World War II was over, the combination of Marshall, Truman, and the Ambassador to Moscow, George Frost Kennan, formulated a sort of policy which was based on not wanting the Soviet Union to expand communism beyond where it had already been enforced. Appointed by President Truman, Kennan served a very short tour as ambassador—less than a year—but his ideas, particularly the doctrine of 'containment,' had a powerful influence on future U.S.-Soviet relations. While he was out of the country in October 1952, Kennan was declared *persona non grata* by the Soviet government for remarks critical of Stalin, and he did not return. In February 1946, he wrote his famous 'Long Telegram,' calling for a policy of containment of Soviet expansion.

Thanks to Franklin Roosevelt, half of Europe became Soviet satellites, but America stopped the expansion of communism in Korea. America attempted to stop the expansion of communism in Viet Nam. Part of that policy was not to allow China, the largest country in the world, to become a member of the United Nations.

But Kissinger formulated a real policy. That's why one could consider Kissinger an asset, even though I certainly did not think that détente would work. It is because the Soviets do not think like Europeans or Americans. Lenin said, "The capitalist, for making an ephemeral profit, will sell us the rope by means of which we shall hang him."

When I first went to New York, it usually it took me the better part of an hour to drive the twenty-two miles from Micky's house in Sands Point, Long Island to the Greek Consulate General on Seventy-Ninth Street in Manhattan. One day, I pulled onto the long Island Expressway at my usual 7:30 a.m., hoping to reach the consulate not later than 8:30 a.m., and to my surprise, there were hardly any cars on the road. I started thinking that I had my days mixed and that it was a Sunday. In ten minutes, I was across the Fifty-Ninth Street Bridge, which was also nearly deserted. When I reached Park Avenue, and saw no traffic, without the thousands of taxis that crisscrossed the area on weekdays, I thought a sudden plague must have hit New York. I reached the consulate an hour before opening time. I asked the sleepy policeman who stood guard at the door what had happened. Where was everybody? He looked at me inquisitively and said, "Yom Kippur." I then realized how Jewish New York—Hymietown, according to Jesse Jackson—is.

In 1973, Anwar Sadat chose another Yom Kippur, Day of Atonement, during which all Jews stay home and pray from sun-up to sun-down, for his assault across the Suez Canal. Sadat was not as charismatic as Nasser, but he was by far a better leader and strategist. Instead of demagoguing the mob into a frenzy, he prepared in total secrecy, methodically and efficiently for the next round against Israel. With the Aswan Dam completed, Egypt was now self-sufficient in energy and had almost doubled her cotton production. The Soviets, against their better judgment, reequipped the Egyptian Army and Air Force after the 1967 debacle, with their best materiel and dispatched thousands of instructors and trainers to make sure the Egyptians would not waste the hardware, but would know how to use it effectively. The Syrians were willing to join Sadat in this venture, but King Hussein refused. Jordan had suffered enough in blood, lost tourist revenue and lost real estate—the West Bank, the only fertile portion that Jordan had.

On a very gloomy, gray Friday afternoon in October 1973, I was walking near the Hammarskjöld Plaza, in front of the United Nations Building, when from every street and avenue, a torrent of people, thousands of them, started converging toward the Plaza. I was told the Israeli UN Delegate would address them. I had no idea what had happened. The Israeli UN ambassador came out, and he said that the Israeli forces were defending the Sinai, that she had suffered heavy losses, and what Israel needed the most right now was blood.

The human avalanche immediately moved down First Avenue to the New York City Hospital three blocks away. I was swept by the crowd and found myself inside the hospital. Everything was prepared as if they had planned it in advance. Dozens of doctors and nurses were taking blood samples to establish the blood type and sticking needles in veins. When my turn came, I said I was O-Positive. "Good," he said, "Unbutton and lift your sleeve."

"Wait," I protested, "I am not a Jew."

"Blood is impervious to religion," returned the Jewish doctor, and stuck the needle. So, I shed a pint of blood for Israel.

The initial Egyptian assault across the defunct canal was a total success. They extinguished a number of bunkers that were defended by female personnel. In two hours, Egypt had established a sizeable beachhead and started building a pontoon bridge that was completed in record time. Soon their heavy armor started rolling and it was not yet ten o'clock in the morning. The Egyptian Air Force also attacked at dawn but did not catch the Israelis entirely by surprise. The radars defending the military airports had intercepted the MIGs, but not in time for all Israeli F-104s and F-105s to scramble. Some were destroyed on the ground.

The Syrian assault on the Golan Heights was not as stealthy nor as well coordinated, because it was preceded by a heavy artillery barrage. When the attack came, the defenders were awake and ready. Because the Israelis were caught by surprise, their losses in the first few days were indeed very heavy, but eventually the fronts were stabilized, and their general mobilization completed.

The Pentagon had seen the Middle East as the future proving ground for its new hardware so most of the three billion dollars in aid that Congress voted for Israel was in the form of state-of the-art American tanks, fighter jets and medium range ground-launched ballistic missiles, GLBM, and submarine-launched ballistic missiles, SLBM. Improvements and modification by the Israelis, who had their own munitions and armament plants, ensured that the Israeli Defense Force was even better equipped and trained than the United States.

There is a school of thought, and I have mixed feelings of its veracity, that the Israelis pretended surprise in order to trap the Egyptians at the Sinai passes and obliterate them. The thought emanates from the efficiency of the Mossad. So good an intelligence service could not be unaware of so gigantic an enterprise involving thousands of tanks and airplanes and almost half a million men. The reason I doubt the accuracy of this is the high number of losses both in human power and airplanes that the Israelis suffered during the first stages of the campaign.

Within the first week, the air war was decided in favor of Israel. Meanwhile, the Egyptians, victorious on land, had transported the bulk of their armor and infantry across the canal and were on their way to Sinai passes for the initial assault on Israel proper. The Syrians had failed to take the Golan Heights, but the battle there was not yet decided. What the Soviet observers could not understand was why the Israelis would not commit their armor in an attempt to prevent the fall of the Sinai. Soon they found out.

The Mitla Pass fiasco was repeated with the same ferocity and, for the Egyptians, lethal results. A perfect coordination of air and ground power stopped and then decimated the Egyptian forces, which became trapped at the Sinai passes. They could neither advance nor retreat. They were immobilized and easy prey of the Israeli Air Force that now dominated the air. The first week of November had a shock for the Egyptians and their Soviet mentors: Israeli forces in division strength had crossed the Suez Canal and were in Egypt. There was hardly a division available to confront. them. Total chaos and panic befell the Egyptians.

Soviet Foreign Minister Andrei Gromyko again started threatening with nuclear war. The paper tower of détente, Kissinger's scheme, was being torn. The United States applied pressure to both Israel and Iran: Israel to withdraw its troops from Egypt, and Iran, under the Shah, to stop the supply of oil. Undaunted, the Israelis launched an assault with Cairo as its objective. The Syrians, in order to help their beleaguered confederates, committed their last reserves and launched a desperate counterattack that cost them dearly, with the Israeli Air Force killing their tanks at will. In those first few days, 50,000 Syrians were lost—comparatively, the number of Americans killed in Vietnam in ten *years* of conflict was 58,135. The Soviet threats became more ominous. The United States suspended all deliveries to Israel in an attempt to strangle them logistically. When the spearhead of advancing Israelis was less than thirty miles from Cairo, the war was over. Kissinger had won.

A rabbi friend of mine in New York told me, "Beware of Jews working for Gentiles. In order to prove their loyalty, they will victimize their fellow Jews."

Kissinger robbed Israel of a decisive and final victory. The horde of Soviet advisors, trainers, and instructors, in disgust, left Egypt. Anwar Sadat attempted to present the demise of his army and air force as a victory. It seems that to an Arab, survival is tantamount to victory. "I am not dead, therefore I won."

The Israelis again harvested almost 600 brand new Soviet tanks at the Mitla Pass, and 100,000 Egyptian prisoners. The only good that came out of the Yom Kippur War was the disgust and contempt of the Soviets for the incompetence and ineptitude of the Arabs, and the change of their policy by distancing themselves from Egypt. It also became crystal clear to them that Israel was there to stay.

Angola, Ethiopia, and Somalia, with surrogate troops from Cuba, became their next targets.

CHAPTER **39**

Meeting Miss Kim

MY COUSIN MICKY'S English first wife, Moira, had returned from Athens with their daughter, Samantha, and had married an American lawyer in New York. He was employed in the legal department of the New York Telephone Company. Her husband, Fred Millbret, and I became more or less friends. Fred had helped me with various contacts in New York.

One day, Fred telephoned me, and said, "Michael, I would like a favor from you."

"What is it, Fred?"

He said, "I know a Korean woman ——, "and he embarked on a description of a paragon of Oriental womanhood." After he finished the encomium about that Korean woman, he declared, "She has tickets for the opening of the Metropolitan in Lincoln Center and she needs an escort, and I suggested to her, you."

"Fred," I said, "If she is one-third fitting to your description, she certainly wouldn't need you or anybody else to get her a date."

"Ah," he said, "you don't understand. She's a Korean aristocrat and she doesn't go out with just anybody. So, I recommended her to you as being the typical Greek gentleman."

I have never considered myself a Greek gentleman, or any kind of gentleman. However, I assumed that she may have been involved in some kind of legal matter with Fred, and I said, "Alright, I'll take her to the Lincoln Center," thinking that I was doing a favor to Fred.

The opening was December 1, 1973, but the previous night had been one of my typically extravagant, expensive, promiscuous nights. I had drunk a lot, eaten a lot, and fornicated a lot, so when I woke up that morning, I felt decidedly unwell. I had a horrible case of diarrhea and I had to go to the bathroom every ten minutes. I wanted to call Fred and break the date—the blind date—with that paragon of Korean womanhood, but on the other hand I felt that I should do Fred's favor. Reluctantly, and weakly, I took the Rolls Royce and went to the address I was given on Seventy-Third Street, somewhere between Lexington and Third, where the Korean woman was living. She was waiting in the lobby of the building, and I saw she was wearing a full-length mink coat that almost touched the ground. She was tall, as far as Korean women go, she must have been at least five feet, seven. I couldn't see what she was wearing underneath the mink, but she was not totally repulsive, as are many Koreans. She had the moon face and the unattractive characteristics of her race, but she was not repulsive. I told her that I felt very poorly—I didn't say that I had diarrhea, but I told her that I had been sick most of the day and that I couldn't eat anything. She had said, "First we will go to a French restaurant where we will meet my other friends, and we shall have dinner at that restaurant."

We went to that restaurant where we met two more couples, who were friends of hers. When she removed the mink, I saw she was wearing a typically oriental sari-type dress, obviously made of silk, and a lot of expensive jewelry. It was obvious that she wanted to make an impression that she was well-to-do. Fred had told me that she was a member of the Korean aristocracy. I didn't know that Korea had an aristocracy. I thought that Korea, whatever little I knew about Korean history, was either subjugated to the Chinese or subjugated to the Japanese. I had never heard of a Korean royalty, and without a crown, I can't imagine how you can have an aristocracy. But I let it go because I didn't know too much about Korea.

The woman, Chayon Kim, had a propensity to drop names. Her various acquaintances resided in South Hampton, New York, and Palm Beach, Florida, and evidently, from what she was saying, she knew the entire membership of the American plutocracy. I couldn't eat much at the restaurant, but in order to be polite, I ordered a very dry steak, of which I ate perhaps one-third. When the bill came, since nobody made any attempt to pay, I gave my American Express credit card. But Kim said, "Don't worry, you'll be reimbursed."

Actually, I didn't worry; money was not my worry at that time. We proceeded to the opera, and the opera was *Traviata*, sung by that magnificent soprano, Anna Moffo, who sang until her death in 2006. I was so sick I could hardly enjoy it, and the longer it lasted the worse I felt. When it ended, and we went out, I thought that if I were hit by the fresh air that I might recover. Exactly the opposite was the case. The moment we stepped out of the Lincoln Center I felt extreme nausea, and I told Kim, "I shall have to lean on you. I'm sorry." I put my hand on her shoulder, but that didn't help, and I collapsed on the pavement. Apparently in 1973, American doctors had not yet been hit by so many malpractice lawsuits because immediately a group of doctors, who had also attended the opening of the Lincoln Center that night, gathered around me. I was wearing a three-piece flannel suit, but no overcoat. A fairly young, and very pretty female doctor took charge.

"First," she said, "we need a blanket, so he won't be lying on the cold pavement."

To my enormous surprise—because after all, it was a blind date, we had never seen each other before that day, or before five hours—Kim took off that magnificent mink coat and put it down on the pavement so that they could roll me onto it. I thought, *if my wife owned that mink, would she take it off and put it down, in December?* I had my doubts. I even wondered if my mother would take off so expensive a mink and put it on the sidewalk. That, I must admit, impressed me.

Standing there was a policeman, a big Irish cop—he looked to me to be a giant—and the doctor that had taken over the ministrations instructed the policeman, "Hit him, here, as hard as you can."

And he did, the cop hit me on the chest, and I thought I would die. The female doctor cajoled, "I'm sorry, but your heart was stopping so we needed that."

Eventually an ambulance came, and they loaded me to go the Roosevelt Hospital which is only a few blocks down the street from the Lincoln Center. Kim insisted to get into the ambulance. I knew she had told me that she had plans for after the opera to go to Sardi's and then there would be a midnight party at the house of one of their friends. But she insisted that she was my date and she felt obliged to come to the hospital in the ambulance.

I had asked her to take the keys, because I had gone to that date with the Rolls Royce, and drive it to a garage. I didn't want the Rolls Royce to remain overnight exposed on the streets of New York, but she said, "Unfortunately I don't know how to drive."

"What do you mean, you don't know how to drive? Everybody knows how to drive."

"No," she objected, "in Korea we had chauffeurs."

So, I gave the key to the policeman and asked him to take the car to the precinct garage, which he actually did.

At the Roosevelt Hospital they smeared my wrists with goo and attached the electrodes to make cardiograms. All the while Kim was standing there as if I were a next of kin. I was taken to the cardiac emergency ward. The electronic device they attached to me registered the heartbeat in a yellow and green line in a black frame. The heartbeat looked okay to me.

Each cubicle in that big ward had a white nylon drape so that it could be enclosed, but the drape was not drawn. One of my fetishes was white stockings. Show me white stockings around well-shaped calves and it would be an instant erection. One of the nurses, a blond one, fit the description, and each time she would pass in front of my bed, the monitor that was registering the heartbeat would start ringing, so all of them would rush to see what's wrong with me. Eventually it dawned upon them that it was the blond nurse that was causing the disturbance, and they drew all the curtains around me so I couldn't see her anymore.

A young intern appeared with a sort of board, and said he was there to take my medical history. I told him I had none, that I had no need for a doctor, and that I felt utter contempt for the medical profession. He said, "You had a major heart attack," and started asking very personal questions. He asked, "What do you eat, smoke and drink on an average day?"

I said, "None of my days is average. It depends on my mood, who I am with, and how I feel." But I told him that I smoked perhaps ten or fifteen cigarettes a day, and perhaps one or two cigars. I am six feet three, I weigh 220 pounds, and I eat enough to satisfy my hunger, and I drink some days nothing, and other days something.

He asked, "Are you married?" I answered, yes. "How often do you make love to your wife?" He was a young man, and an American, but that was a stupid question.

"What do you mean, 'how often,'" I said, "it is not in the frequency, it is in the duration."

Still, he persisted, "How often do you make love to your wife?" "Perhaps four times a year," I answered.

He said, "Is that all?"

"That's how often I see her. She lives in Greece, I live in New York."

He continued, "Any extra-marital activities?"

I responded, "As many as I can get."

So, the young intern decreed that I should reduce smoking, eating, drinking, and fornicating. I queried, "If I do all that, what will be the advantage?"

He asserted, "You will live longer."

"Who wants to live longer under such conditions? Forget it."

It was three o' clock in the morning and I fell asleep. Next morning a nurse told me it cost two hundred dollars per day. Exorbitant, I thought. When the cardiologist came on his rounds, he told me, "We shall keep you here ten days under observation." I told him I declined, but he said, "You don't have a choice; we won't release you until we have determined what the further therapy should be." I insisted I was not staying ten days. I was leaving. He was adamant, "We contacted your wife, and she gave us consent to keep you here."

In surprise, I said, "What do you mean, 'my wife?'"

"The Korean lady that brought you."

I retorted, "She's not my wife, I didn't know her until yesterday."

"We assumed she was your wife. Nonetheless, you are unable to leave, and, no, we shall not give you your clothes."

"I don't care, I have diplomatic immunity, and I can walk naked on the streets of New York."

Yielding, he said, "If you want to leave here, you must give us the name of your doctor, so he can have the responsibility."

I knew a doctor in New York with whom I used to play bridge. His name was Douglas Lake, and he was a peculiar case of a doctor. He used to be the surgeon of a Canadian destroyer and when his Canadian destroyer was in port, he jumped ship and remained in the United States. And now Douglas Lake was a venerated plastic surgeon and darling of the New York plutocracy. His practice was three adjacent suites of the Westbury Hotel, and he was very wealthy. I said, "The only doctor I know is Douglas Lake." Lake told them to let me go. He knew that I would leave anyway.

I felt on top of the world. Before releasing me from the hospital, they called Kim—evidently, she had left her name and telephone number—and she came in a taxi. She chided, "I told them to keep you here."

"Yes, they thought you were my wife. I feel alright, and I'm very hungry. We shall now go to my favorite restaurant in Long Island. Where is the Rolls Royce?"

"The policeman has it," she answered. We went to the police precinct, and they had indeed taken care of the Rolls Royce. I donated a hundred dollars to the widows and orphans of the precinct, and I drove to a restaurant I knew in Long Island, which belonged to Lithuanians. We had a good steak and accompanied it with a good claret. On the way back I felt that, since Kim had done what in my eyes was an enormous gesture of putting that precious mink on the pavement, I was obligated to her.

At that time, I had rooms at a beautiful hotel in New York called the Alray. On the ground floor of the Alray was a famous French Restaurant called Henry IV. The Alray Hotel was on Sixtieth Street between Madison and Fifth, on the East Side. It was not a big hotel, but a very nice hotel. All the rooms of the Alray are suites. When we came back to New York, I invited Kim to my room. Not that I desired her, not that she attracted me sexually, but I thought that I was obligated. But, thank Zeus, Kim declined. I thought that I had done my duty, I had invited her.

Because I was not in America at the time, I don't know how Kim managed to penetrate the innermost sanctuary of American plutocracy in Southampton, Long Island. She was staying at the house of Woodward who had been accused of having murdered her Whitney husband. Even though they caught her with the pistol smoking, she was acquitted. That Woodward woman, and the Whitney's, and a number of other American plutocrats, all were Kim's friends, and she had lived in all their houses. I know that American upper crust are fascinated by all kinds of aristocracy, true or imaginary. If Kim claimed to be the niece of the Korean Emperor, apparently, they would believe her.

At a future time in my life, Miss Kim was to play a pivotal part, when she determined to establish a Korean War Memorial in Washington, DC and invited me to join her in that endeavor.

CHAPTER **40**

Job Insecurity

BY LATE 1973, I had determined that my career as a Greek diplomat might not last very long. My chief, Colonel Papadopoulos, had promised that the military dictatorship would last for as long as it was necessary. Pursuant to that promise, he was gradually withdrawing from the active governance of Greece to allow elections and a political government. The plebiscite in Greece, with a majority of eighty-nine percent of the people, determined that Greece should be a republic rather than a monarchy. Colonel Papadopoulos had assumed the more or less decorative post of President of the Republic.

The government now comprised a cabinet of politicians who belonged to the party of Spiros Markezinis, who was a right winger, and, in my opinion, a brilliant man. His party, called the Progressive Party, was the smallest political party of Greece, and was right of center, ideologically speaking. When the military junta took control in 1967, the Progressive Party was the only party in the Vouli, the Greek parliament, willing to work with the junta at all. Spiros Markezinis was briefly appointed Prime Minister of Greece in October 1973, as Papadopoulos resigned as Prime Minister to take the title of President. Markezinis' time in this post was short lived, as other members of the junta forced out both Markezinis and Papadopoulos a month later, on November 17, 1973, following a bloodily suppressed student uprising at Athens Polytechnic University.

Once we had a cabinet comprising of politicians, the army was still in charge of Greece, but not on a day-to-day basis. This government, however, didn't last very long. When Papadopoulos was removed from power, in what amounted to a second coup, Brigadier Ioannides, also said to be a CIA agent, and head of the Military Security Police, arrested Papadopoulos in November. Ioannides installed a puppet of his own in his place, reverting Greece into a military dictatorship. Under his leadership, repression increased.

Following the collapse of the Papadopoulos government, Markezinis remained active in the political scene, playing a crucial role in the negotiations in early 1974 that led to the return of democratic government under Konstantinos Karamanlis' National Unity government.

The beginning of the unraveling of the military dictatorship was when inflation, which in the rest of the world was almost galloping, finally came to Greece. It created a malaise with the people who had been quite happy all those years to have price stability and zero inflation. The problem with a police state which regulates prices, and is determined to maintain absolute price stability, is that you combat inflation—the first six years of the military dictatorship, inflation was zero, and prices were maintained at the same level as in 1967—but it is extremely difficult to maintain in a country that depends so much on imports. It came as a boomerang to punish the military dictatorship in Greece, because after six years, it was obvious that one could not police the stability of prices, and inflation did hit Greece. A powerful economy, like the United States, might under the same conditions succeed in maintaining inflation to zero indefinitely, but not in a country that depends so much on imports.

I started feeling the clouds gathering when I was given an assignment that nobody else wanted. I was to go to West Africa to renew the fishing treaties that Greece had with the various West African countries. Greece needed those fish treaties because Greek fishermen, in a combination of stupidity, ignorance, greed and defiance of the law, had created an Aegean Sea almost devoid of life. For many, many years, taking advantage of the German occupation, and then of the civil war in Greece, they got into the habit of using explosives for fishing. They also used nets with very small holes—nets of narrow gauge—which meant they were capturing the very young fish. The explosives killed not only fish, but also the fish banks of the eggs of the fish. Because of those practices, the Aegean was practically without life. The Greek fishing fleets had to go to West Africa to do the fishing, and for that, of course, we needed fish treaties with the various West African nations. So, when I was given an unpopular undertaking, and I was sent to renew those fishing treaties, I felt that that was the beginning of the end.

I was to renew the fishing treaties that Greece had with all the West African nations, starting with Morocco and Mauritania, all the way to Cameroon. I went to Lagos, in Nigeria. The first thing I saw, the morning I woke up and got out of the hotel to go to the ministry and negotiate the re-signing of the treaty, was garbage. The garbage collectors, I was told, were on strike, so there were heaps of garbage all over Lagos. It was a huge city at the time, with 5,000,000 inhabitants. In one heap of garbage, I saw a hand protruding out of the trash. They also had cadavers in the garbage.

In Ghana, the capital, Accra, is situated on the Atlantic Ocean. I observed in the harbor of Accra, two Russian trawlers which seemed to be in very good shape. It was the same type of vessel that the Russians were using allegedly to fish, but in reality, as supporting vessels for their fleet of nuclear submarines operating outside the territorial waters of the United States. I was surprised because those ships, even though they were still in good shape, looked as if they had been abandoned.

I repaired at the hotel, the Hotel Hilton of Accra, and early the next morning I heard splashing, and women giggling, and speaking a language I couldn't understand. My window was adjacent to the swimming pool, so I opened the drape to see. There were about six young women, none a beauty, none even good looking, but six relatively young women, laughing and having a good time. It was a little after seven o'clock in the morning. I put on my swimming trunks and went outside to join them.

"Does any one of you speak English?" I began. All of them more or less could, but two of them spoke very fluent English. "Where are you from, Girls?"

"From Moscow," came the reply. "And what are you doing here?" I queried.

"We are the prostitutes of the Hilton Hotel." I didn't know Hilton was hiring prostitutes. That was new to me, but they explained, "We are not on a payroll, but they allow us to entertain the guests."

"Did Hilton import you from Moscow?" I was becoming more curious.

"No, they didn't," one answered. "We married Ghanaians who were students at the Lomonosov University." It was translated Lumumba University, after Lumumba, the Communist leader of the Congo. "We married Ghanaian students in hope that life in Ghana might be better than life in Moscow. What we found in Ghana was that life with the families of our husbands is even worse than the worst in Moscow."

"Yes," another spoke up, "and when we divorced and applied to the Soviet Embassy in Accra to be repatriated to Russia, the Soviet Union said they didn't want us. We are stuck here in Ghana, and this is how we make our living."

I had an idea. "See those two trawlers over there?" I pointed. "Yes. They've been there for three years now," they noted. "Well," I said, "they are Russian. Why don't you ask the Ghanaian government to let you run them and go fishing? Instead of fishing johns, fish for fish, and sell them, and you'll make a good living." They began contemplating the idea.

Later, I went to the ministry to discuss renewing the fishing treaty with

Greece. They told me they were sorry, but they had already committed themselves with Star-Kist, saying, "You can't fish the Ghanaian waters this year. Star-Kist is going to fish." I was a little disappointed. Then I asked them, "What about those two trawlers?" "What about them, do you want to buy them? It seemed to me they were hopeful. I said, "Not necessarily, but why are they idling there?" "The Russians gave them to us as a gift," they replied, "but they didn't give us a crew." When I asked why they didn't sail them themselves, they said helplessly, "Nobody knows how to sail those vessels."

I advanced, "If I find people to sail them, will you sell them on credit to those people?" They declared yes, they would.

I returned to the Hilton Hotel and found the girls. "Girls, you can get those ships for nothing. Just get on board, familiarize with the vessels, read the manuals, and go into business as fishermen."

I don't know if they did it or not, but I did plant the seed. I thought Hilton might not like it because it will be deprived of its prostitutes.

I found that in Africa, American Negroes were resented because when American Negroes would go in some official capacity in Africa, they would patronize the Africans. The Africans resented that because they considered the American Negroes a lesser kind of person because they come from slaves, whereas the ones in Africa are the ones who sold them initially. And they didn't like to be patronized by the American Negroes.

The oil crunch of 1973 created a big demand for cars with lower gasoline consumption. Gas stations in New York would sell gas on Tuesdays, Thursdays and Saturdays to cars which had odd numbers, and on Mondays, Wednesdays and Fridays to cars that had even numbers. Sometimes one had to go to New Jersey to buy gas. Even after the price of oil quadrupled, from $2.50 a barrel to $10, the price of gas, which was between forty-five to fifty cents, went to sixty cents per gallon; it didn't quadruple. It was relatively petty. But it created a tremendous panic. It was the lines at the gas stations that created it. Somehow, I got into that mode. I had developed a high opinion of American Motors since their flagship, the Ambassador, had an engine that was a facsimile of the Rolls Royce, so I bought a Matador which was a six-cylinder engine and consumed less. I had the Matador less than two weeks. It was usually parked in one of only two spaces available for parking in Beekman Place, between Irving Berlin and Huntington Hartford Buildings. It got stolen.

The insurance company paid me the invoice amount I had paid minus ten percent. It was February 1974, and to my surprise, Hertz, which features Ford products, was having its annual auction in New Jersey. It was unusual because it was just February. Usually those auctions occur in April, because Hertz auctions all cars two years old, or which have 12,000 miles. I decided, since I had the money the insurance had paid me, to go and buy a car from Hertz.

The cars were displayed in classes: there were the Ford Fairmont's, there were the Ford Torino's and there were the Ford LTD's. The used car dealers were bidding for the whole lot, say twenty cars or thirty cars. Then I saw, all alone, nobody even looking at it, a Ford Thunderbird which was last year's model. No dealer would even consider it because it was a gas guzzler with a big eight-cylinder engine and got something like nine miles to the gallon.

In order to be allowed to go to into the auction, one had to pay a fifty-dollar entry fee which would be deducted from whatever one bought. If one didn't buy anything, one forfeited those fifty dollars. I managed to find a Hertz employee to ask him about that Thunderbird. He said, "It's $3,500." That was less than half what the car was worth. "What year is it?" I inquired.

"It's a '74, it's less than six months old." It was only February of 1974, and I wondered, why do they sell it. He told me, "Because it has 13,000 miles. It was rented to only one person who drove all those miles. He went from New York to Alaska, or wherever he went."

"Where do I bid?" I asked, and he answered, right here, so, I posed, "I bid $3,500, less the fifty dollars I have paid."

He said, "Sold."

Nobody would touch the gas guzzlers. At that time Thunderbird had the biggest Ford engine in it. That car was a combination of ugly colors. It was a diarrhea brown with a black vinyl top and a disgusting black shiny upholstery of some kind of cheap nylon. But it was brand new, it was big, it was impressive. I had that unsightly big Thunderbird for about a week, and I was at the United Nations. At the cafeteria was a new Iranian, just arrived in New York. Ford gave a fifteen percent discount to diplomats, and he was shopping. "I went to the Ford dealership, and I wanted to buy a Ford Thunderbird, and they didn't have one. They said I have to wait six months," he lamented.

When I asked him what color he would want it to be, he said, "I love that light brown with the black vinyl top."

"Come with me." I took him to the cavernous, probably the largest garage on earth, below the United Nations building, and there sat the Thunderbird, which I had thought of naming 'Diarrhea' because that was the color. I said, "Is that the color?"

"Yes!" he enthused, "Exactly that. That's what I want." I told him, "You can have it. It's this year's model, and it has about 12,000 miles." "No matter, how much do you want?" he asked, and I replied, "Fifty-seven hundred." He bought it.

It was the beginning of 1974, and I had conceived the idea of putting together a business network that could make a lot of money for me in a very short period of time. I needed $200,000 to get into the oil business, which was my target if I were to remain permanently in the United States. I was making the preliminary moves to generate a business based on export of beef from the United States to Italy and Greece.

Back when my father was a traveling man, the big hotels, the famous hotels, would stick their label on a guest's suitcase, and my father was a collector of such labels of great hotels. It was a silent show-off. When one went to the railroad station, or to the pier to board the ship, —of course back then very few people traveled by air—it showed how well traveled you were. My father had taught me that, whether one had stayed in the most expensive room of the hotel, or the cheapest room of the hotel, one got the same label. I learned that, and it was a good idea, so I always went to the most expensive hotel, but the cheapest room.

The one time that I decided it was not such a good idea was at the Danieli Hotel in Venice. The Danieli Hotel is famous because it used to be Dandolo, a palace of the Doge of Venice. It is a grand hotel. When I asked that they put me in the cheapest room, the room they put me in was where the doge kept his servants, so it was a small room with no window, and it felt claustrophobic. Instead of a bed it had a cot. It had the tiniest black and white television, probably the smallest one I had ever seen—not that it made much difference, because the television was in Italian—my Italian is not particularly fluent, I can get by, but that's about it. So, I thought, *Danieli, you lost me.*

I also possibly became a father, I don't know. The consul general of the Greek consulate in Venice was a very close friend of mine, and he had a girlfriend, an Italian. I went to visit him to introduce him to my idea of creating a network. When one is a diplomat, automatically one establishes good contacts with important people, because the important people are mostly snobs and they want to invite members of the diplomatic corps to their various functions and brag to their friends, "I had the ambassador of such and such at home yesterday."

His girlfriend had a best friend. The best friend, Valeria, when I was in Venice, was on a rebound. She had broken up with her boyfriend. So, I was at the opportune moment in the opportune time. She was an interesting, good-looking woman. Valeria was from one of the famous, but newly impoverished, families of Venice, and she was working for a shipping company, called Adriatica, that belongs to the Vatican. After a couple of months, she sent me a letter in New York, and it said, "I am pleased to announce that I am pregnant, and you are the father."

I answered and pointed out, "In view of the fact that you are married and still live with your husband under the same roof, and in view of the fact that you had just broken up with your boyfriend, what makes you think that I am the father? If, however, you want to go to Switzerland and have an abortion, I will contribute to one-third of the cost."

That's when she wrote back that she was very happy to be pregnant. She said that she had been married for nine years and didn't have a child, and that was one reason why she was separated from her husband. She insisted it was mine. I said, "Alright, when you are about to deliver, I'll come to Venice, and if it's mine, I'll divorce my wife and marry you." The family did not appear to be impoverished. They lived in the ancestral palace, or palazzo, and she had a bedroom in the one wing of the palazzo and her husband in another. They did live under the same roof, but they hardly saw each other, because the palazzo had about thirty bedrooms.

When she gave birth, I was there, at the clinic. I went there from New York. It was full term, it was nine months, and a couple of hours. Out of her came an ugly dark thing with hair all over the place. It looked like a monkey, only it didn't have a tail. In fact, I turned it around to see if it had a tail. The tail would fit perfectly, it would be like a Rhesus monkey. I said, "I couldn't possibly have sired that. Impossible."

I looked for several marks and signs that are germane to my family, certain moles in certain places, none of those. I didn't find anything that even remotely would indicate that I was the sire. I told the obstetrician, "It can't be mine."

The obstetrician was also taken aback, how so beautiful a woman could possibly give birth to so ugly a thing. It didn't even look human. It had hair all over. Valeria could enter a beauty contest and become Miss Italy, perhaps not then, when she was twenty-nine, but when she was twenty. She was tall, she had bluish gray eyes; the eyes were kind of cold. She was a dish. The obstetrician, such a nice Italian gentleman, a Venetian, said, "All we need is a drop of blood."

I am O-positive. Valeria was O-positive, and that thing was O-positive, so that means I and another 200,000,000 men could be the father. Now we needed a drop of blood from the husband, and a drop of blood from the boyfriend. The husband, to my very great surprise, came and gave a drop of blood. He was B-negative, which of course explains why they couldn't have a child for nine years. Mama nature wants a baby, but she doesn't want a deranged baby. O-positive and B-negative won't produce a good child. Now it was up to the boyfriend to come and give us a little blood and he vehemently refused because he was angry that she had told him that it was not his.

"Listen, Giovanni," I told him over the telephone, "I have seen pictures of you, and if I see you on the Rialto or the San Rocco Bridge, I'll punch you in the nose and that will cost you much more than a drop of blood, so get yourself here to the hospital and give us a drop of blood." He didn't. That was 1974, before DNA tests became available.

The obstetrician advised, "Well, you have to wait until the baby becomes five years old, and then you will go to Switzerland and have a chromosome test." I couldn't understand why you couldn't have a chromosome test when it's a baby.

Valeria was angry that I denied paternity. I knew, very well, a lawyer. I brought the lawyer, and he wrote the papers that said after the baby was five years old we would undergo the chromosome test, and if indeed it was mine then I would marry Valeria. That was not good enough for Valeria. She was irate because I disputed, but I meant what I said. For about three months I sent her checks for one hundred dollars which were never returned, so obviously she kept the money. Then I found out that she married her boss, one of the directors of Adriatica, and he adopted the Simian. So, I was freed. I know Venice quite well.

It is extraordinary that of the two women who claim that I sired their babies, one is Valeria, and the other is Valerie.

But Valerie was much later.

CHAPTER 41

Becoming a Fugitive

ON MY LAST day in Greece, I was on a sailboat. The dictatorship had already fallen. Constantine Karamanlis, two weeks earlier, on July 24, had returned from France on board the private plane that French President Giscard d'Estaing placed at his disposal. Karamanlis had already taken over the Greek government and had withdrawn Greece from NATO. All these things had happened.

It was the ninth of August 1974, and I remember it because the big thing on Eurovision on that day was the abdication of President Richard Nixon. For the first time in history, an American president had resigned. While I was tuned into Nixon's abdication speech, the news reported that all my superiors had been arrested but one—one had managed to leave Greece in the meantime—and they were facing charges of high treason. When I heard they were facing charges of high treason, I thought I had better get out of Greece because of what the verdict would be with me. If they were to kill my superiors, I might be glad to get sixteen years or something like it.

I immediately unloaded our guests in Corinth, and my wife and I sailed to Sicily. That was my last day in Greece. I left everything behind. From Sicily, I went to Rome, and from there I returned to New York. On my desk was a piece of paper which said, 'Upon receipt of the present, you are ordered to immediately return to Greece.'

I went to the United Nations and asked if I could remain in the United States without asking for political asylum. I was told that as a member of the Delegation to the United Nations, I could stay in America indefinitely as long as I did not accept paid or unpaid labor. However, that apparently changed at some time because the Immigration and Naturalization Service considered me an illegal alien after a while, but I don't know how long that while was.

That's another story.

TO BE CONTINUED

I will discover America from oil wells to ostriches, and in the halls of Congress campaigning for a Korean War Memorial, from a J.C. Penney heiress to penniless, from wealth to welfare, on my road to Ithaca.

www.ingramcontent.com/pod-product-compliance
Lightning Source LLC
Chambersburg PA
CBHW061932220426
43662CB00012B/1875